AF521875

WILD INDIA

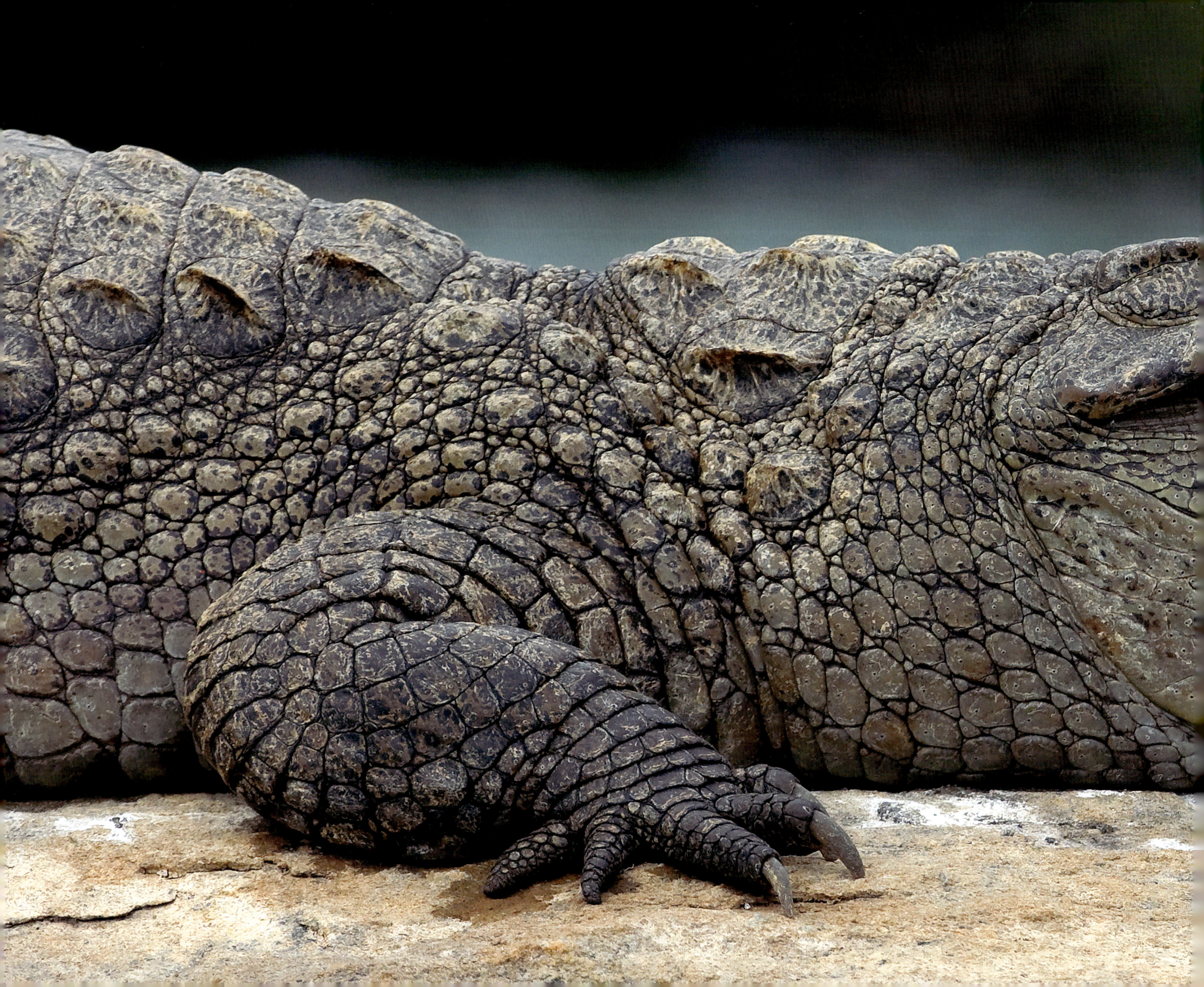

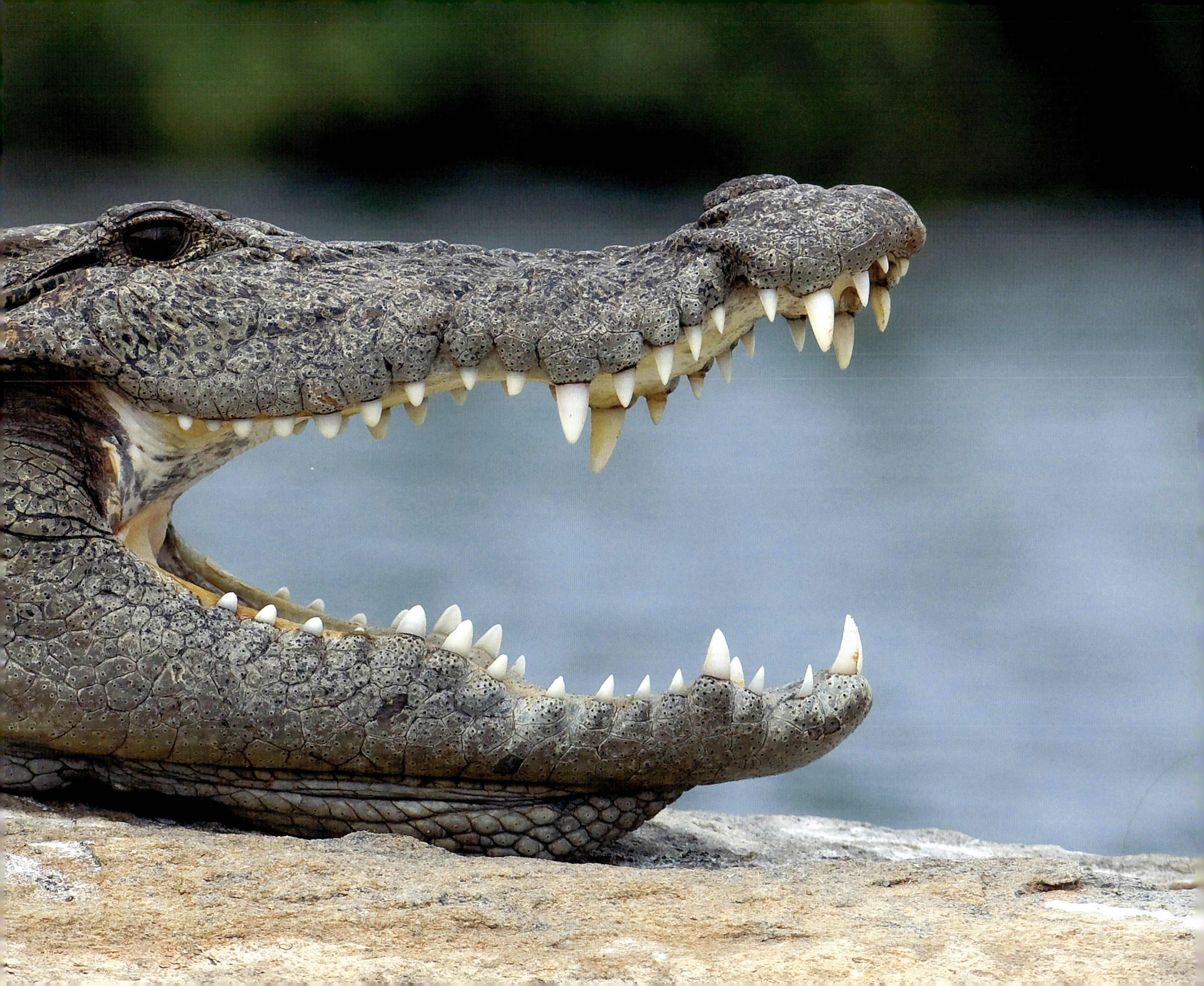

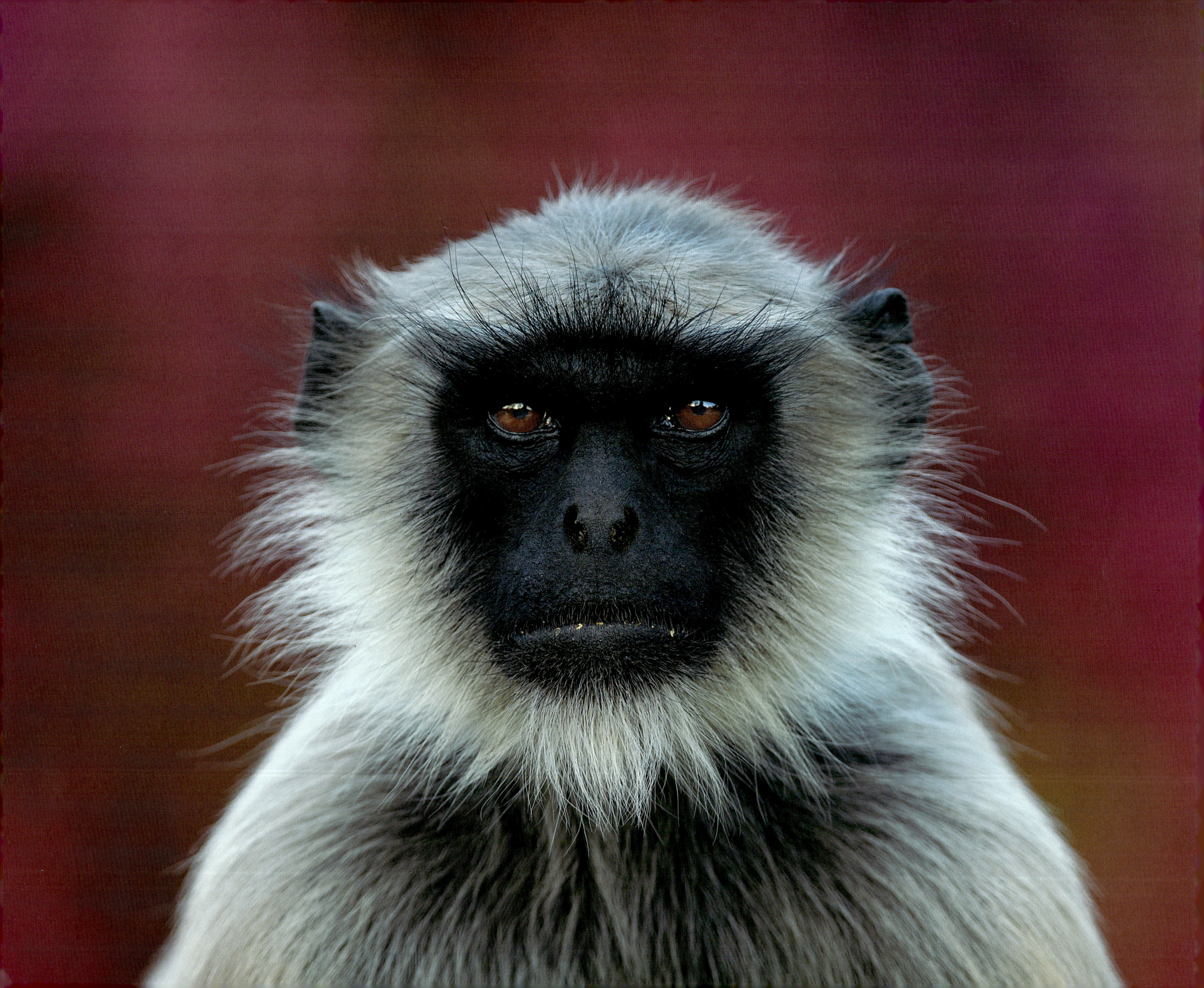

AXEL GOMILLE

WILD INDIA

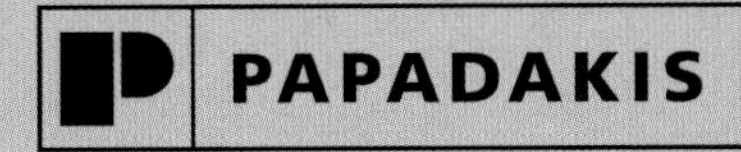

First published in Great Britain in 2017 by Papadakis Publisher

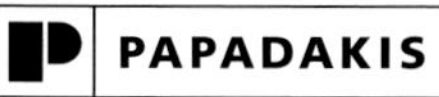

An imprint of Academy Editions Limited

Kimber Studio, Winterbourne, Berkshire, RG20 8AN, UK
info@papadakis.net I www.papadakis.net

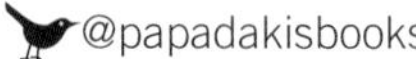@papadakisbooks 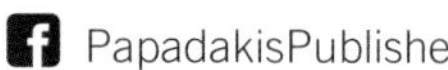 PapadakisPublisher

Publishing Director: Alexandra Papadakis
Design Director: Aldo Sampieri

ISBN 978 1 906506 63 6

A CIP catalogue record of this book is available from the British Library.
Printed and bound in China.

Page 2-3: A marsh crocodile or mugger basks on a rock in the Cauvery river in Karnataka. The range covered by these huge reptiles extends from Iran over the entire Indian subcontinent to Sri Lanka.

Page 4: A Bengal hanuman langur rests in the city of Jodhpur in Rajasthan, while a carpet of flowering Bougainvillea adds unusual colour to the scene.

CONTENTS

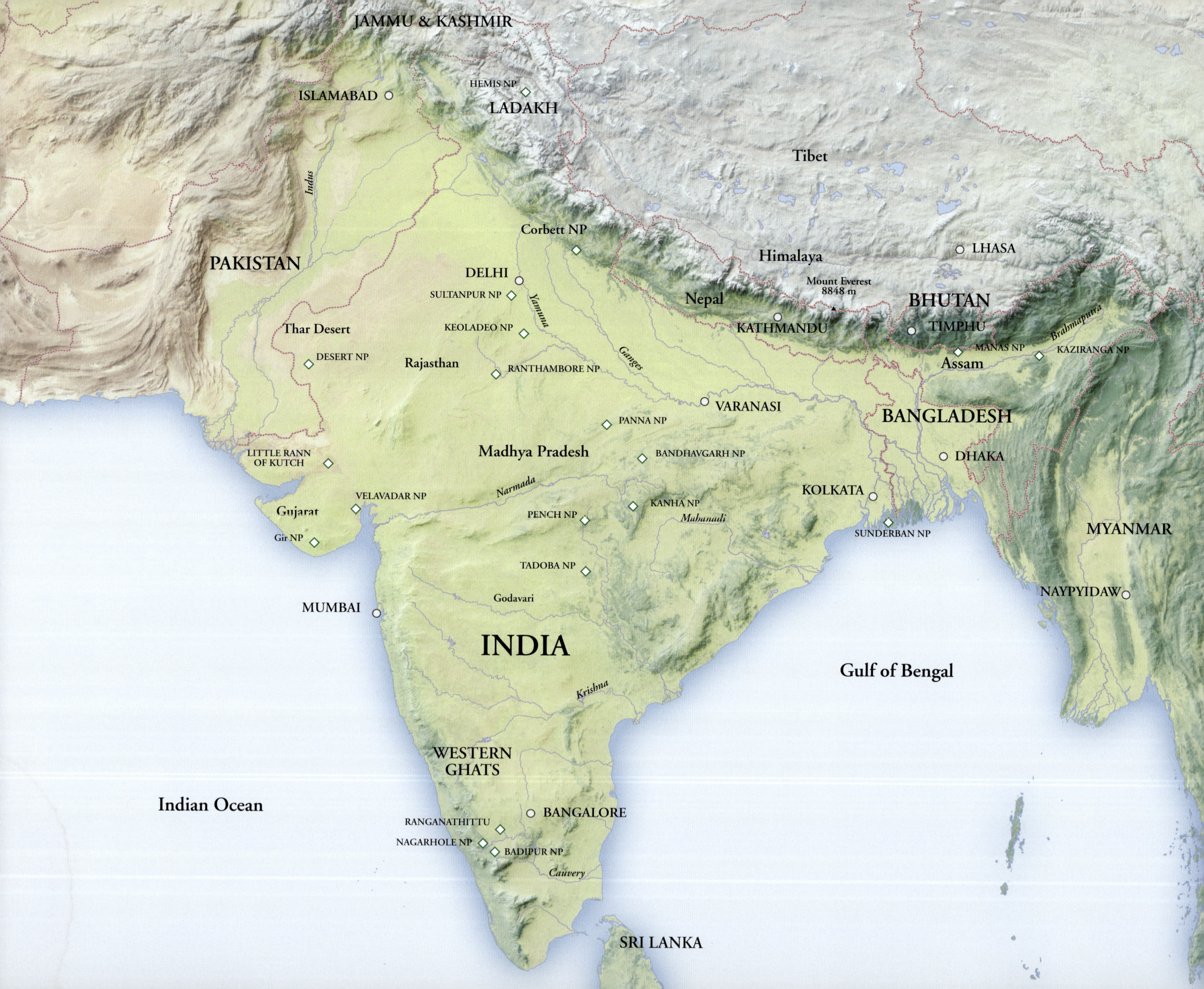

JAMMU & KASHMIR
HEMIS NP
ISLAMABAD
LADAKH
Tibet
Indus
PAKISTAN
Corbett NP
LHASA
Himalaya
DELHI
Mount Everest
8848 m
SULTANPUR NP
Yamuna
Nepal
BHUTAN
KEOLADEO NP
KATHMANDU
TIMPHU
Thar Desert
Ganges
Brahmaputra
MANAS NP
KAZIRANGA NP
DESERT NP
Rajasthan
Assam
RANTHAMBORE NP
VARANASI
PANNA NP
BANGLADESH
LITTLE RANN
OF KUTCH
Madhya Pradesh
BANDHAVGARH NP
DHAKA
Narmada
KOLKATA
VELAVADAR NP
KANHA NP
Gujarat
PENCH NP
Mahanadi
MYANMAR
Gir NP
SUNDERBAN NP
TADOBA NP
NAYPYIDAW
MUMBAI
Godavari
INDIA
Gulf of Bengal
Krishna
WESTERN
GHATS
Indian Ocean
BANGALORE
RANGANATHITTU
NAGARHOLE NP
BADIPUR NP
Cauvery
SRI LANKA

WILD INDIA

AXEL GOMILLE

My first encounter with Indian wildlife was through my first visit to a cinema. As a six-year-old boy, I watched the Disney animation of Rudyard Kipling's *The Jungle Book* and was fascinated by *Baloo* the bear, *Shere Khan* the tiger, and *Hathi* the elephant. This sparked my desire to track down my heroes from *The Jungle Book* in real life, something which I was to achieve years later as a photographer and zoologist.

Prior to venturing into the jungle, I arrived in Delhi, a gigantic metropolis with more than 16 million inhabitants. There were people everywhere, and the streets were gridlocked. Mumbai and Kolkata are similar in these respects. Today, more than 1.2 billion people live in India, and its population is expected to exceed that of China by 2028, making it the most populous nation in the world.

Given such an environment, one must ask if there can there be any space left for wildlife? Surprisingly, animals are a common sight, and I saw parrots in gardens, monkeys on rooftops and antelopes out in the fields. Of the world's 37 species of wild cats, 14 of them occur in India – more than in any other country. By comparison, the entire African continent only has ten different species of wild cat. In total, about 350 species of wild mammals, 540 species of reptiles, and 1200 species of birds have been recorded in India.

One reason for this remarkable diversity lies in the size and geography of the Indian subcontinent. Such a wide range of habitats and extreme landscapes ensures that the biodiversity of India is one of the richest on Earth. The distance from the desert in the west, close to the Pakistani border, to the rainforests in the east, close to Myanmar, is around 3000 kilometres, which is roughly as far as the distance from the tropical coasts of southern India to the snow-capped peaks of the Himalayas in the north. The mountain ranges of the Himalayas act as a mighty barrier, redirecting monsoon winds, saturated with moisture from the Indian Ocean, over the Indian subcontinent. The climate of central India is characterised by a wet monsoon season with a long dry period, although this does not apply to the Thar desert and the rainforest regions of the western Ghats and the northeast.

Such wide ranges of habitats and extreme landscapes ensure that the biodiversity of India is one of the richest on Earth. Among the mammals endemic to the Indian subcontinent are sloth bears, nilgai and blackbuck. The last populations of the Asiatic lion and the khur, a subspecies of the Asiatic wild ass, also live in India. India is home to the world's largest surviving populations of wild tigers and Indian rhinoceros. If the fate of these endangered species is to be decided somewhere, it will be in India.

Although India's ecology and wildlife have suffered in the past from human encroachment, today, some 150,000 square kilometres of wilderness is protected across numerous parks and sanctuaries, with the *Wildlife Protection Act* and *Project Tiger* playing a crucial role in conservation. Religion also continues to influence how people treat their environment: Hinduism as India's prevalent religion teaches respect for all forms of life, and some wild animals, such as monkeys, elephants or cobras, are even considered to be holy. These traditional virtues still have their place in modern India.

I found my work as a naturalist in the tiger reserves of Kanha and Bandhavgarh fascinating. Over a period of about 25 years, I have explored different parts of the country with my camera in my hand and one of the results is *Wild India*. This has been my personal discovery and subsequent presentation of some well-known characters from *The Jungle Book*, together with some of the lesser-known species that also deserve our attention. Despite the growing human population and its associated problems, the natural heritage of India is still overwhelmingly spectacular.

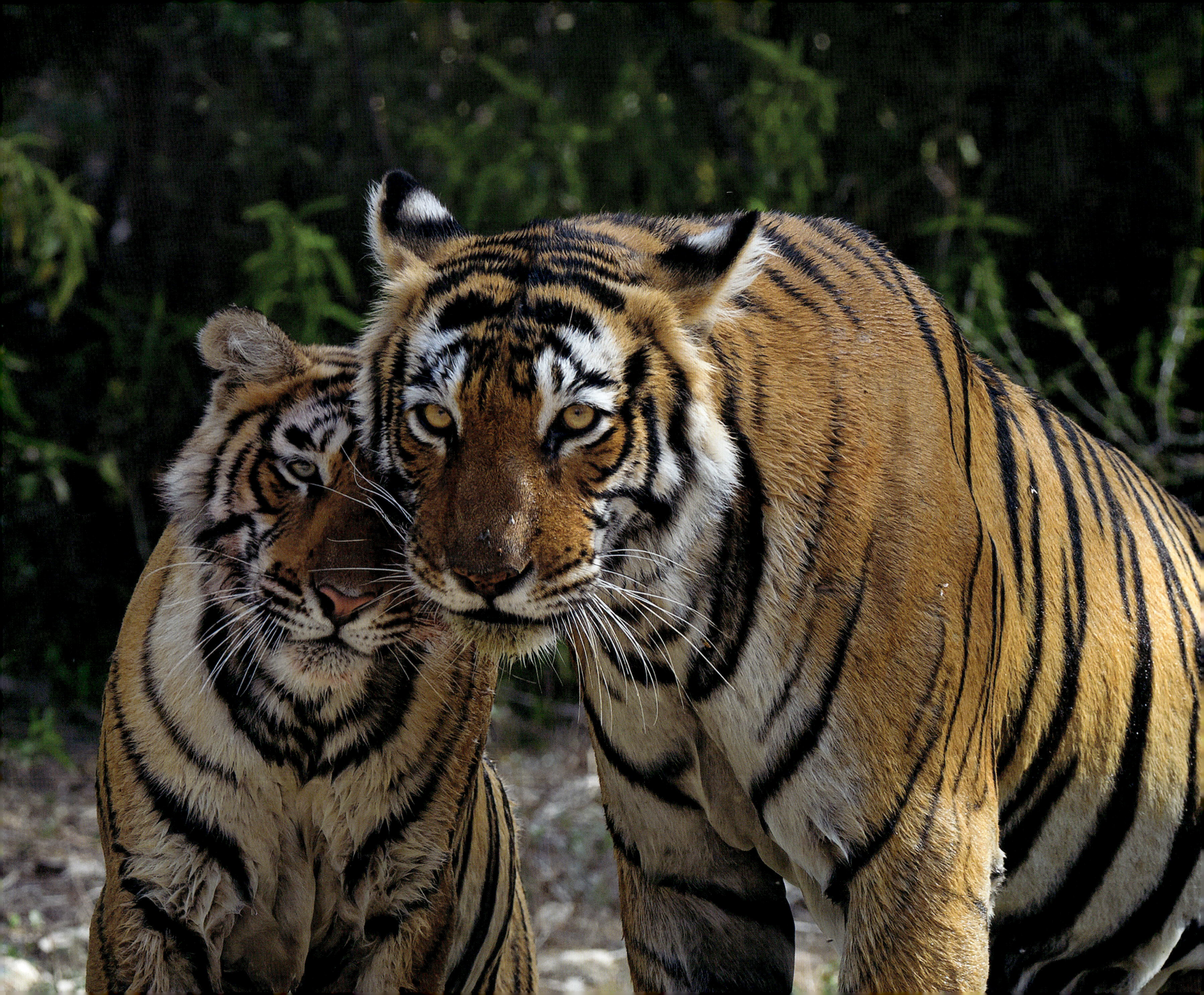

JUNGLES

The jungles of India are habitats for some of the most rare and exotic species of wildlife in the world. A jungle often evokes an image of dense and overgrown vegetation; a hostile and impenetrable place. In fact, jungles are biodiversity hotspots, teeming with wildlife. Plant growth depends on the amount of annual rainfall, creating rainforests in the northeast and in the Western Ghats, running parallel to the west coast of India, and monsoon forests or seasonal tropical forests in central India.

No animal symbolises Indian wildlife as strongly as the tiger. The tiger is considered to be the king of the jungle, and is the most powerful predator on the Indian sub-continent. Seeing them in the wild is an unforgettable highlight when travelling in India. Monkeys, wild boar, deer and wild cattle, such as the mighty gaur can also be found, while predators include leopards and the rare Asiatic wild dogs.

Much of the jungle areas of India are now protected. Today, there are 50 tiger reserves covering a total area of over 70,000 square kilometres. Such major projects to conserve tigers and their habitats have benefited other jungles species.

A Bengal tigress caresses one of her larger cubs in the Ranthambhore National Park in Rajasthan. Tigers most commonly have litters of two to four cubs.

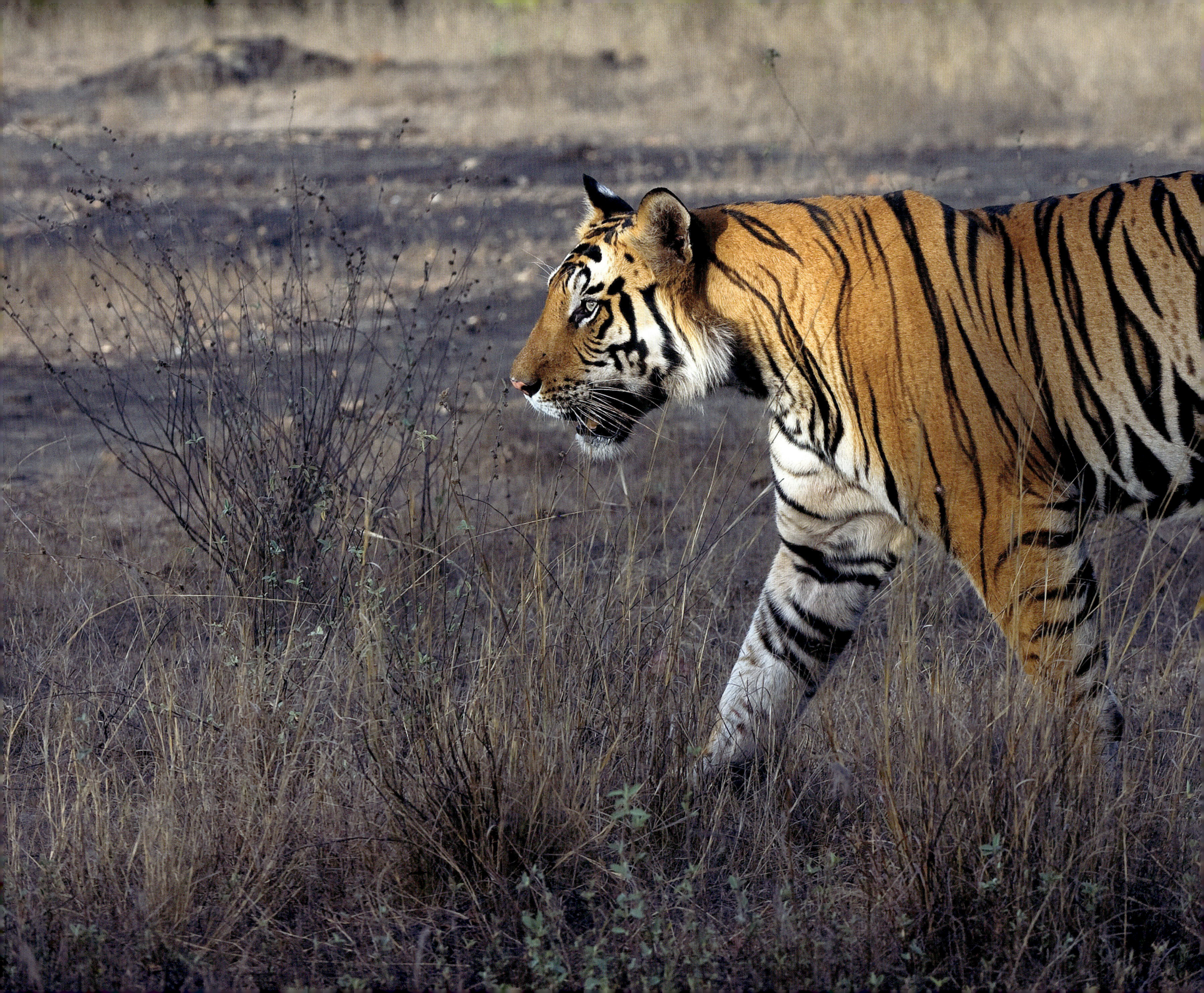

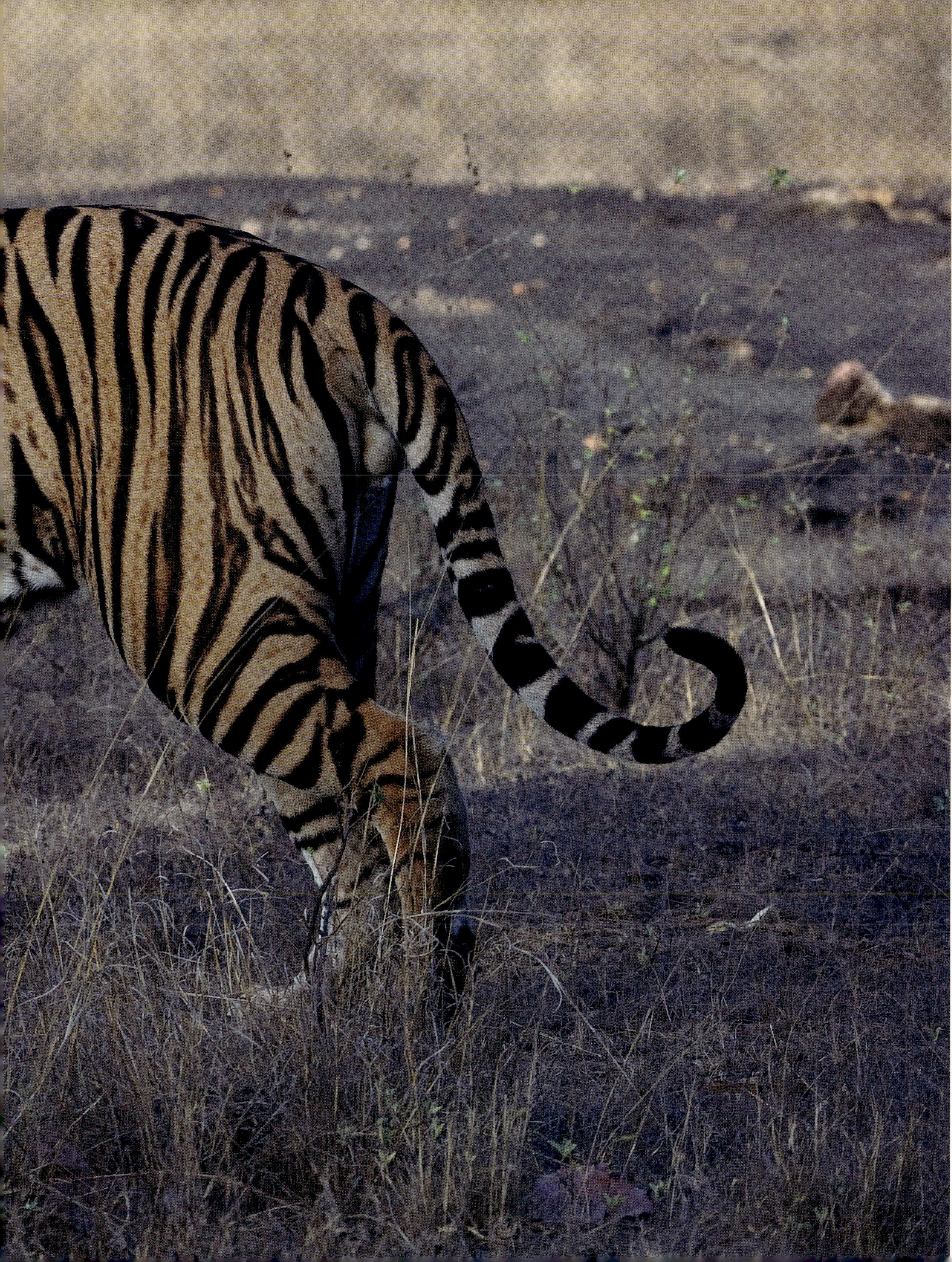

Male tigers, such as this particular one (left) from the Bandhavgarh National Park in Madhya Pradesh, will occupy comparatively large territories, overlapping smaller areas that are occupied by several females, and therefore making it more likely for the males to breed.

Overleaf:
Once the former hunting grounds of the Maharajas of Jaipur, the Ranthambhore National Park, in eastern Rajasthan, is a haven for wildlife. Its grounds offer prime habitat for tigers and it is widely regarded as one of the best places in India to see them. The national park was named after the historic Ranthambhore fortress, whose ruins dot the park.

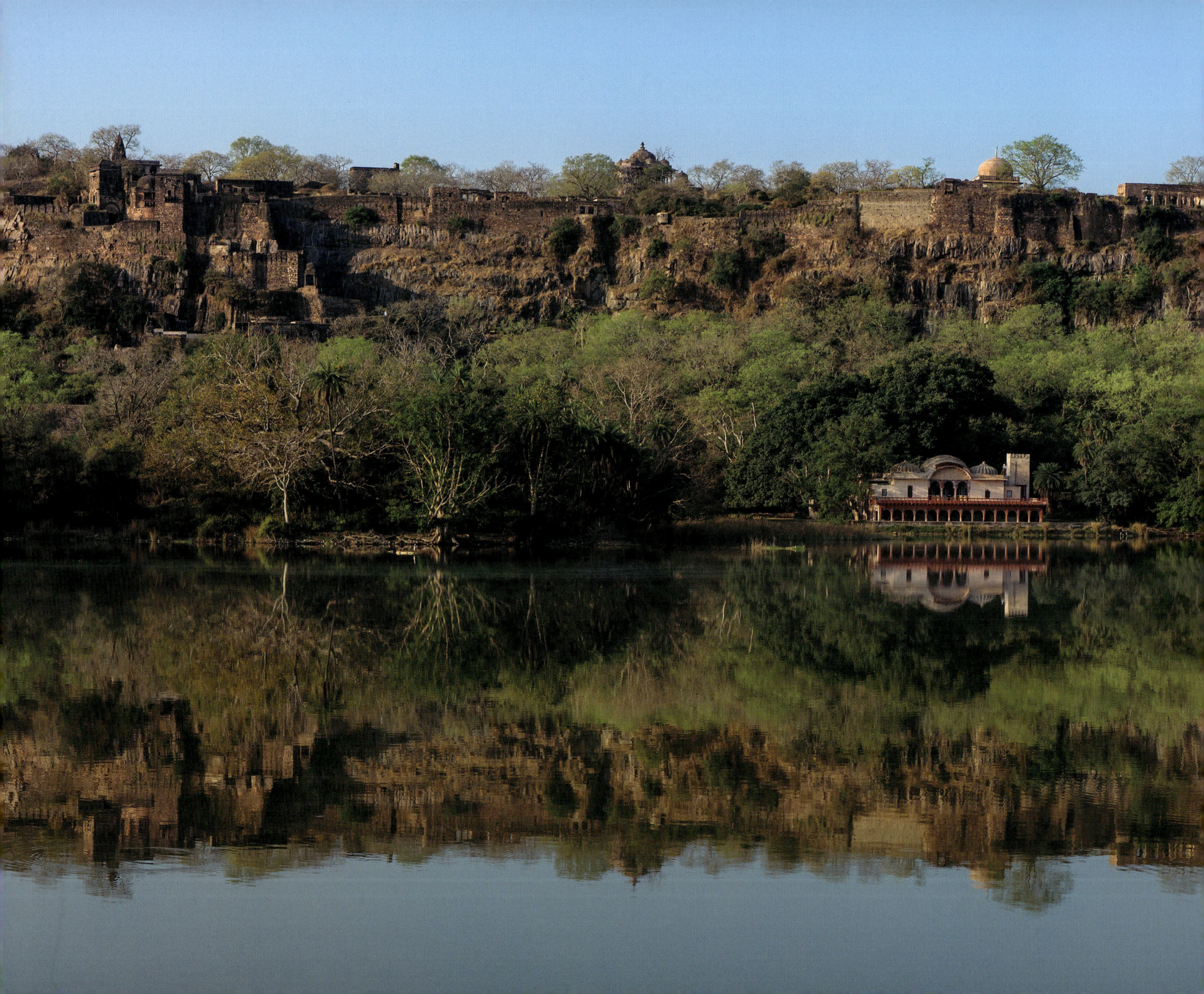

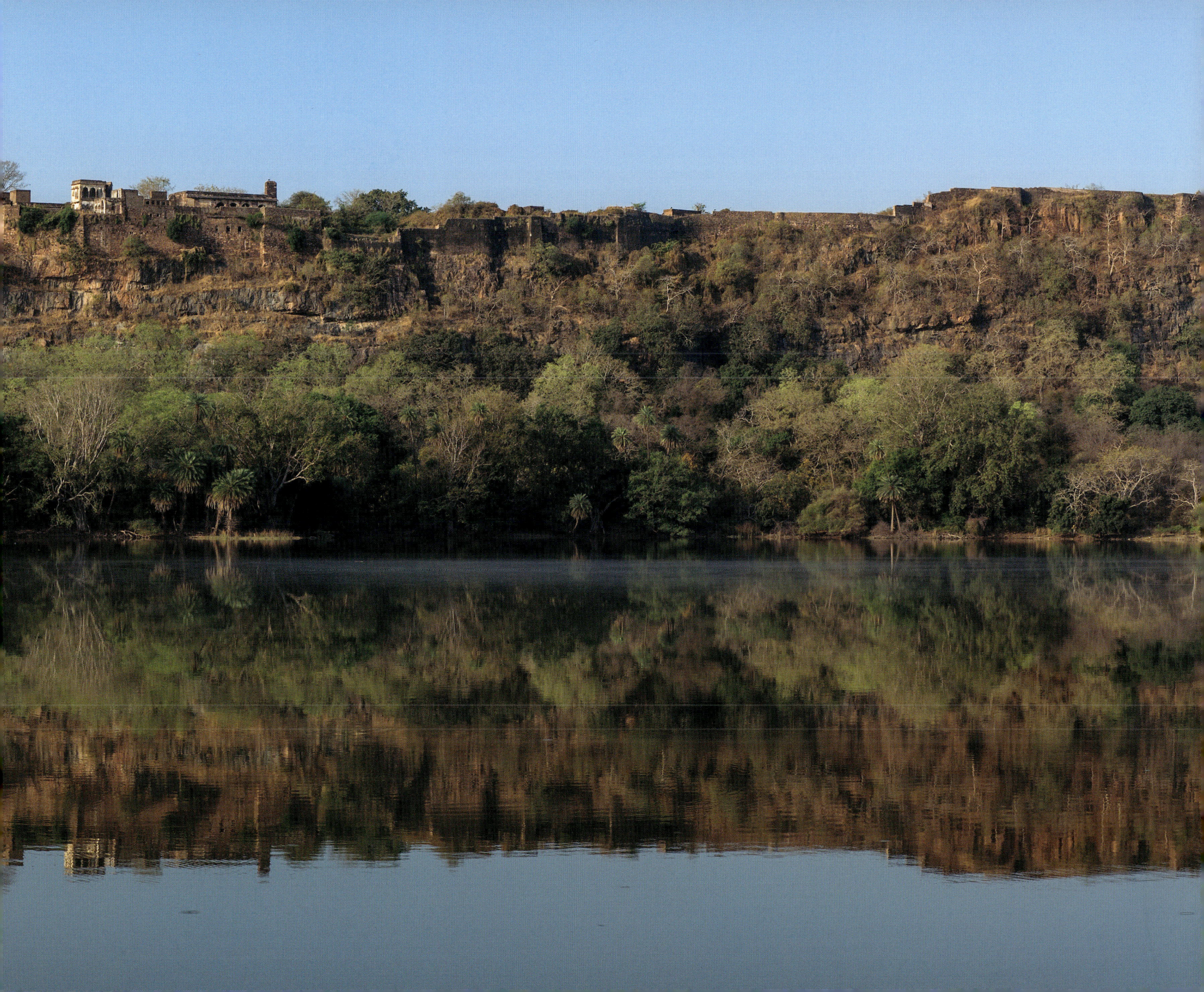

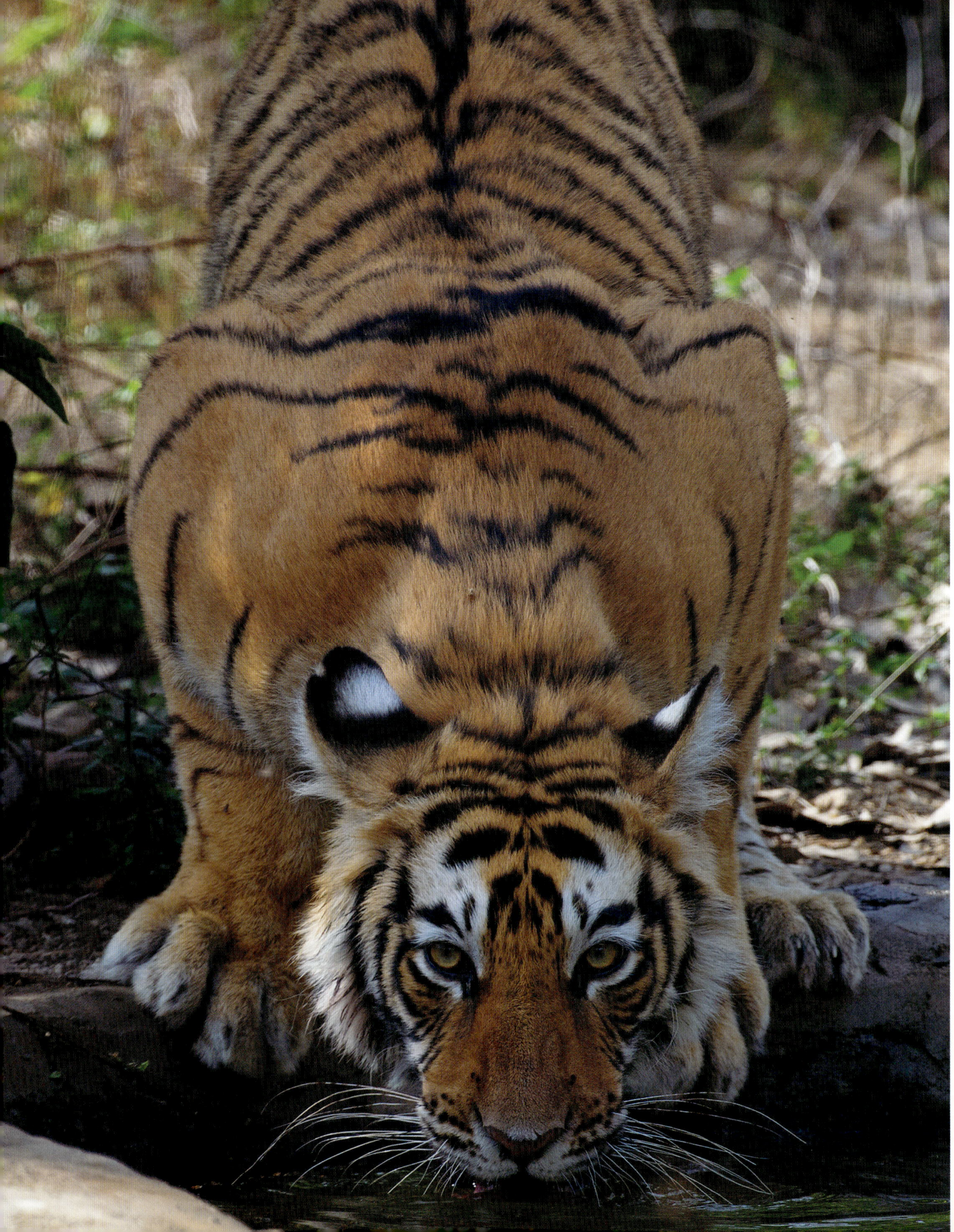

Water can be in short supply in many parts of Ranthambhore. The forest department therefore created concrete water holes so as to keep water supply plentiful for the animals. Tigers use them for drinking (left) and for cooling off, as in this case of this mother and her large cub (opposite).

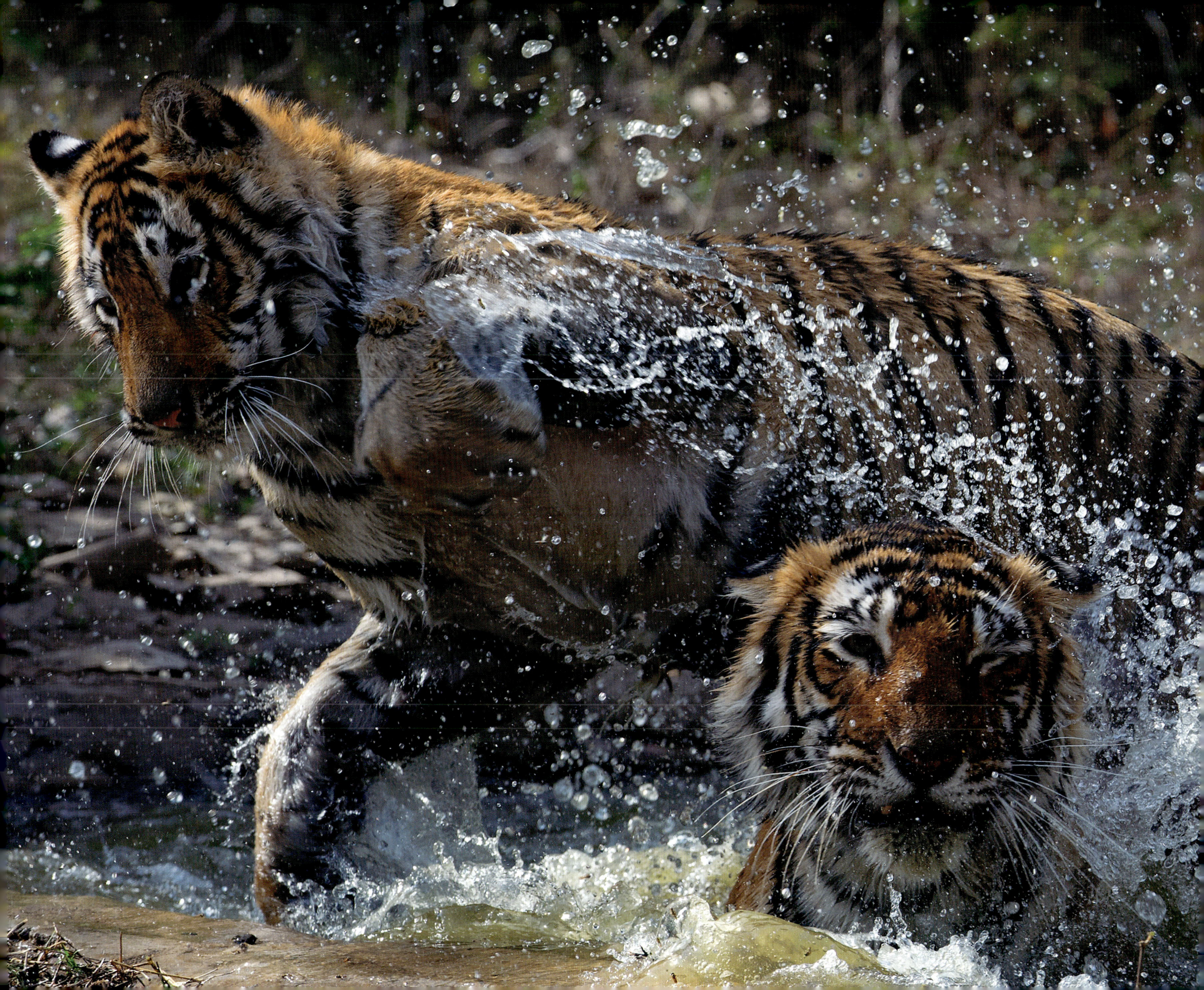

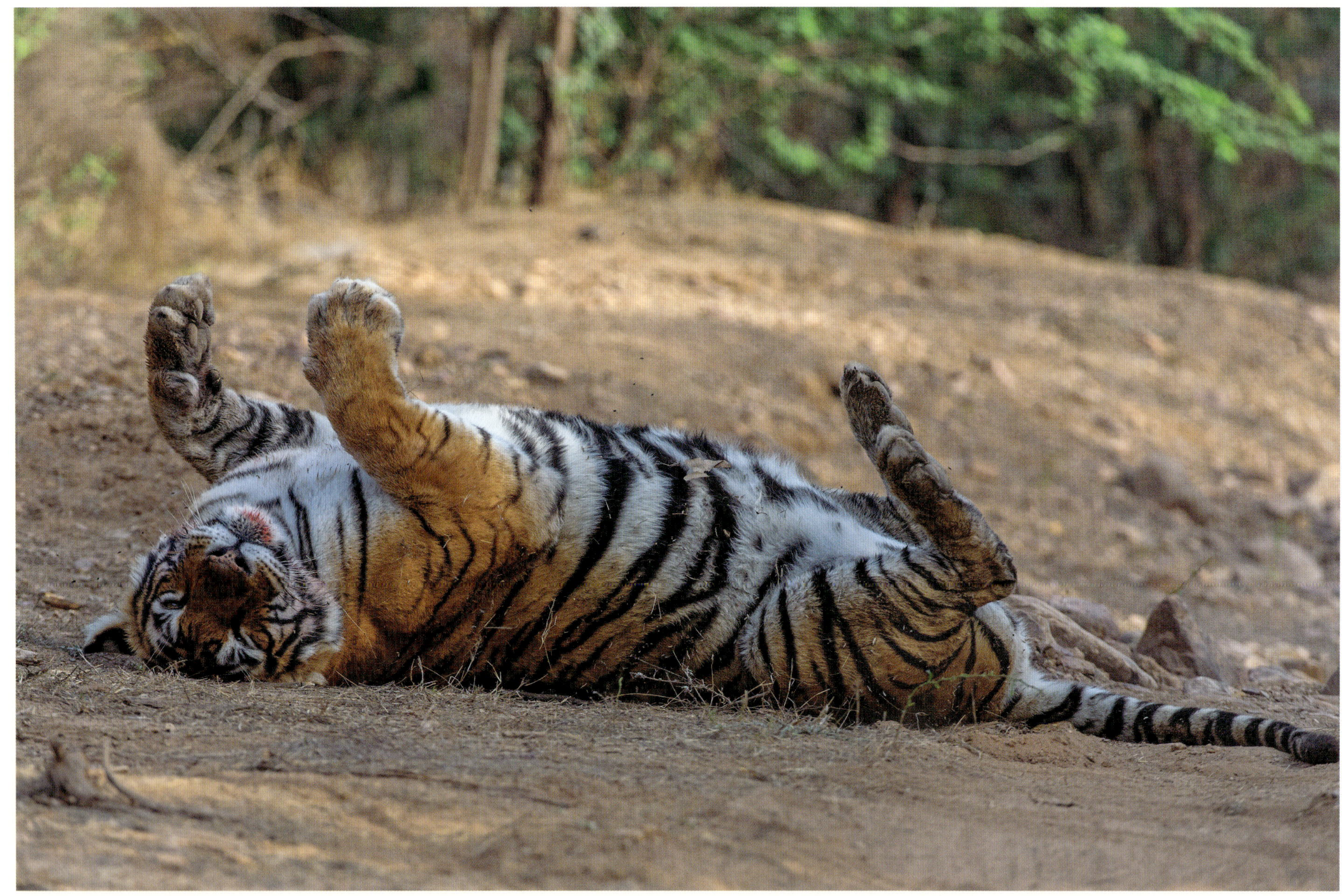

Tigers will usually find a shaded area in which to relax during the heat of the day, leaving hunting to be done at night. This tigress (opposite) remains alert to her environment, following the movements of other animals.

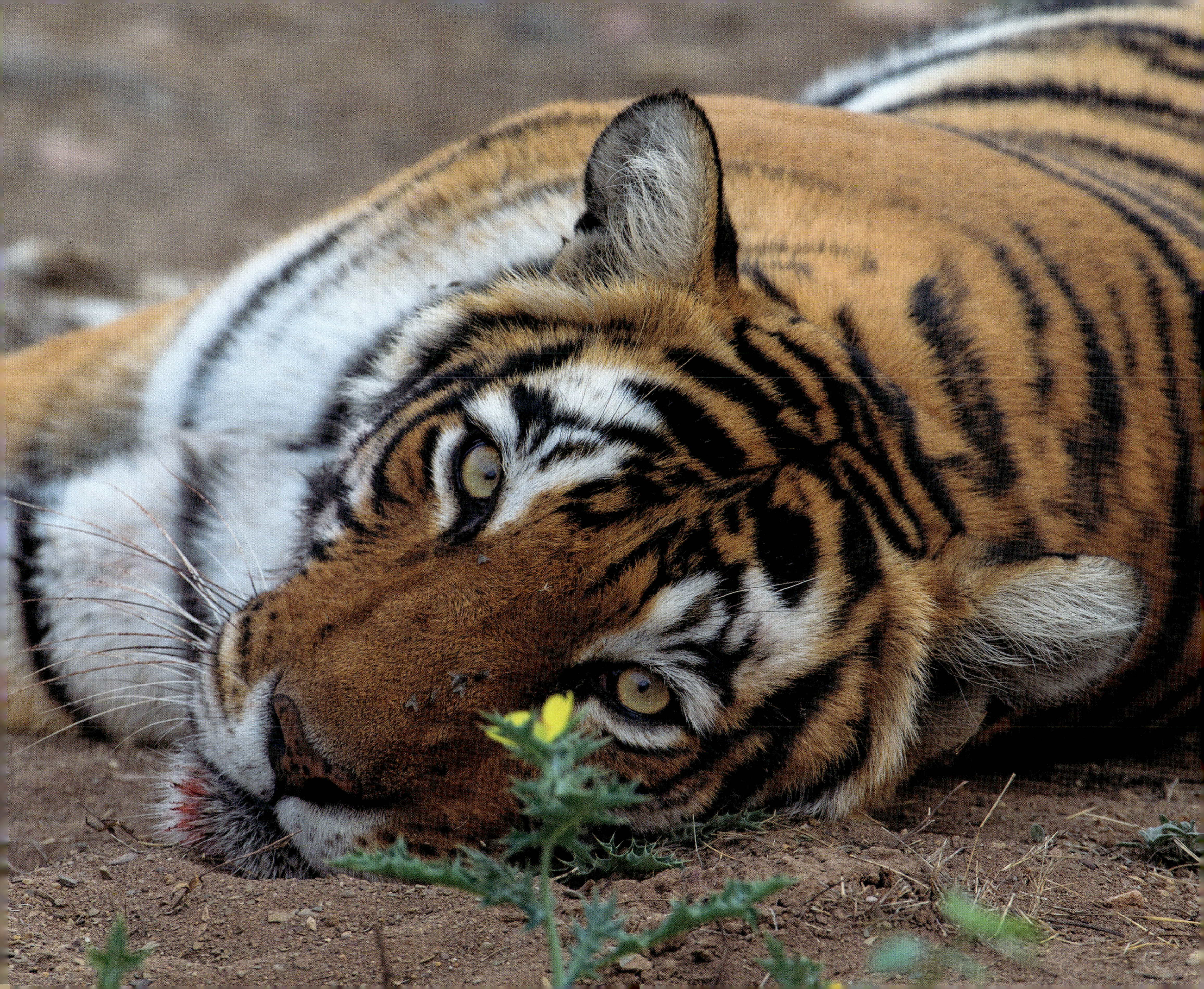

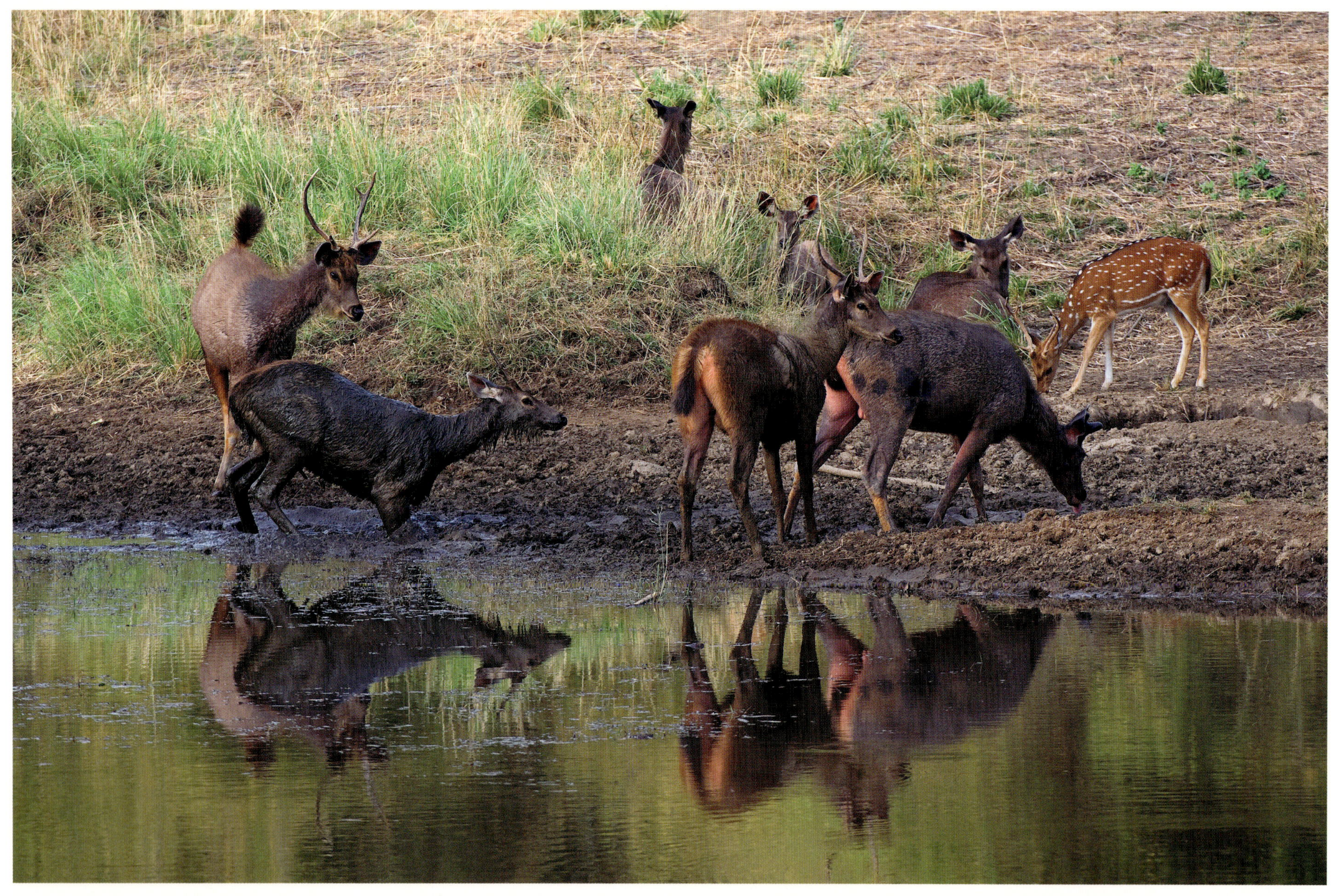

Sambar deer are a favoured prey for tigers. Particular caution must be paid by the deer during the evenings, which is when tigers, such as this large male in the Ranthambhore National Park (opposite) start patrolling their territories.

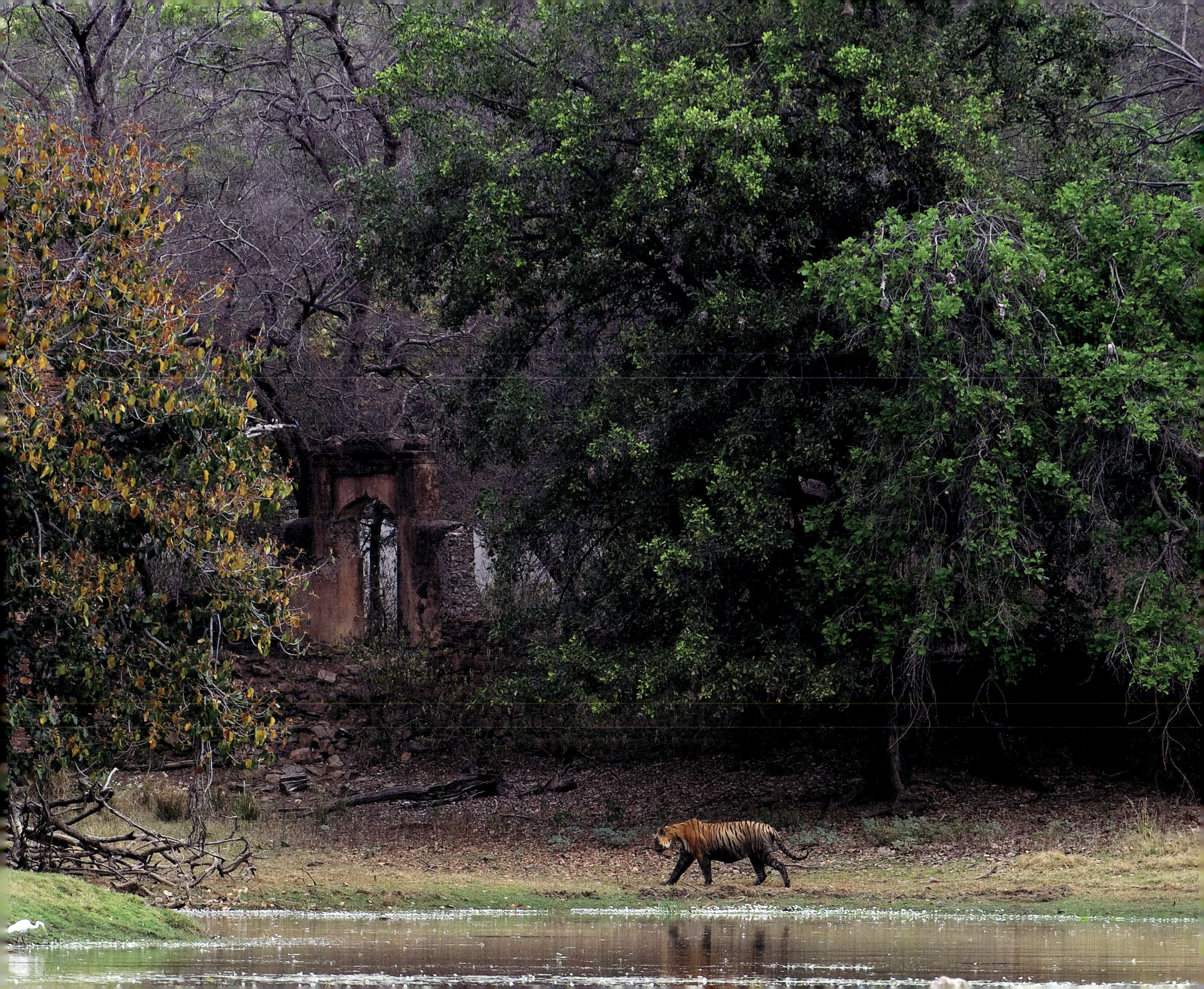

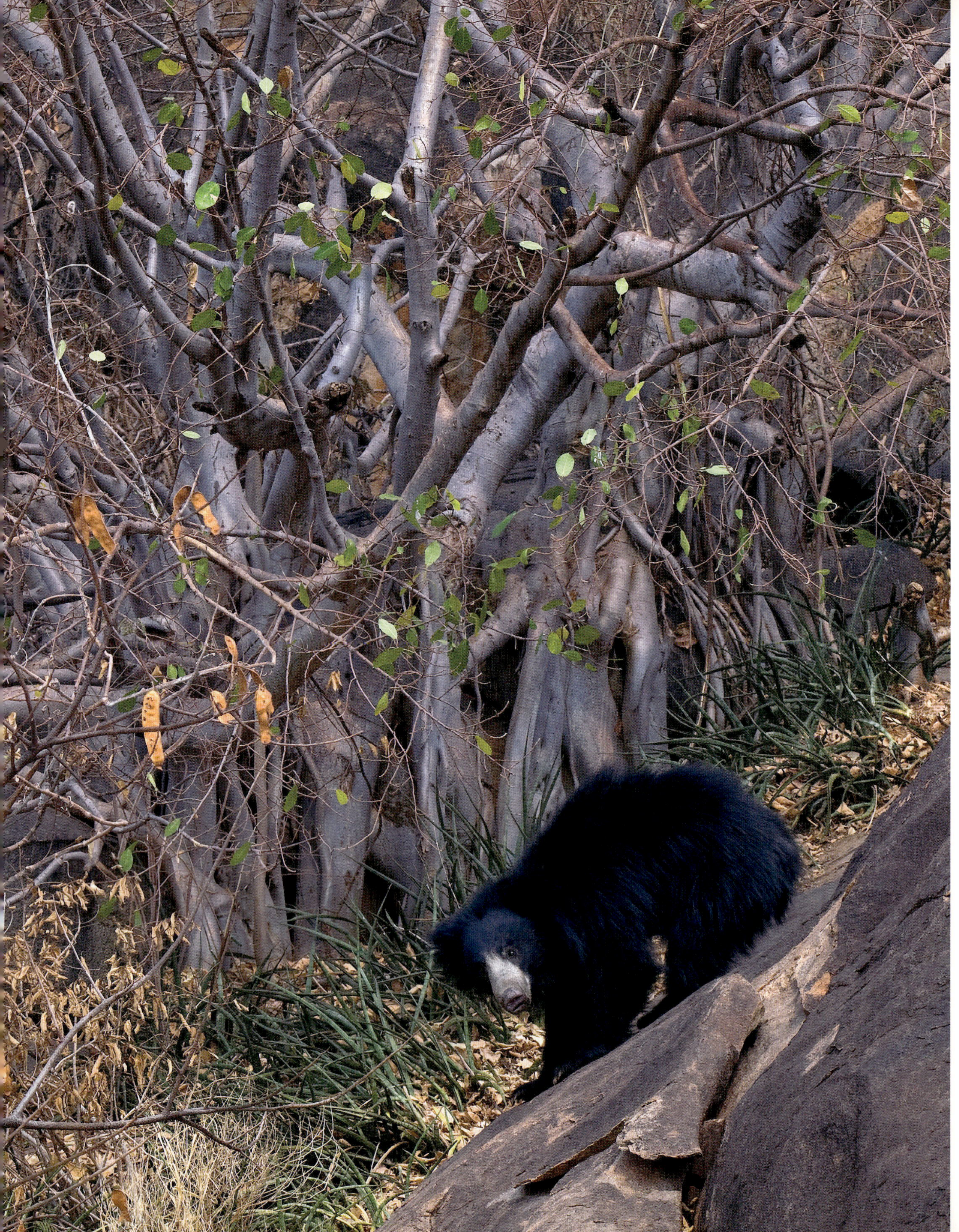

The sloth bear (left) was the inspiration for the fictional character *Baloo* from Rudyard Kipling's *The Jungle Book*. The bear occupies a variety of habitats, including rocky hill country and jungle. Indian peafowl (opposite) are characteristic birds of India and often occupy the same territories as the sloth bears. This male is perched on a huge banyan tree.

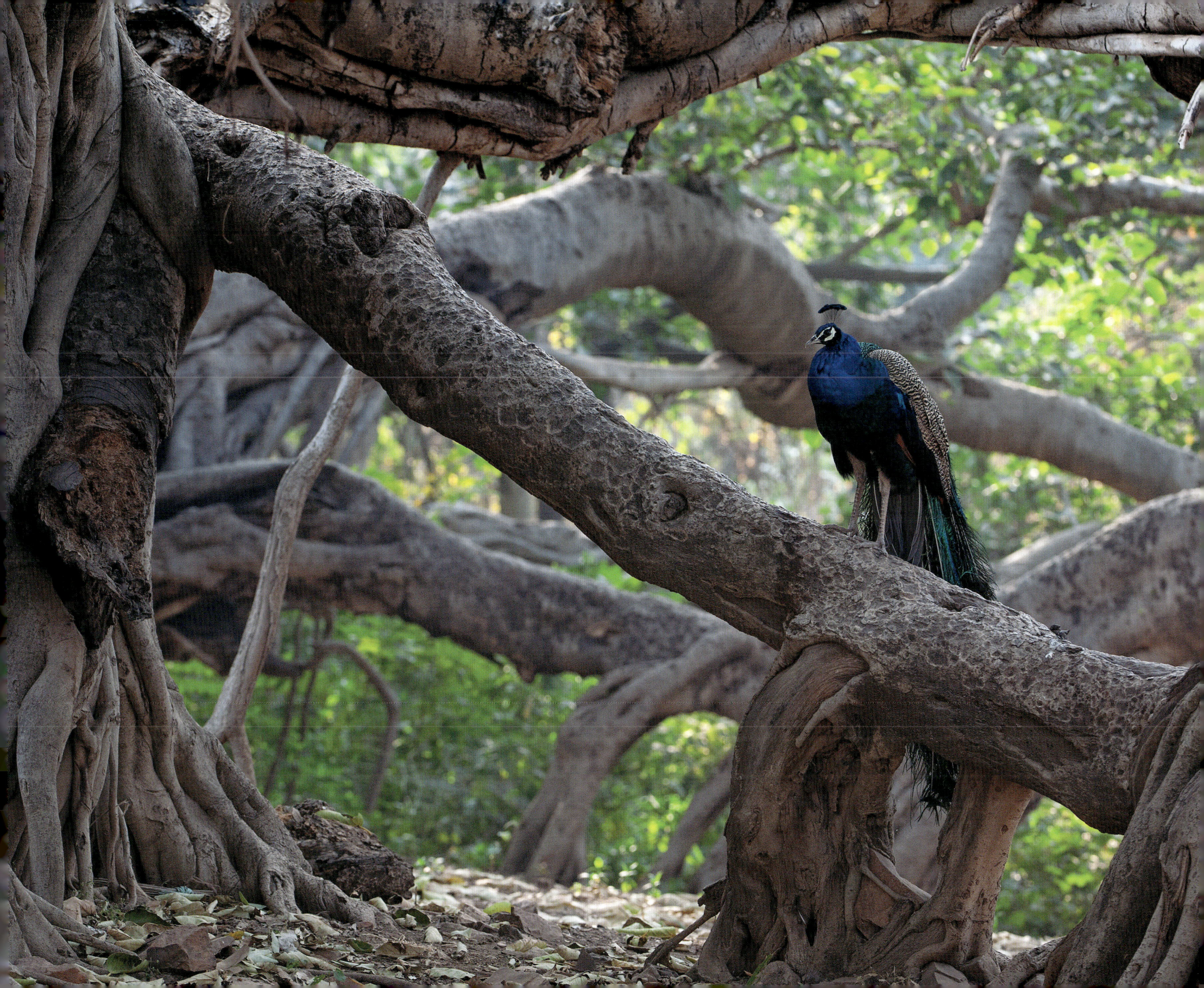

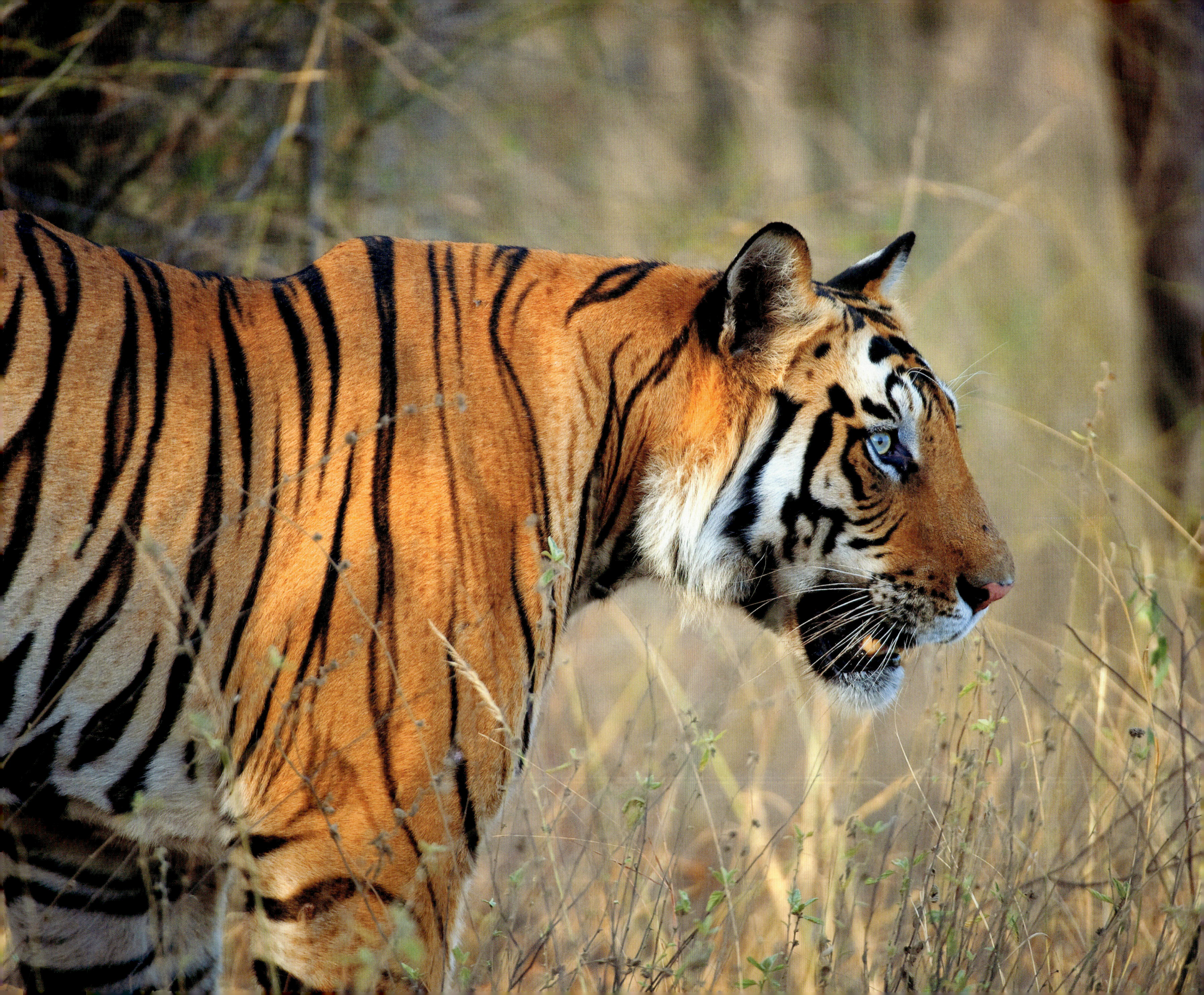

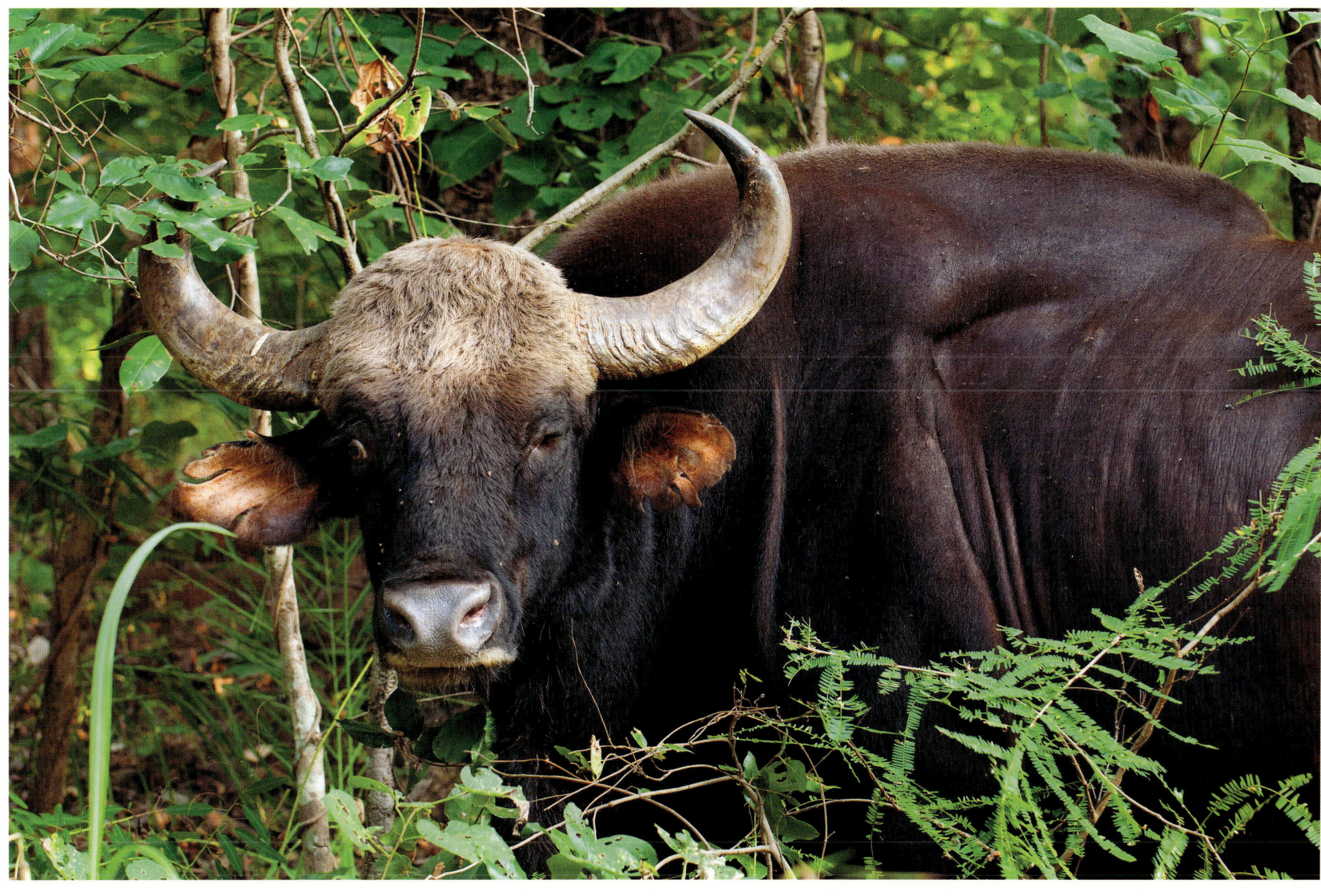

The gaur is one of the largest wild cattle species in the world. Massive bulls like this one (above) from the Kanha National Park in Madhya Pradesh are fierce fighters and can weigh up to a thousand kilograms. Tigers (opposite) have been known to attack and kill these large herbivores, although they tend to hunt smaller prey, such as deer or wild boar.

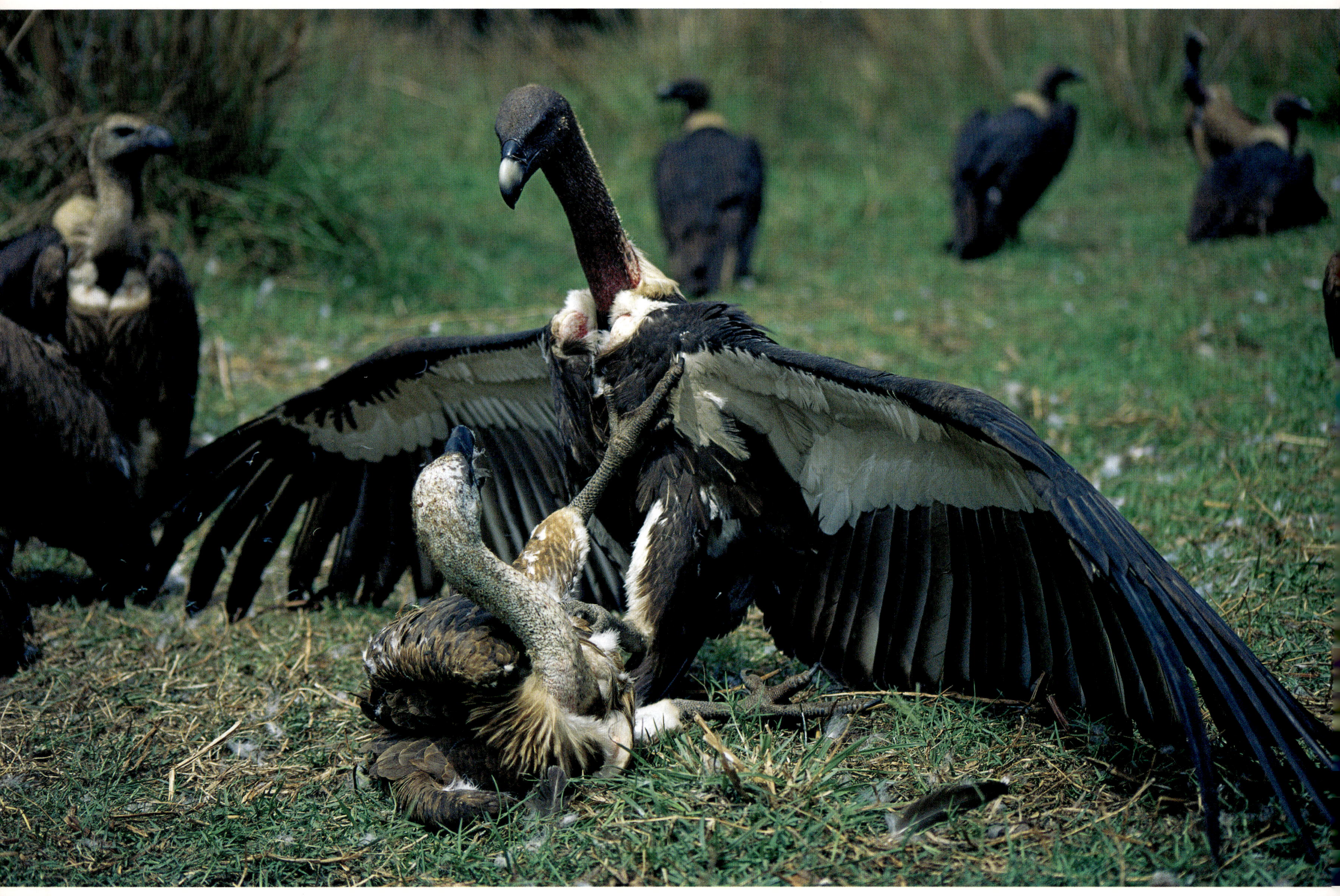

There is a whole array of scavengers that benefit from the leftovers of a tiger kill. Here, white-rumped vultures fight over a carcass (opposite). Although they do not maintain a strict hierarchy, the hungriest bird will act most aggressively in order to get its share. This young tiger cub (right), cannot yet make a kill on its own and is still dependant on the care of its mother.

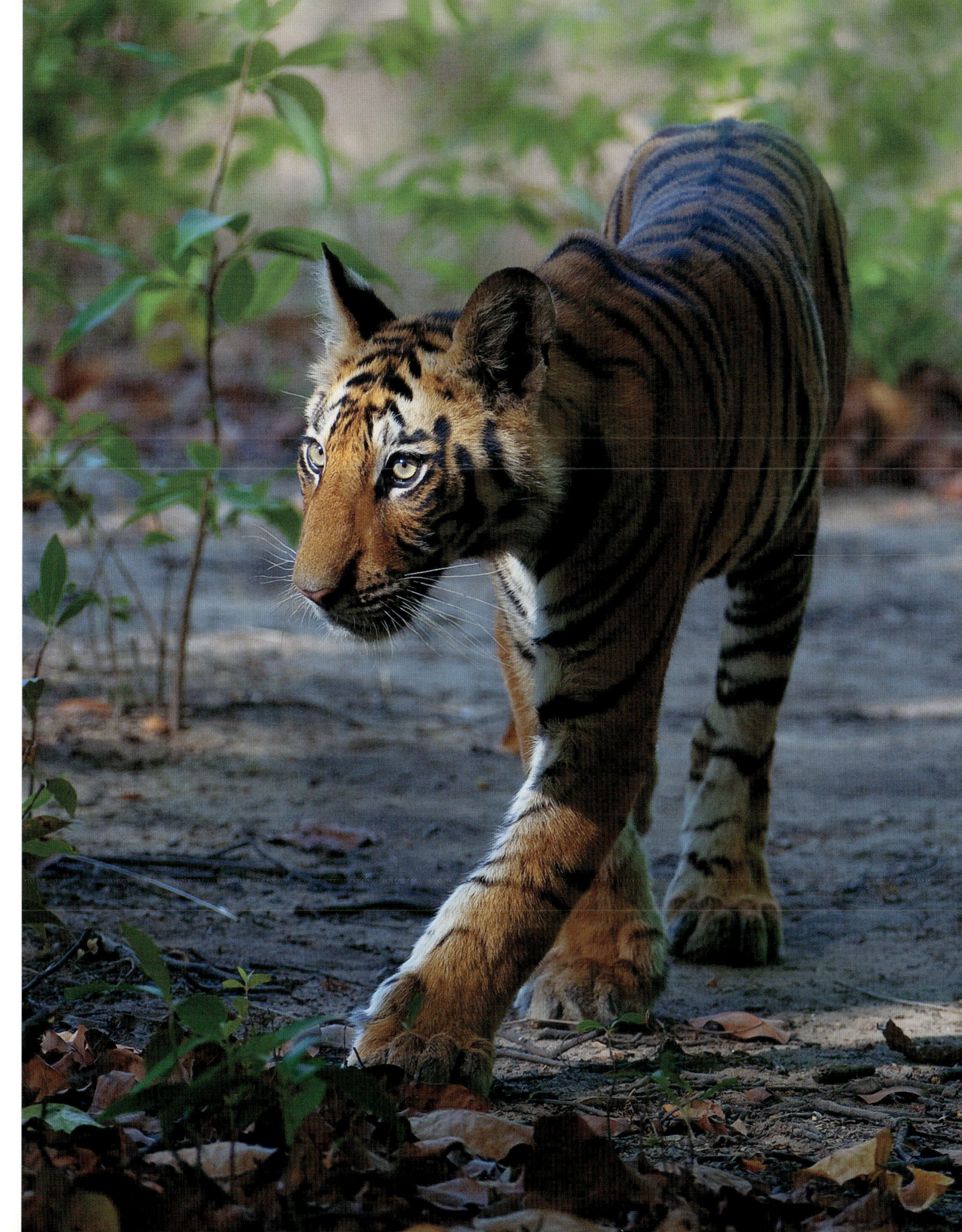

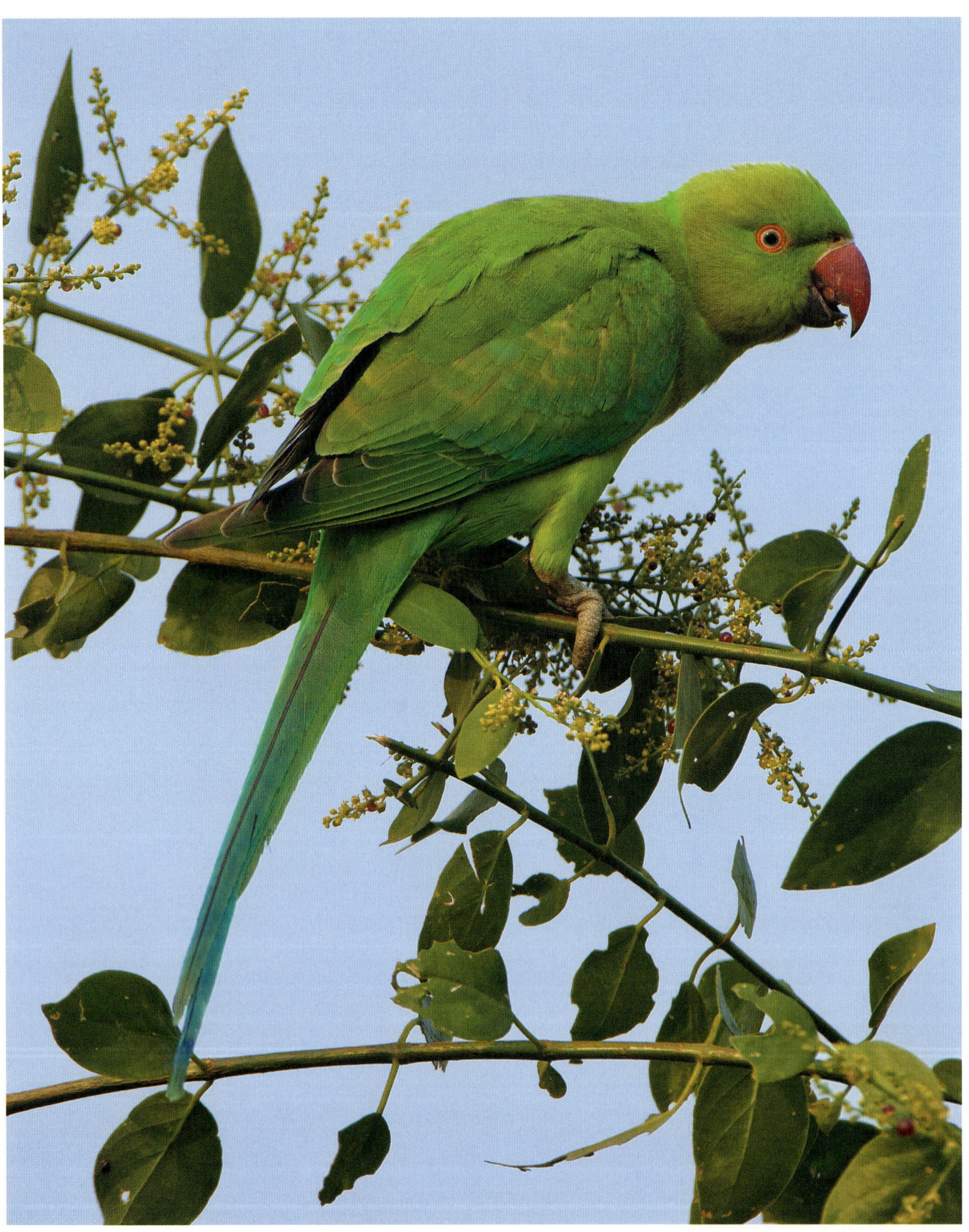

The rose-ringed parakeet (left) and the Indian flying fox (opposite) are common species that are widespread throughout India. While the parakeets eat buds, fruits, vegetables, nuts, and seeds, flying foxes feed mainly on ripe fruits, playing an important role in regenerating plant growth by dispersing seeds within their droppings.

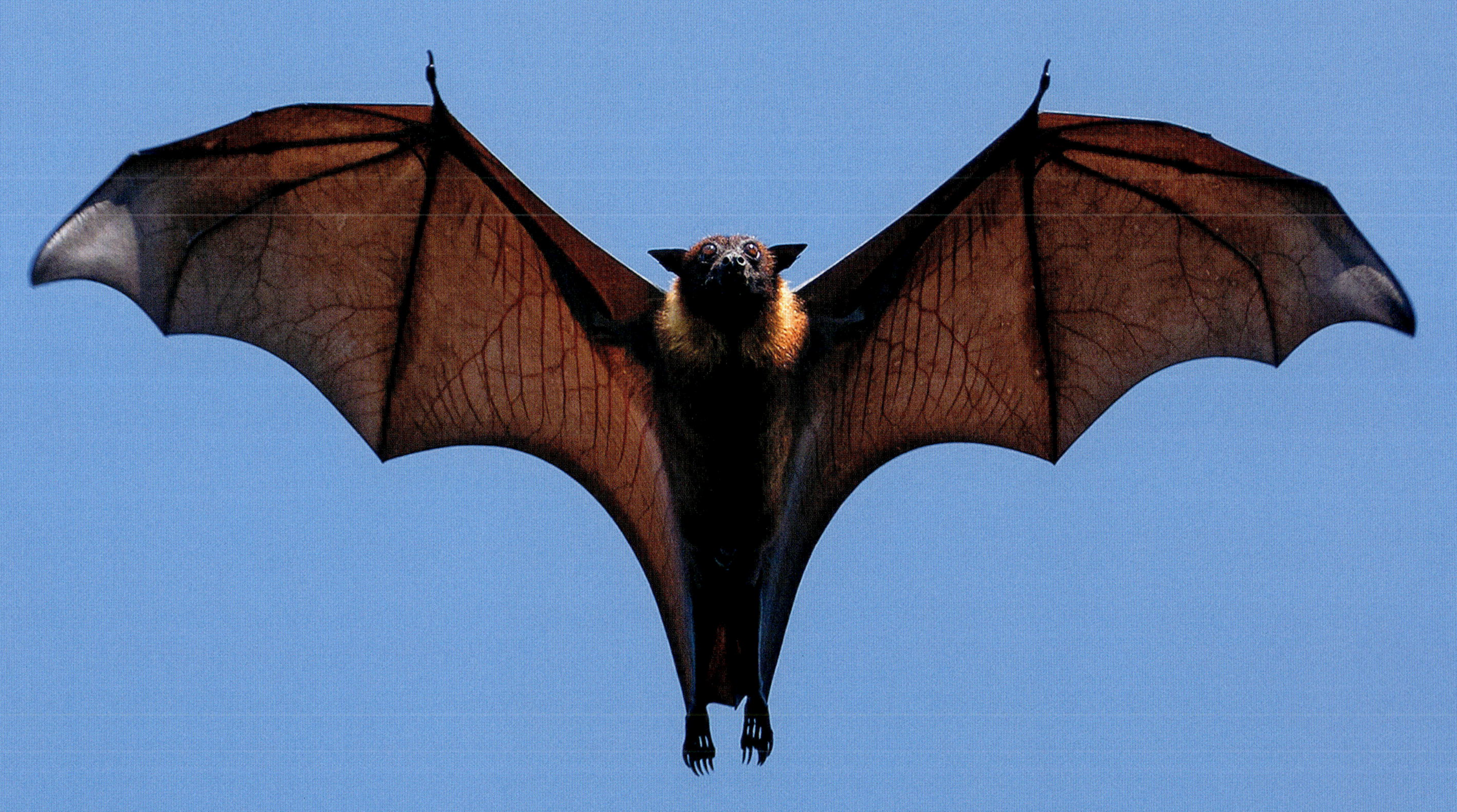

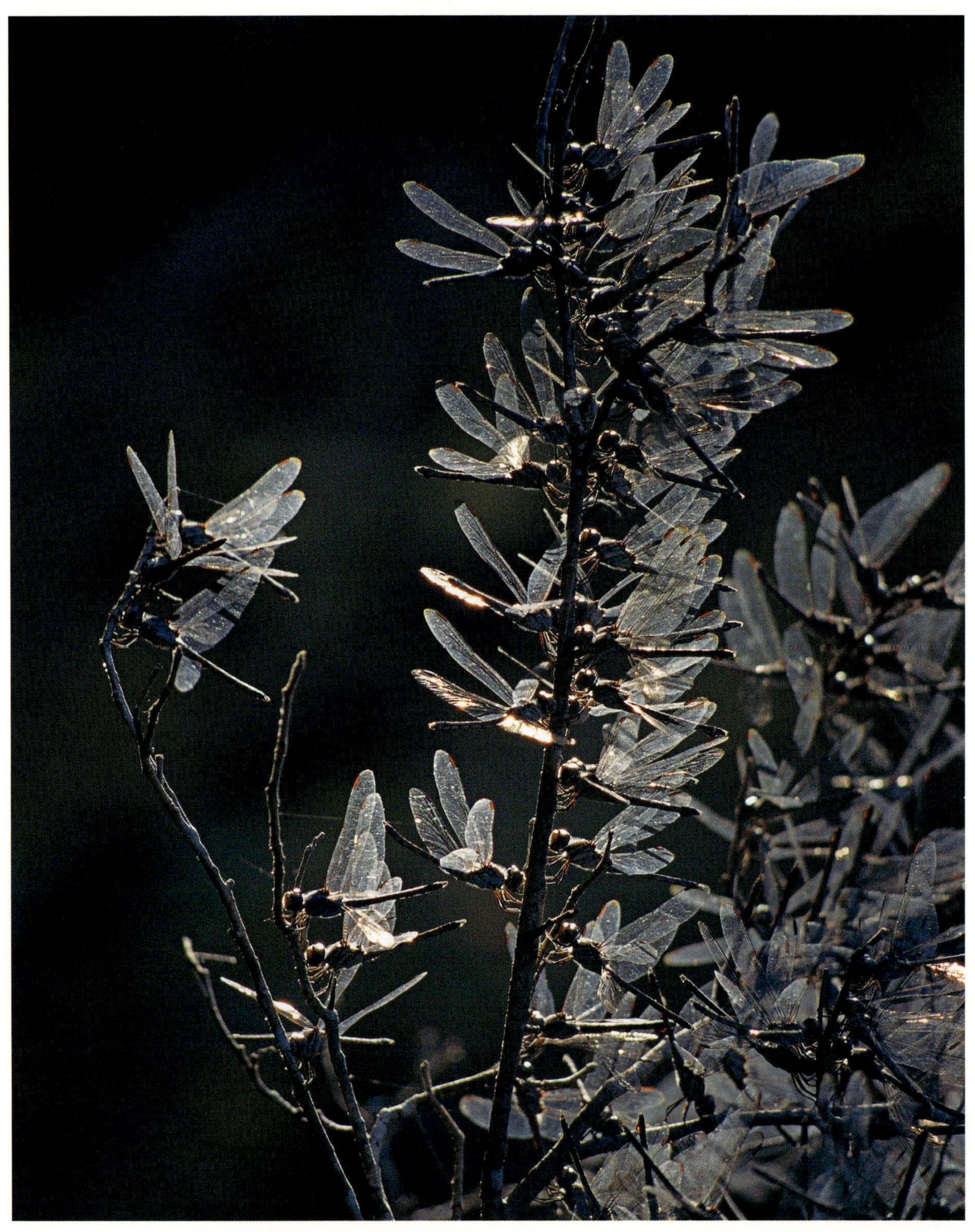

Dragonflies are predominantly diurnal hunters that rest in solitary at night. At times, the jungle offers a surprise, such as this sleeping community of dragonflies in the Kanha National Park in Madhya Pradesh. What appears to be leaves are actually wings. Once warmed up by the morning sun, the dragonflies will dart away in different directions.

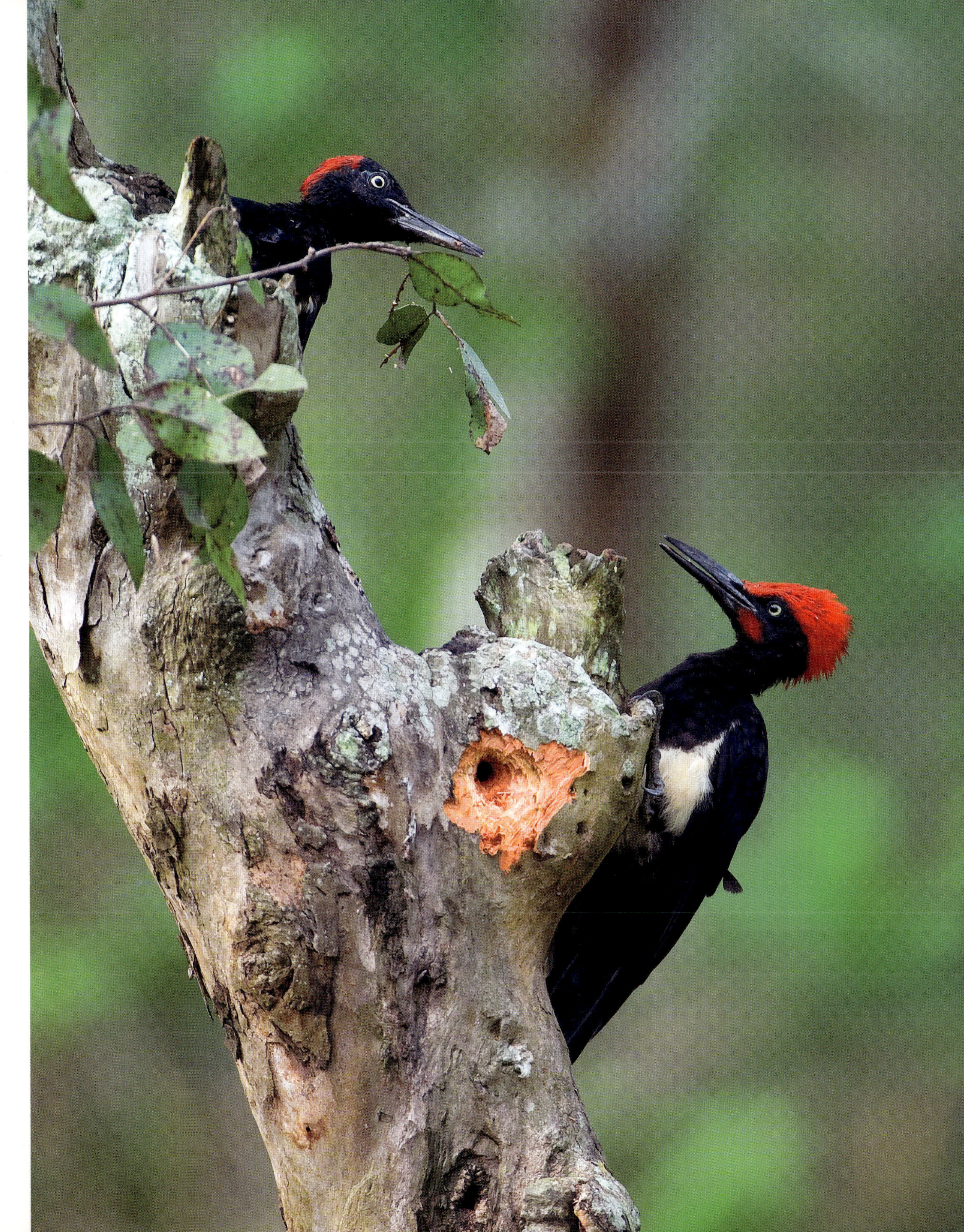

White-bellied woodpeckers are among the largest living species of woodpecker. They prefer natural forests with a mixture of young and old trees, such as in the Western Ghats of South India. The male has a red crown and red moustachial stripes, whereas the female's red plumage is restricted to the hindcrown.

Tigers once ranged widely from Turkey across to the east coast of Russia. Over the past century, their numbers have been in serious decline as they lost the vast majority of their historic range, dropping from around 100,000 to some 3900 alive in the wild today, half of which are in India. This female, from the Kanha National Park in Madhya Pradesh, has contributed several litters to a population where each and every animal counts.

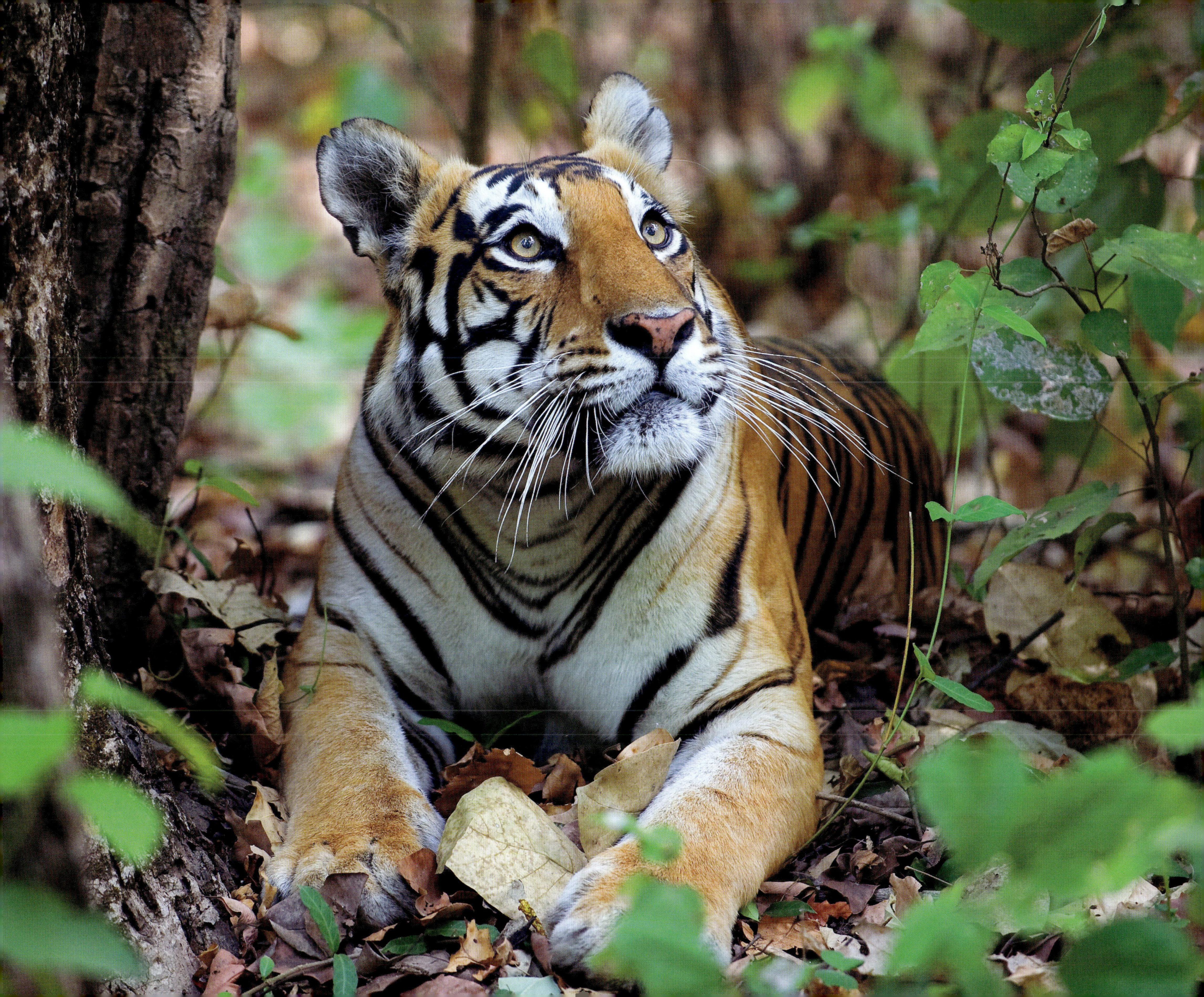

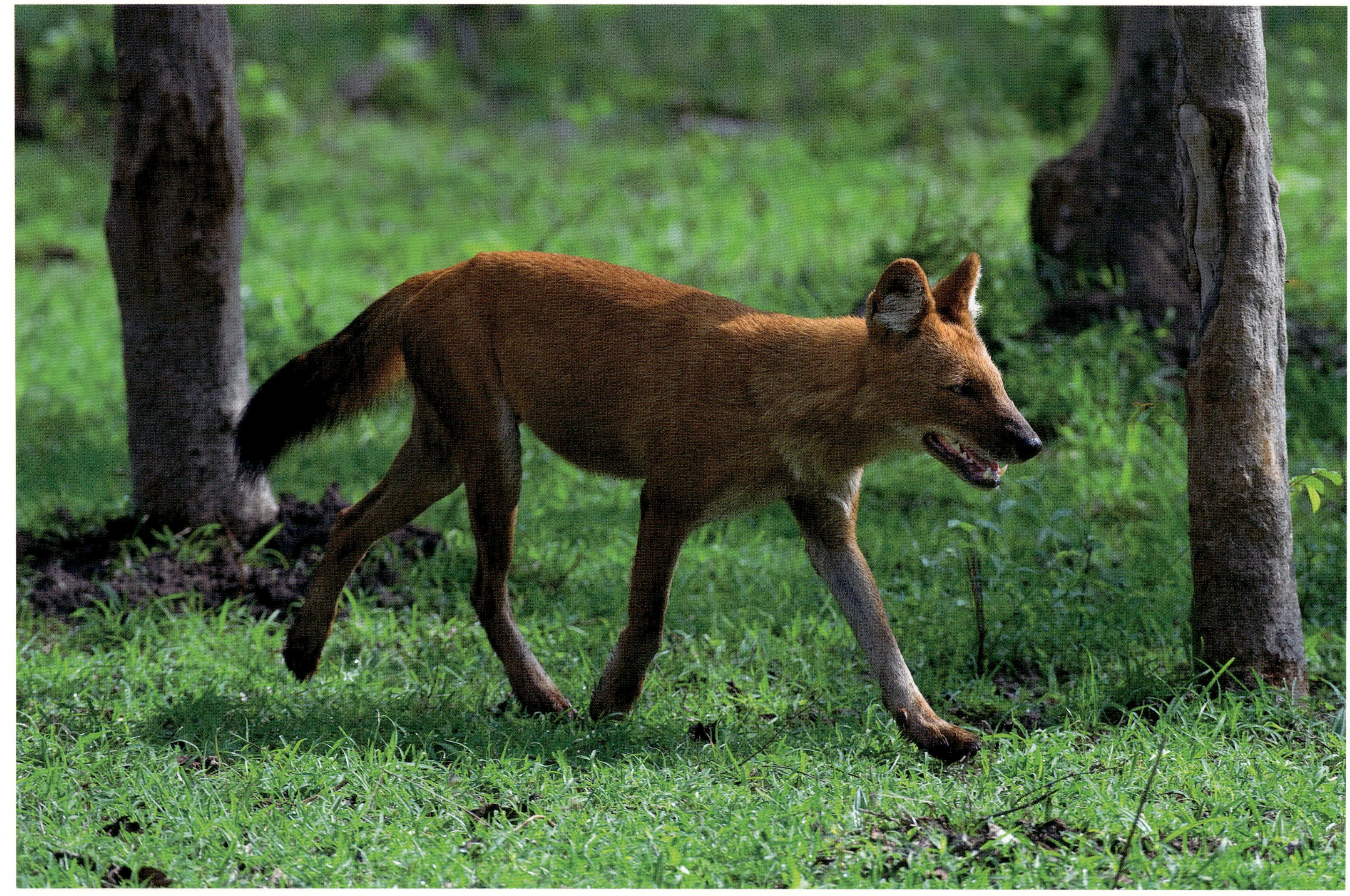

Asiatic wild dogs, also known as dholes, are extremely efficient predators. This photograph (opposite) shows them having brought down a spotted deer in the Nagarhole National Park in Karnataka. Asiatic wild dogs can form large packs, and on some occasions they can even attack tigers. Today, their numbers are in serious decline, and the species has been listed as being endangered.

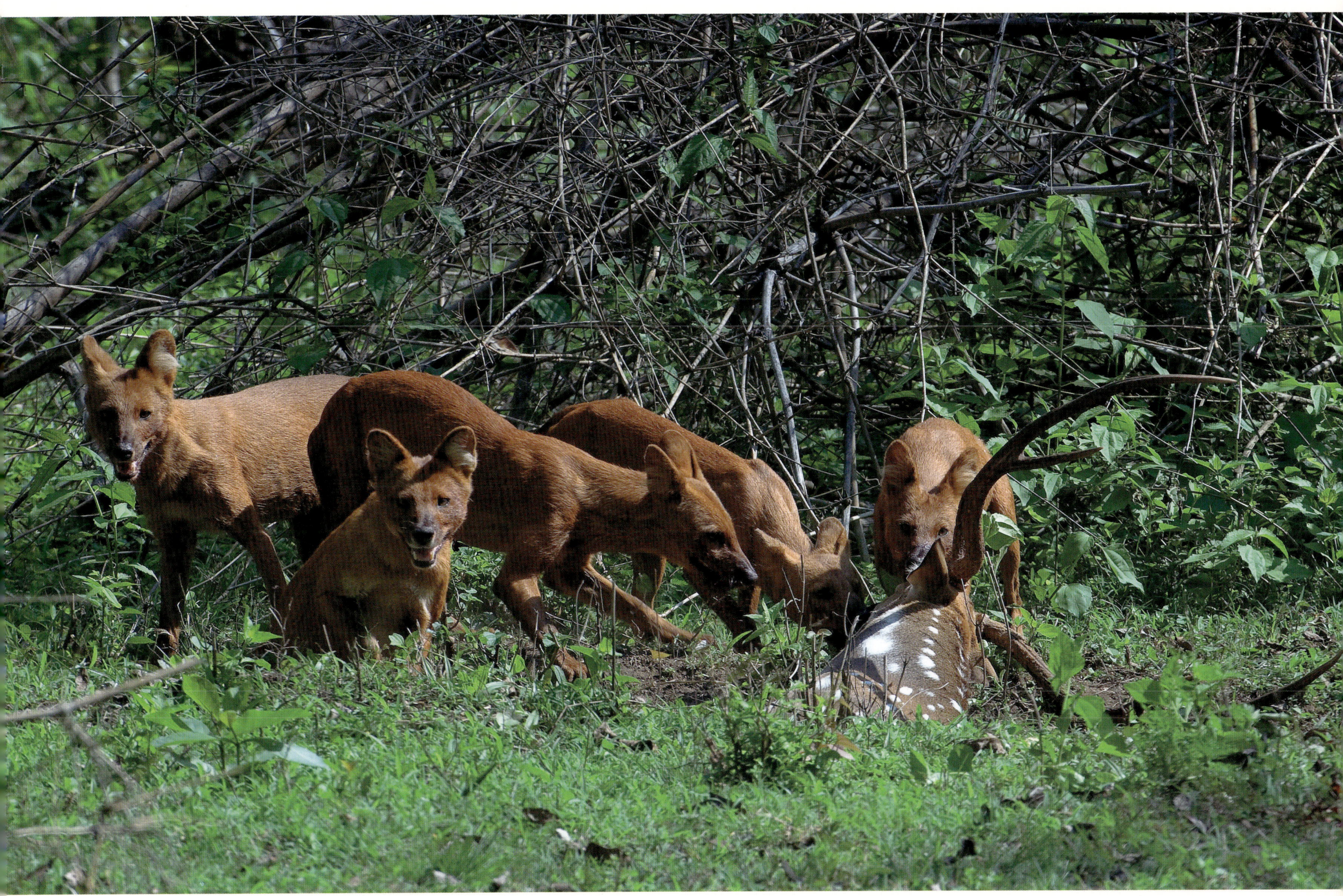

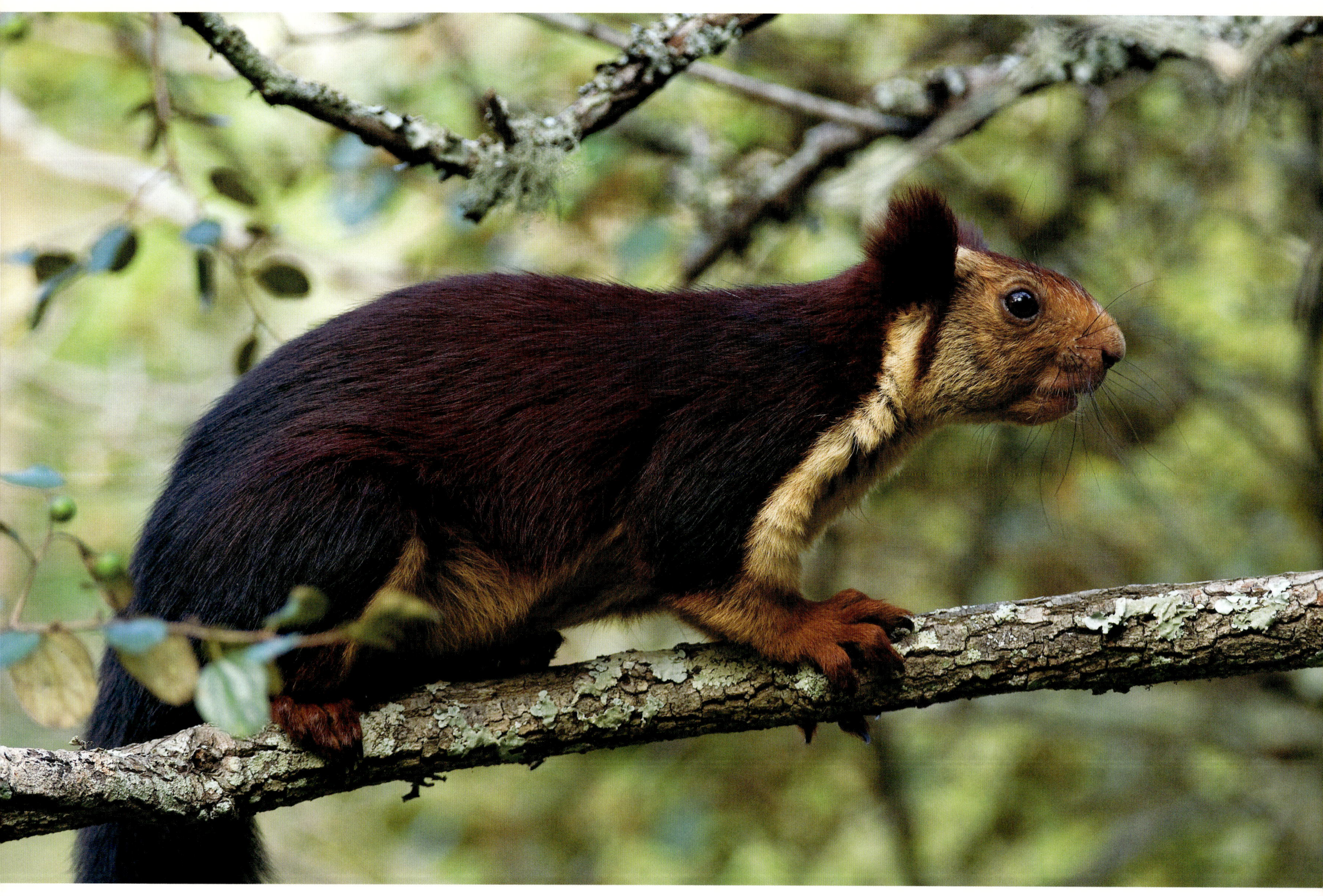

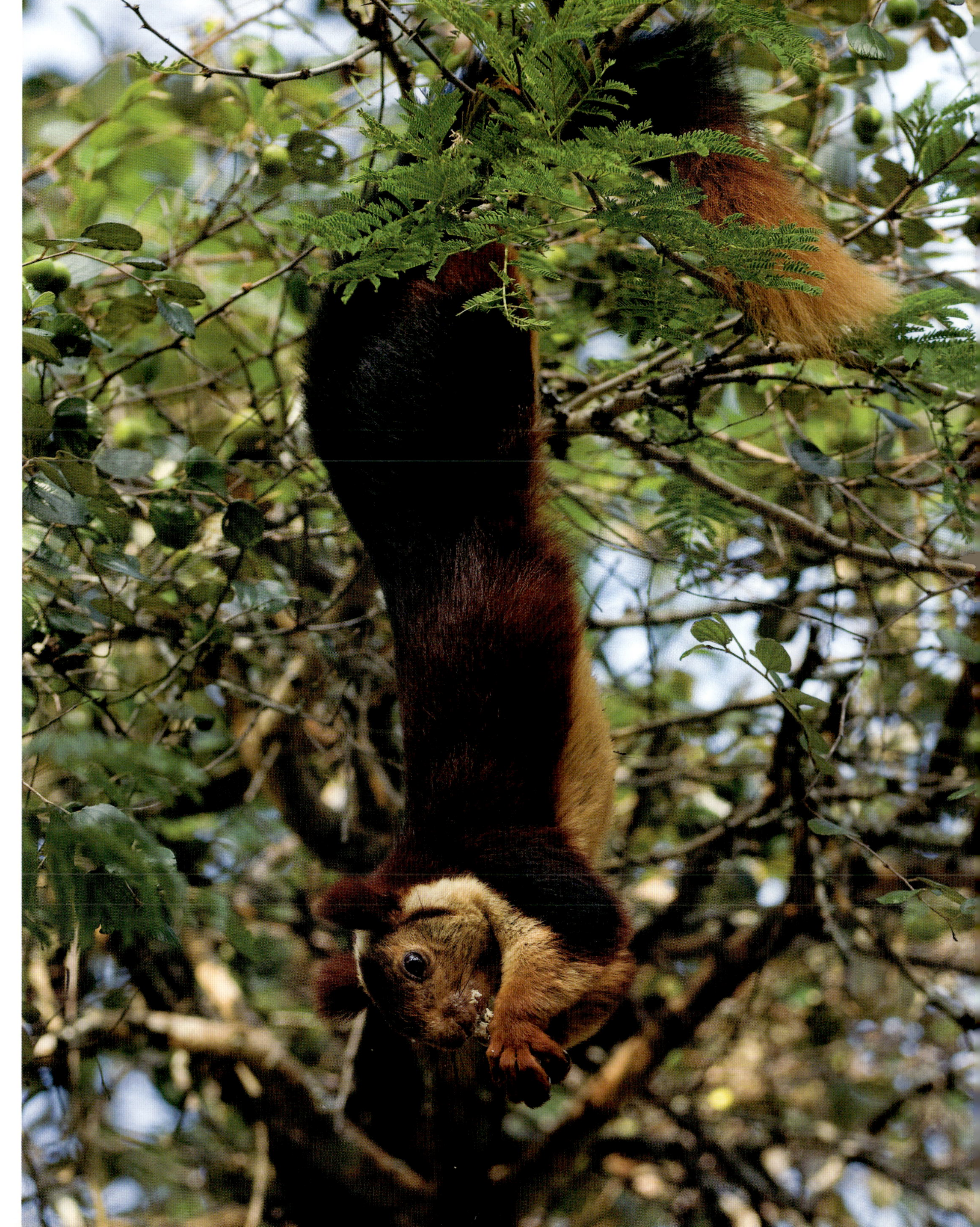

The Indian giant squirrel is aptly named; it can reach to be the size of an average house cat. These large rodents are very agile climbers and with a jump span of up to six metres, they rarely leave the trees. This particular one (right) is cracking open a nut while hanging upside down a tree in the Western Ghats of South India.

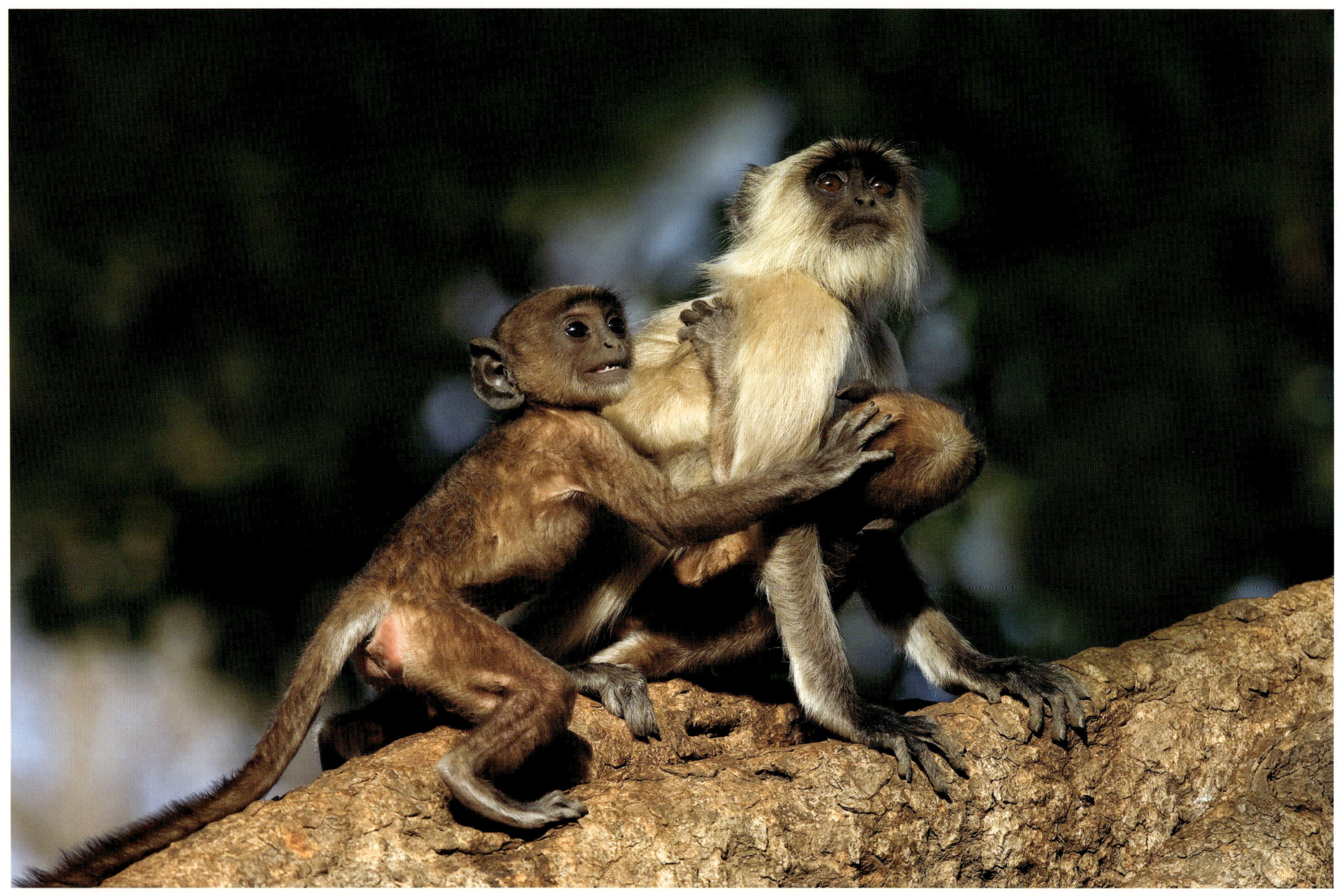

Even when playing up in the trees, these young Bengal hanuman langurs are not safe; the canopy is also a retreat for leopards (opposite), who like to hunt primates whenever a good opportunity arises. In areas where leopards and tigers co-exist, leopards will take refuge in the trees in order to avoid their stronger relatives, who can be a danger to them.

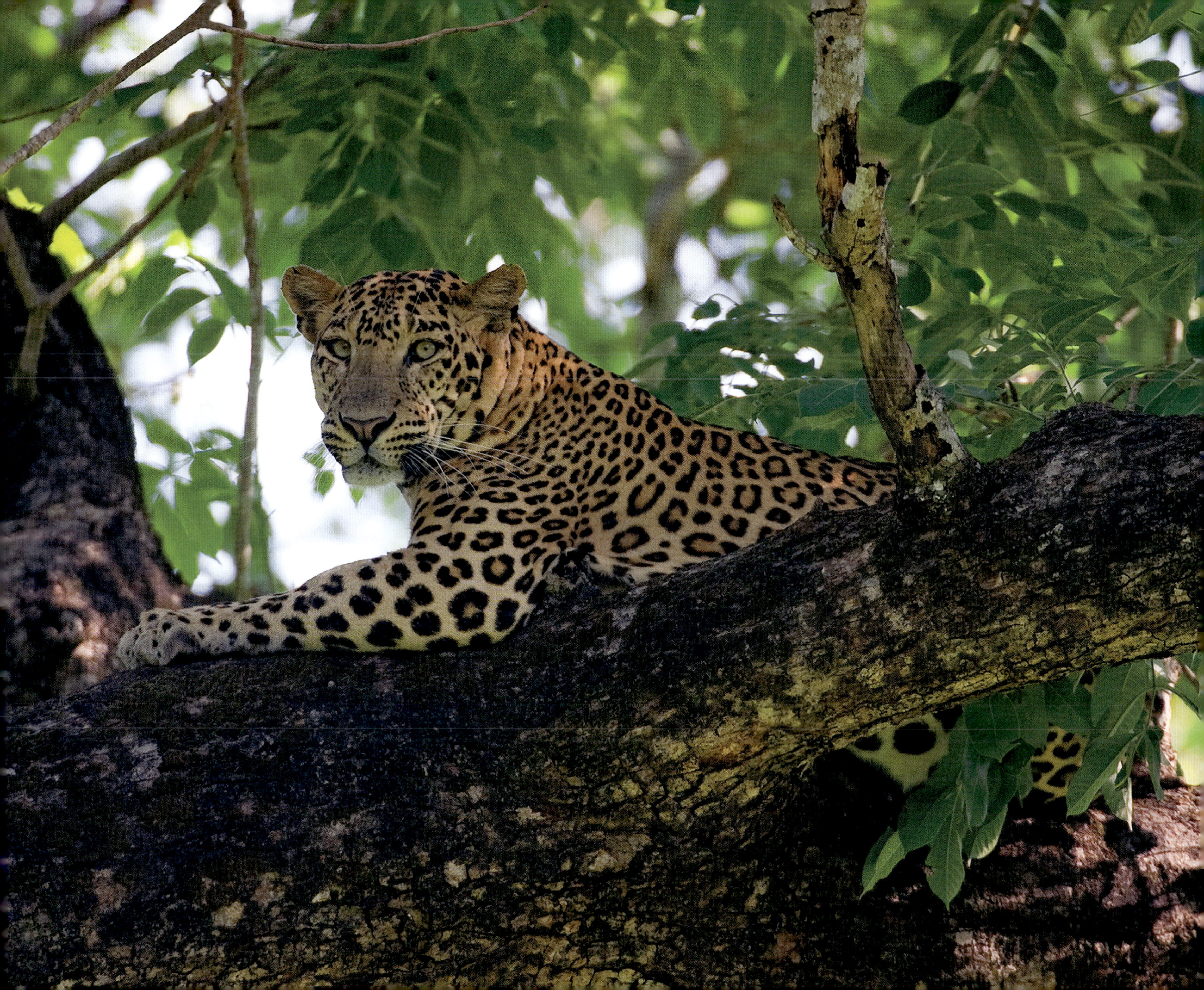

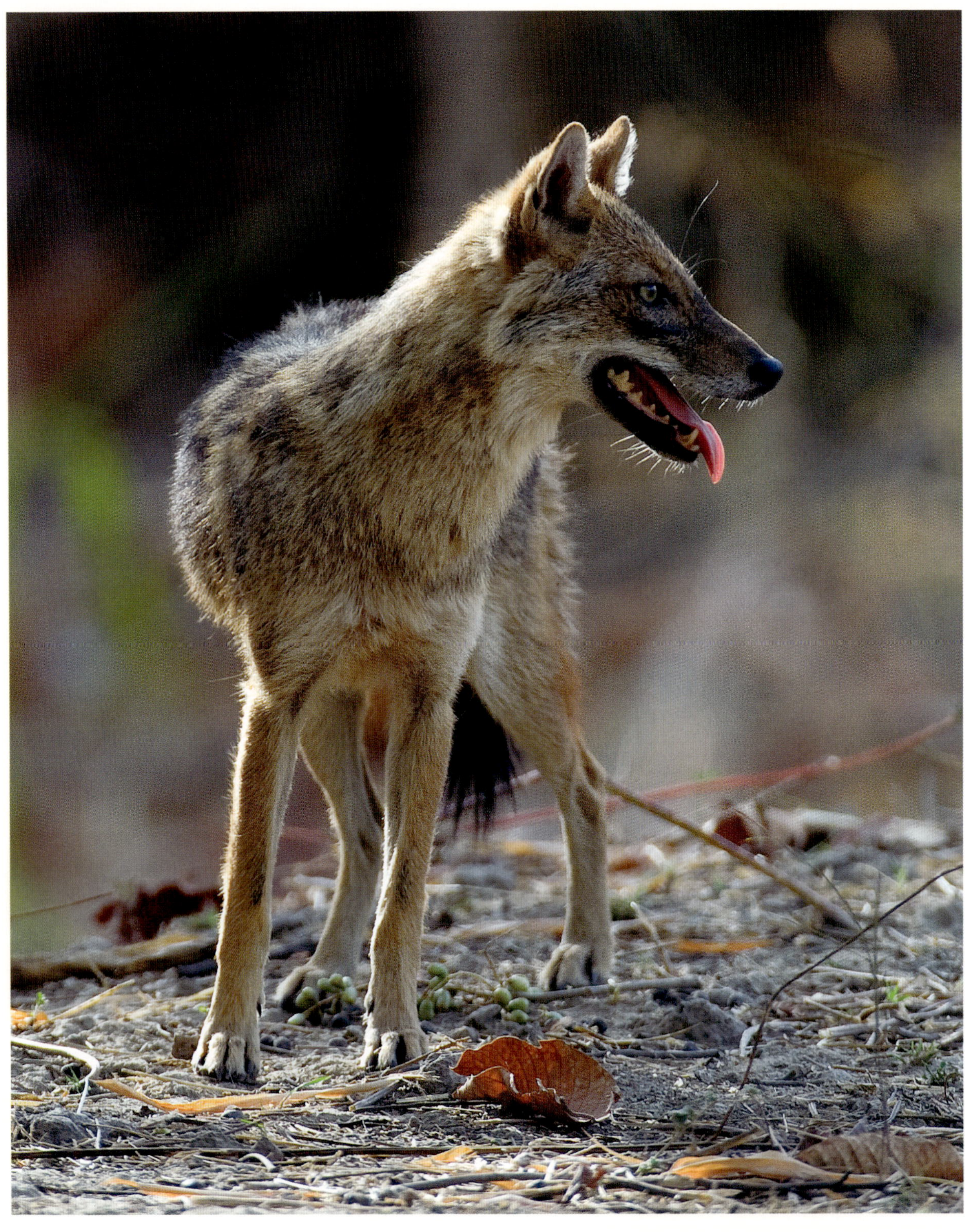

The golden jackal (left) has the undeserved reputation of being a scavenger, yet it is also a skilful hunter. It is not picky and takes anything it can overcome, including rodents and reptiles. An adult Indian python, (opposite) however, would be more than a match. This huge snake grows to an average of between three and four metres long, and jackals have been recorded as a rare prey.

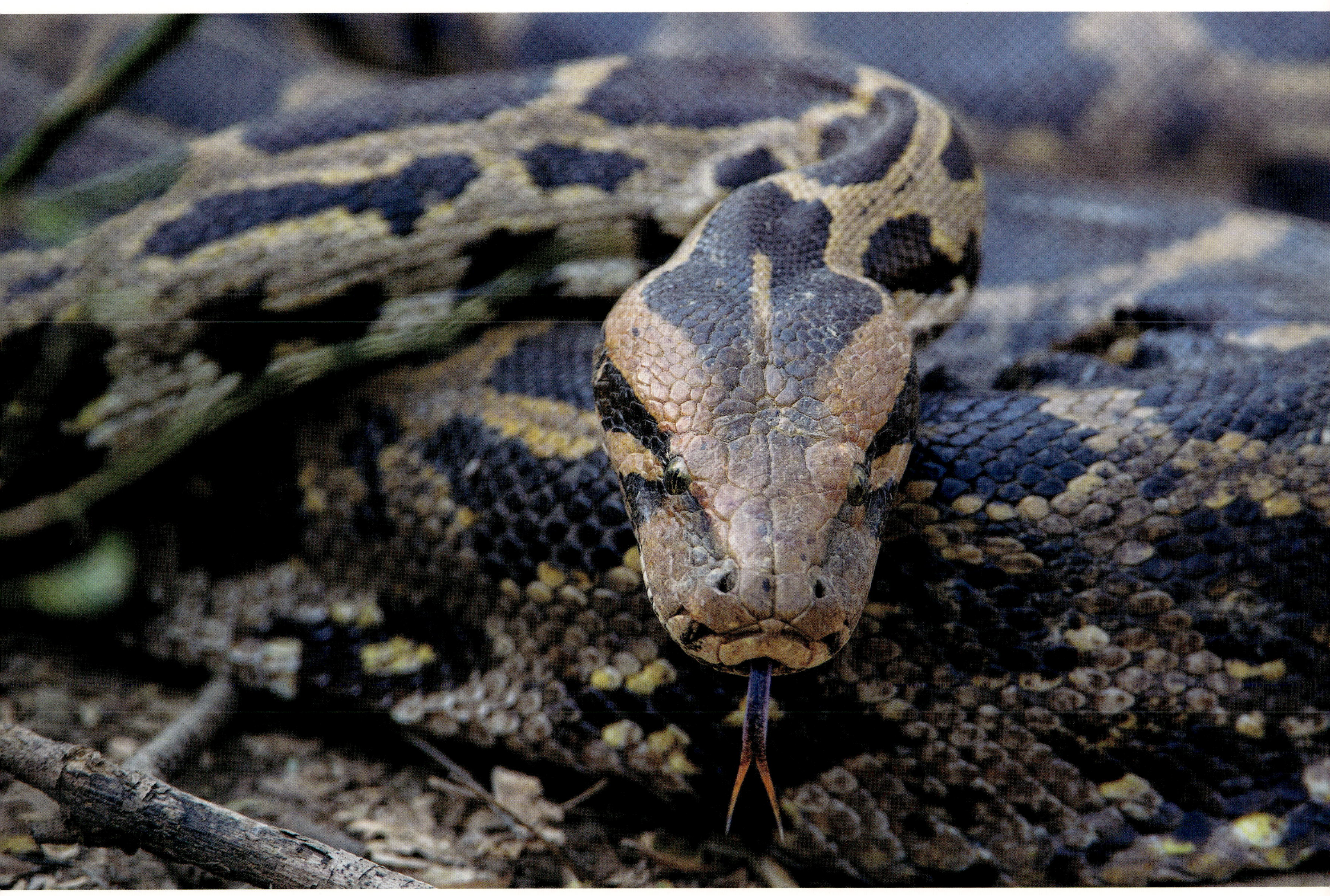

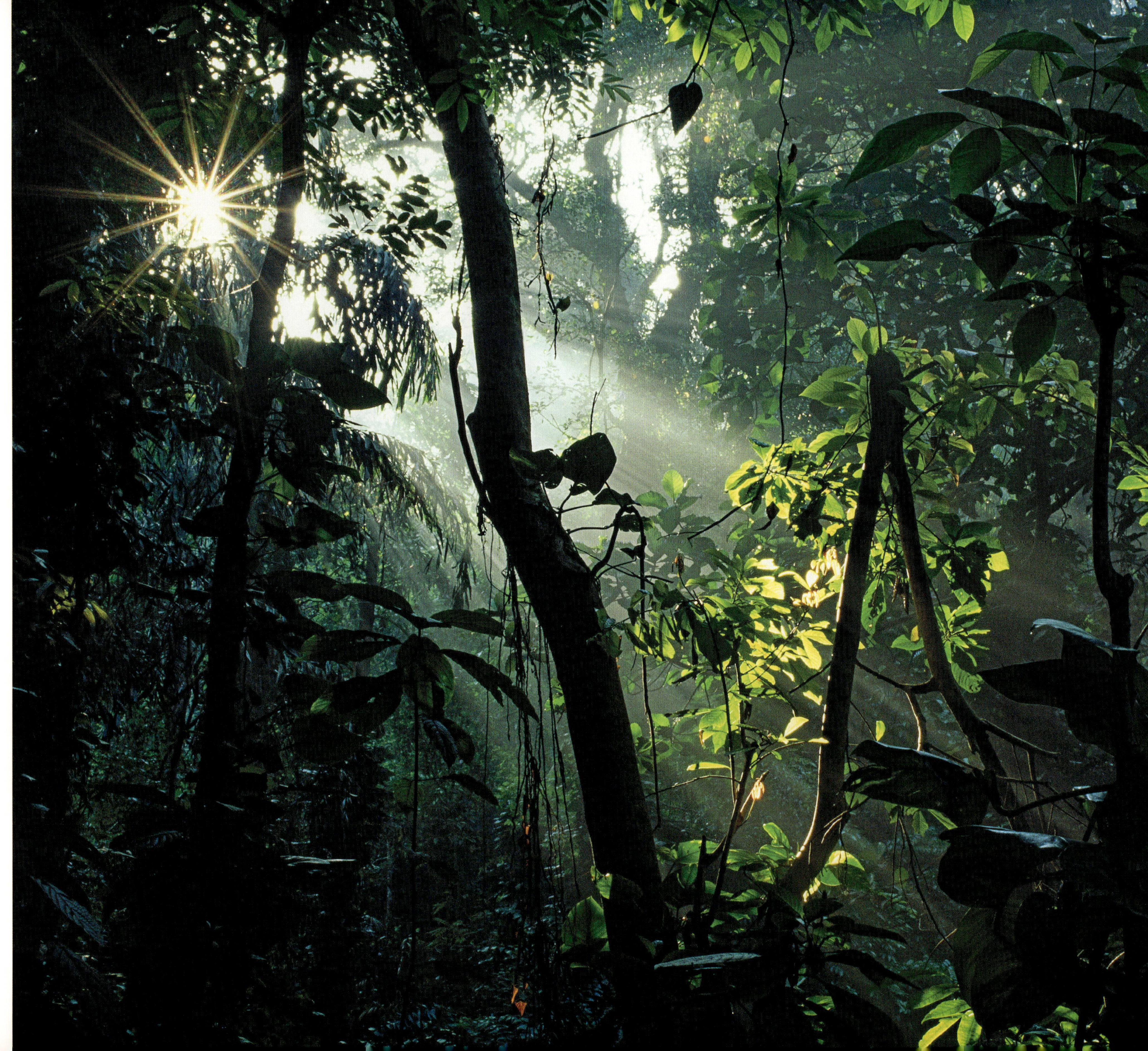

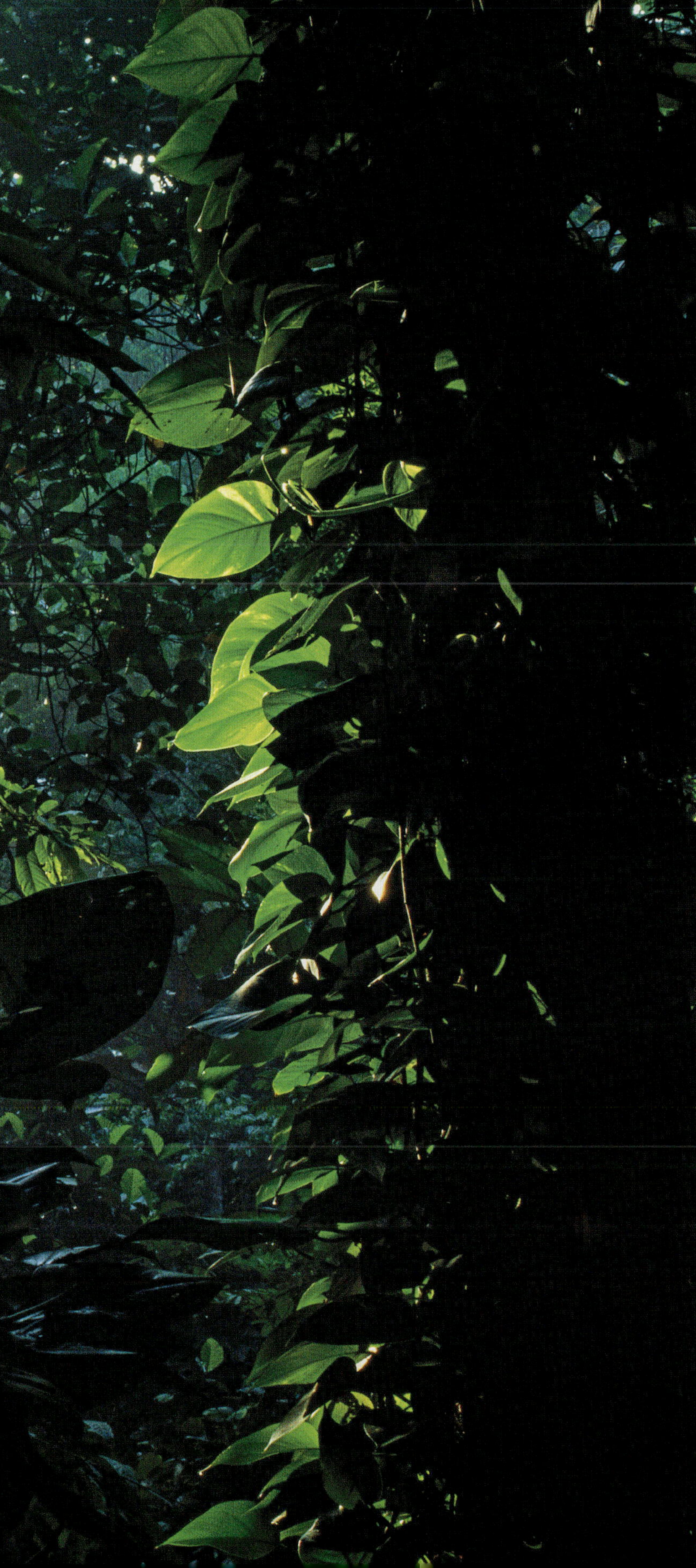

A jungle often evokes an image of dense and overgrown vegetation, a hostile and impenetrable place. In fact, jungles are biodiversity hotspots. Plant growth depends on the amount of annual rainfall, creating rainforests in the northeast and in the Western Ghats, running parallel to the west coast of India, and monsoon forests, or seasonal tropical forests in central India.

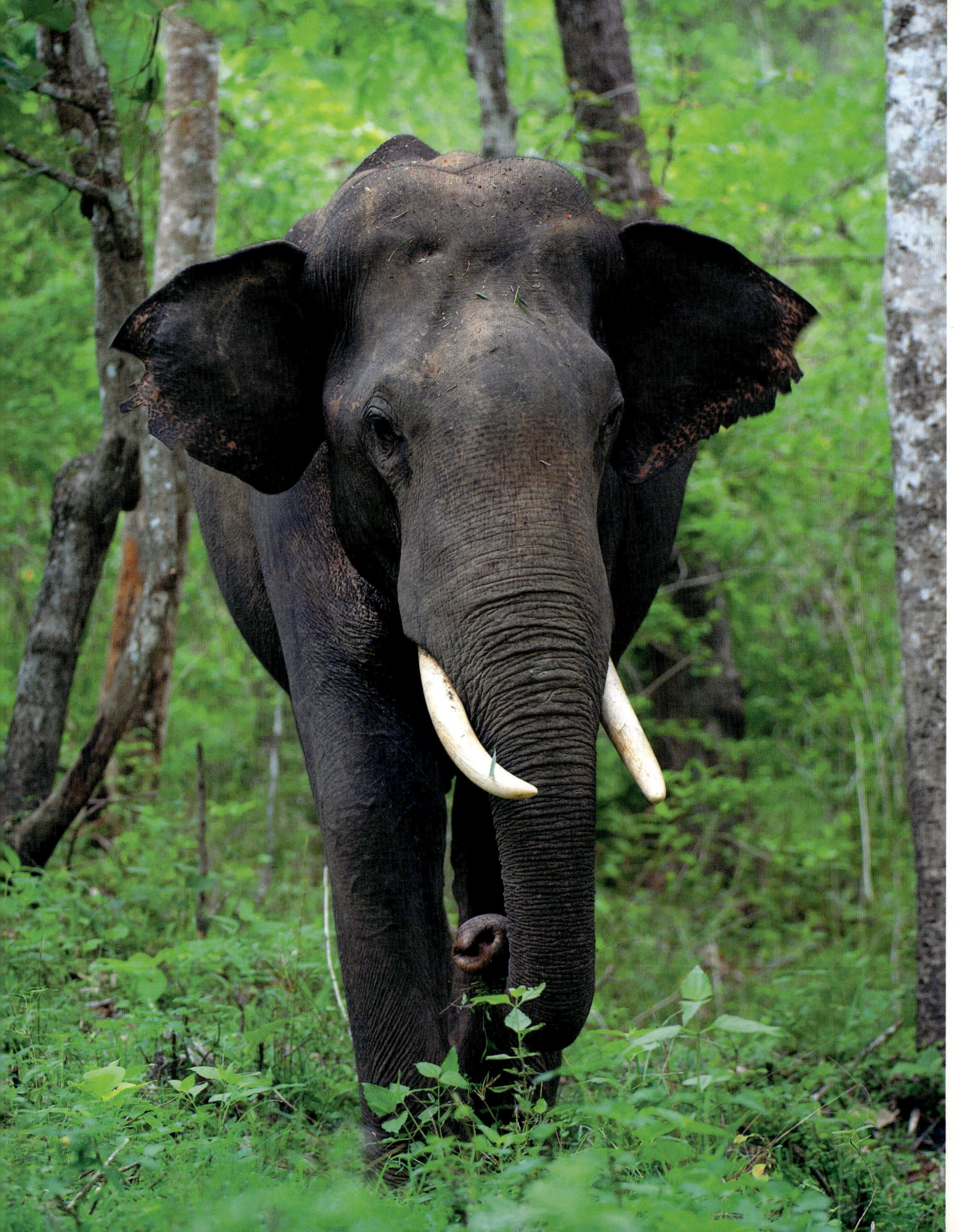

Asian elephants need large areas of land with intact forests in order to sustain themselves. Their depleted population has disappeared from many parts of India and their distribution is now patchy. They still roam areas such as the Western Ghats, the Terai belt at the foothills of the Himalayas, and the forests of northeast India. The females (opposite) lack tusks, whereas the males (left) can bear large tusks, adding to their prehistoric appearance, such as this tusker from the Nagarhole National Park in Karnataka.

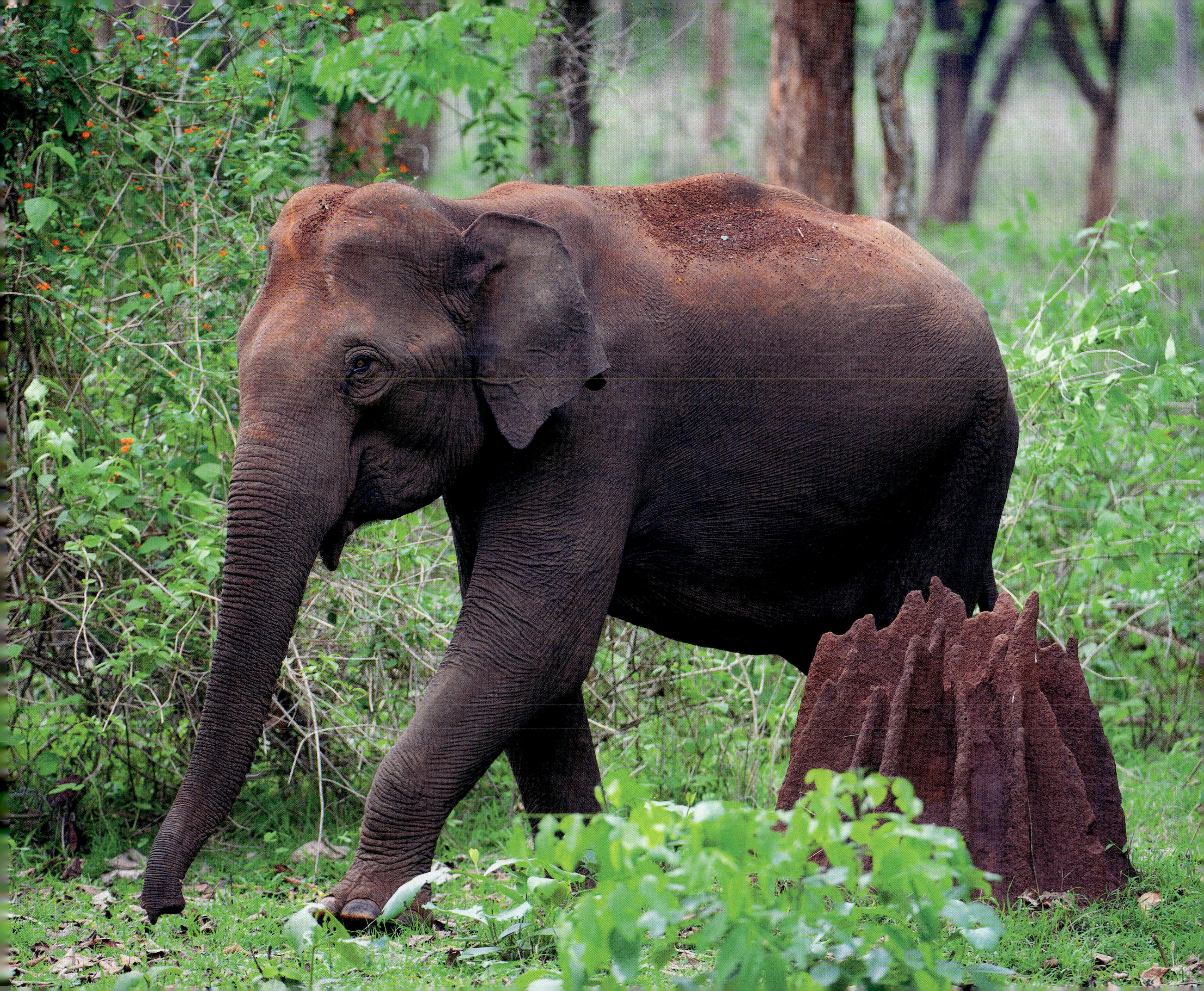

46

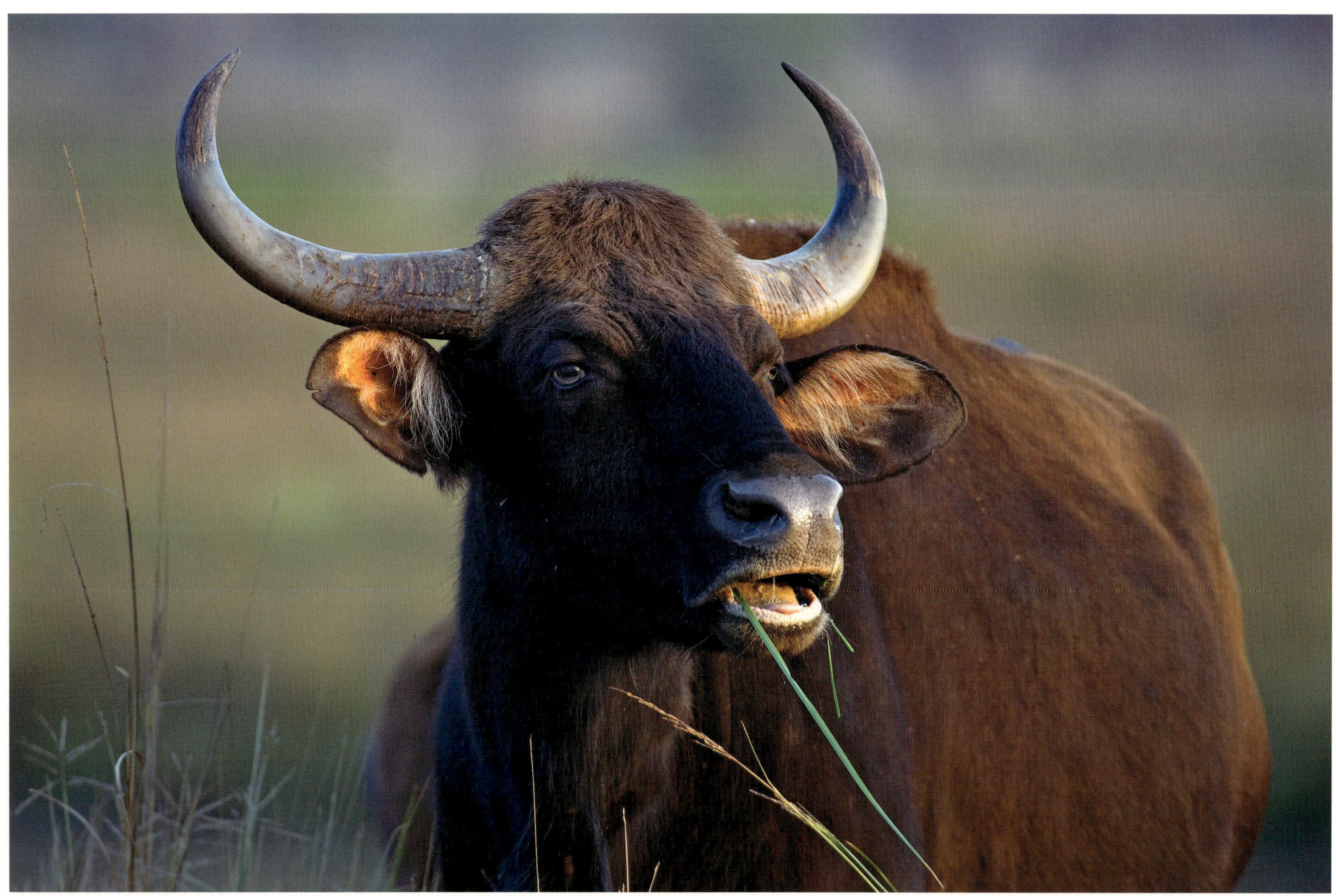

Both Asian elephants (opposite) and gaurs are herbivorous heavyweights. They consume a large number of plants, which in turn shapes their environment, creating clearings in dense vegetation or keeping them open, allowing sunlight to reach new seedlings and helping the forest regenerate naturally.

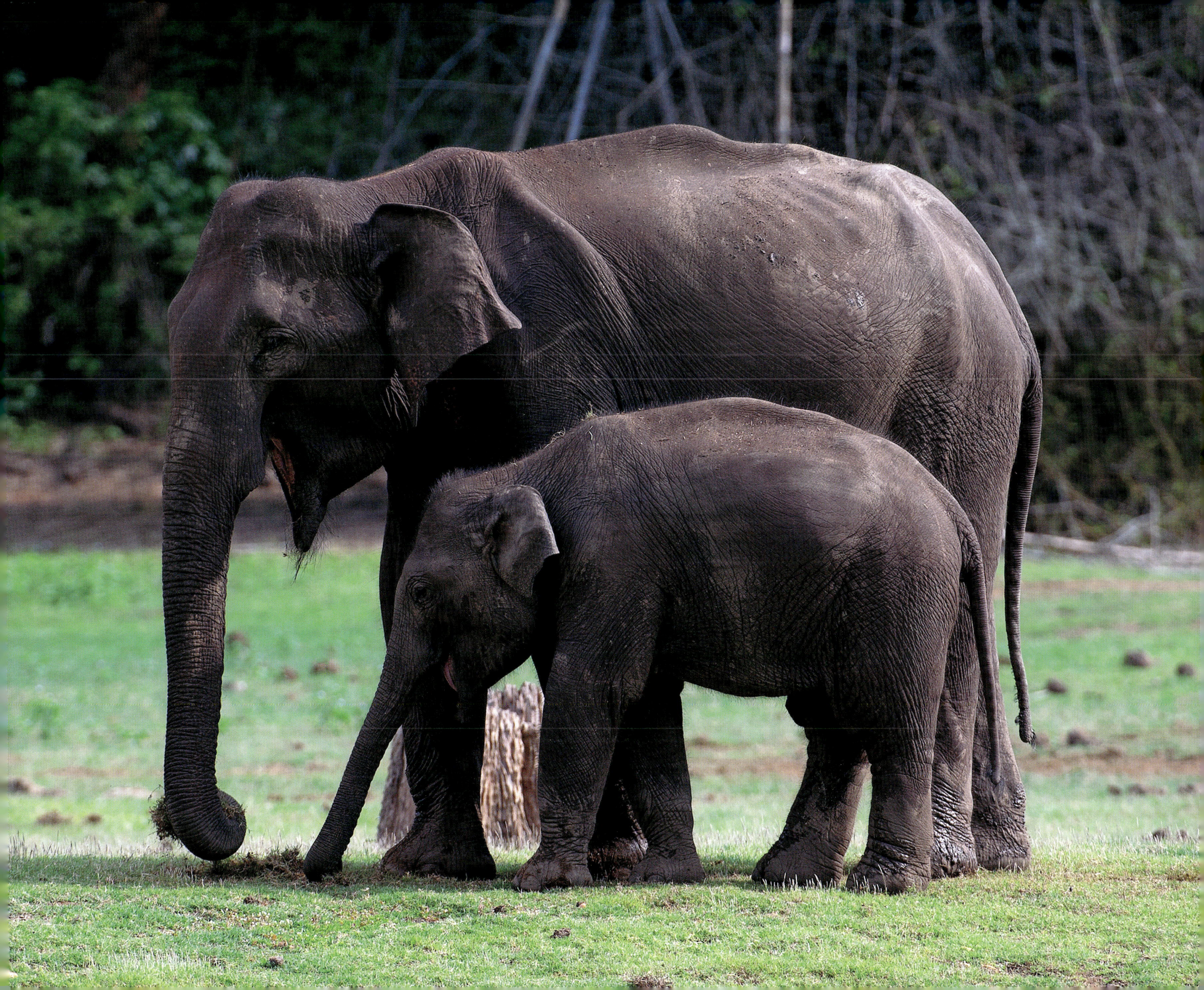

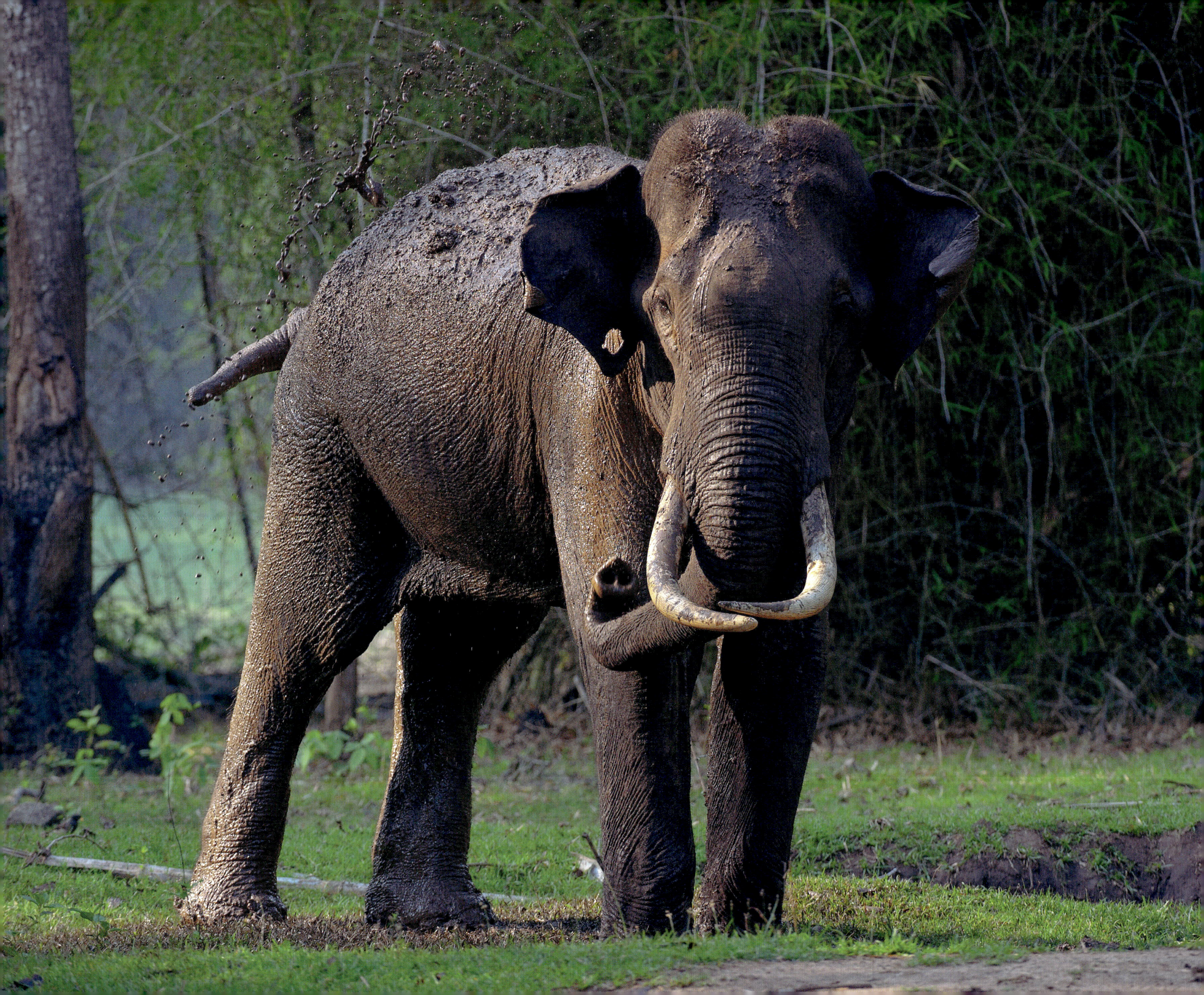

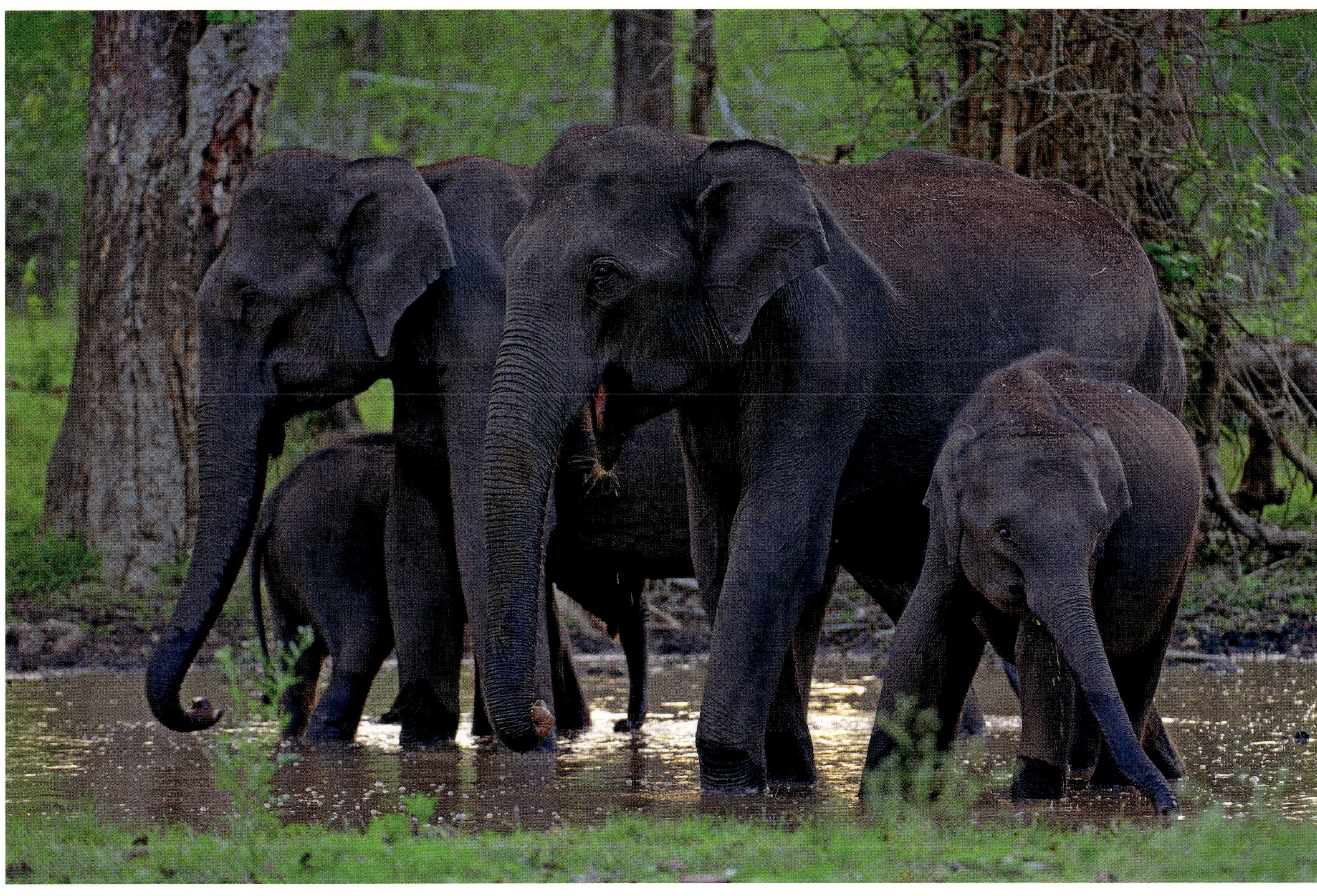

Asian elephants drinking from a forest pool (above) in the Nagarhole National Park in Karnataka. The herd is a family unit, constituting an older matriarch, several females which are most likely related, and their offspring. The calves learn their way around in the jungle by copying their mother's behaviour. Elephants only breed every four to five years, and will have only very few young in their lifetime, investing much time for each calf. Young males leave the herd once they reach sexual maturity, with bulls (opposite) leading a mostly solitary life.

Overleaf:
The Manas National Park lies in northeast India in the state of Assam. Political unrest from the 1980s until 2003 resulted in largescale damage to the wildlife inhabiting this area. The habitat has proven to be good for large mammals such as tigers, Asian elephants and the Indian rhinoceros, and conservationists hope that animal numbers will recover now that the situation has calmed. The wildlife of the Manas National Park connects to neighbouring Bhutan, also home to a large network of protected areas.

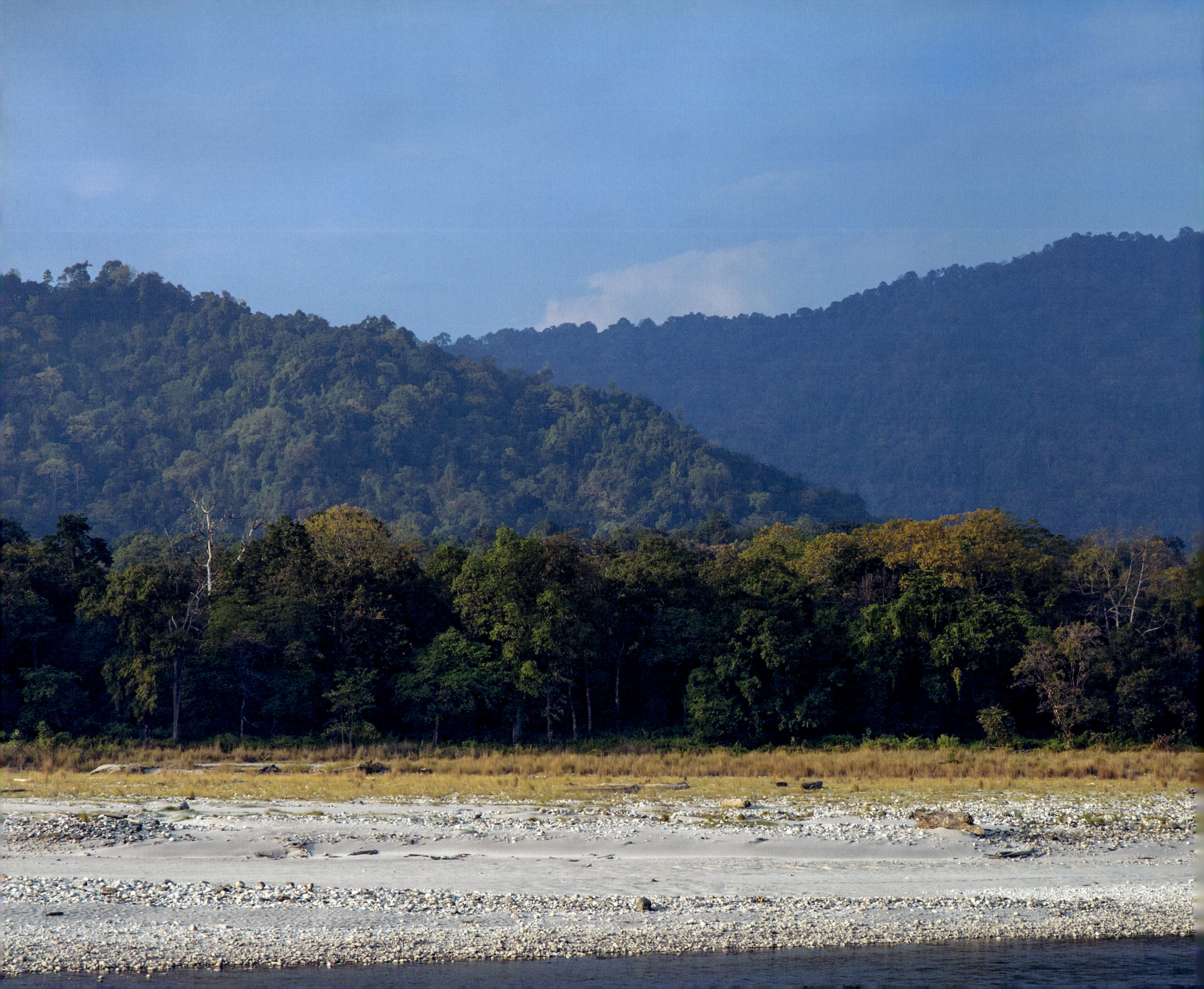

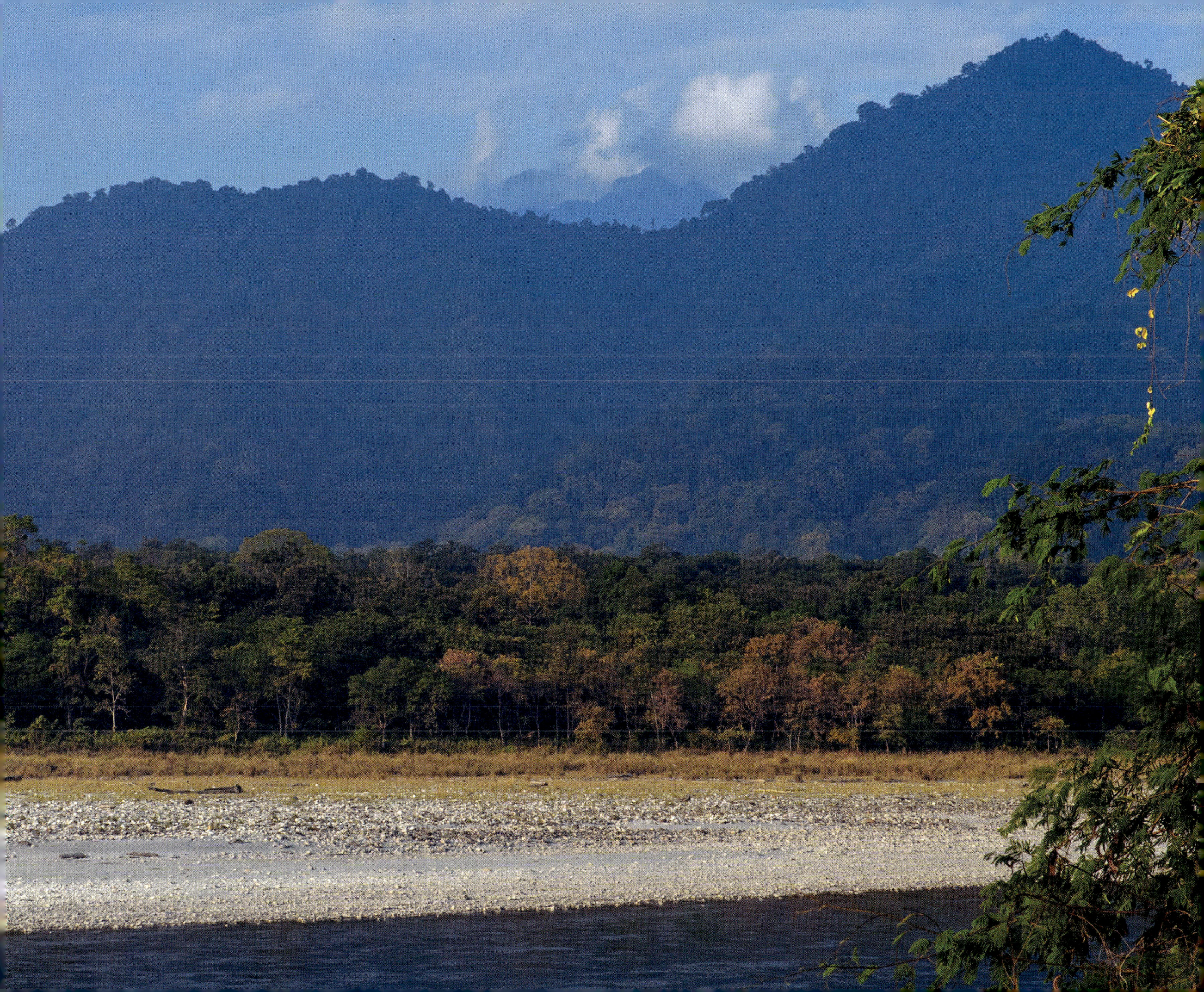

The tiger is the world's largest cat species. Some big males can weigh 250 kilograms and can grow up three metres from nose to base of tail. Such sizes gives the tiger a natural dominance, placing them firmly at the top of the food chain in the areas in which they occupy.

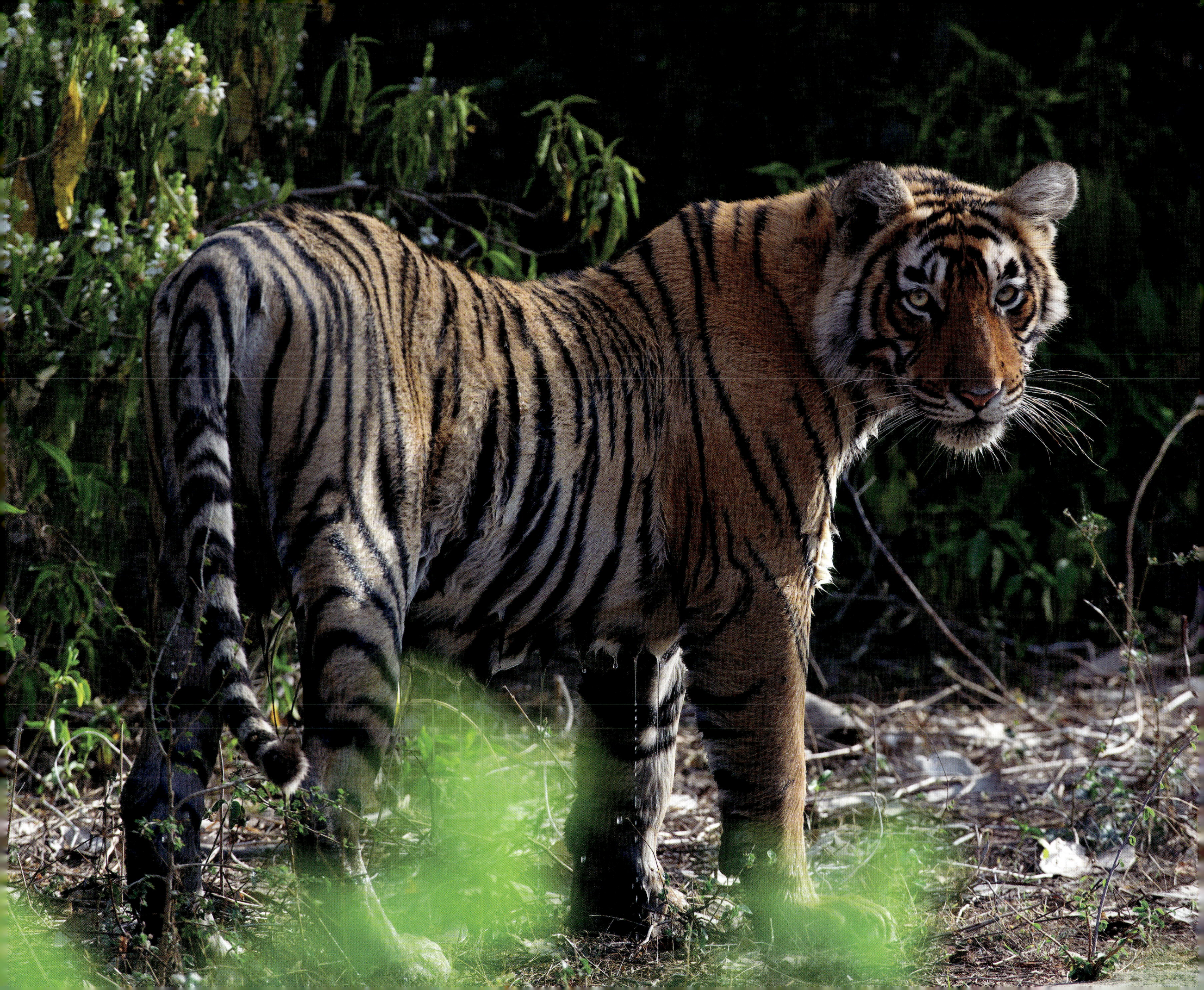

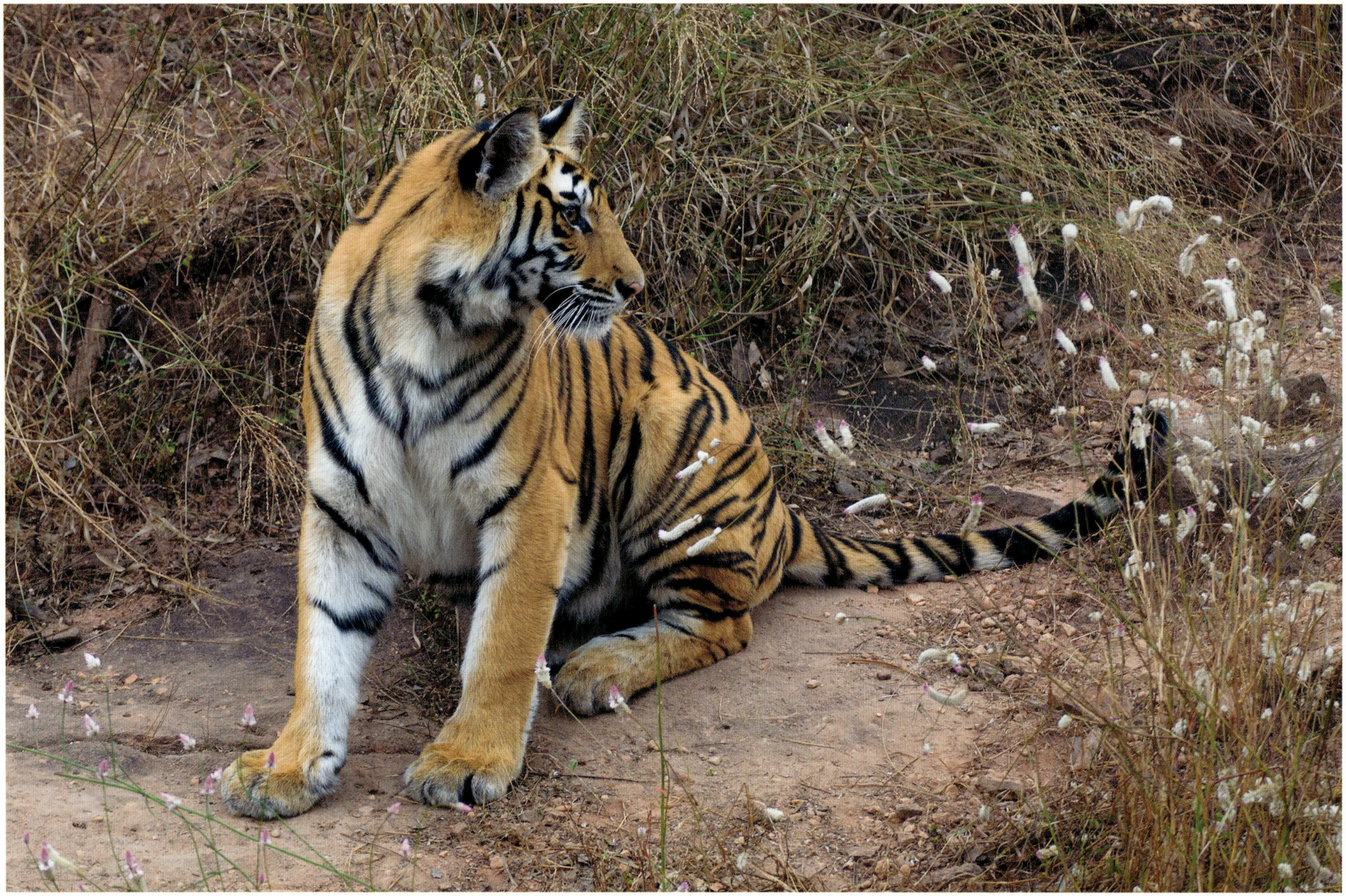

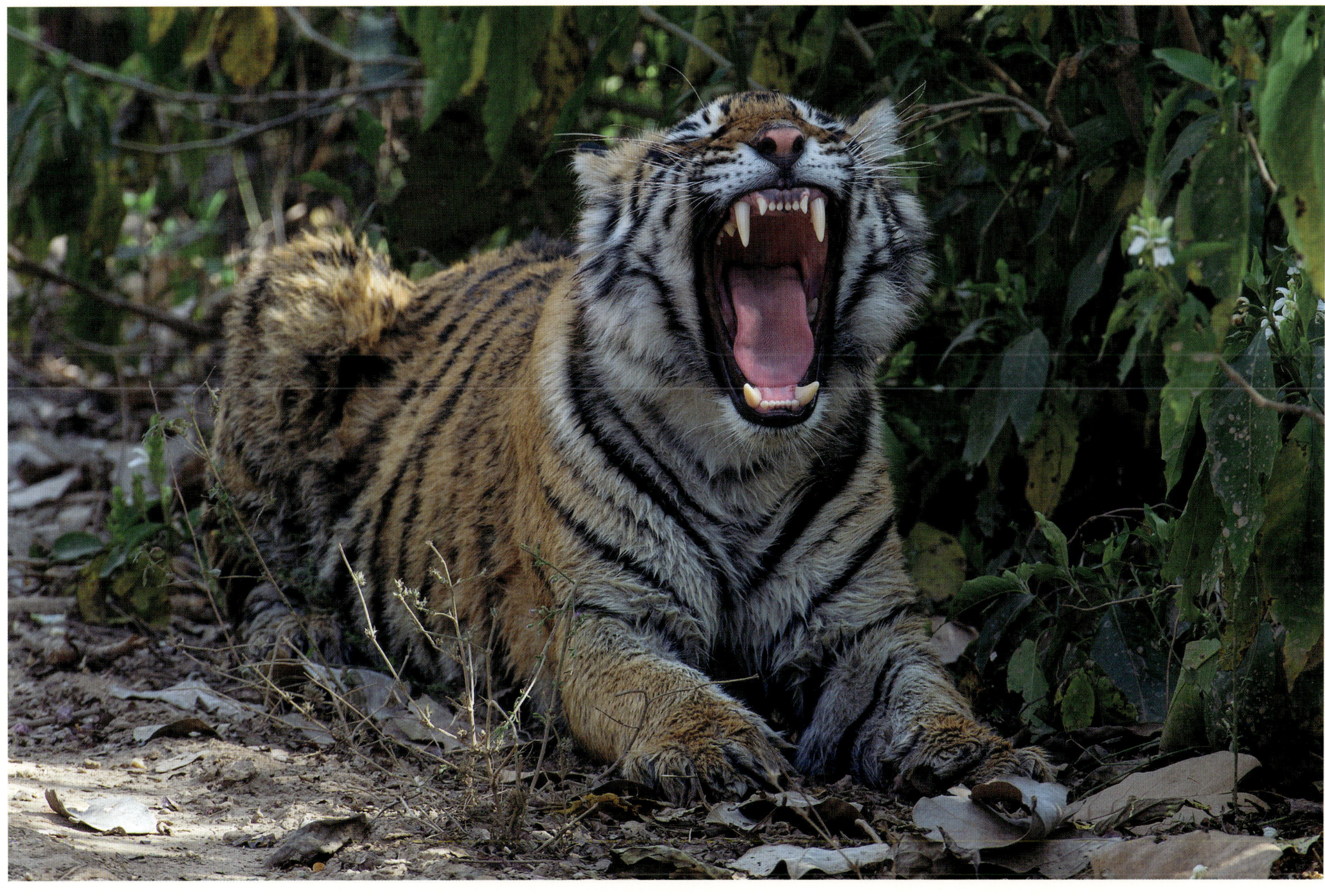

Young tigers, such as these from the Ranthambhore National Park (top) and the Bandhavgarh National Park (opposite) in Madhya Pradesh, depend on their mothers until they are around 18-20 months old, after which, they will become solitary hunters, defending their own territories. They can travel over long distances, and if suitable vegetation corridors exist, have the potential to recolonise former tiger habitats.

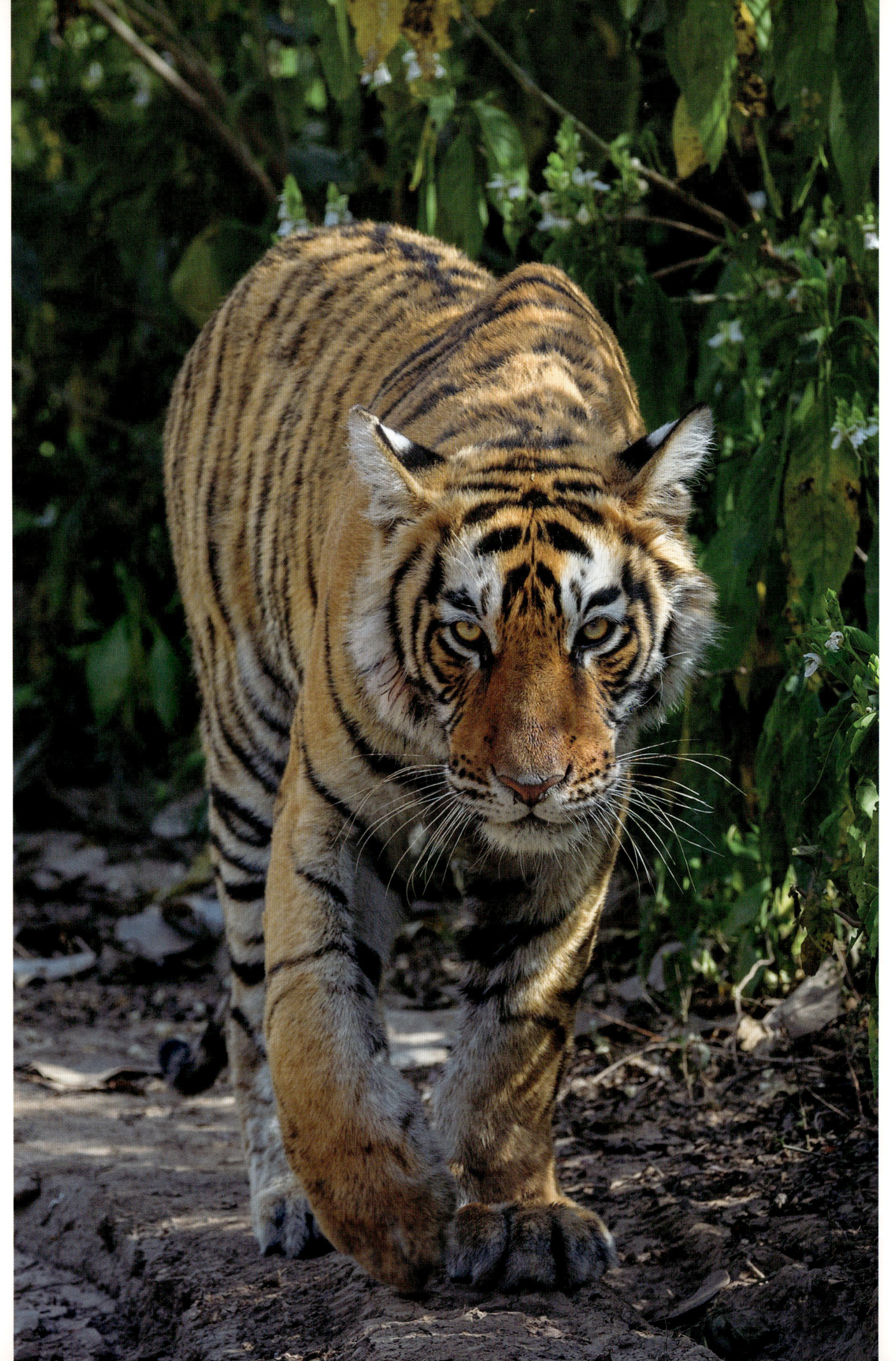

Negative news of poaching, habitat destruction and the chances of survival of wild tiger populations is all too frequent. Although these threats are serious and alarming, there are also positive developments. Tigers are very adaptable, and populations can recover fairly quickly, especially if there is enough prey, they have safe retreats, and there is no pressure from humans. Hundreds of young tigers are growing up in India's protected areas, such as these from the Ranthambhore National Park in Rajasthan, who will, in turn raise successive generations.

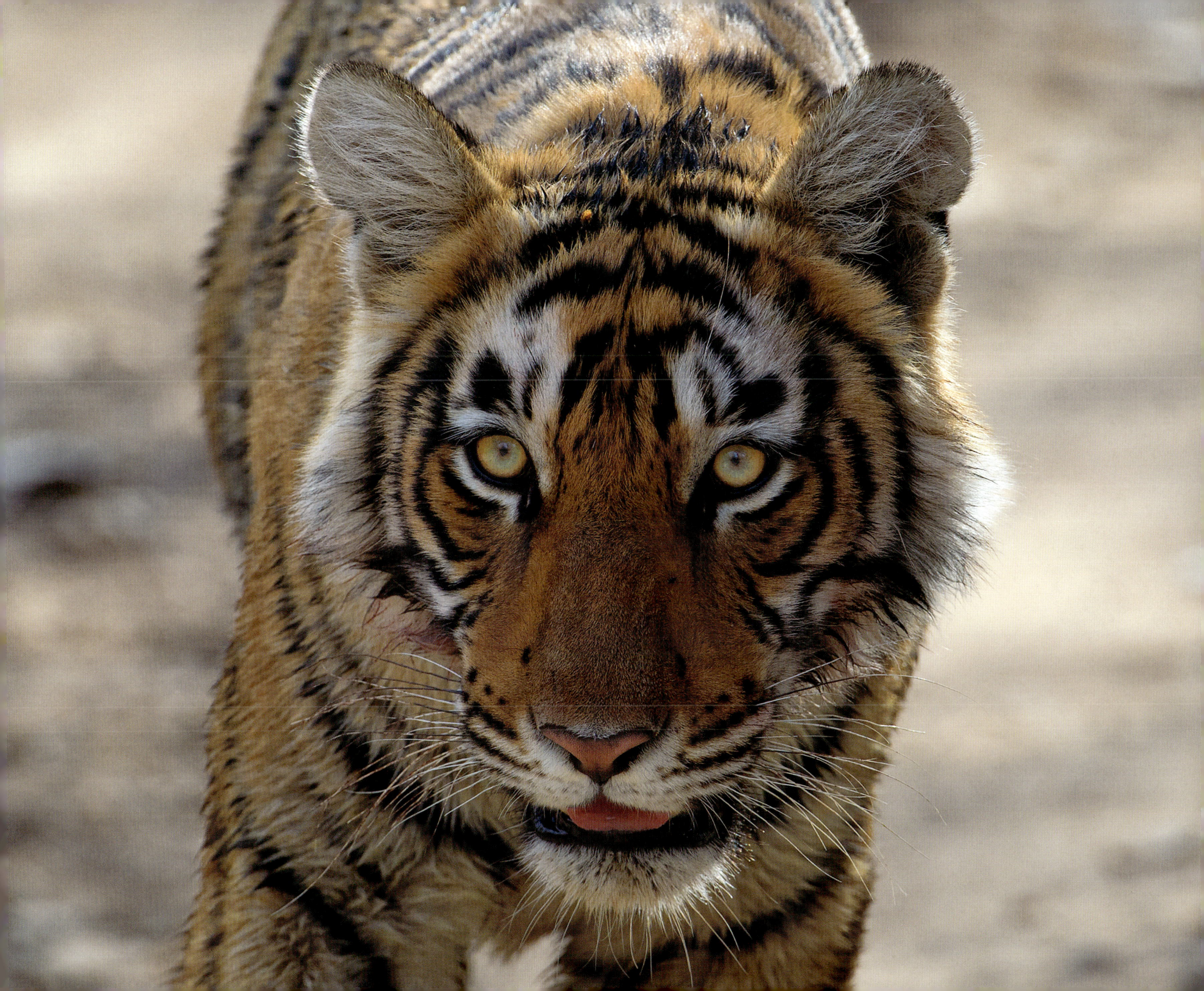

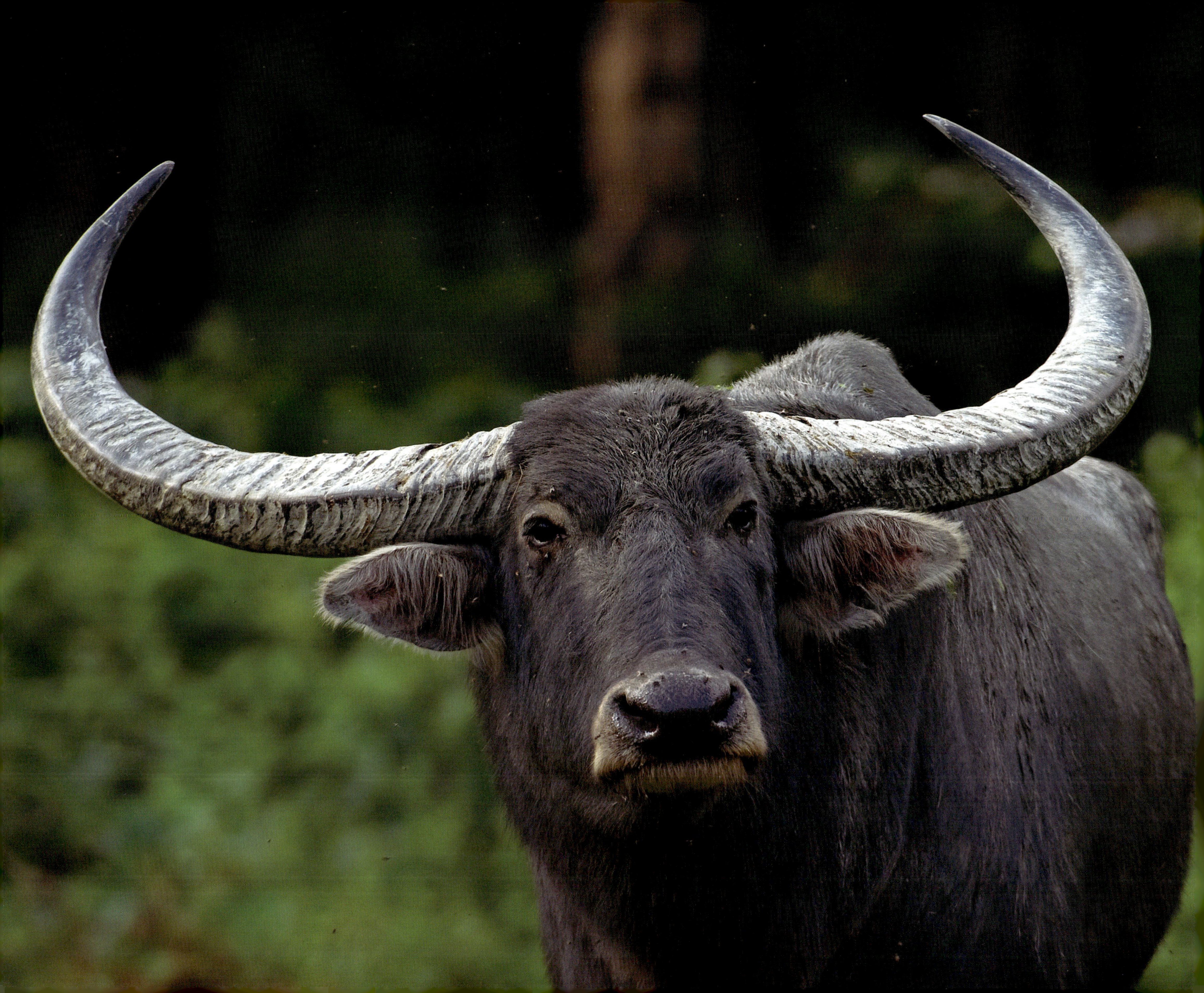

WETLANDS

Water is life – especially in dry environments or during the dry season, where wildlife depends on permanent water bodies to survive. It is no wonder that wetlands are magnets for wild animals who come to quench their thirst or to cool down.

Wetlands boast a wide variety of residents. Crocodiles have ruled tropical rivers and lakes since time immemorial. In India, the marsh crocodile is the most common species, and can be found in bodies of freshwater across the country. India's warm climate favours a rich diversity of reptiles, including turtles and monitor lizards. Rich plant growth in swamps or floodplains as found in the northeast in Assam, attracting large herbivores such as the Indian rhinoceros or Asian wild buffalo, and offering sufficient food for these animals to sustain their heavy bodies. Bird life is especially rich in wetlands, with a wide variety of notable species such as herons and storks, pelicans and kingfishers, ibises and spoonbills.

A reliable supply of water is crucial to all of these species, and without this, even a tropical wetland paradise can be deserted in a short time.

The wild Asian buffalo is an ancestor of the domestic water buffalo. It bears huge heavy crescent-shaped horns that can measure up to a total of two metres along the outer edges, exceeding the size of the horns of any other living bovid. It is listed as an endangered species and only a few isolated populations still survive.

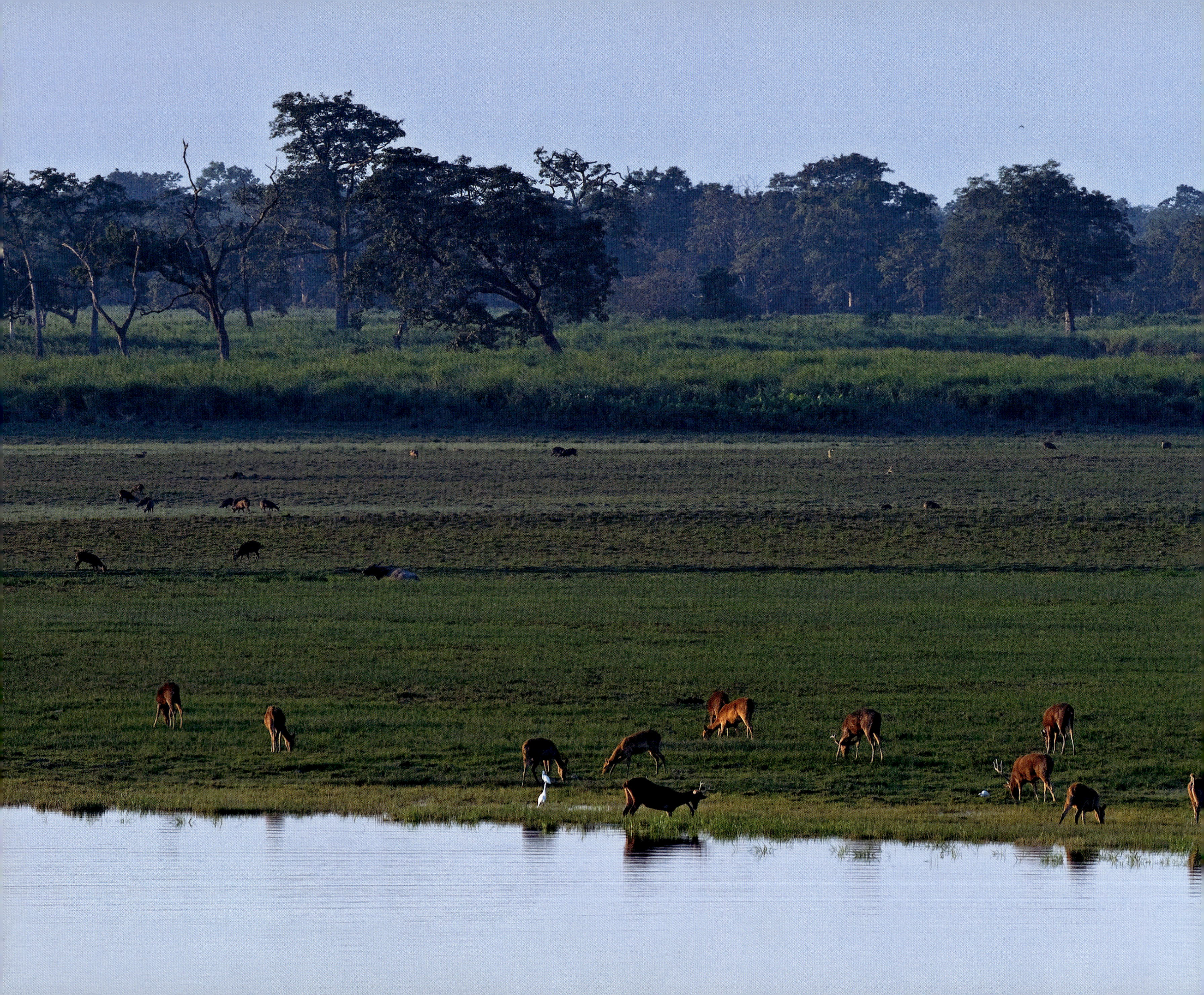

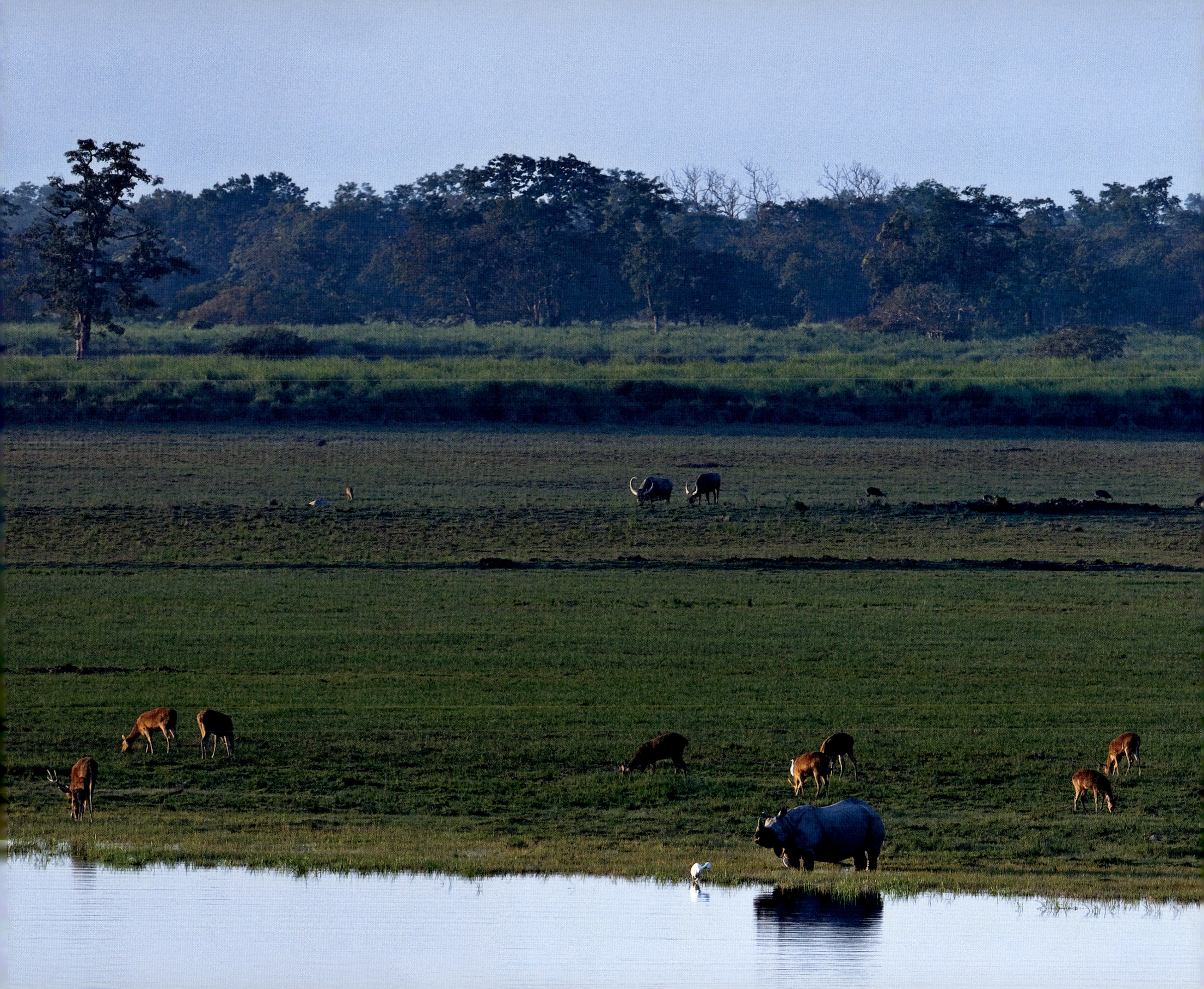

Previous spread:
Marshlands offer good grazing and attract many herbivores. Here, an Indian rhinoceros, wild Asian buffalos, swamp deer or barasingha, and hog deer have gathered on the floodplain of the Brahmaputra river in the Kaziranga National Park in Assam. Such a scene is a window into the past, giving an impression of how the big Indian river systems looked before man began to alter them.

Right:
The Indian rhinoceros is identified by a single horn and grey hide with skin folds, giving it an armour-plated appearance. They boast sharp hearing and an acute sense of smell, but have relatively poor eyesight, which can lead to them making sudden charges when encountering intruders or moving objects at close quarters. The species was close to extinction in the early 20th century, but has made a remarkable comeback thanks to rigorous conservation efforts. Today, there are about 2600 Indian rhinos, with around 70 per cent of the global population living in the Kaziranga National Park in Assam.

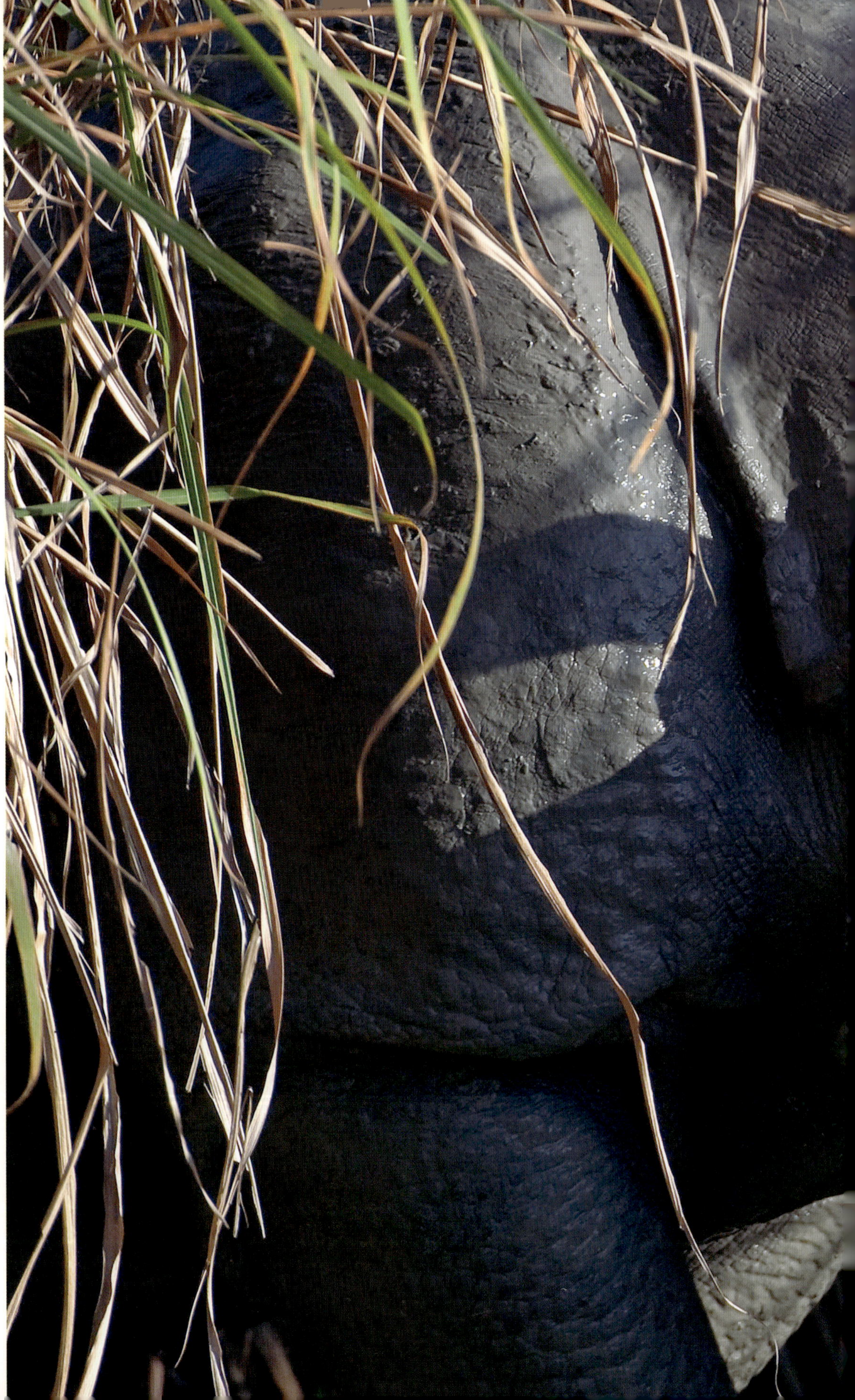

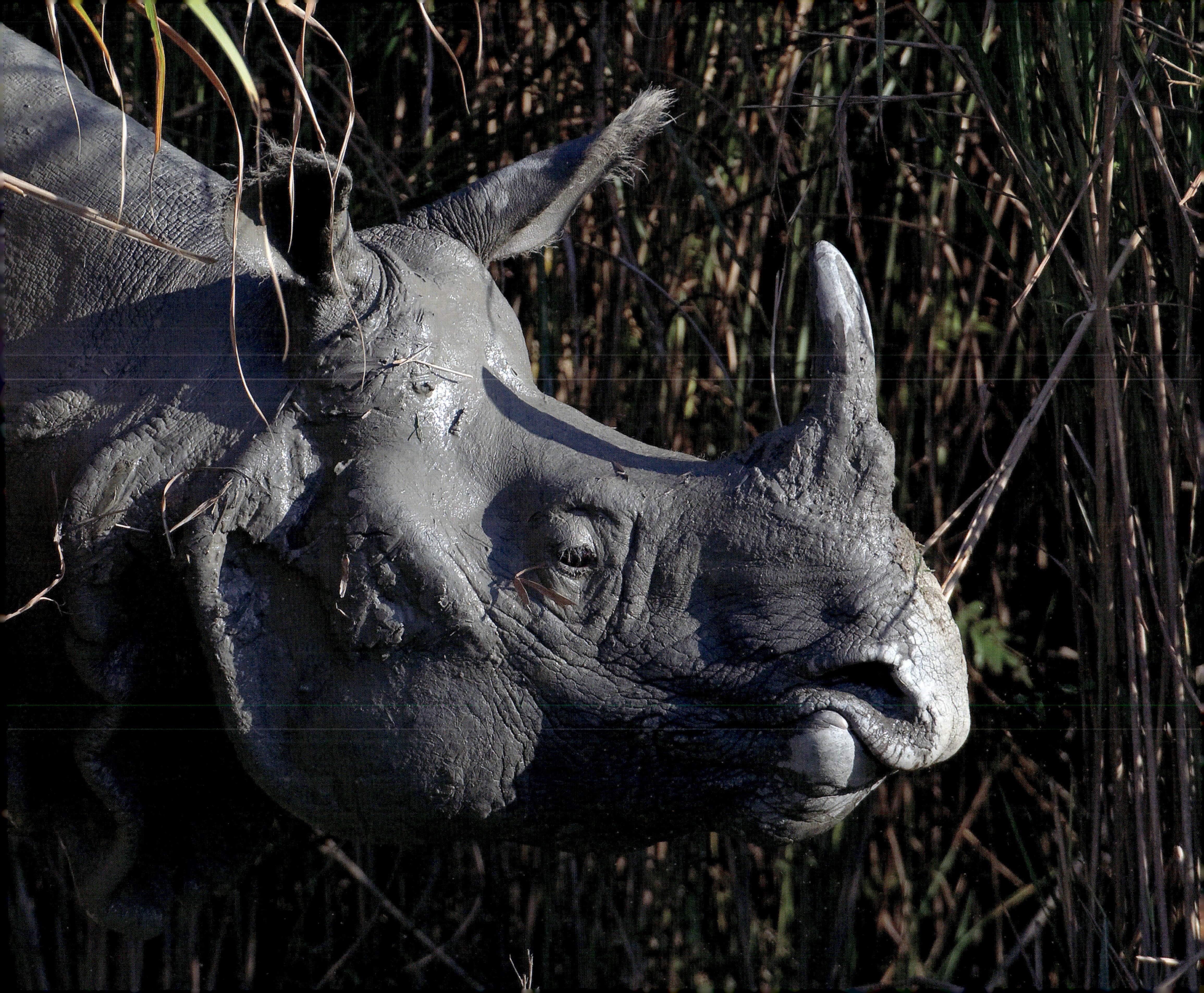

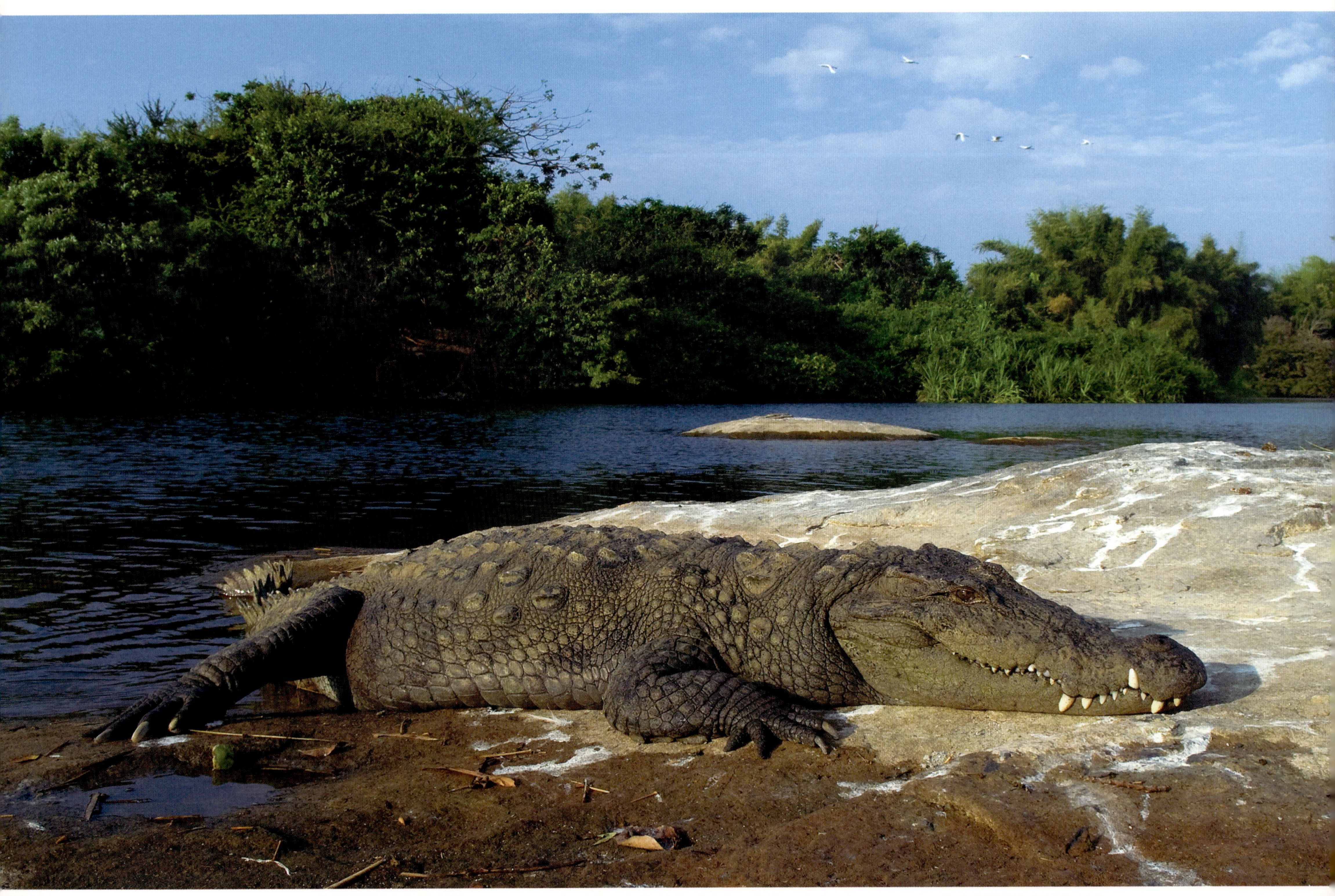

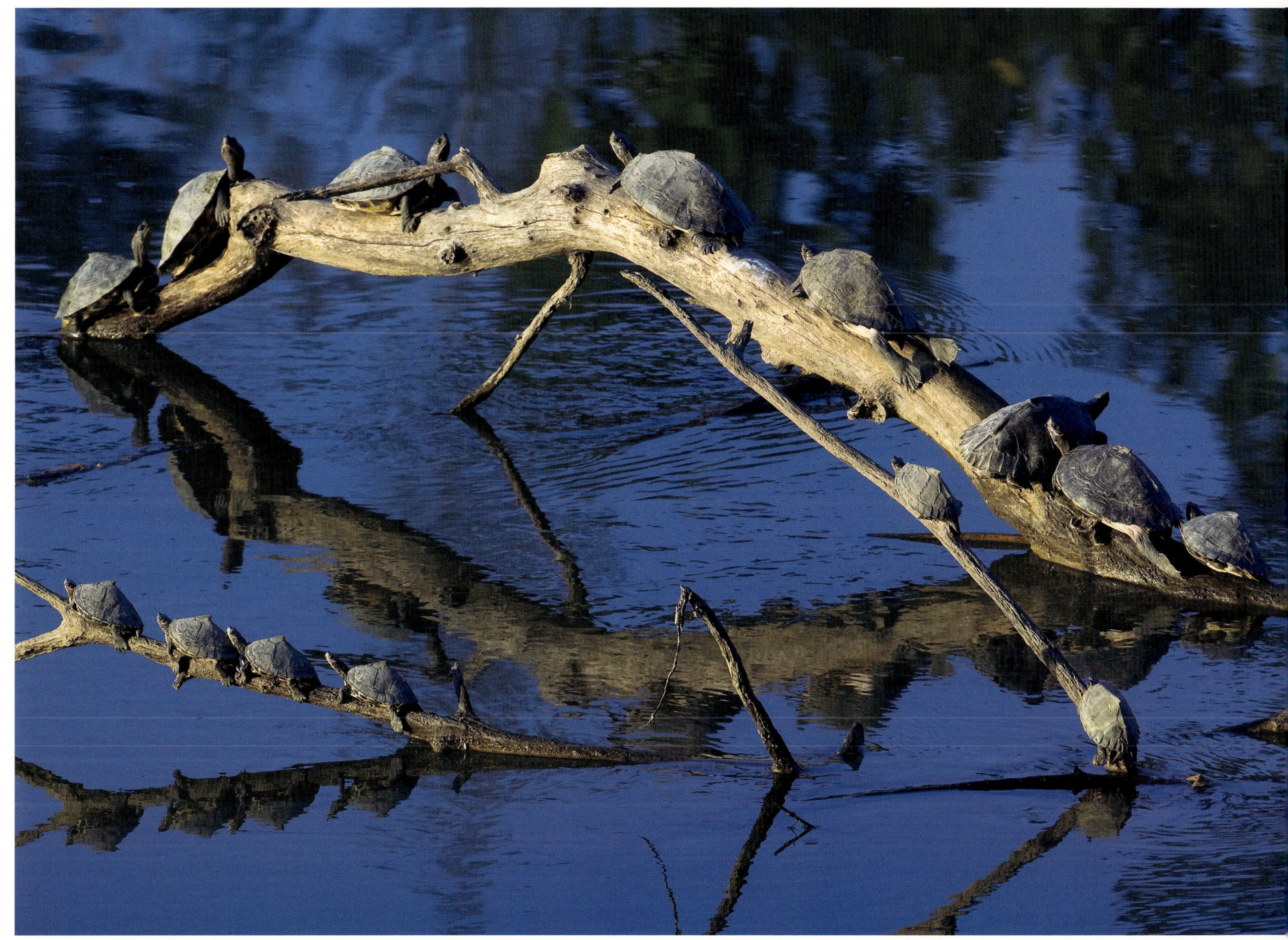

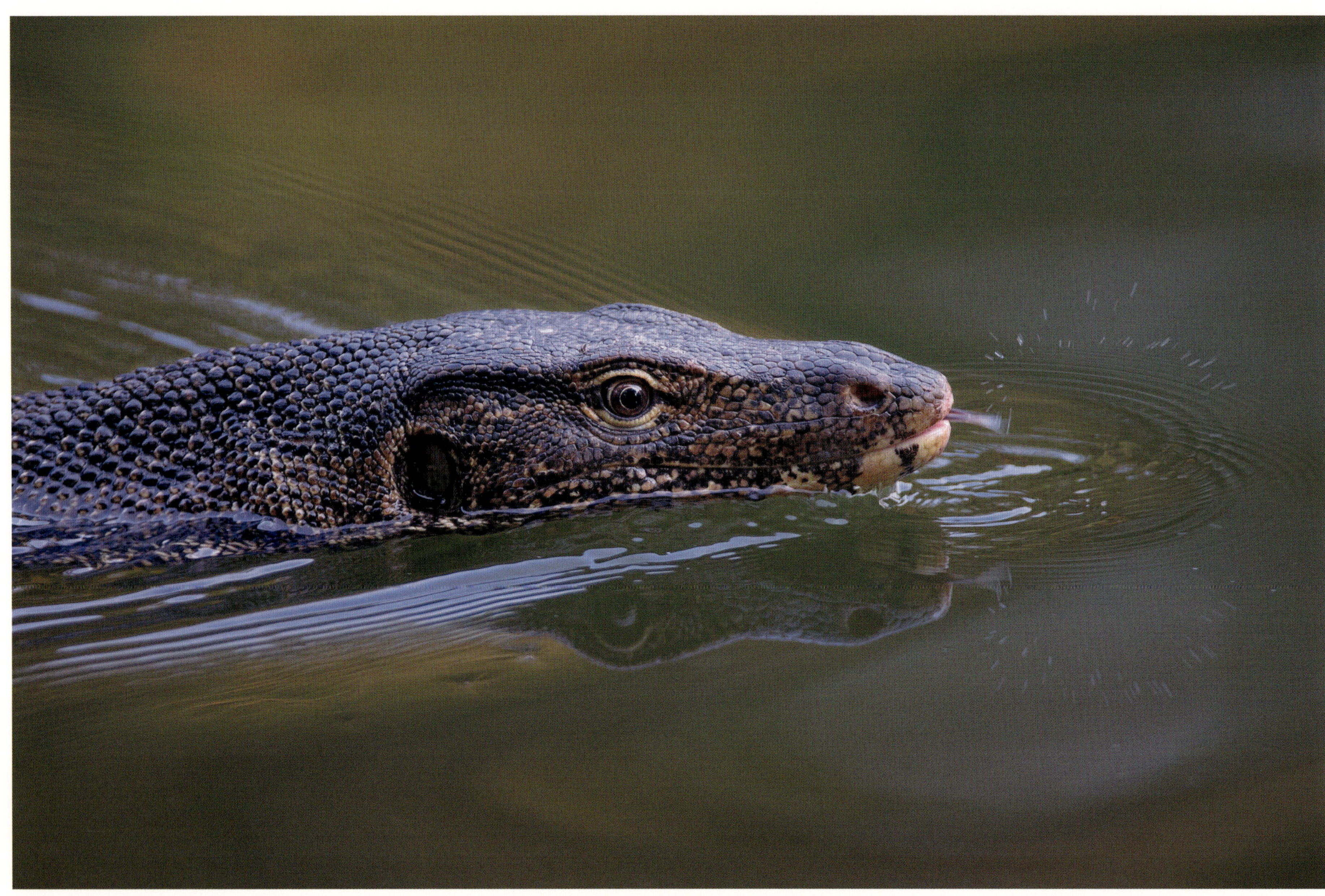

Previous spread:
Reptiles are cold-blooded, meaning that their body temperature takes on the temperature of their surroundings. They will bask in the sun in order to warm up and increase their metabolism. Here, fourteen Assam roofed turtles crowd together on a fallen tree, while a marsh crocodile or mugger rests on a rock in Cauvery river.

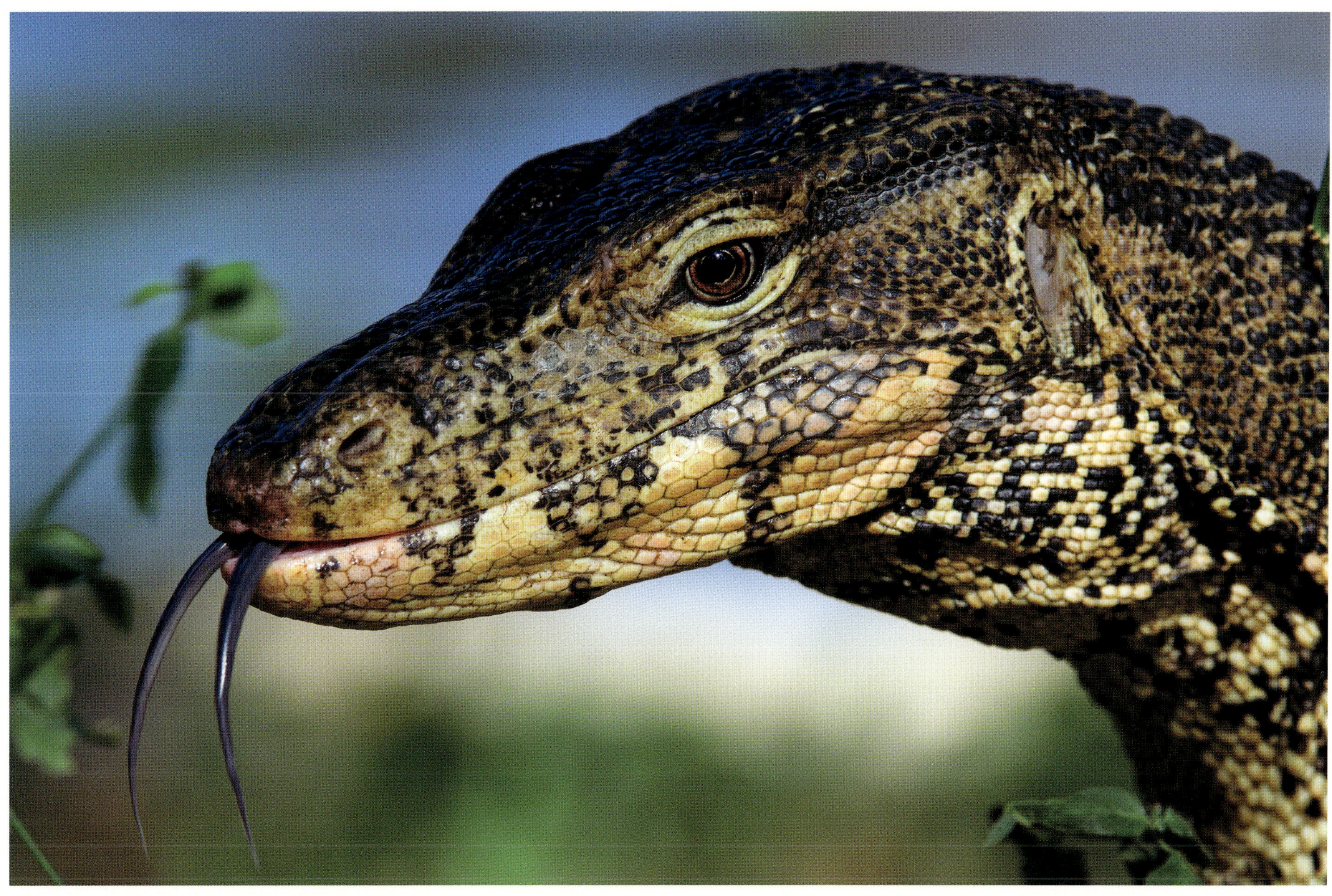

The water monitor is an impressive reptile that can grow to up to two and a half metres long. It likes to forage in and around the water (opposite), flicking its tongue (above) to taste the air, enabling it to detect prey, such as crabs, fish, rodents or birds. The water monitor has a large range, extending from northeast India to Indonesia.

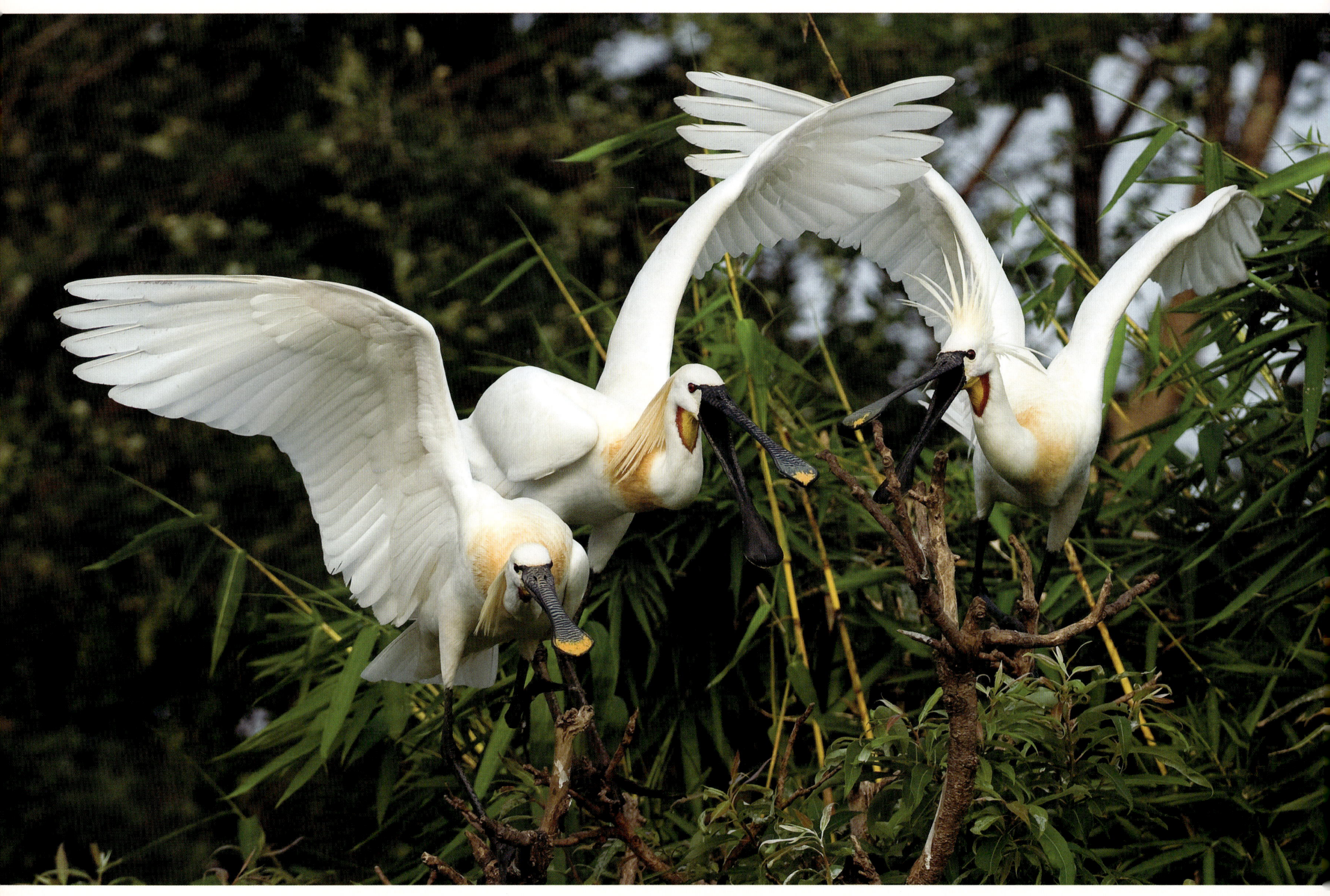

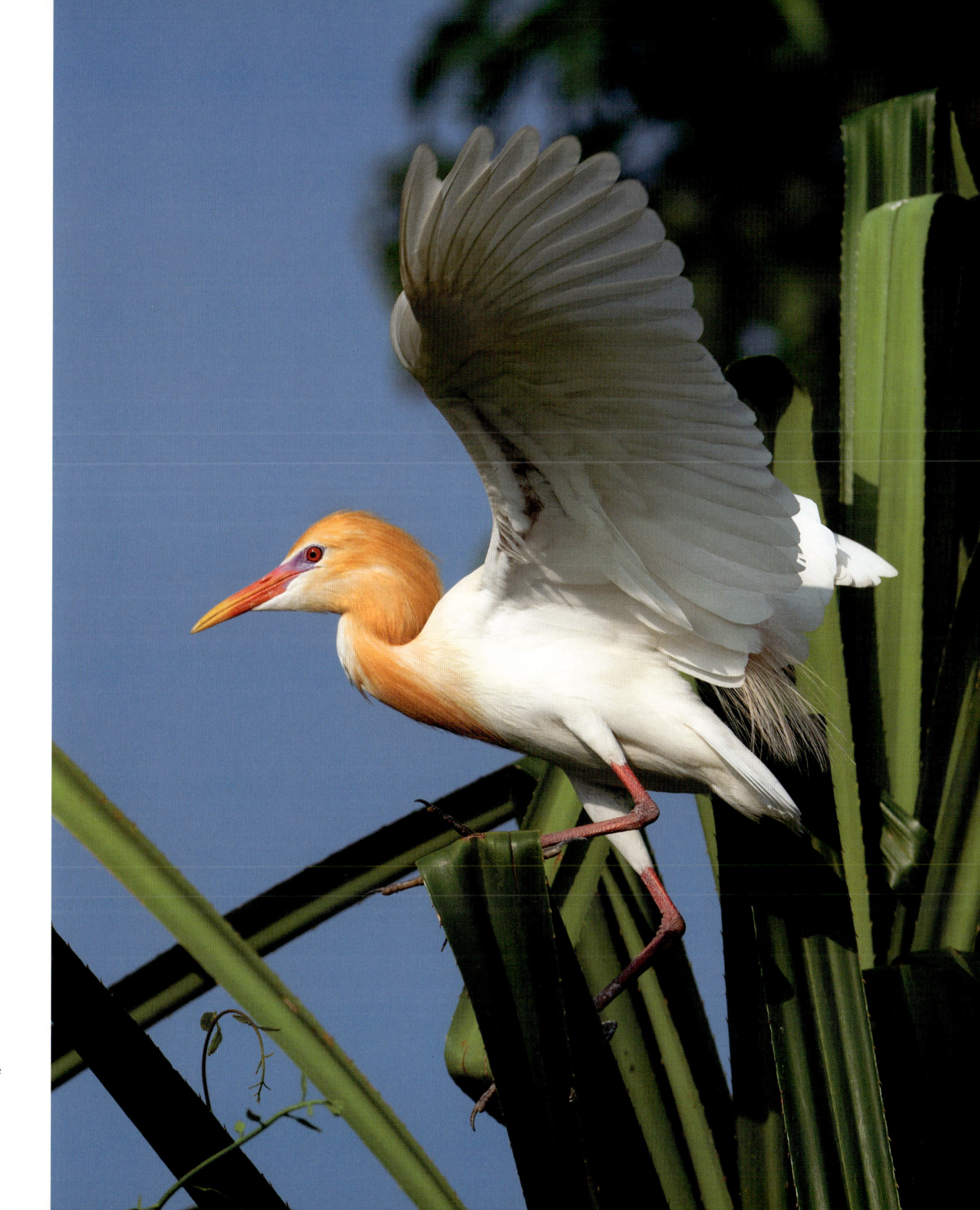

Eurasian spoonbills squabble in their colony (opposite). During courtship, they display their colourful yellow breast patch. Cattle egrets also show a striking coloration during breeding time (right). Non-breeding adults have plain white plumage and a yellow bill.

Asian openbill storks are widespread in India and breed in many places, such as the Ranganathittu Bird Sanctuary in Karnataka. The large gap in its bill is thought to be an adaptation for handling snails, a favourite prey.

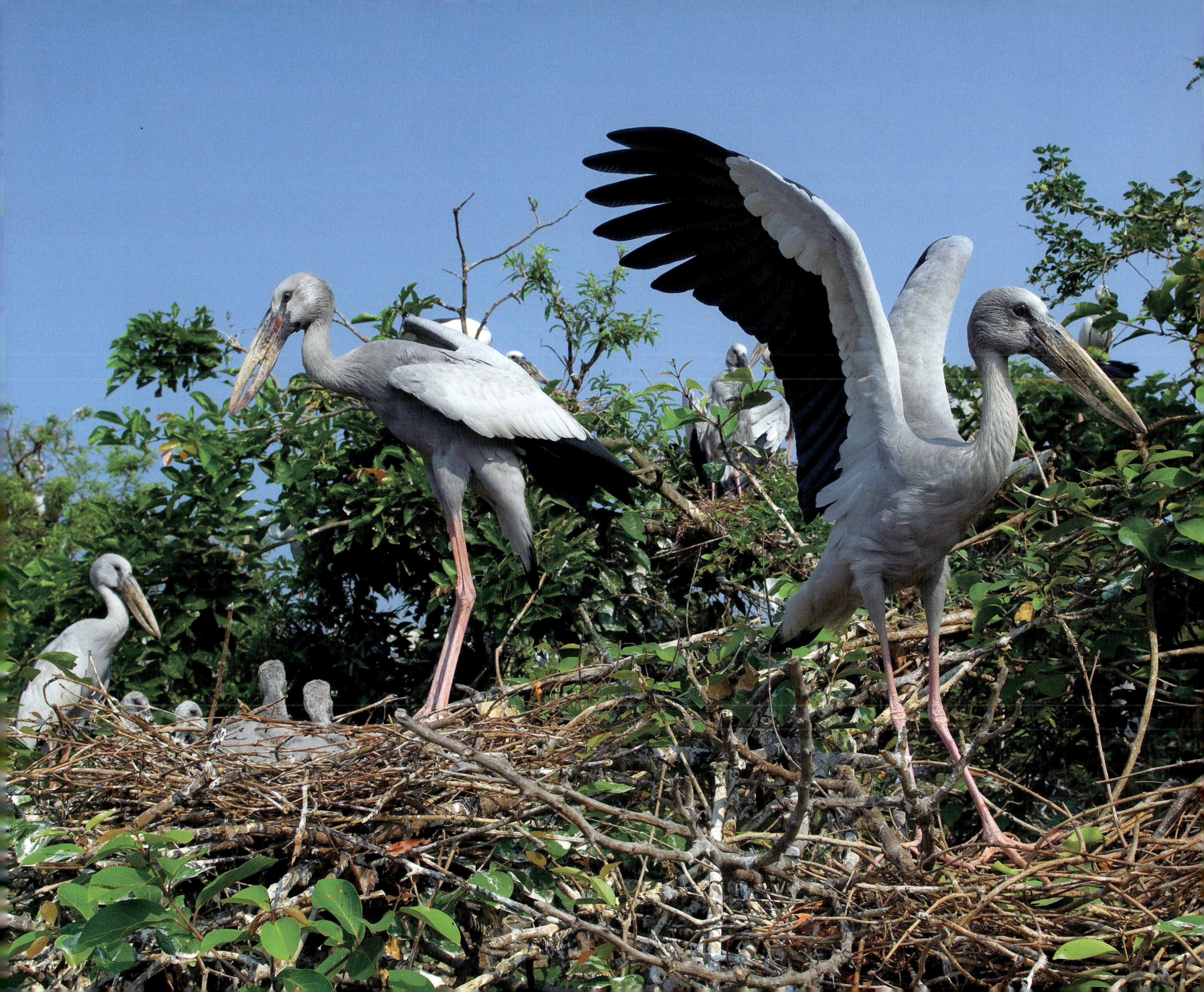

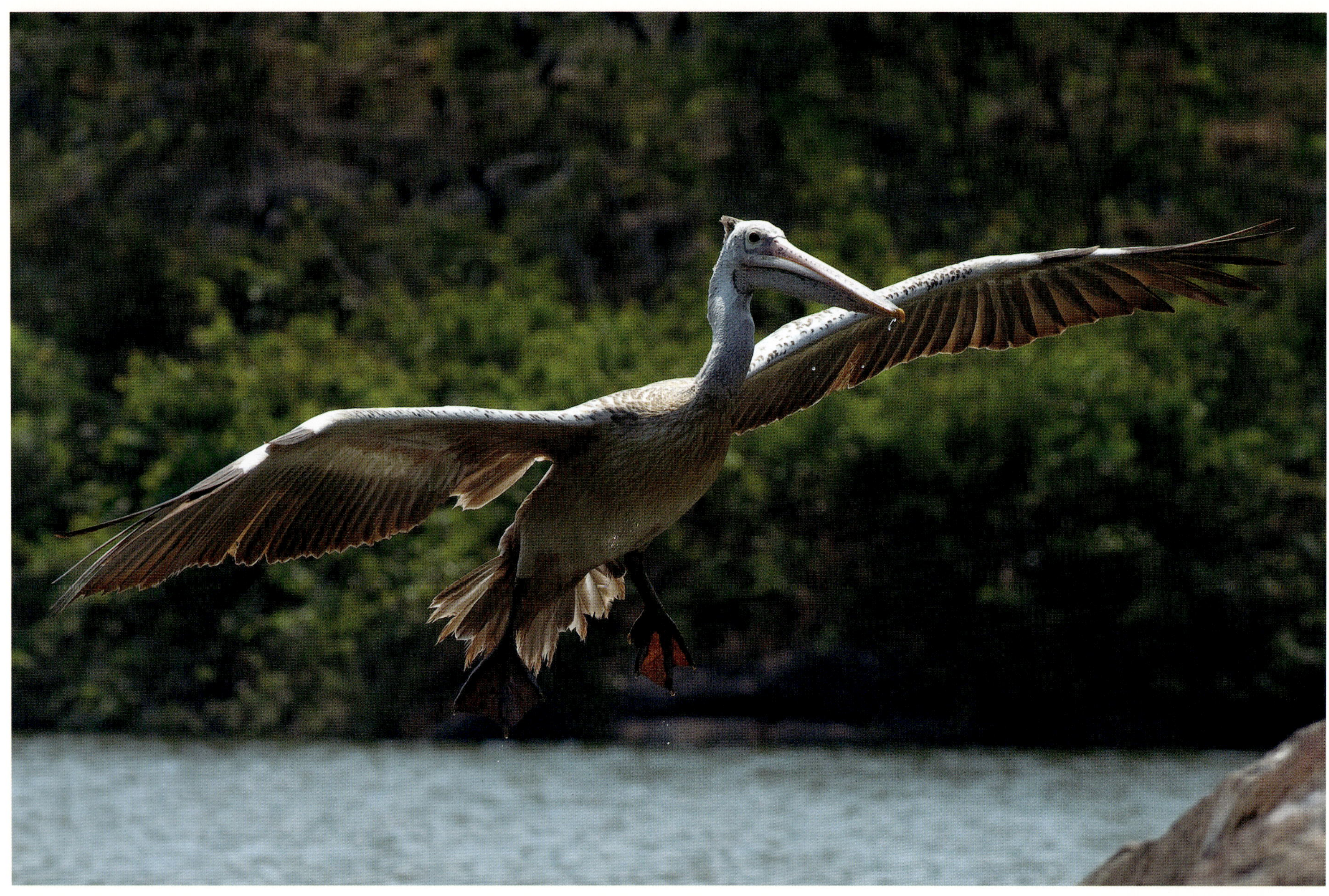

A spot-billed pelican reduces its speed, turning wings and body in order to land. They will also skim their webbed feet across the water surface in order to slow down. As with vultures or storks, their broad wings enable them to soar effortlessly and cover large distances.

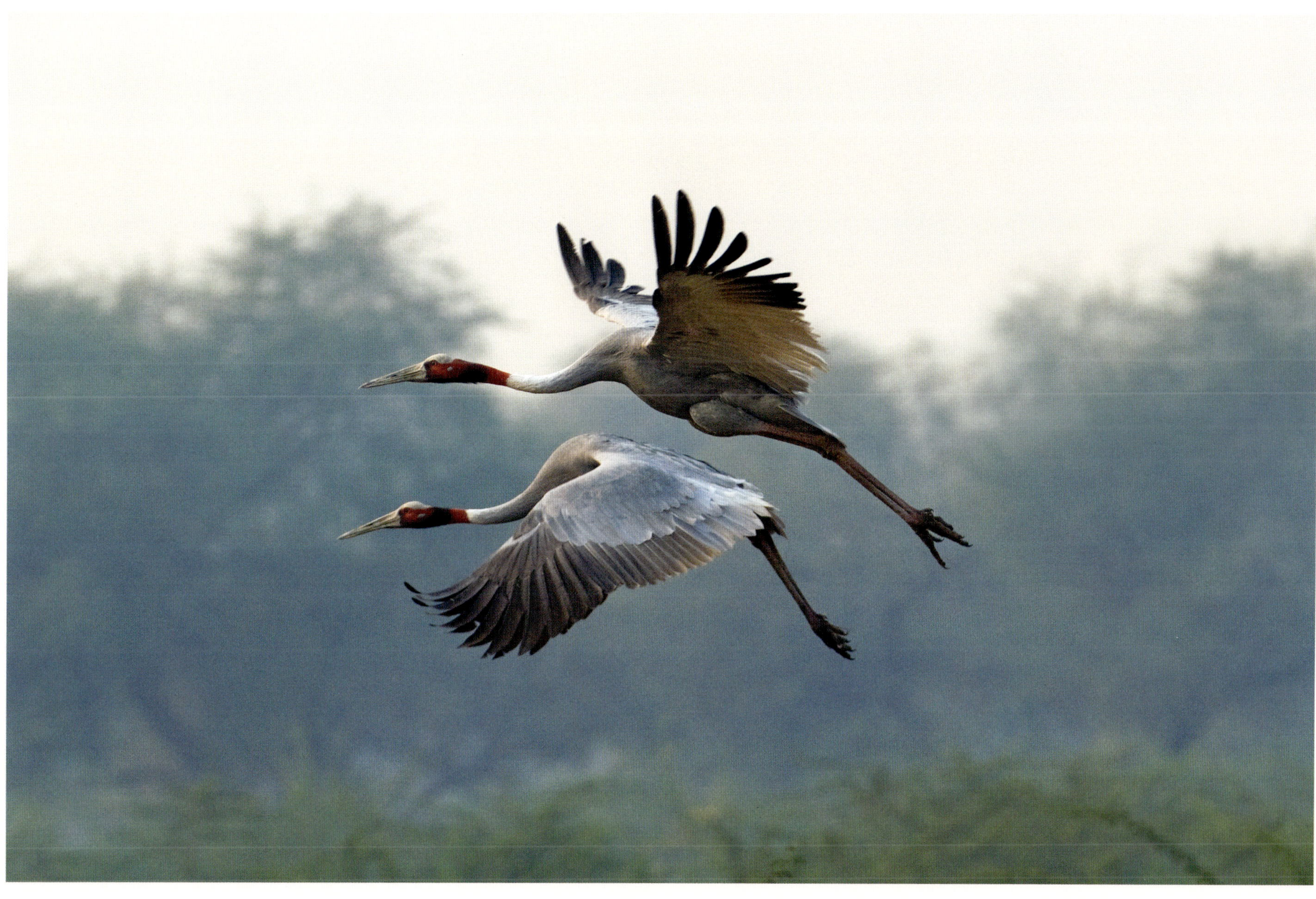

A pair of sarus cranes take wing in the Keoladeo National Park in Rajasthan. The sarus crane is the largest of all crane species, measuring up to 160 centimetres from beak to tail, with a wing-span reaching up to two and a half metres. Cranes are venerated in India, often appearing in poems and folk songs, as they are believed to bond for life.

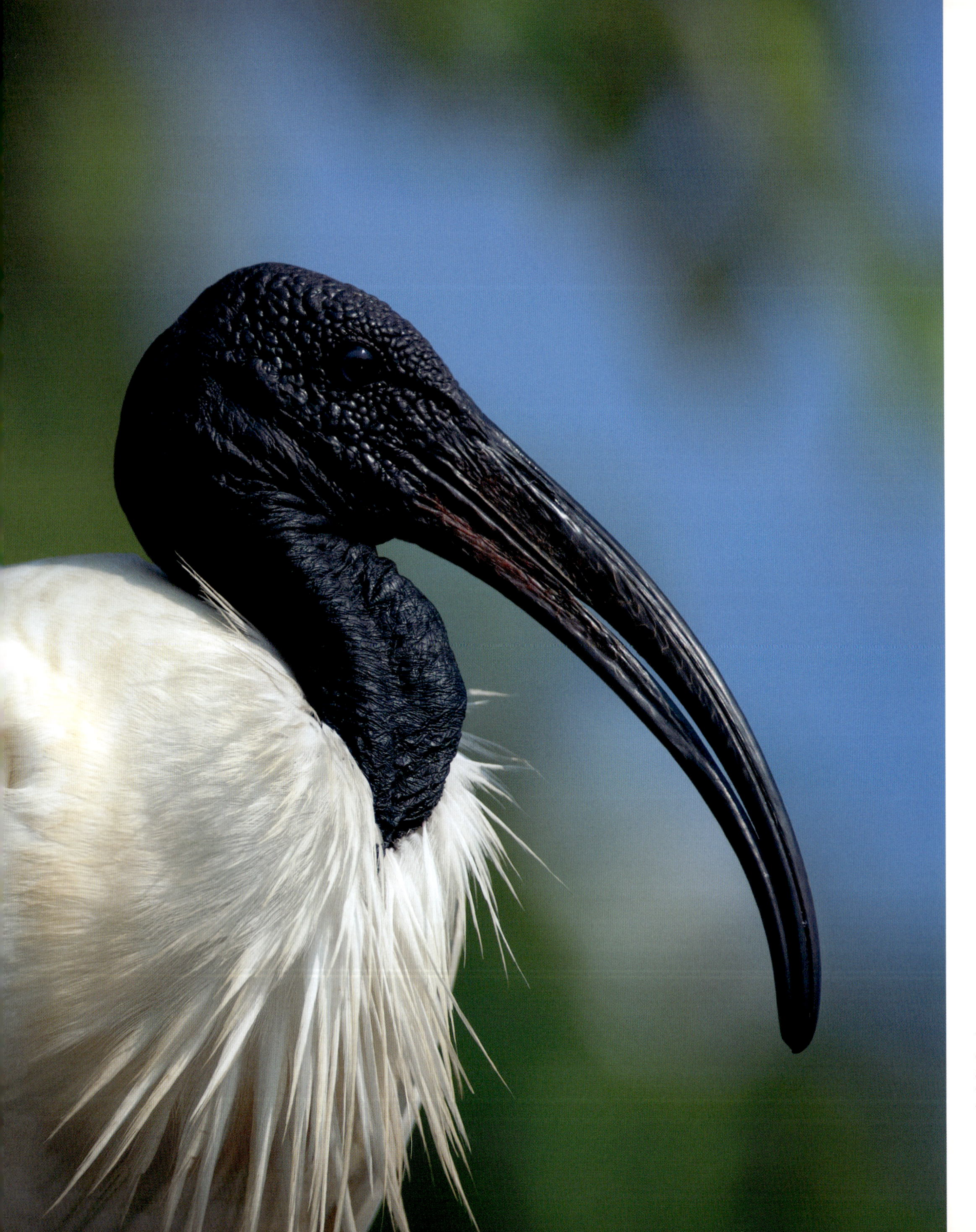

The pied kingfisher (opposite) catches small fish by plunge-diving daringly into the water. The black-headed ibis (left) is not as specialised and feeds on various water creatures such as a variety of fish, insects or frogs. Many species of birds co-exist in the same habitat by exploiting different food sources.

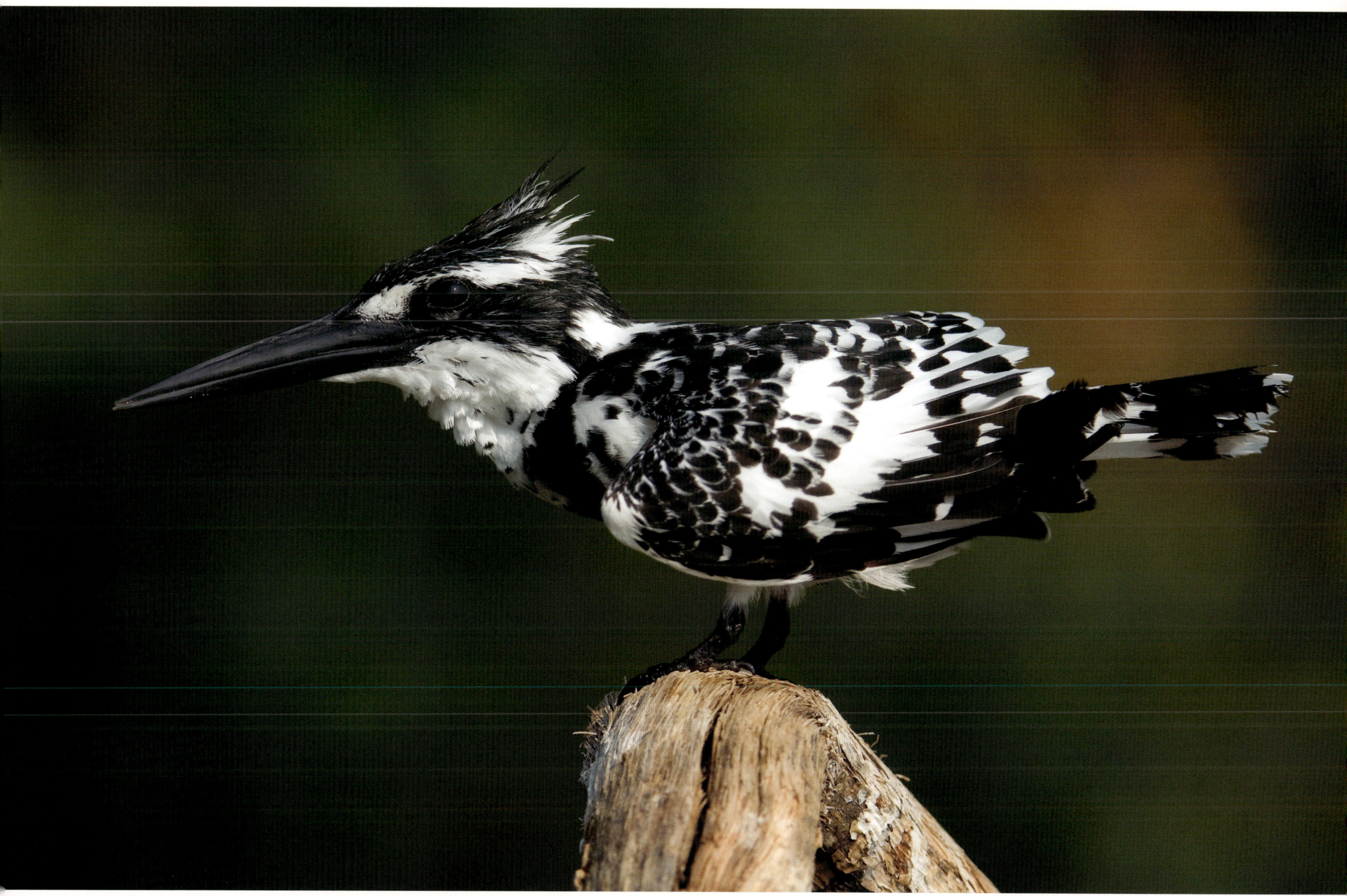

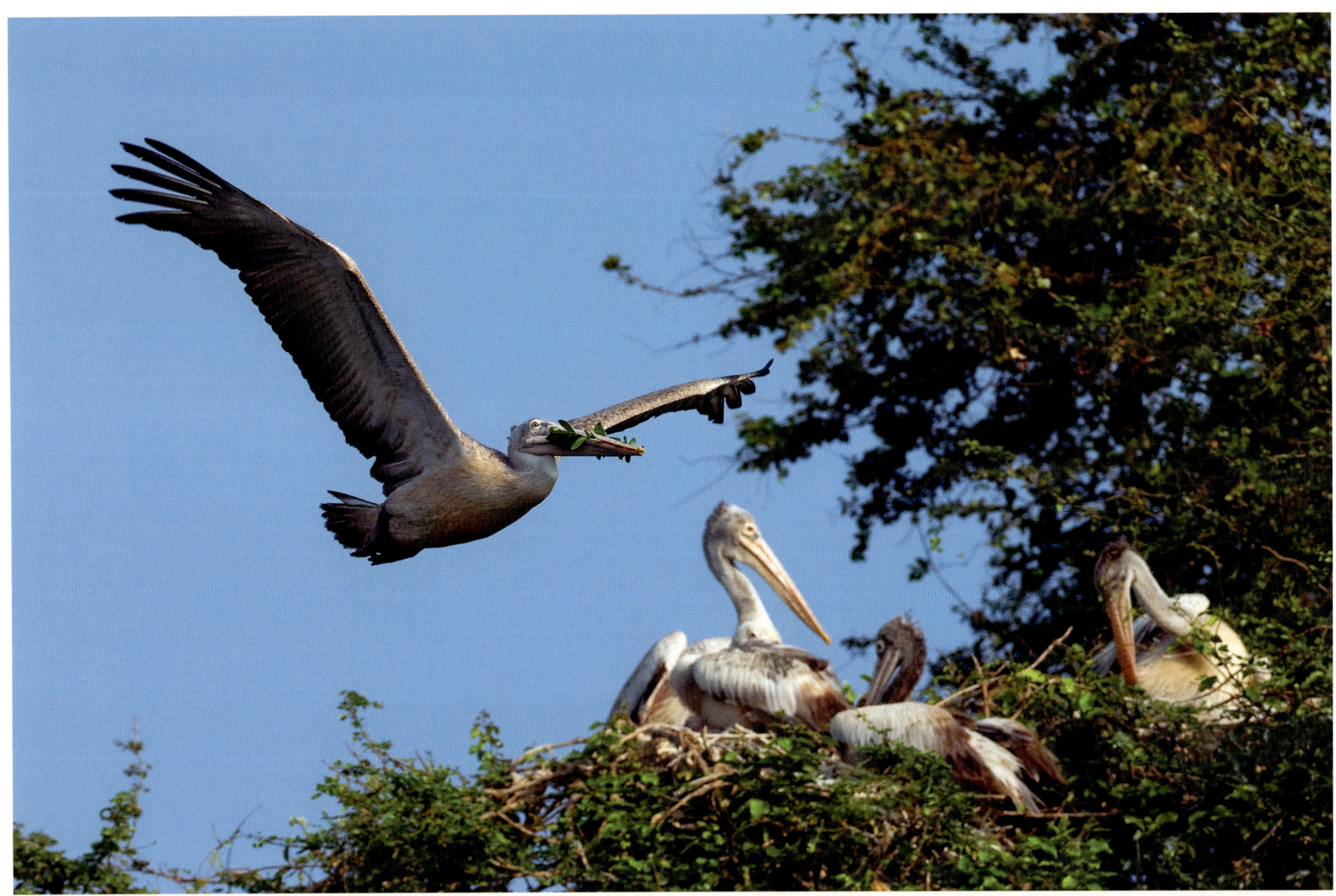

Nests of spot-billed pelicans (above), Asian openbill storks and painted storks (opposite) cover the trees in the Ranganathittu Bird Sanctuary in Karnataka. Such a density of breeding pairs is living proof of the importance of the bird sanctuary and the habitat that it offers.

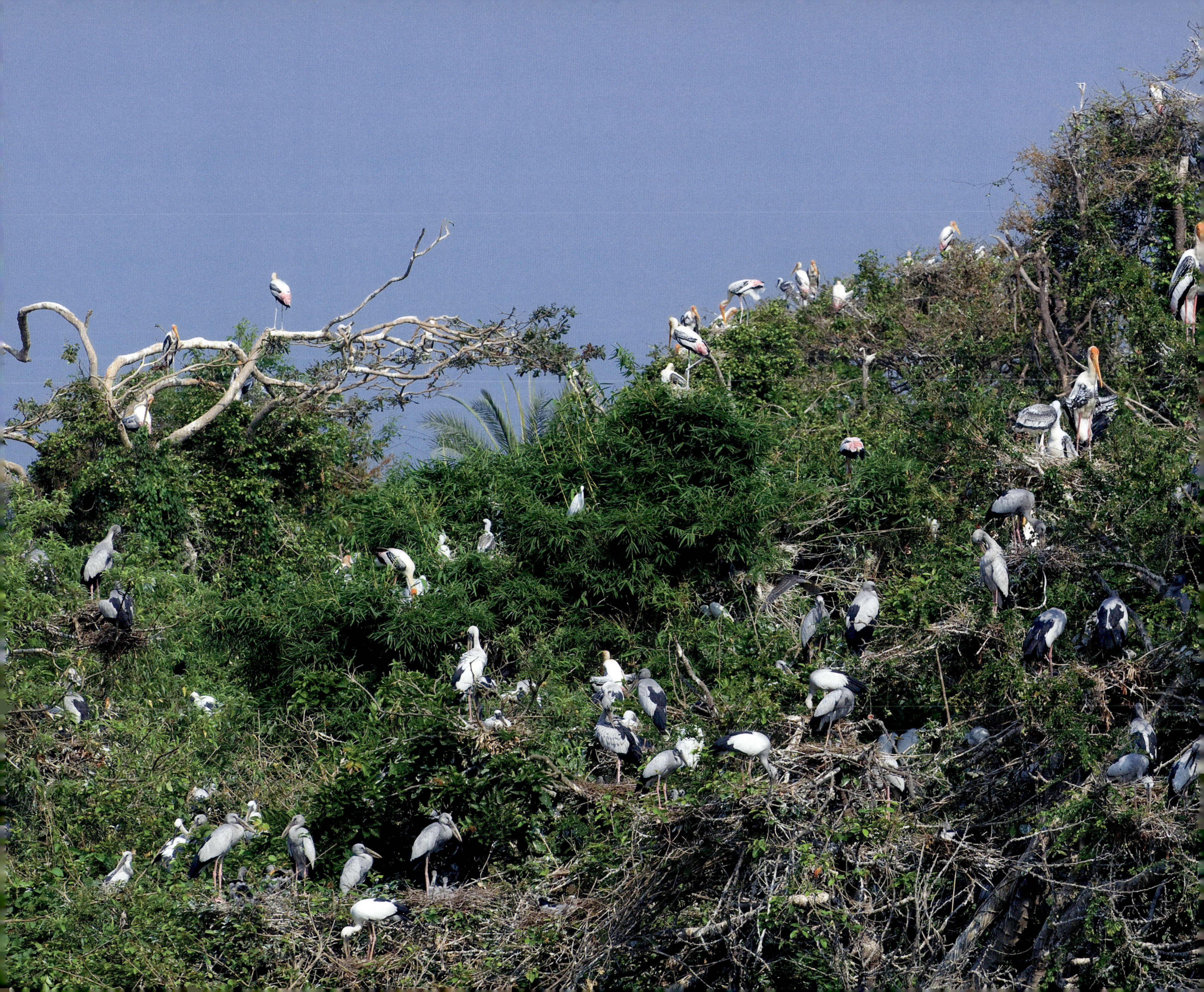

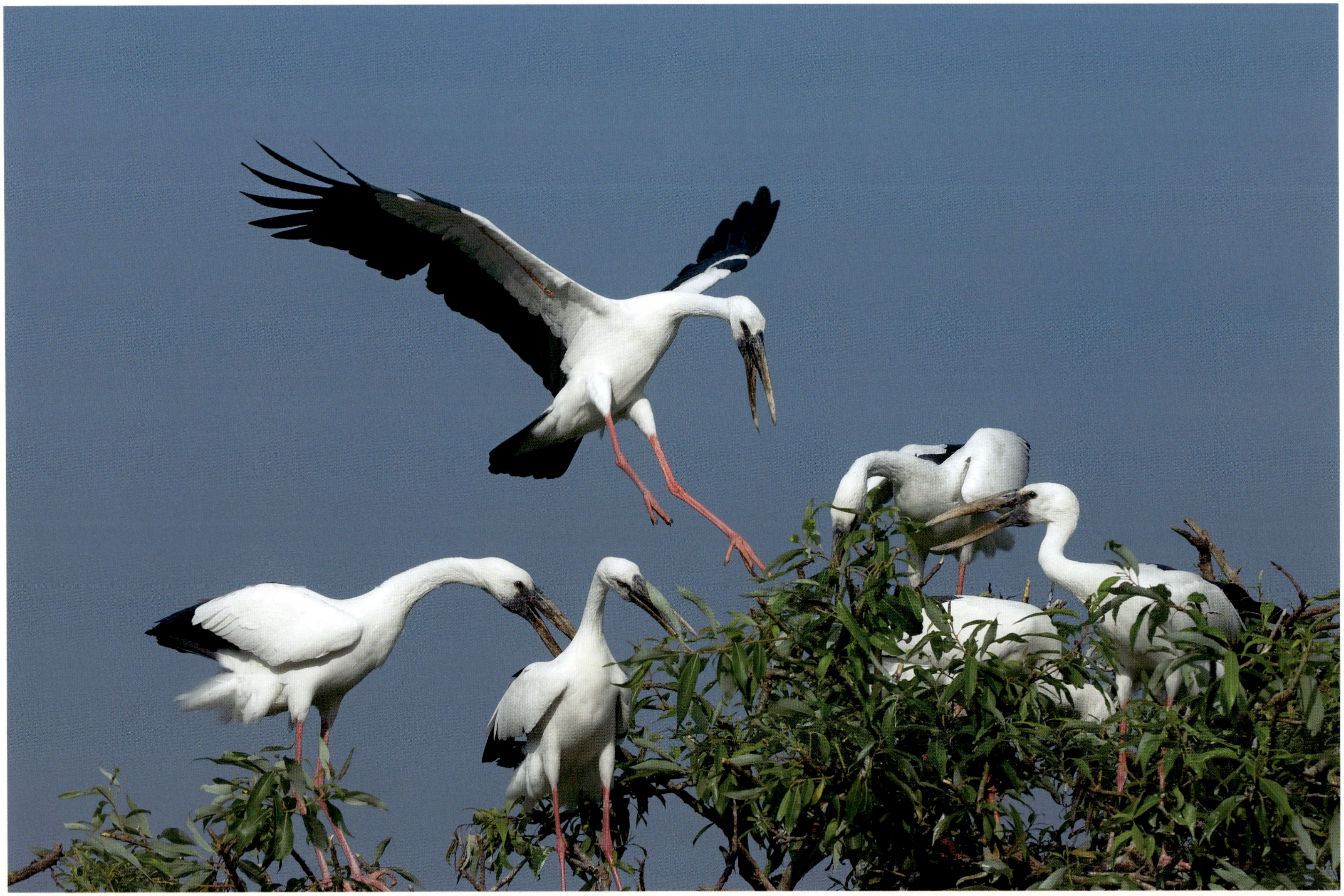

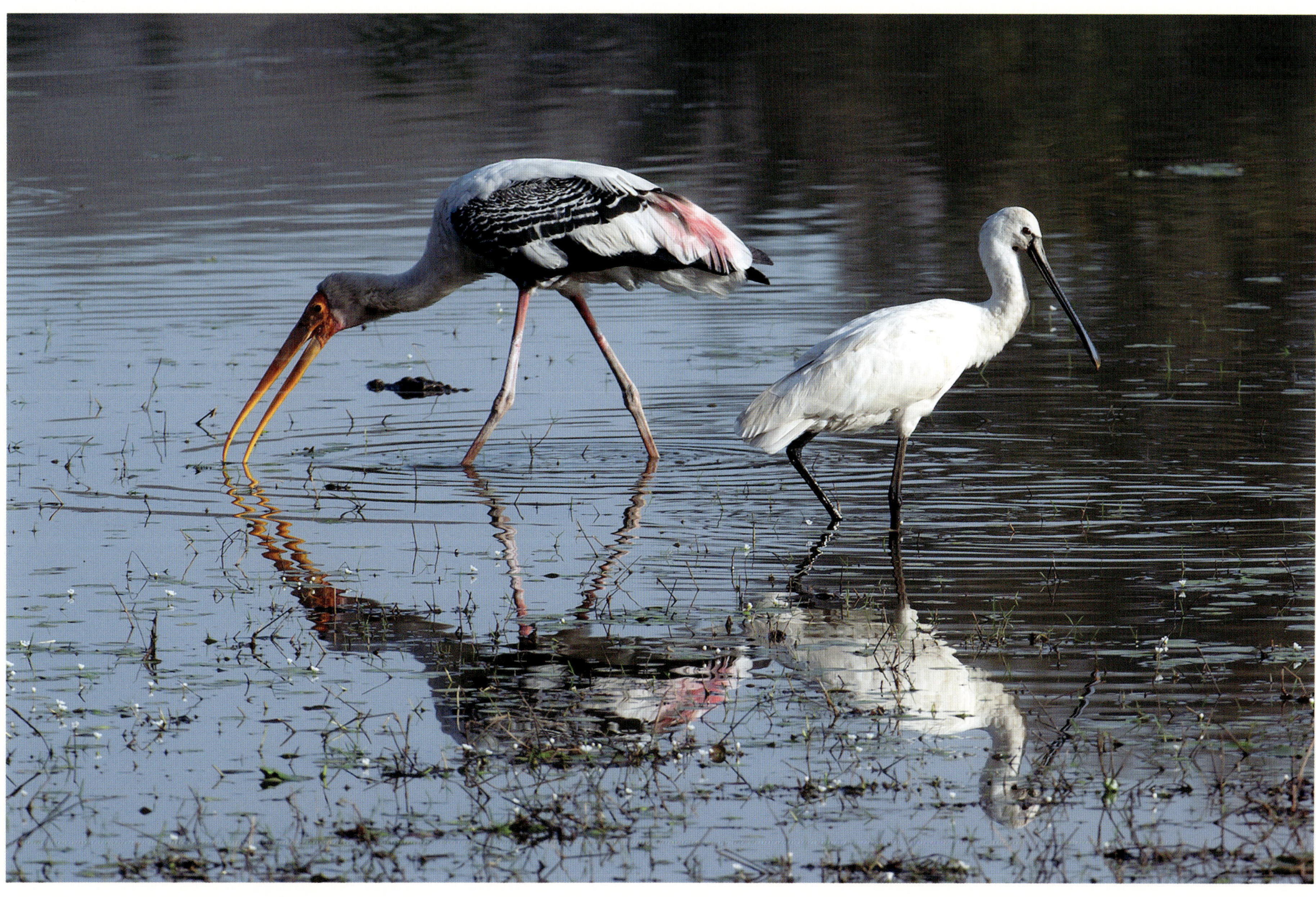

A painted stork and a Eurasian spoonbill are foraging (above), while a baby marsh crocodile or mugger slowly drifts away in the background. As juveniles, these reptiles can fall prey to large water birds, but this will change as the years pass. Any birds, including Asian openbill storks (opposite), must be cautious when close to adult crocodiles.

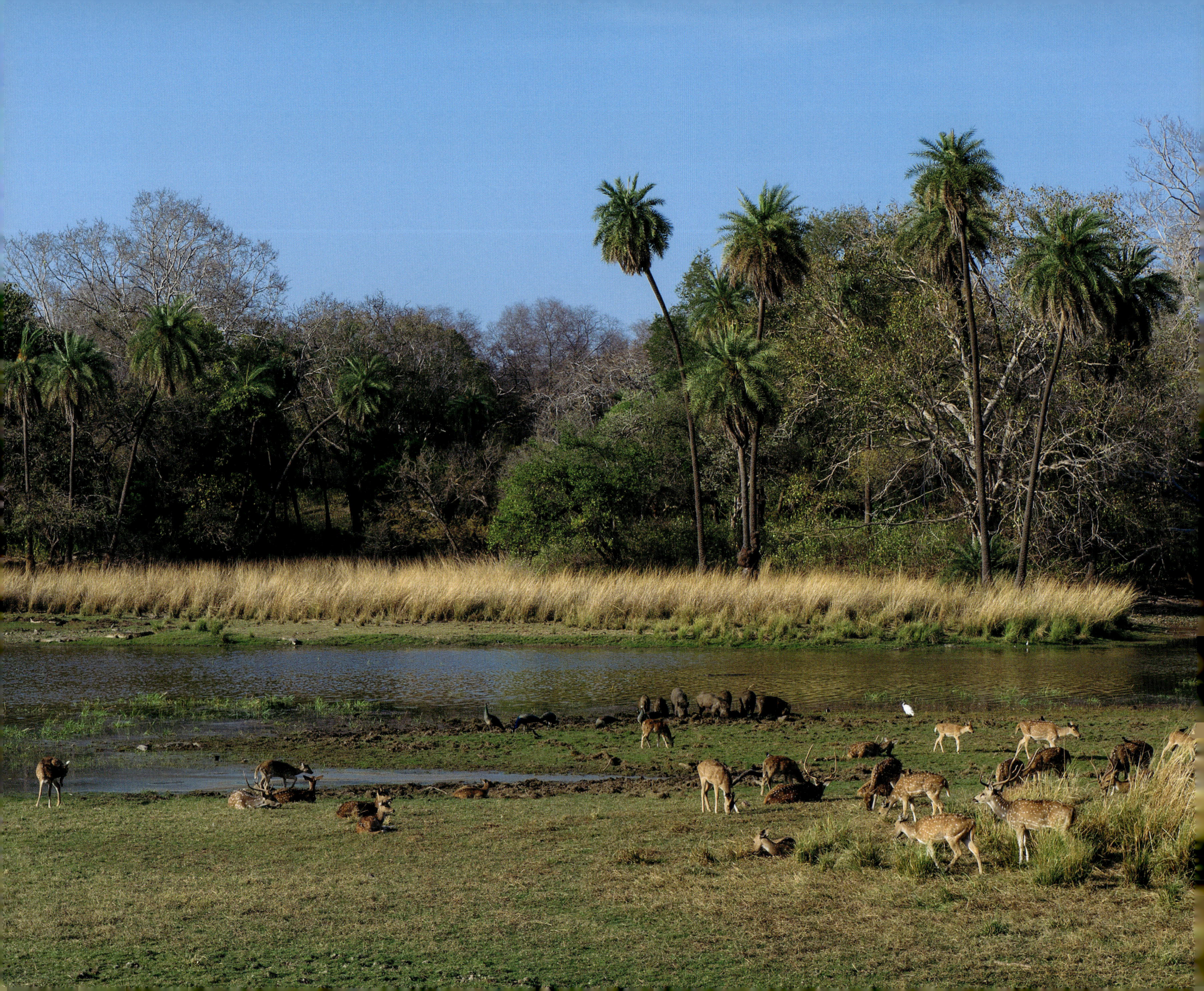

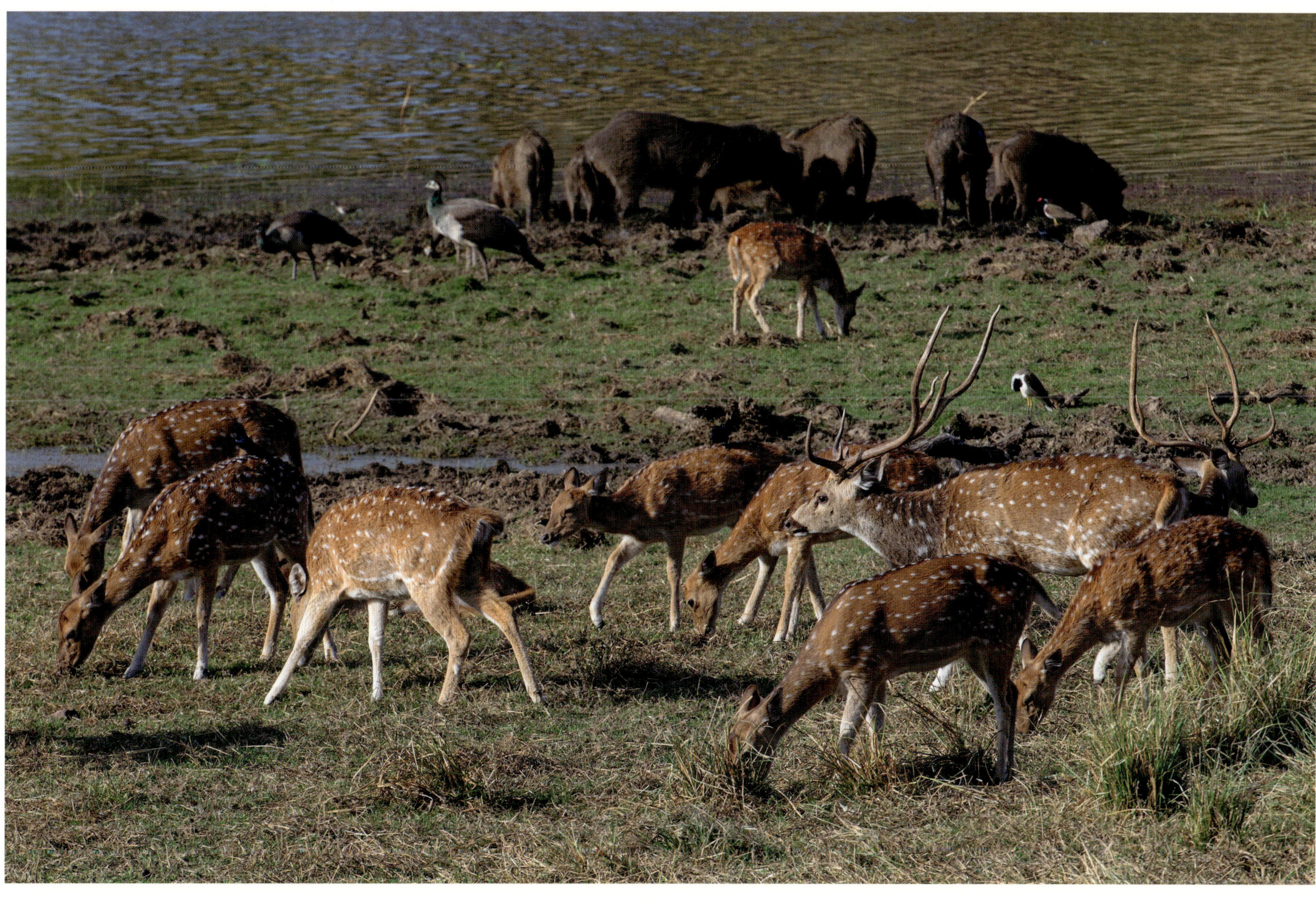

Permanent water bodies are essential for survival during the dry season, attracting wildlife from all surrounding jungle areas. Here, spotted deer and wild boar forage and quench their thirst at the shores of this lake in the Ranthambhore National Park in Rajasthan.

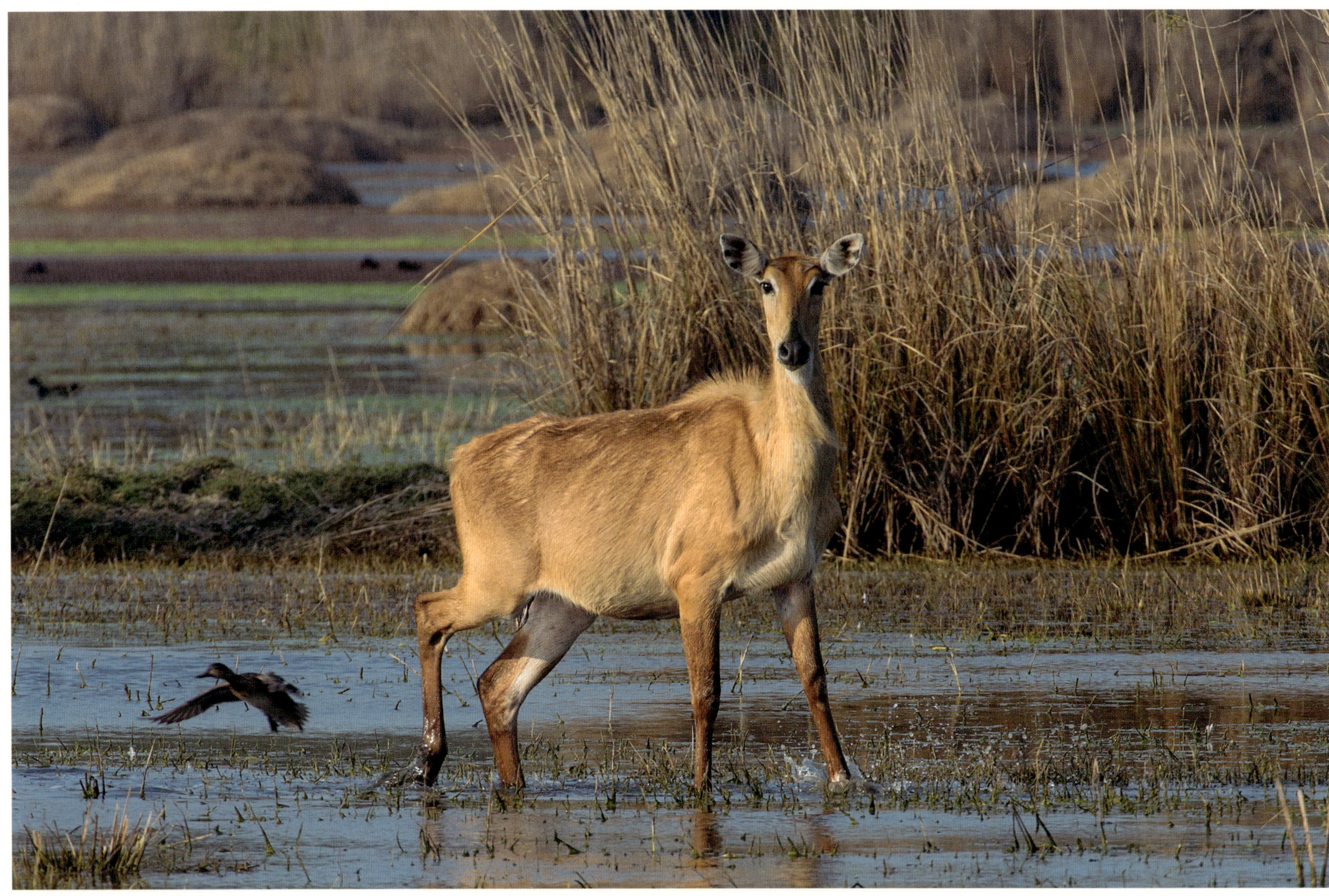

The nilgai is India's largest antelope and can reach the size of a horse. It is widespread, commonly living in dry parts of the country, though able to cope with wetlands such as in the Sultanpur National Park. Females are a tawny colour (above), while adult males have a bluish-grey coat, earning them their name which translates as 'blue cow' (opposite).

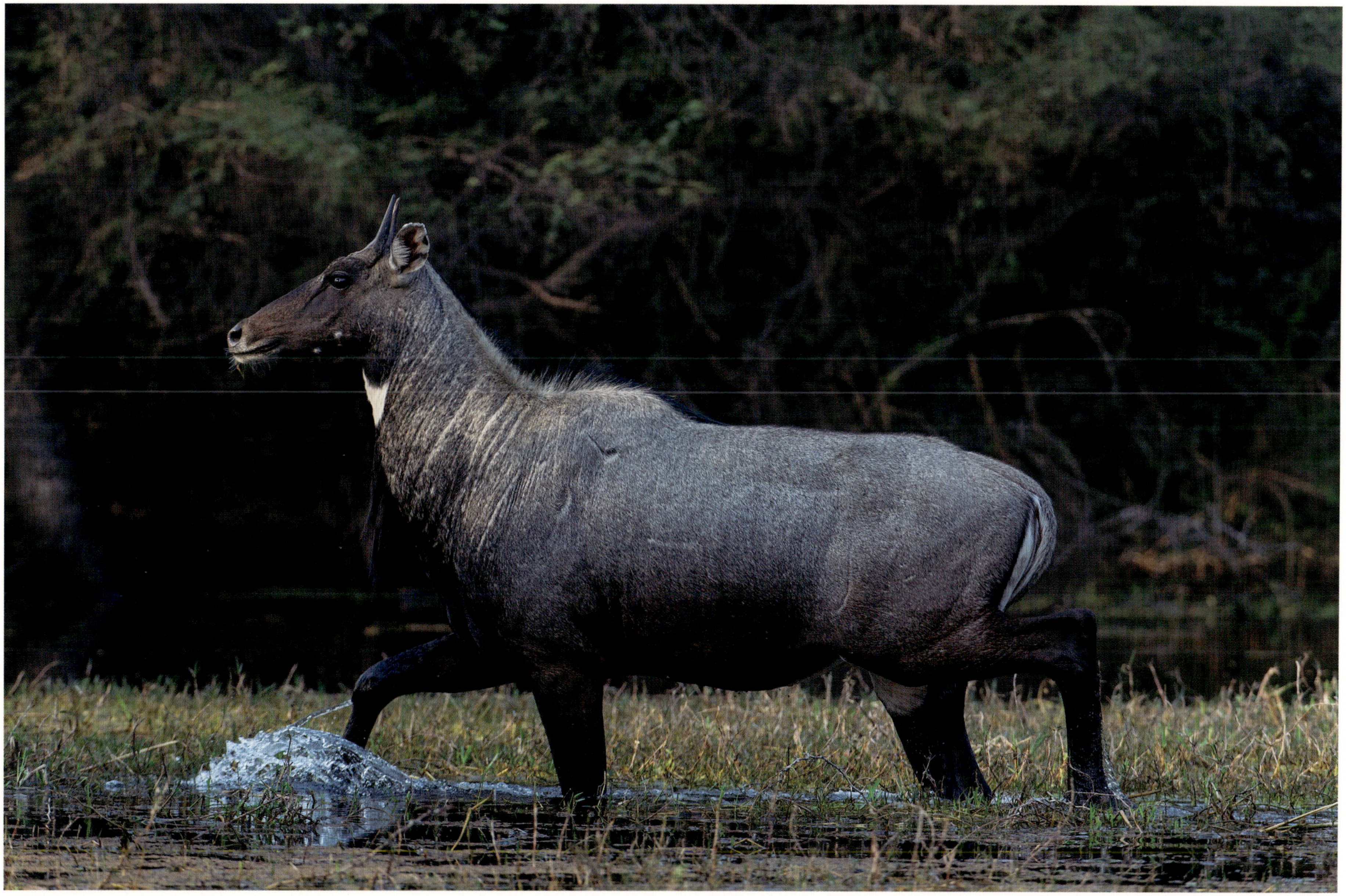

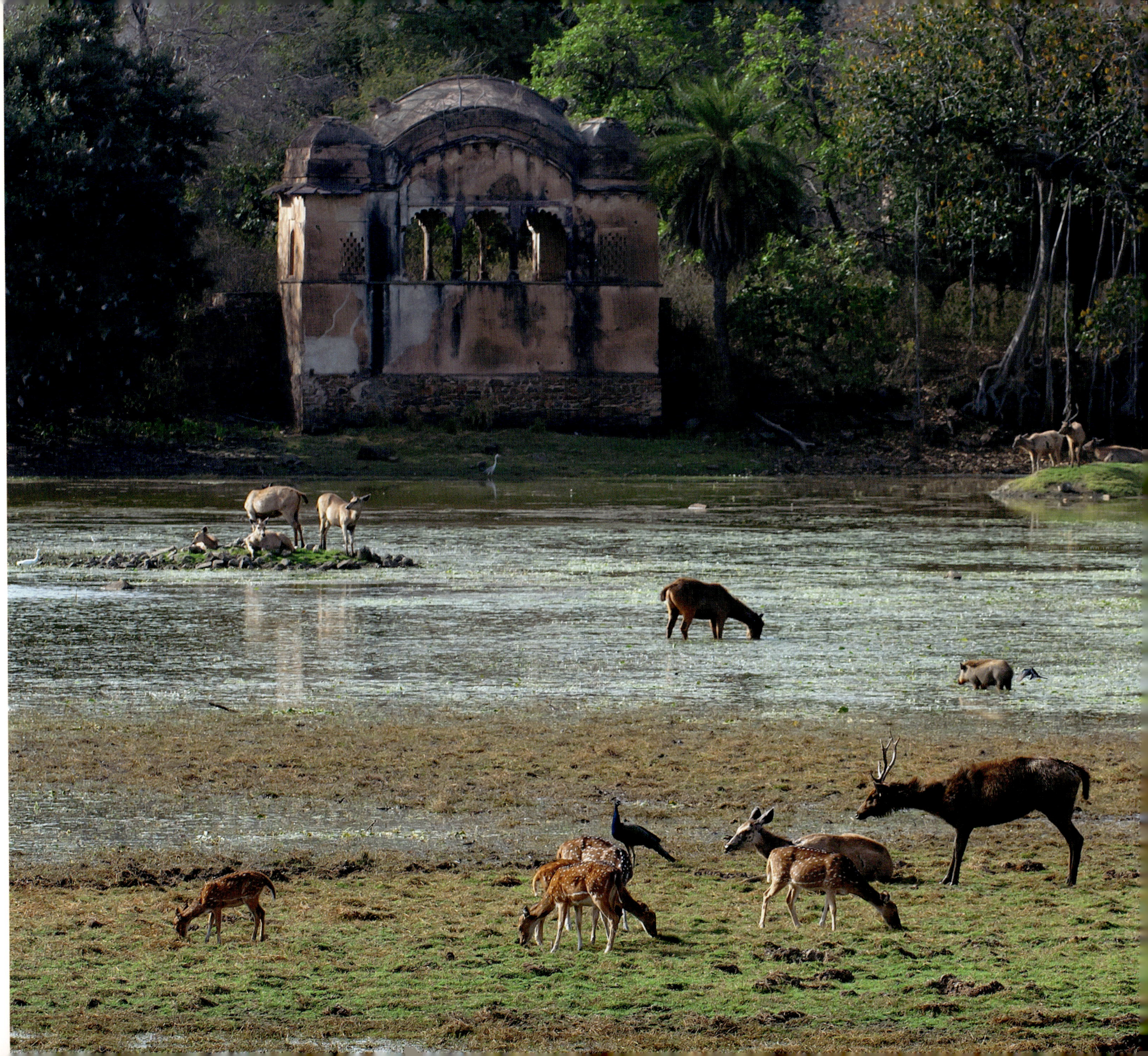

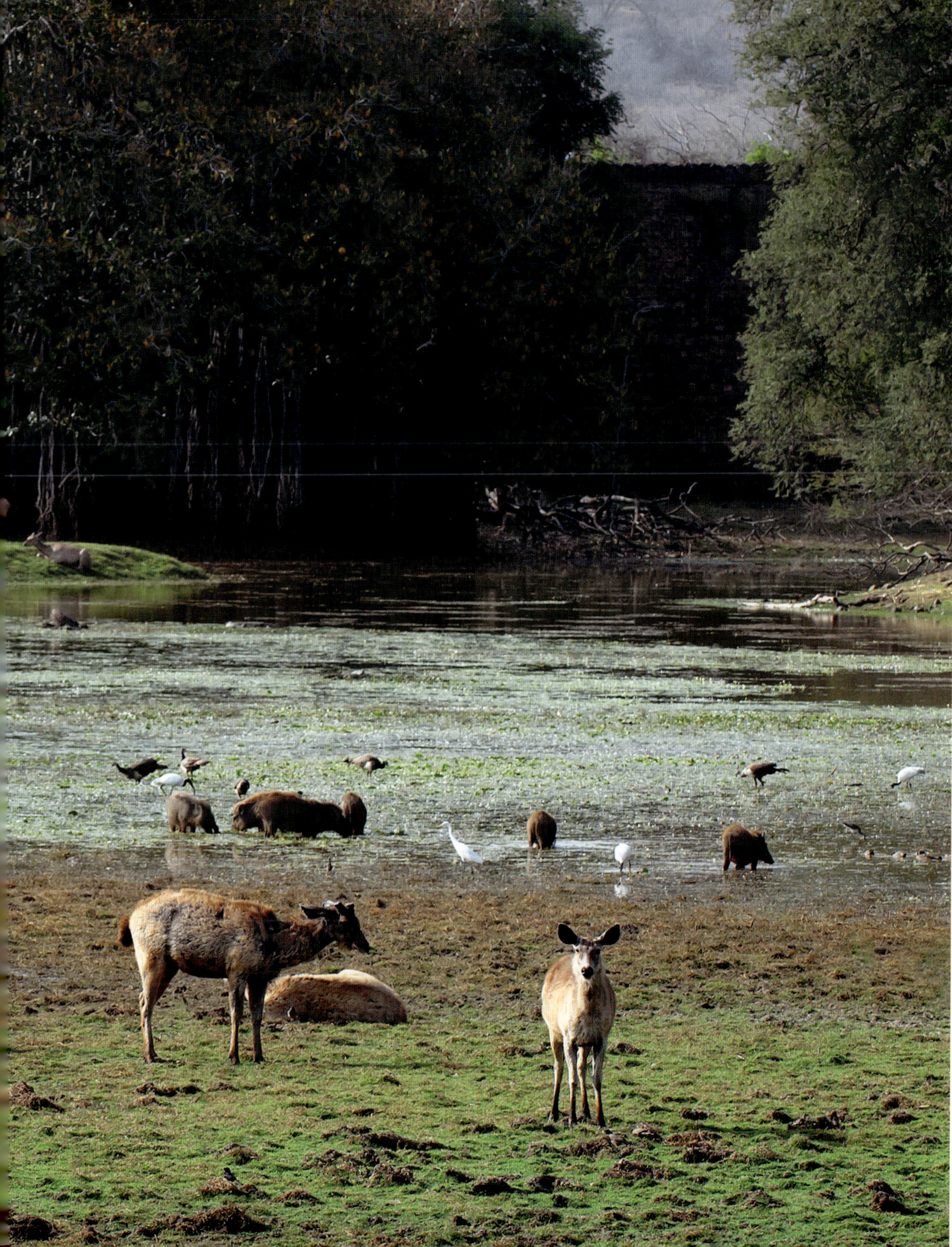

Ruins dot the park at Ranthambhore which was once one of the former hunting grounds of the Maharajas of Jaipur. As a national park, the sambar deer, spotted deer and wild boar no longer need to fear people, however, they must still watch out for predators.

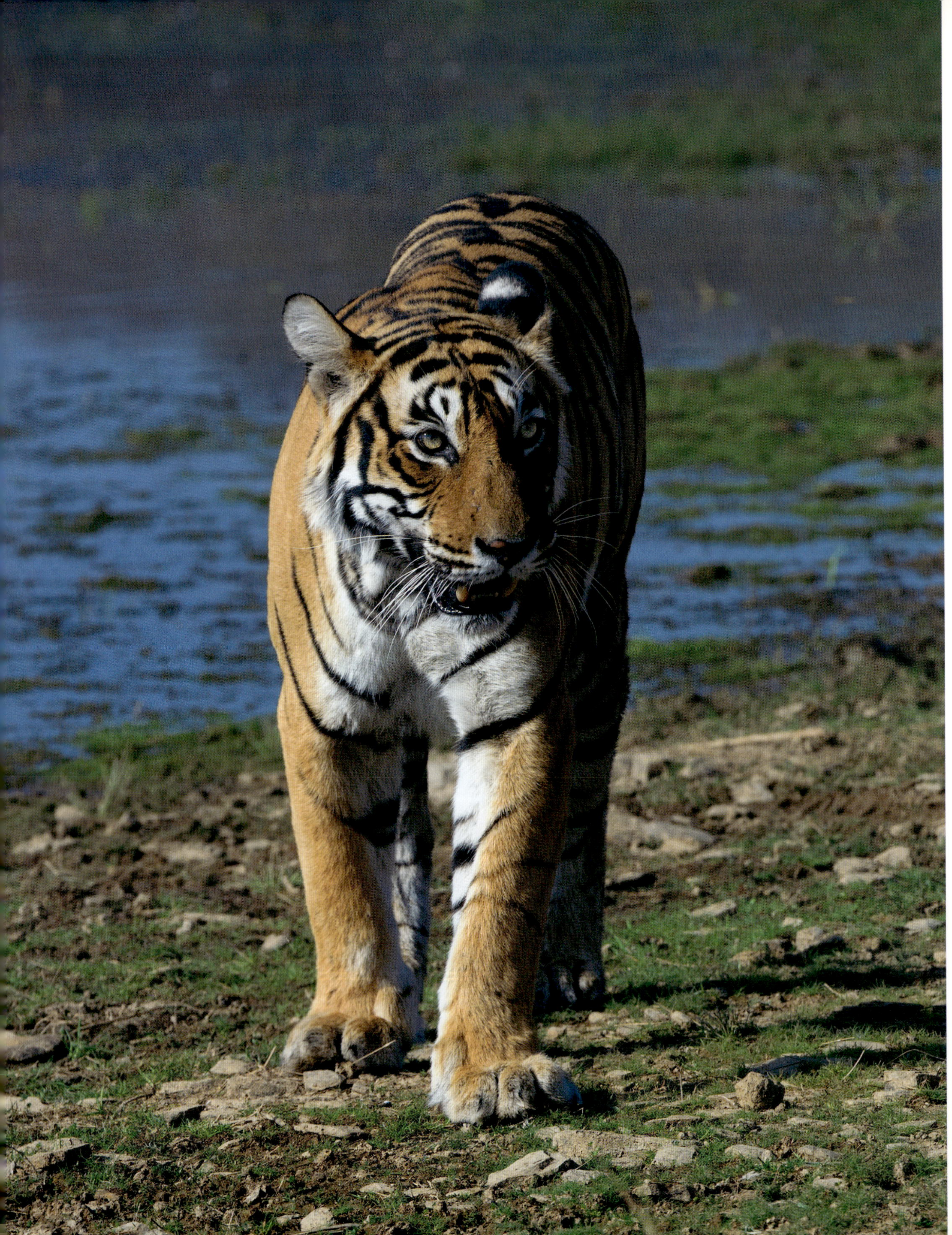

Large concentrations of prey animals (opposite) attract predators such as tigers. In the Ranthambhore National Park, the best territories for the tigers are located around the lakes.

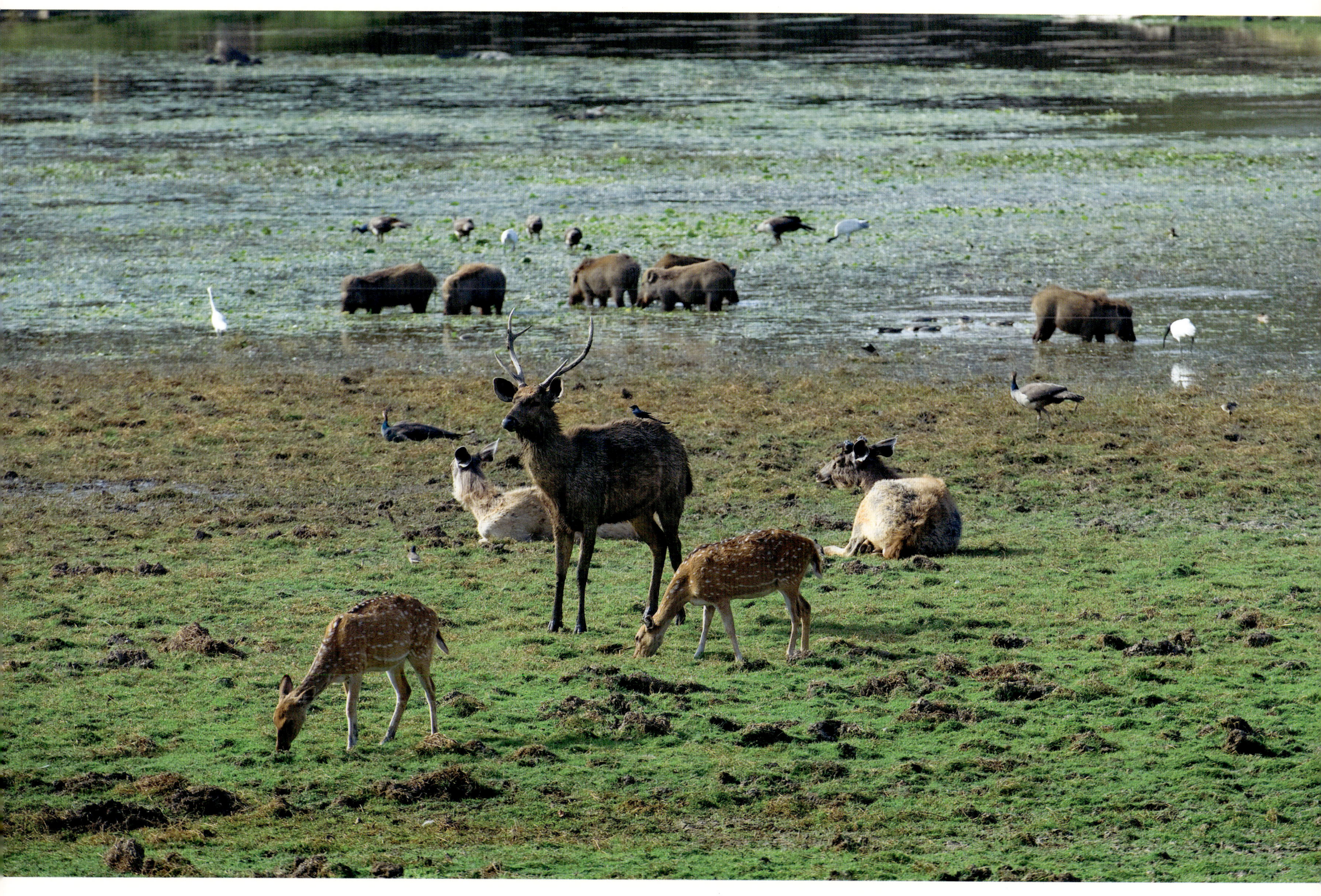

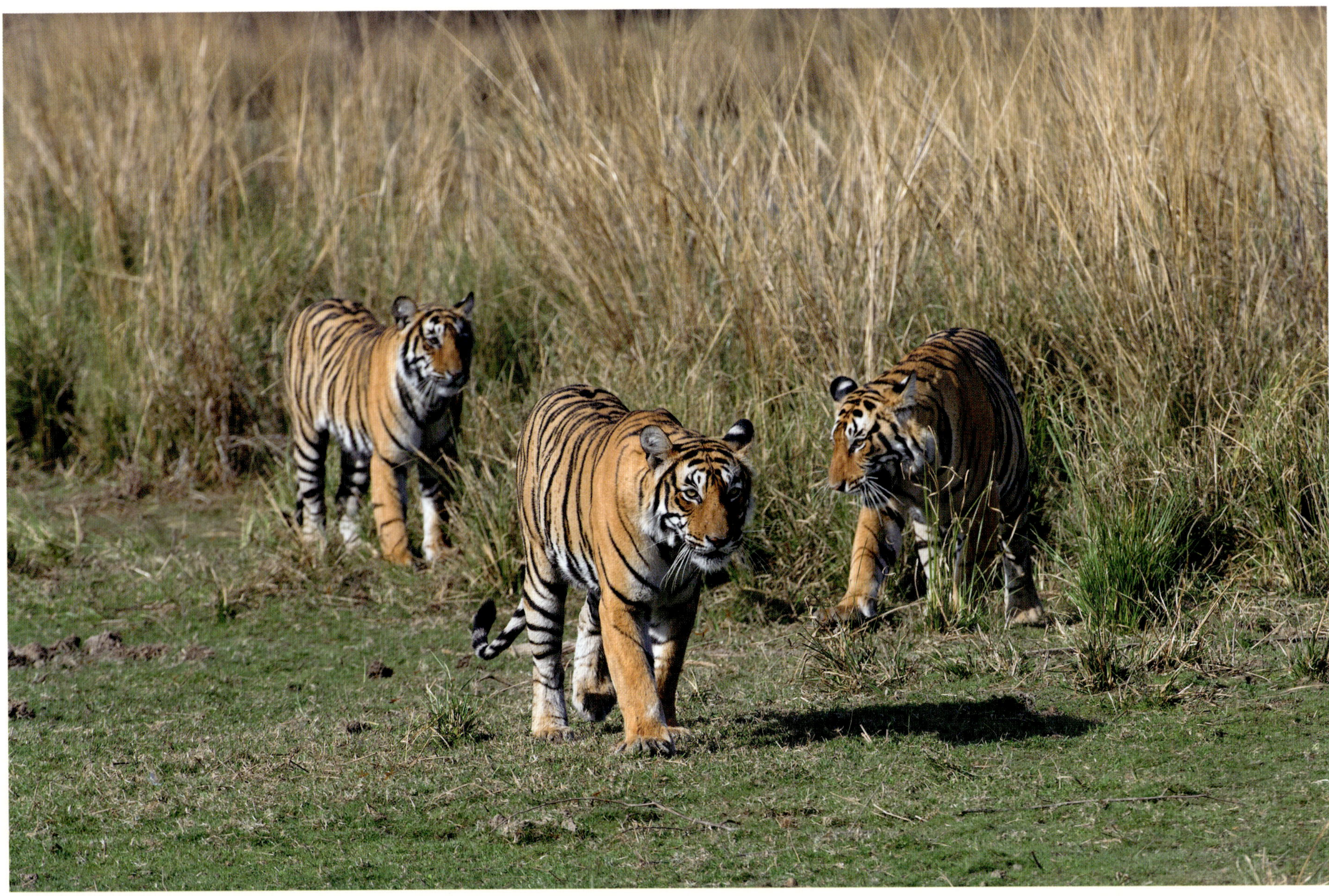

A tigress and her two large cubs leave their hiding place among the tall grasses in search for a drink (above). The vegetation around the lakes offers excellent cover for both hunting and relaxing. Any potential prey must maintain caution here, as a tiger can appear at any time (right).

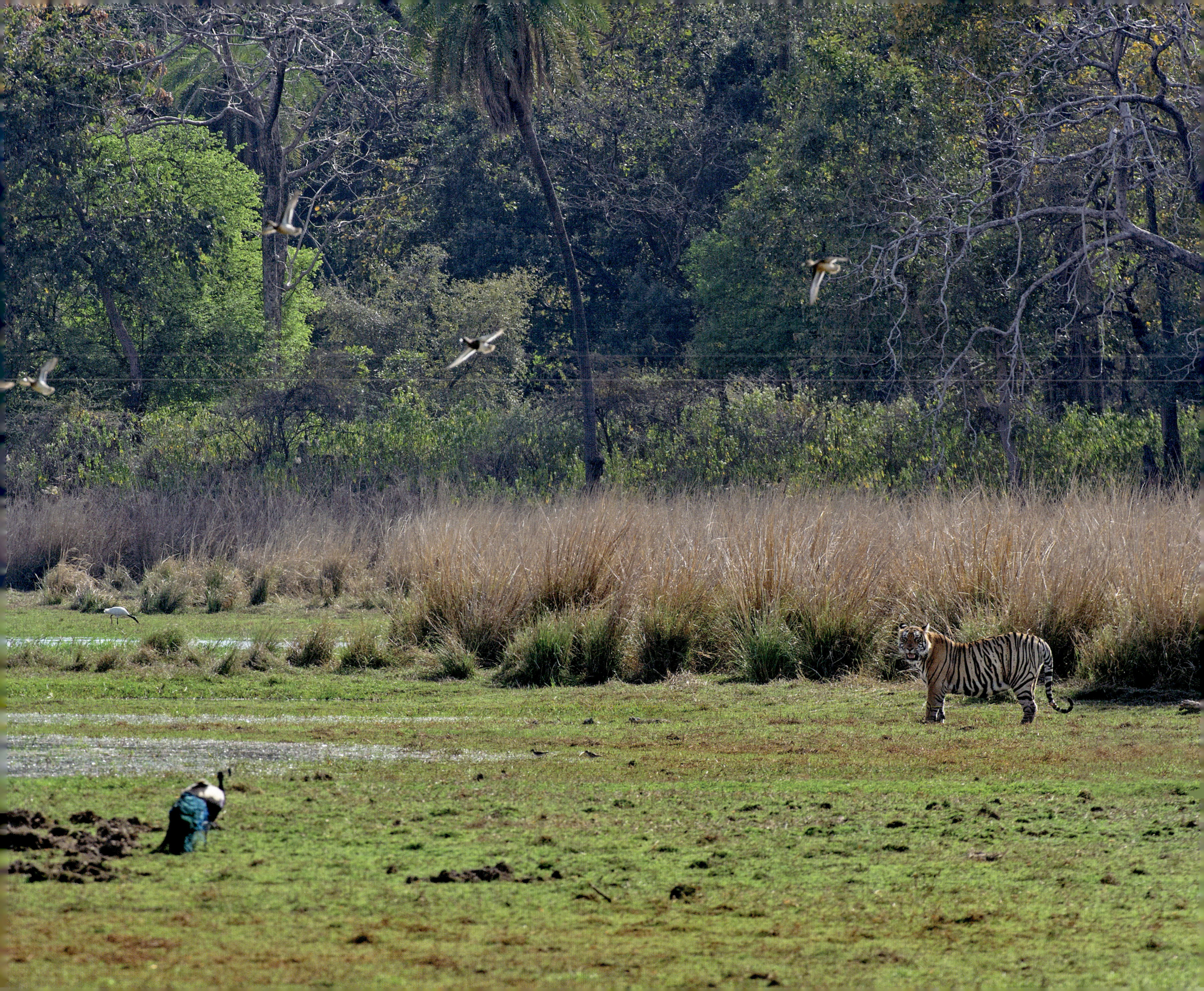

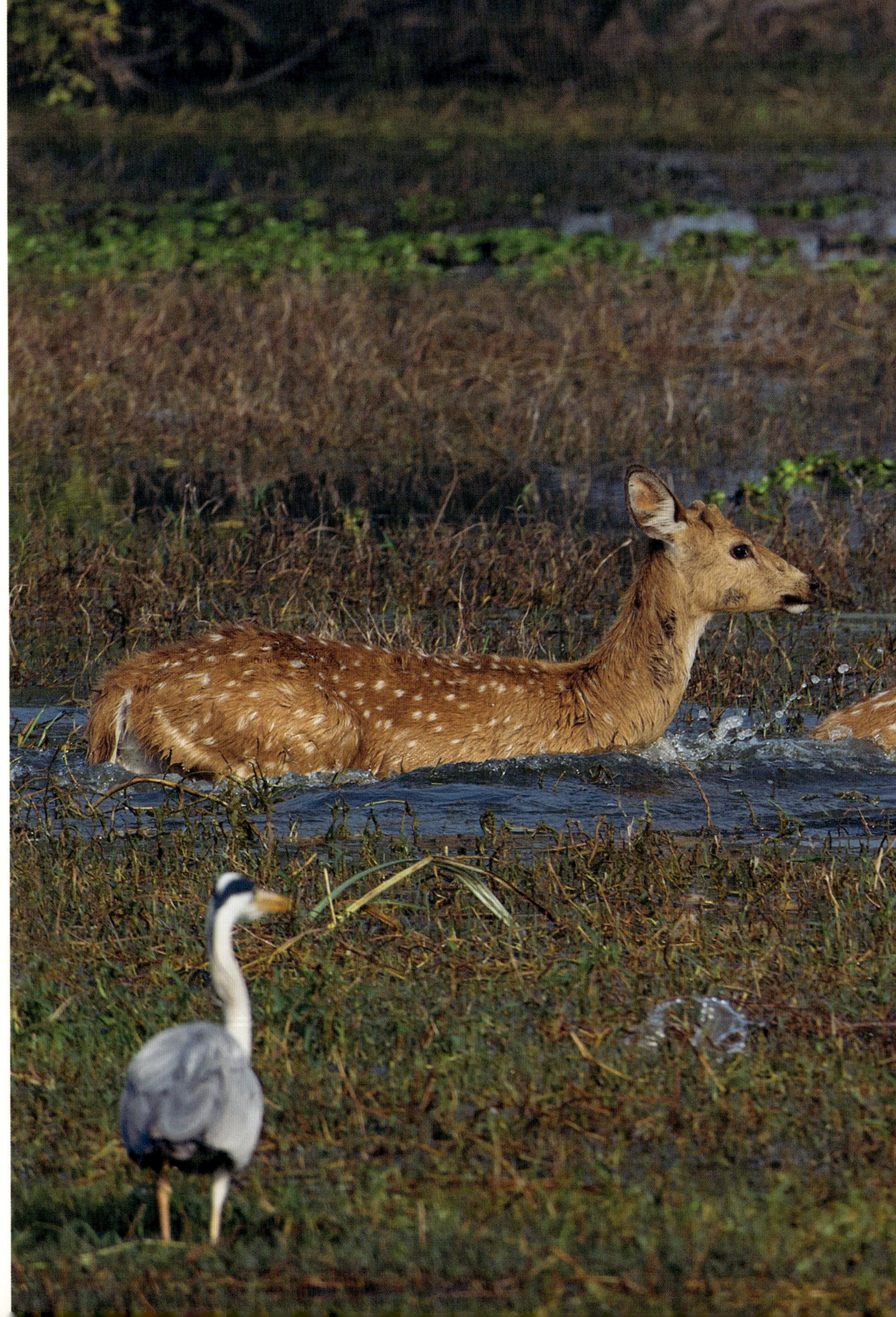

Spotted deer cross a swamp at the Keoladeo National Park in eastern Rajasthan. While the adults are able to reach the ground and walk, the fawns are forced to swim. Any such commotion is of no bother to the birds, who know that these herbivores pose them no threat.

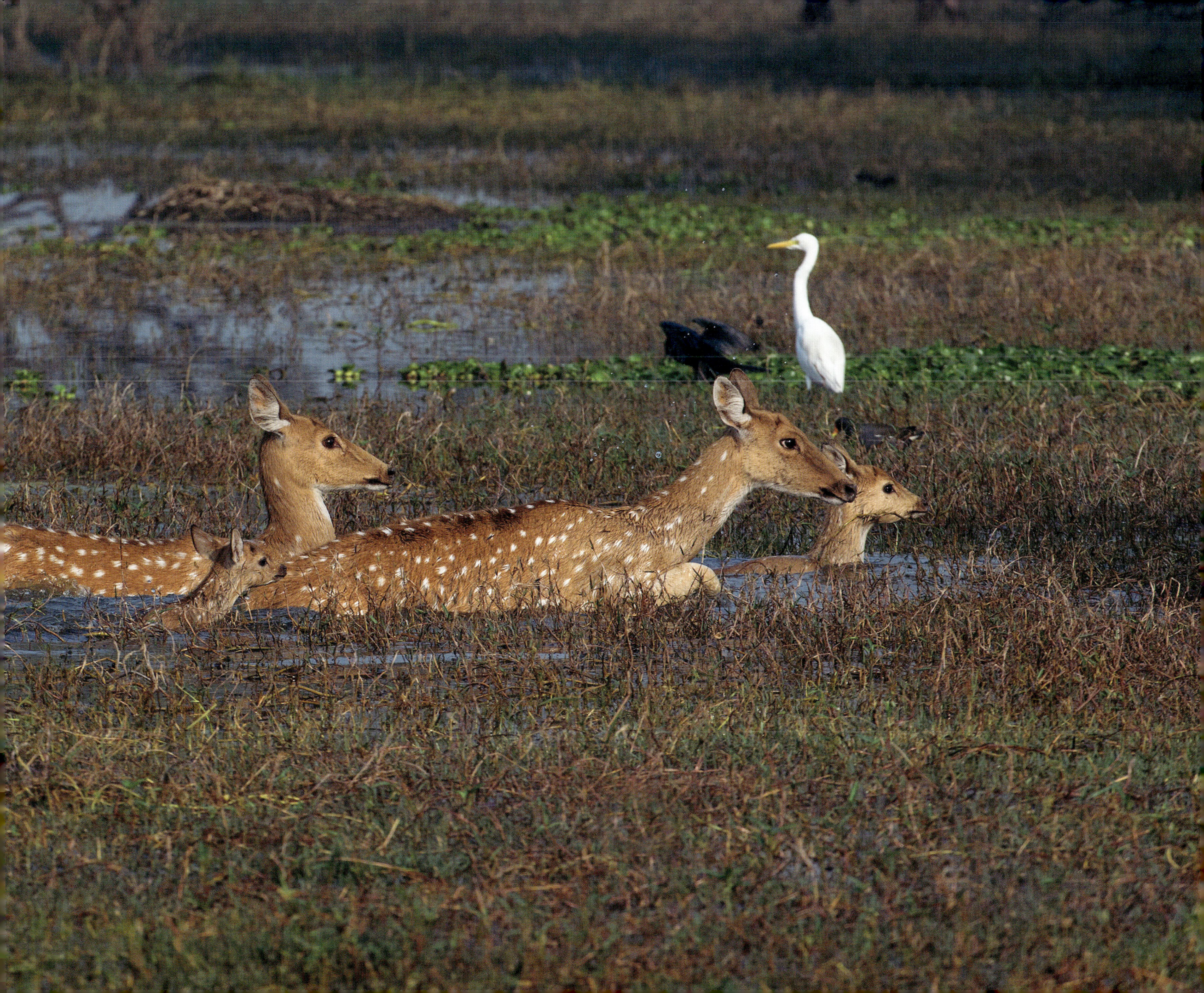

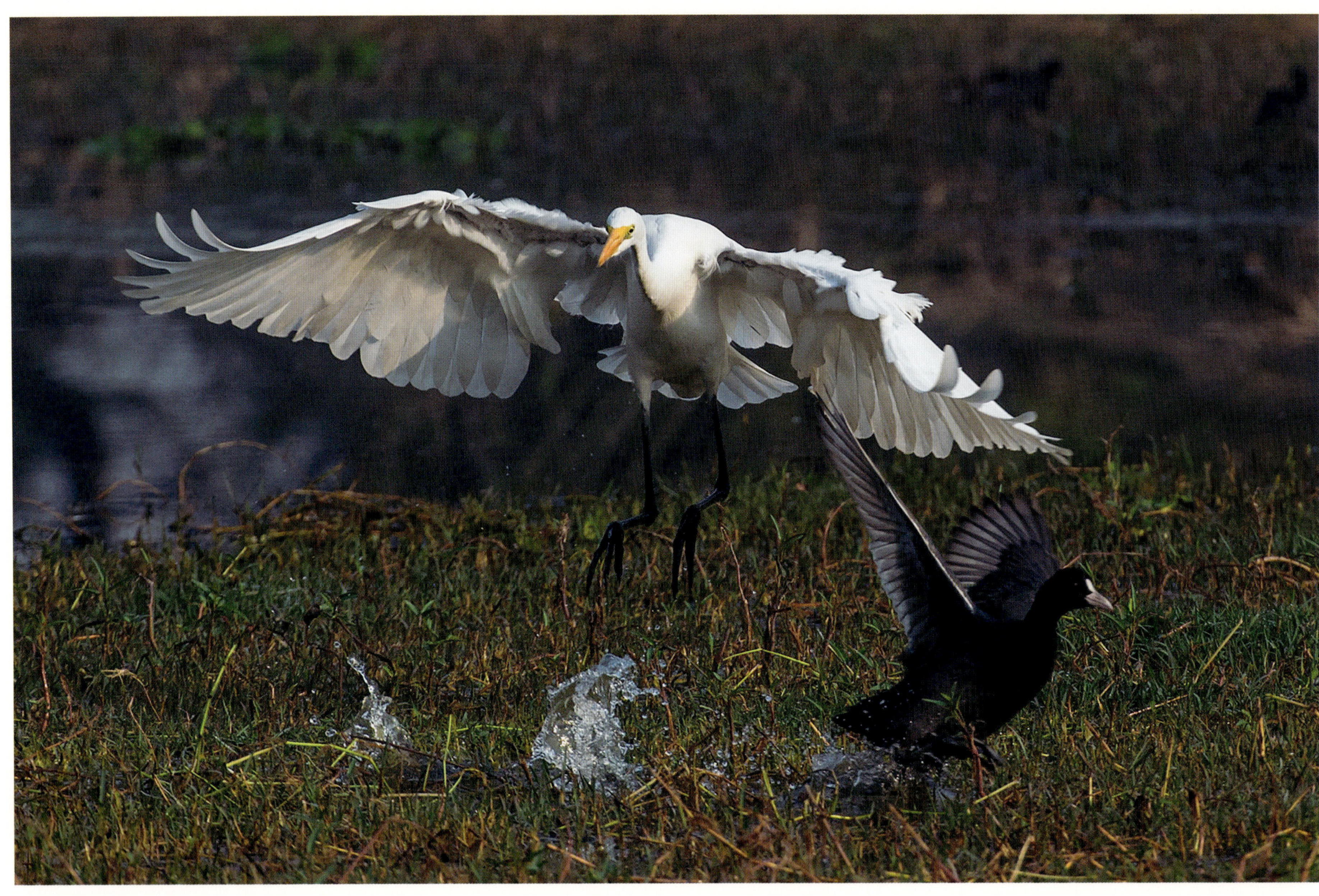

A great egret tirelessly chases away smaller birds such as a Eurasian coot (above) and a common moorhen (opposite) at the Keoladeo National Park.

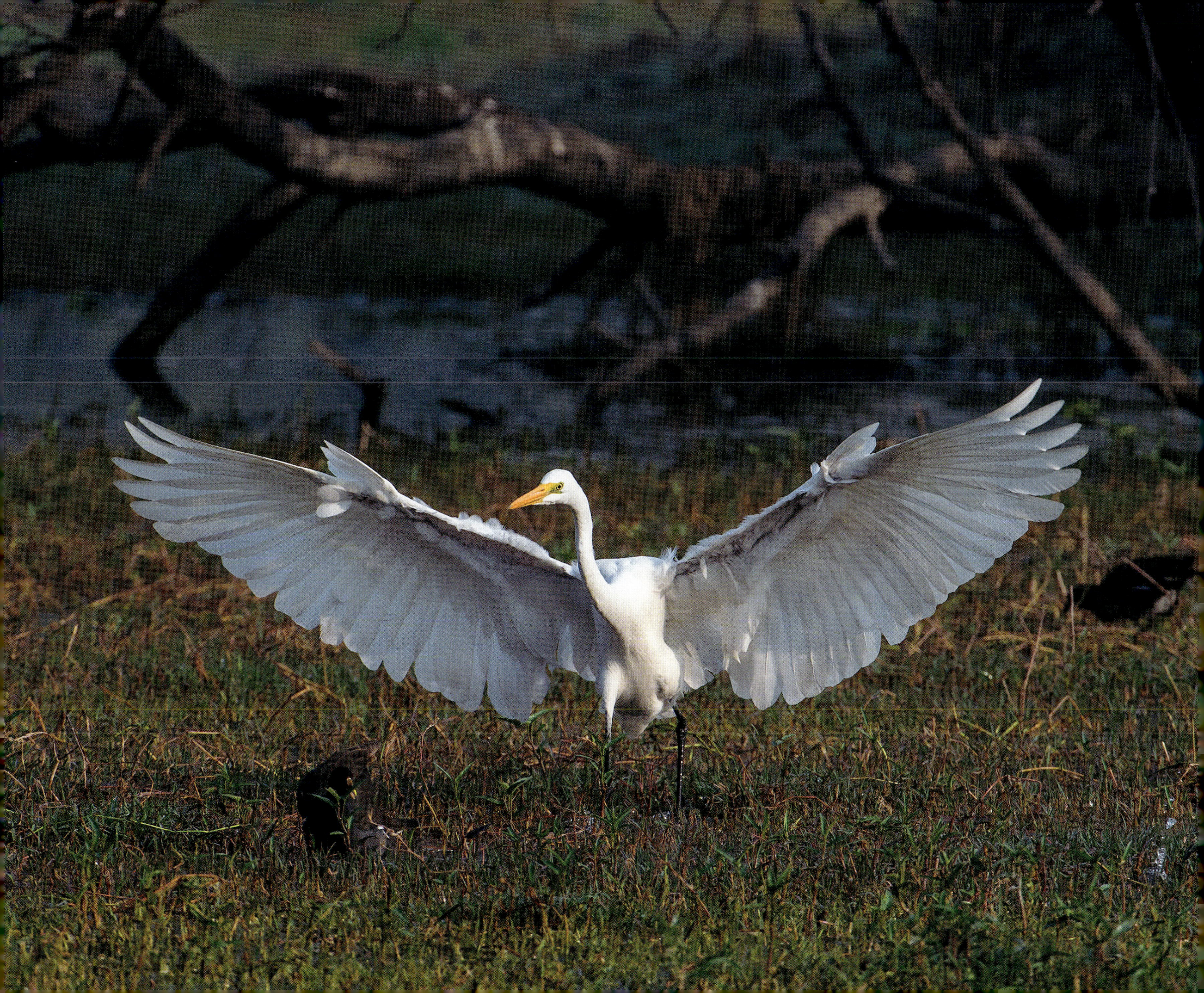

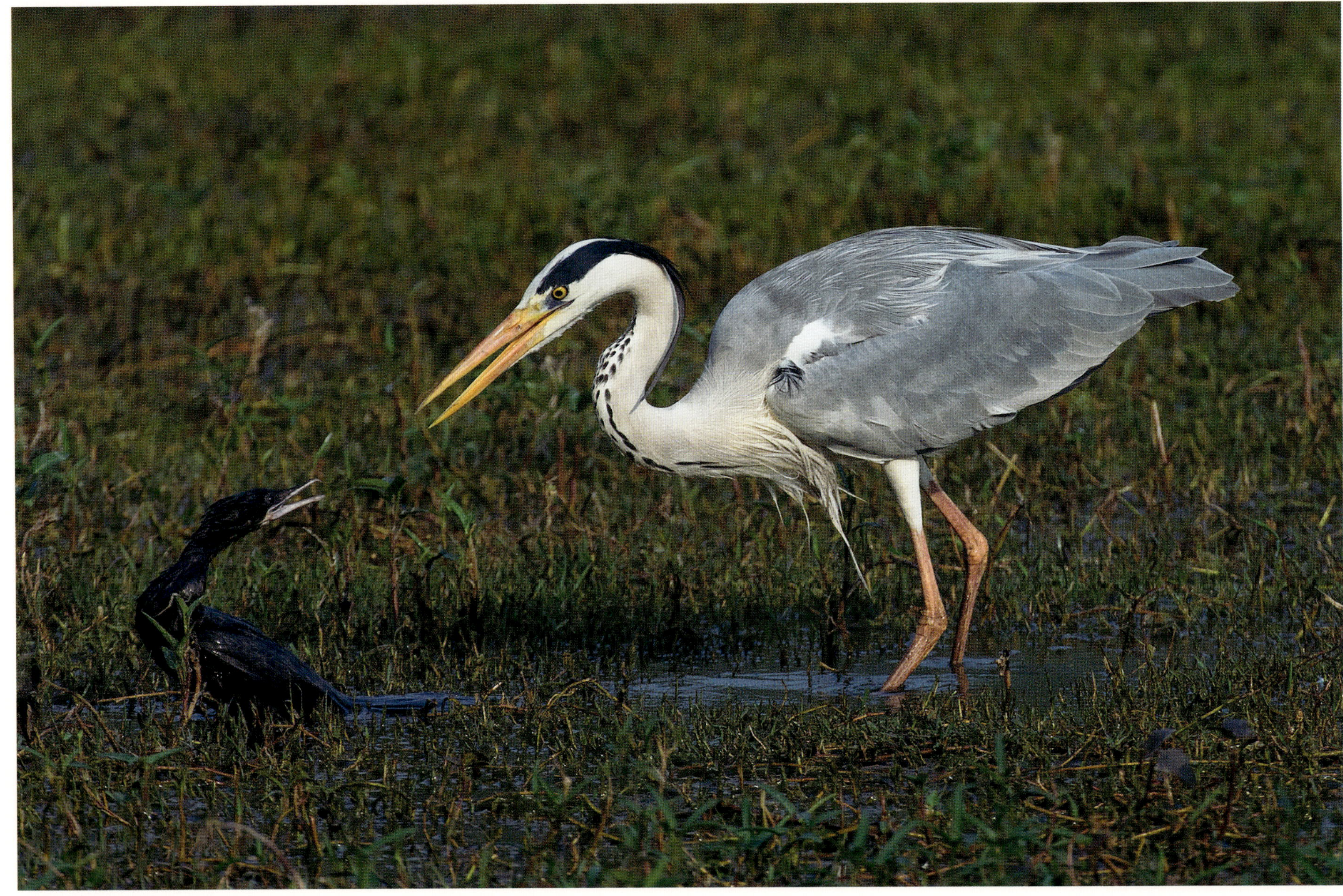

Many different species of water birds often live peacefully next to one other, but here, a grey heron displays aggressive behaviour, threatening a little cormorant with its spear-like beak (above). Although the grey heron can take on much larger prey, the food ranges of both birds overlap to a certain extent, and so the heron will want to see off the rival bird. After foraging, the grey heron flies away to roost (opposite).

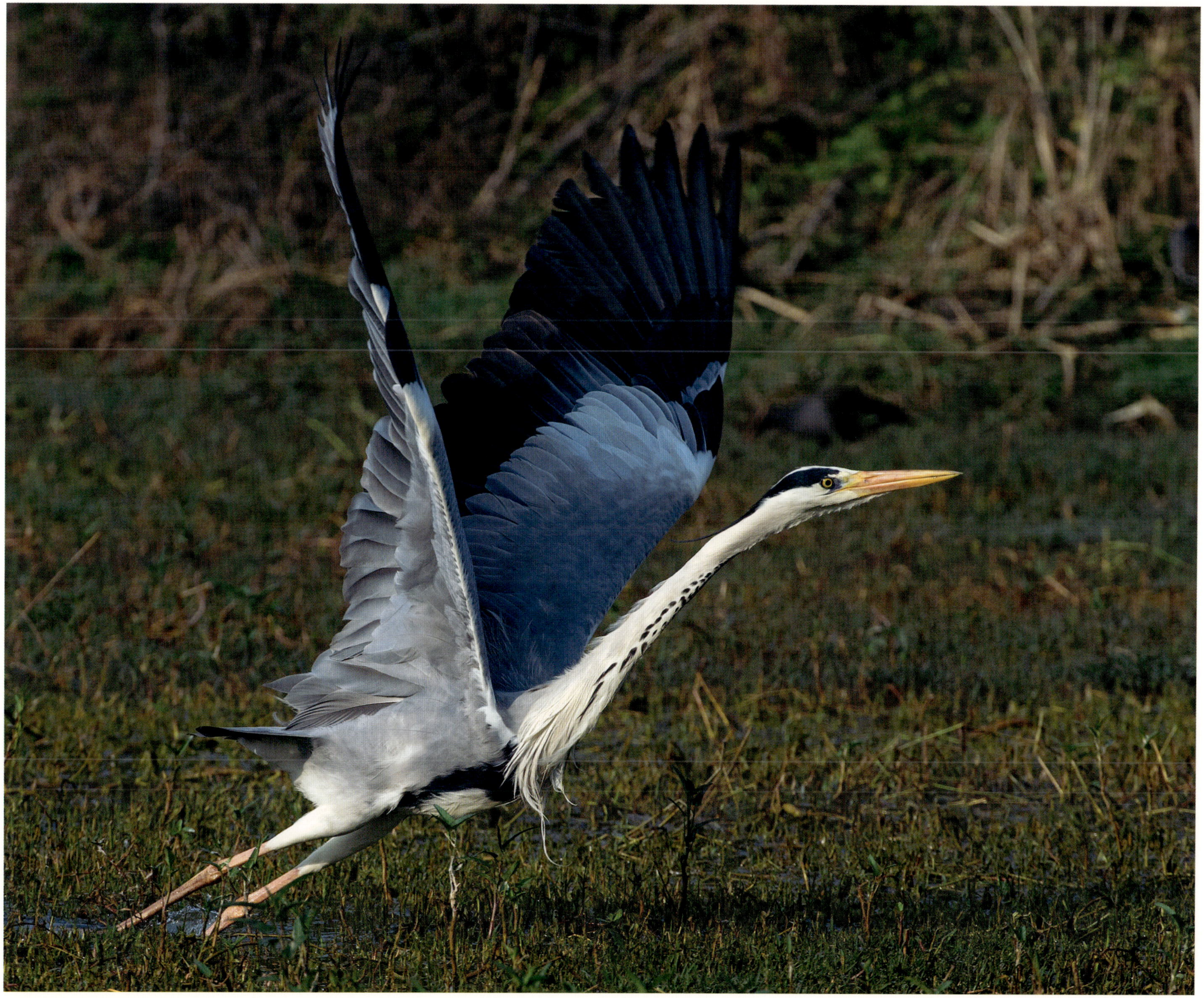

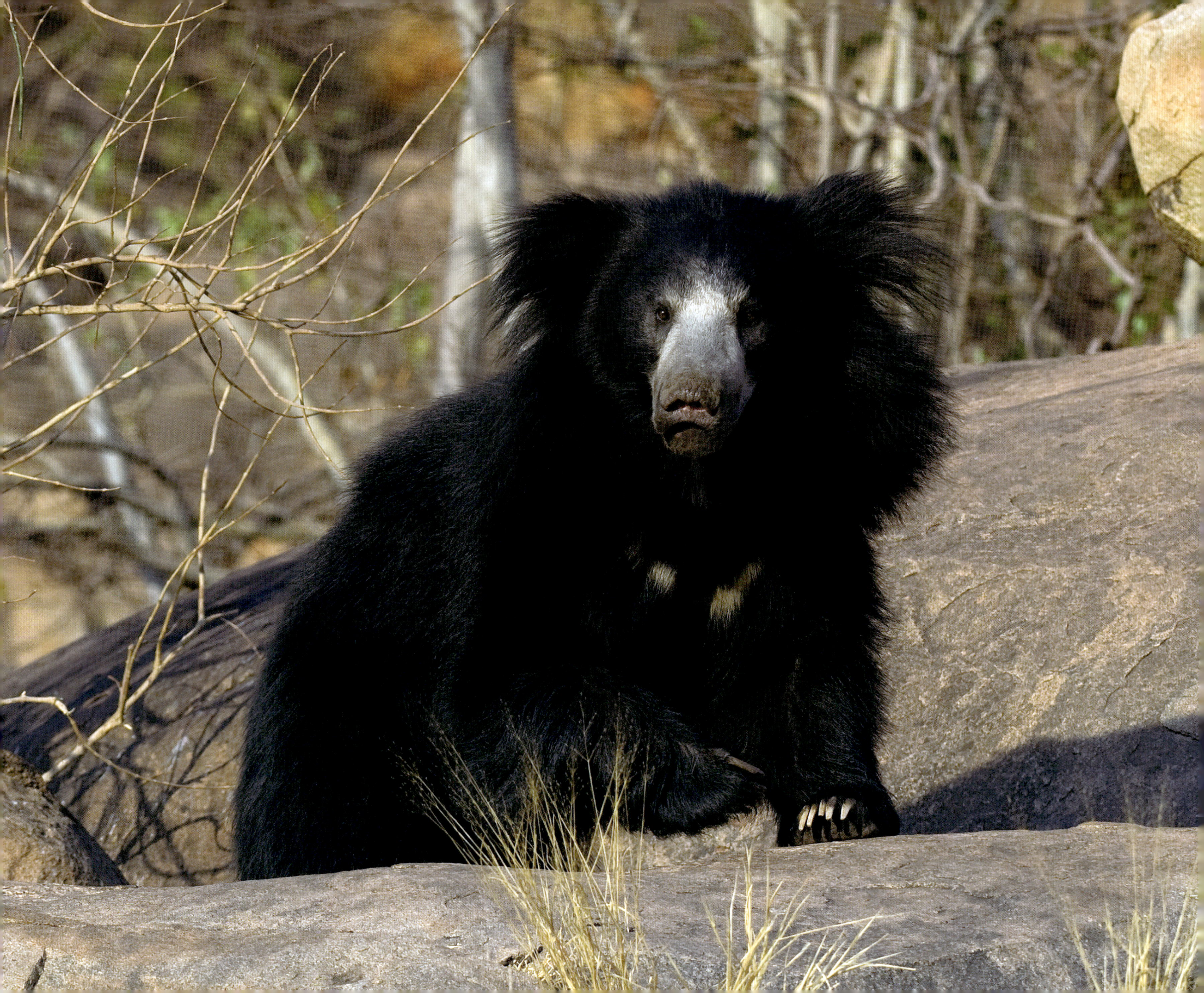

DRYLANDS

The Thar desert dominates the northwest of India. It is a very dry region, with sand dunes surrounded by areas of semi-desert conditions. Most parts of India receive very little rain apart from during the monsoon season. After the rain has ended, the country starts to dry up until the onset of the next monsoon, forcing many creatures to cope with heat and a lack of water for a very extended period of time.

Boulder-strewn landscapes are found in parts of Karnataka and Rajasthan. These are areas where sloth bears and leopards find shelter in secluded caves among the rocky hills. The plains – grasslands reminiscent of African savannahs – are populated by blackbucks, with rare wolves following in their tracks. Large flocks of birds, such as the many thousands of demoiselle cranes, spend their winter in the dry northwest, while Asiatic wild asses called khur take refuge in a saltpan in Gujarat, in Little Rann of Kutch.

Large parts of India's drylands have been cultivated by man, especially the grassy plains, however, land that proved unsuitable for agriculture has suffered less under human pressure and thus remains an important habitat for wildlife.

The sloth bear is endemic to the Indian subcontinent. This particular male lives in a remote part of Karnataka. Note its long shaggy fur and the powerful claws, both of which are key characteristics of the species.

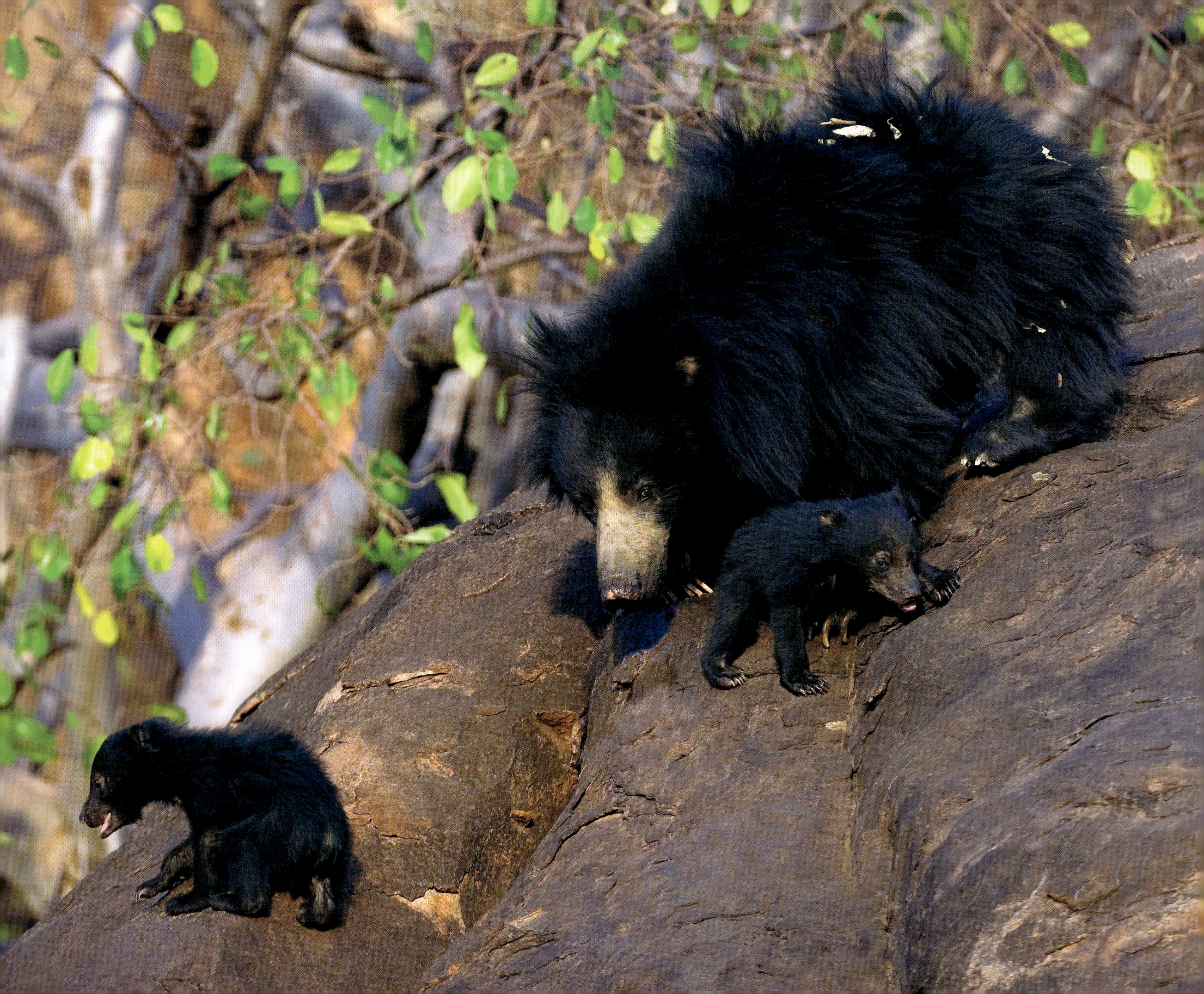

Sloth bears commonly have a litter size of two. During the first months, the cubs are completely reliant on their mother. Some will stay with her for up to two and a half years before searching out new ranges. Sloth bears were once found from the southern foothills of the Himalayas to Sri Lanka, however, their present distribution is patchy, roughly corresponding to areas with remaining forest cover.

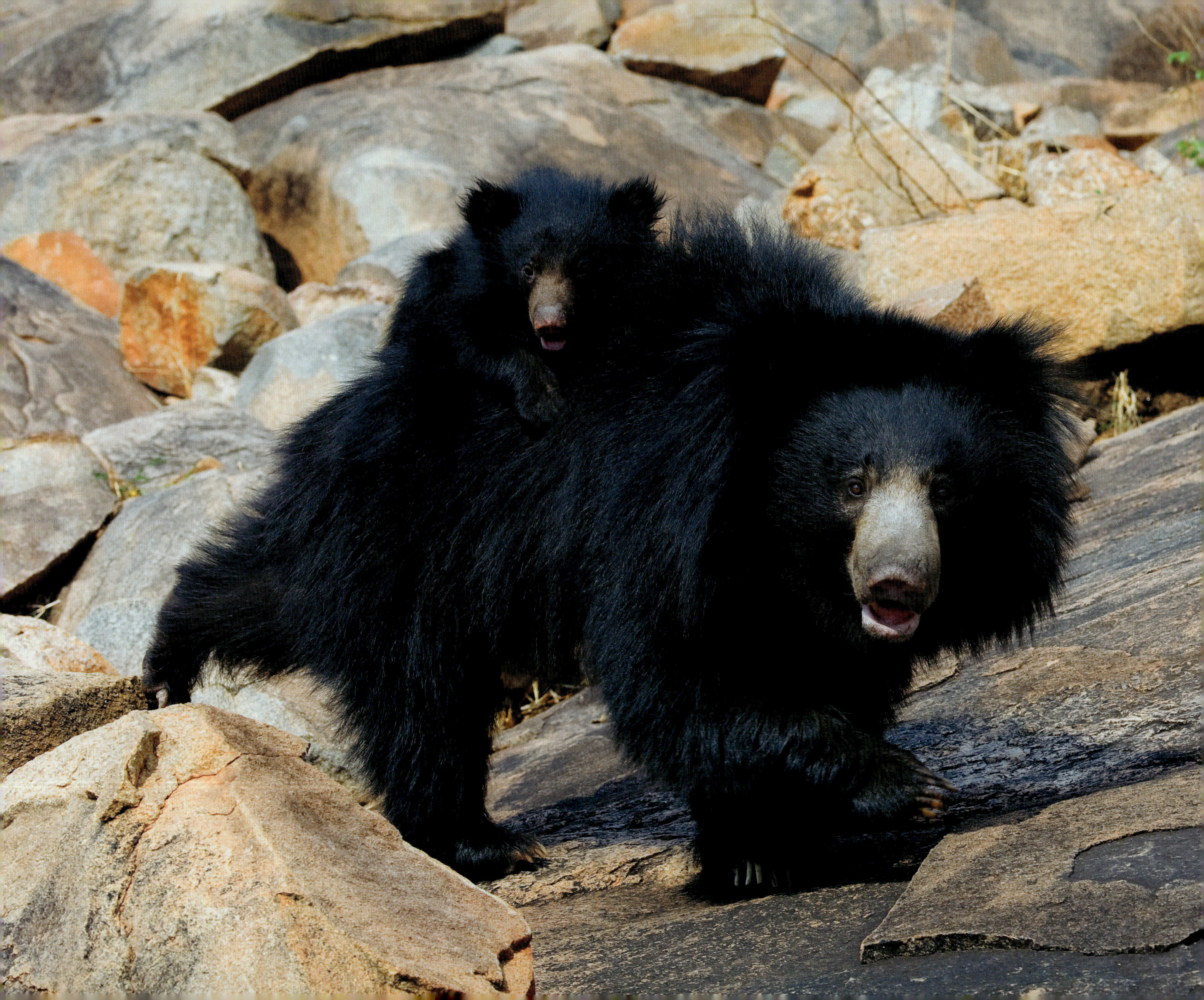

Young sloth bears typically ride piggyback on their mother. The mother's long fur helps them to get a better grip, providing a comfortable and safe way for them to travel. The sloth bear is the only bear species to carry its young this way.

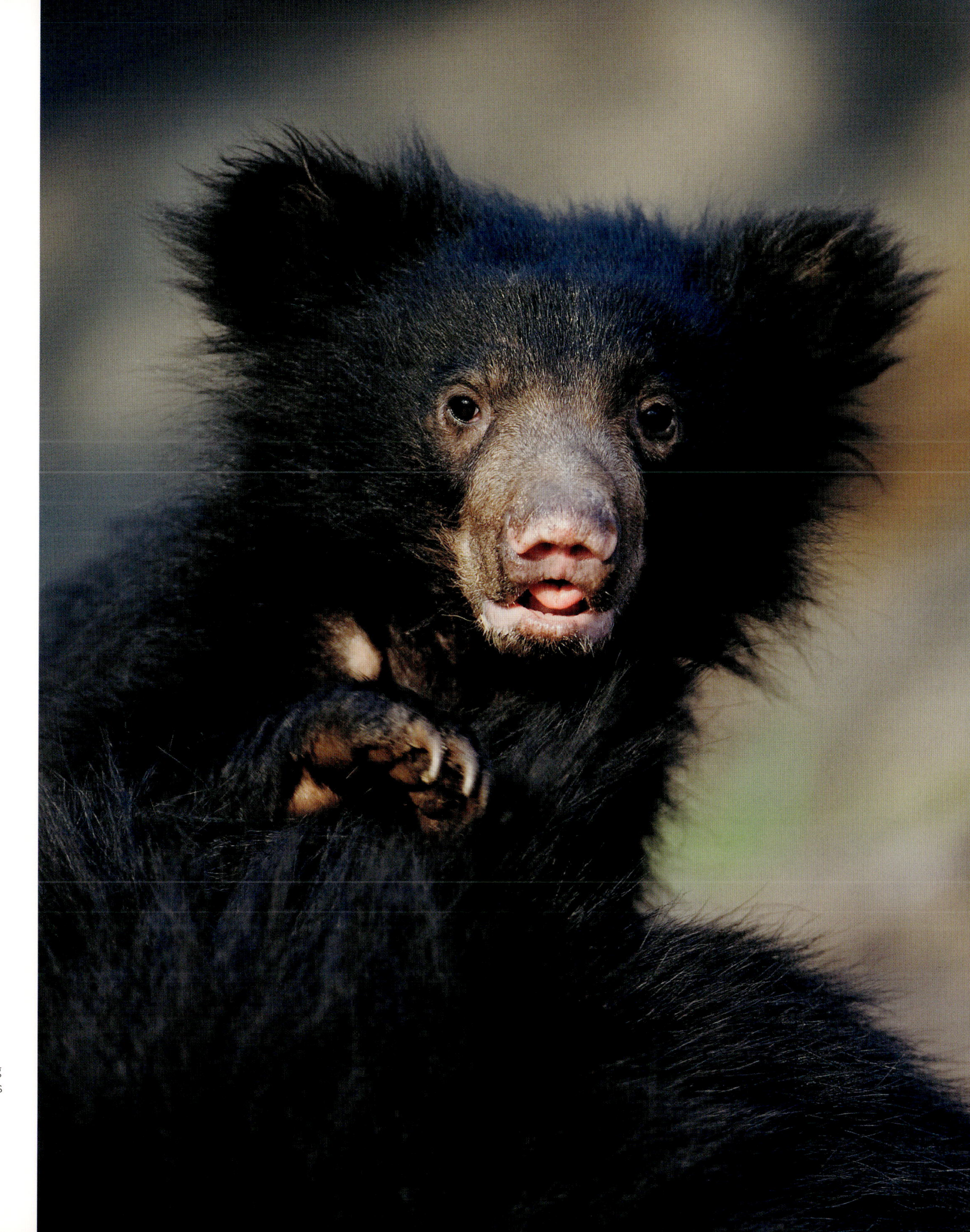

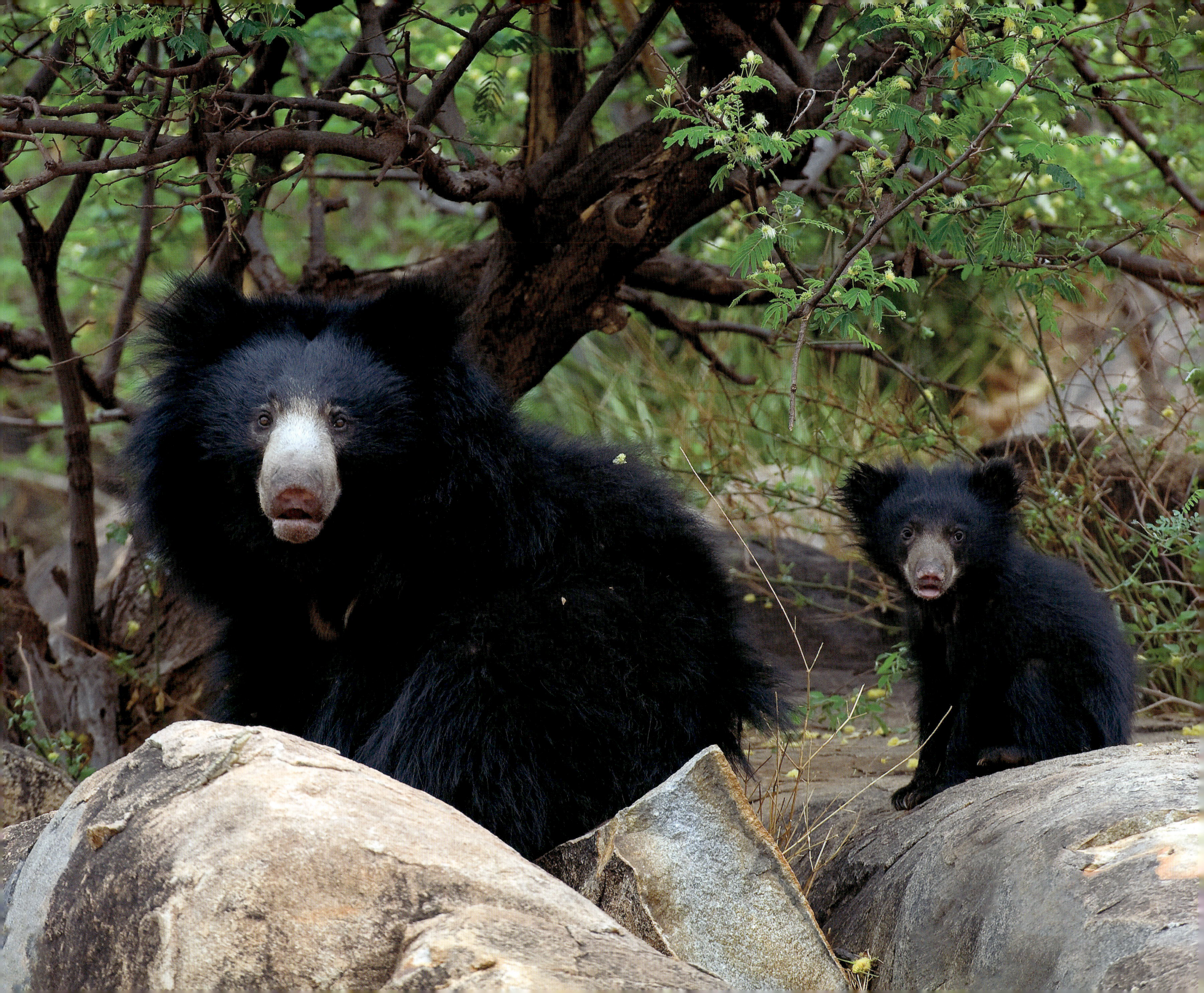

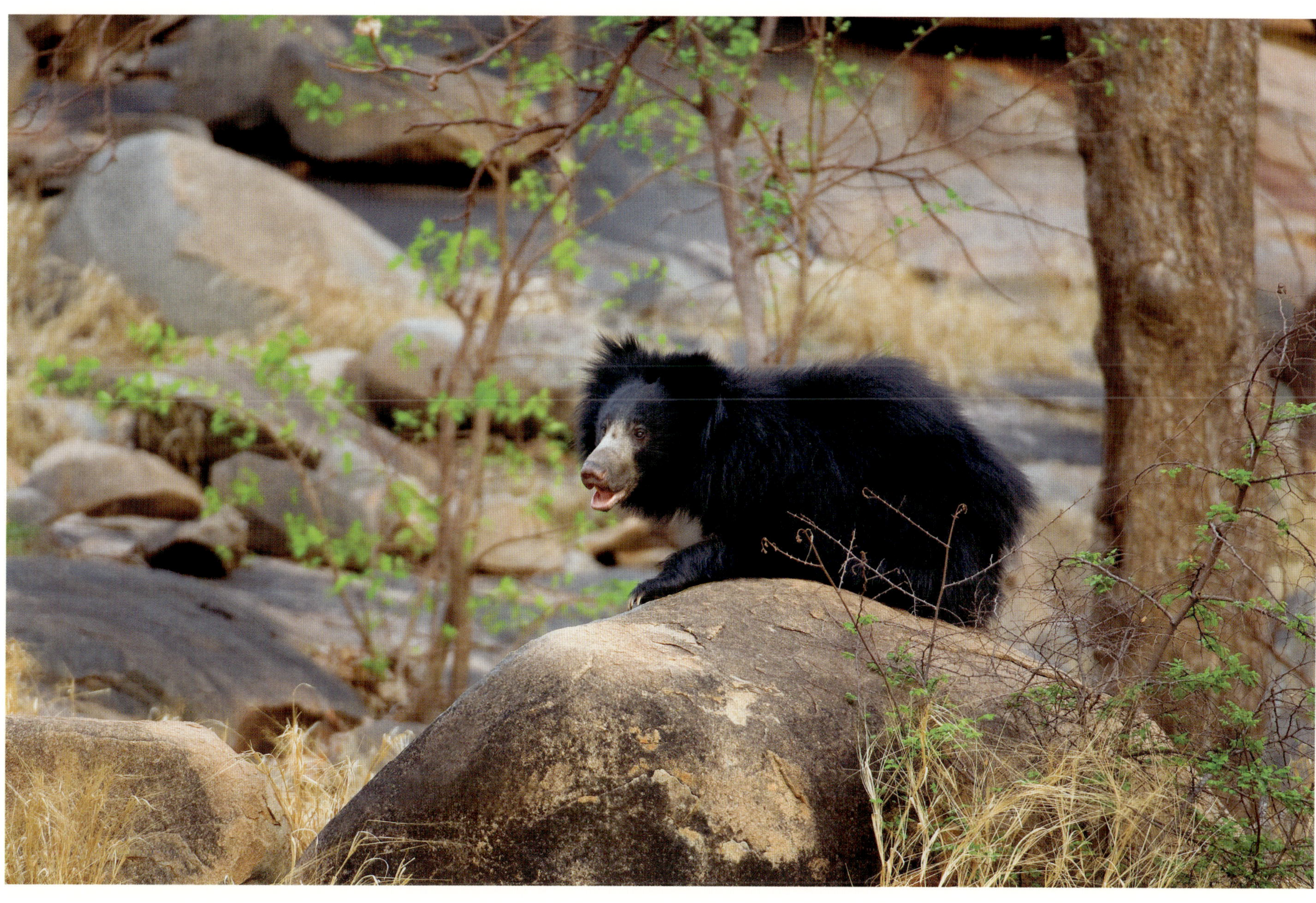

Unlike other bear species that live in colder parts of the world, sloth bears do not hibernate. Inhabiting warmer areas at lower elevations allows them to forage year-round (above). Cubs learn from their mother where to find rich food sources (opposite).

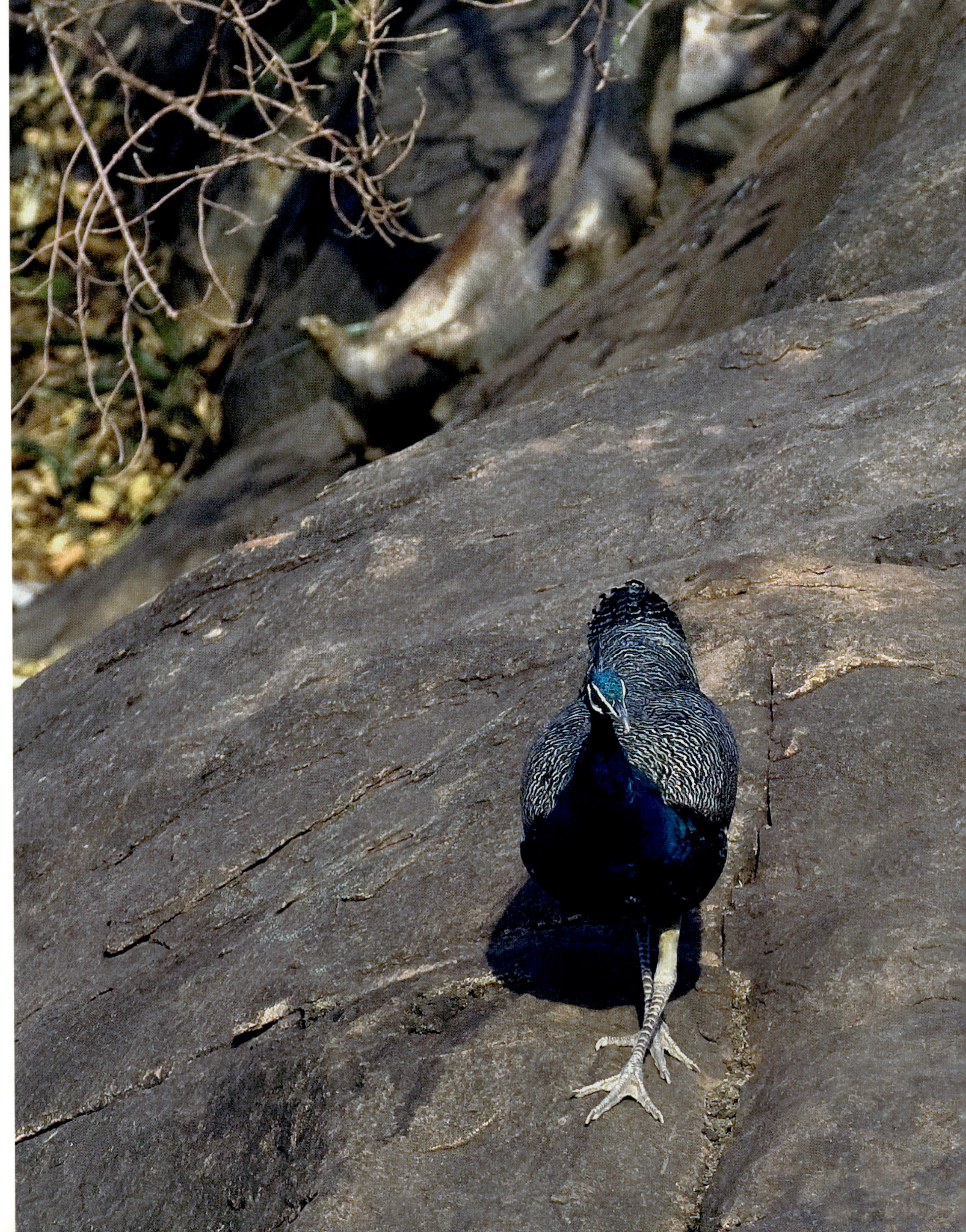

Like all cubs, young sloth bears are inexperienced. Getting to know the world they live in is crucial, and they have to learn to tell the difference between friend or foe. This Indian peacock however, is completely harmless to them.

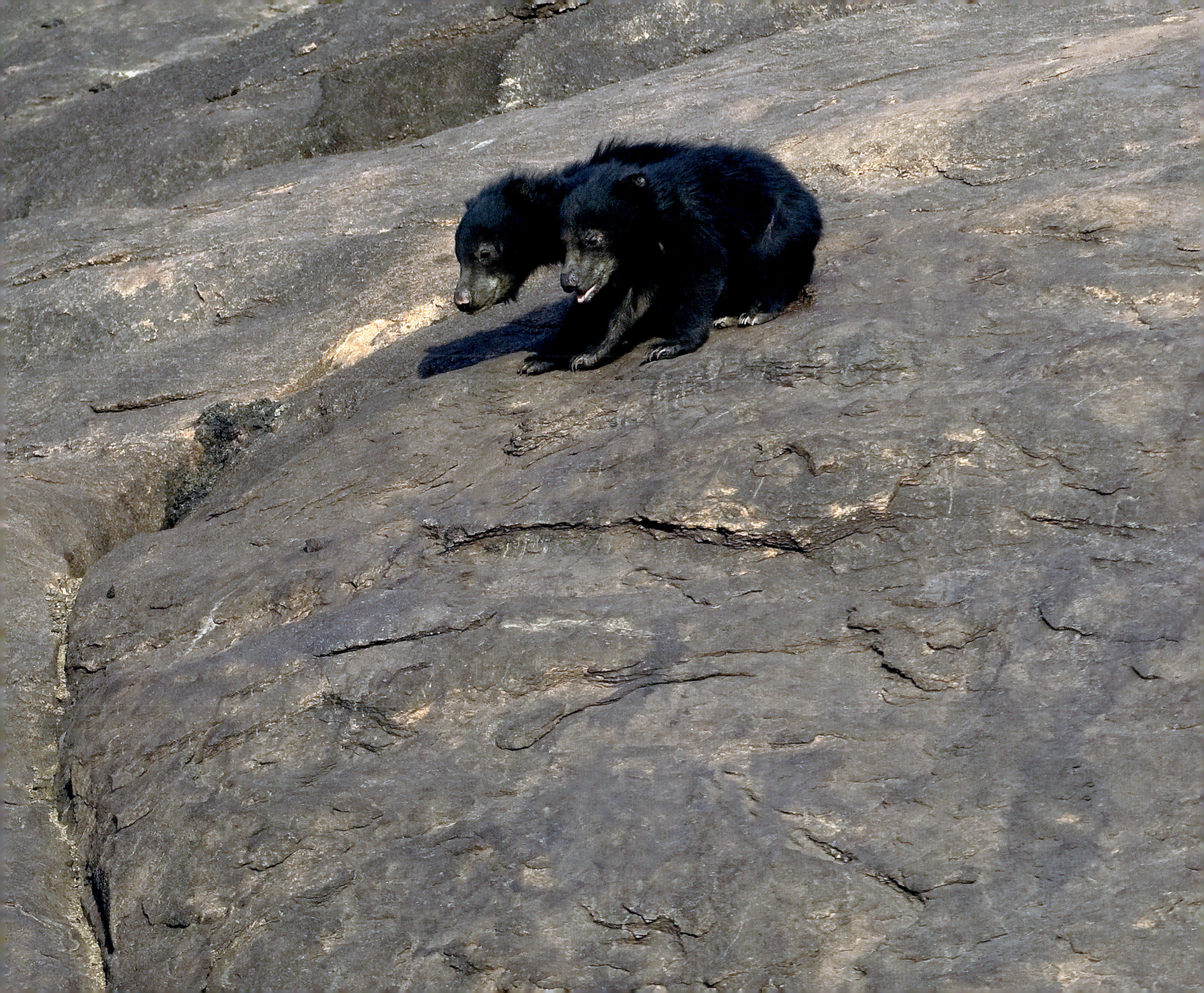

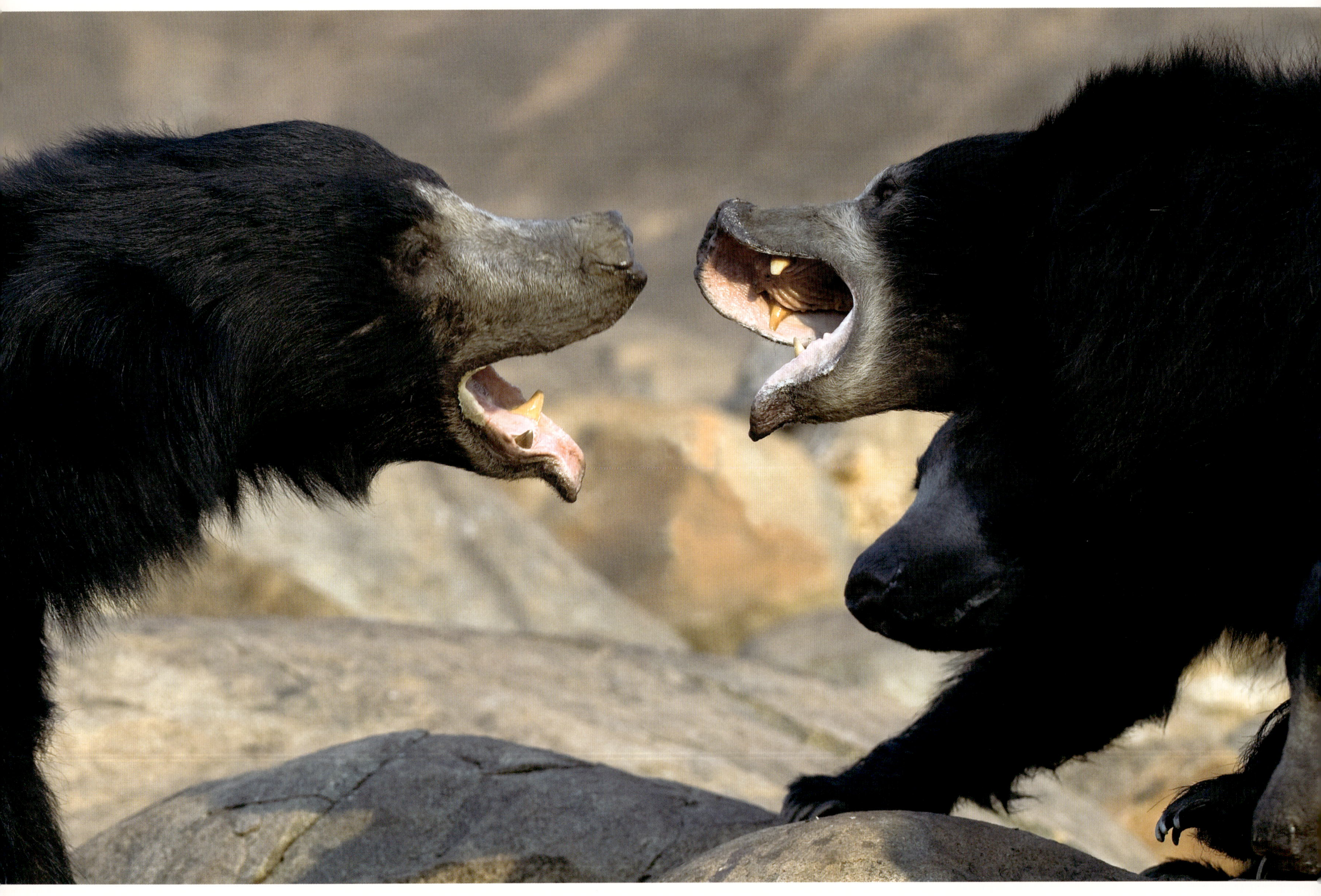

107

Little is known about the ecology and behaviour of wild sloth bears. Here, a mother defends her yearling cubs against a rogue male. Although there are no confirmed records, infanticide in sloth bears seems likely.

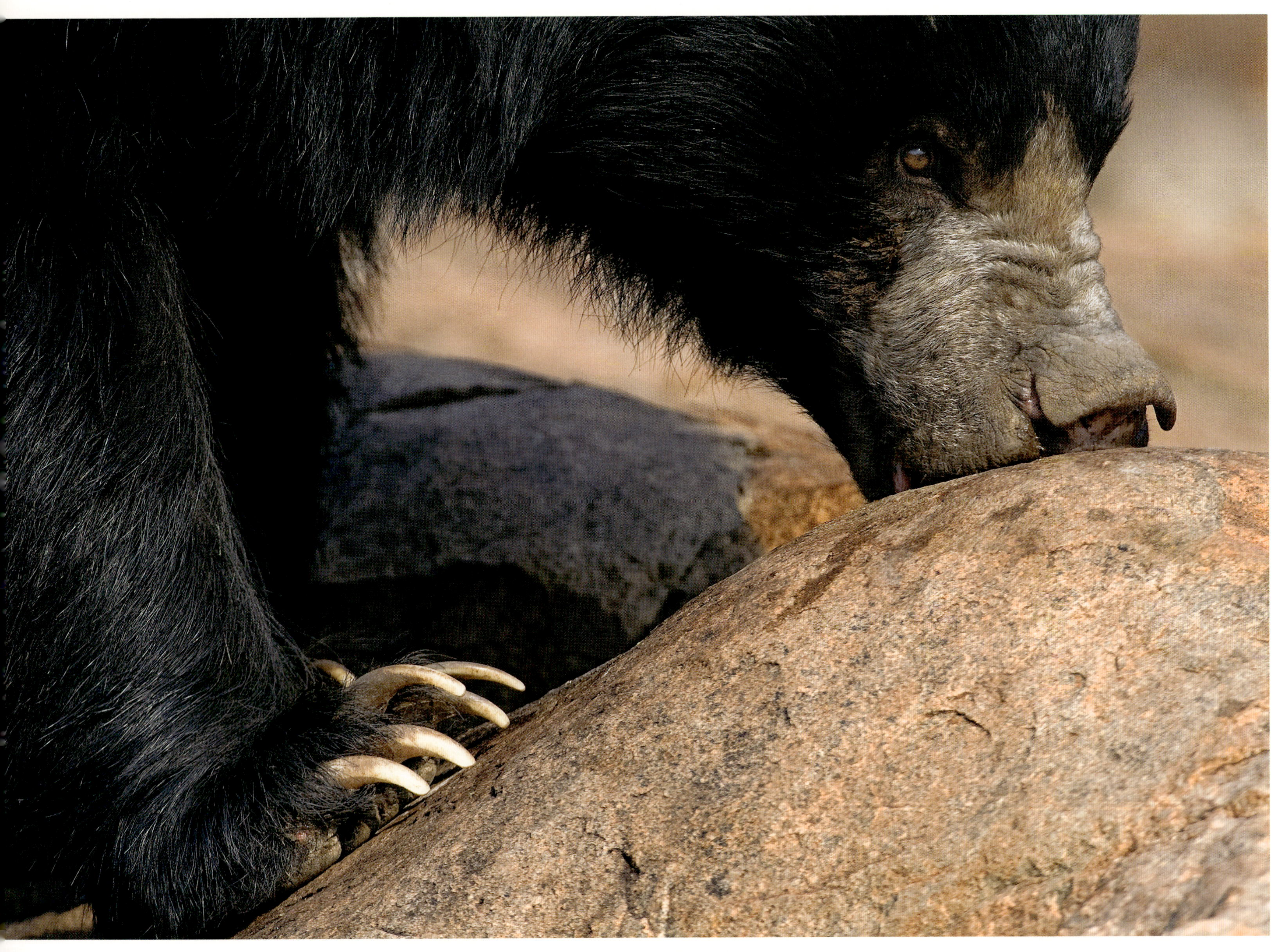

Sloth bears (opposite) feed predominantly on ants and termites. Their massive claws enable them to tear open termite mounds and they use their long snouts to suck up insects. Depending on the season, they also eat a variety of fruits. In some areas, they share the same habitat as bonnet macaques (right) who also have a taste for fruits, although the macaques will always retreat when a sloth bear is approaching.

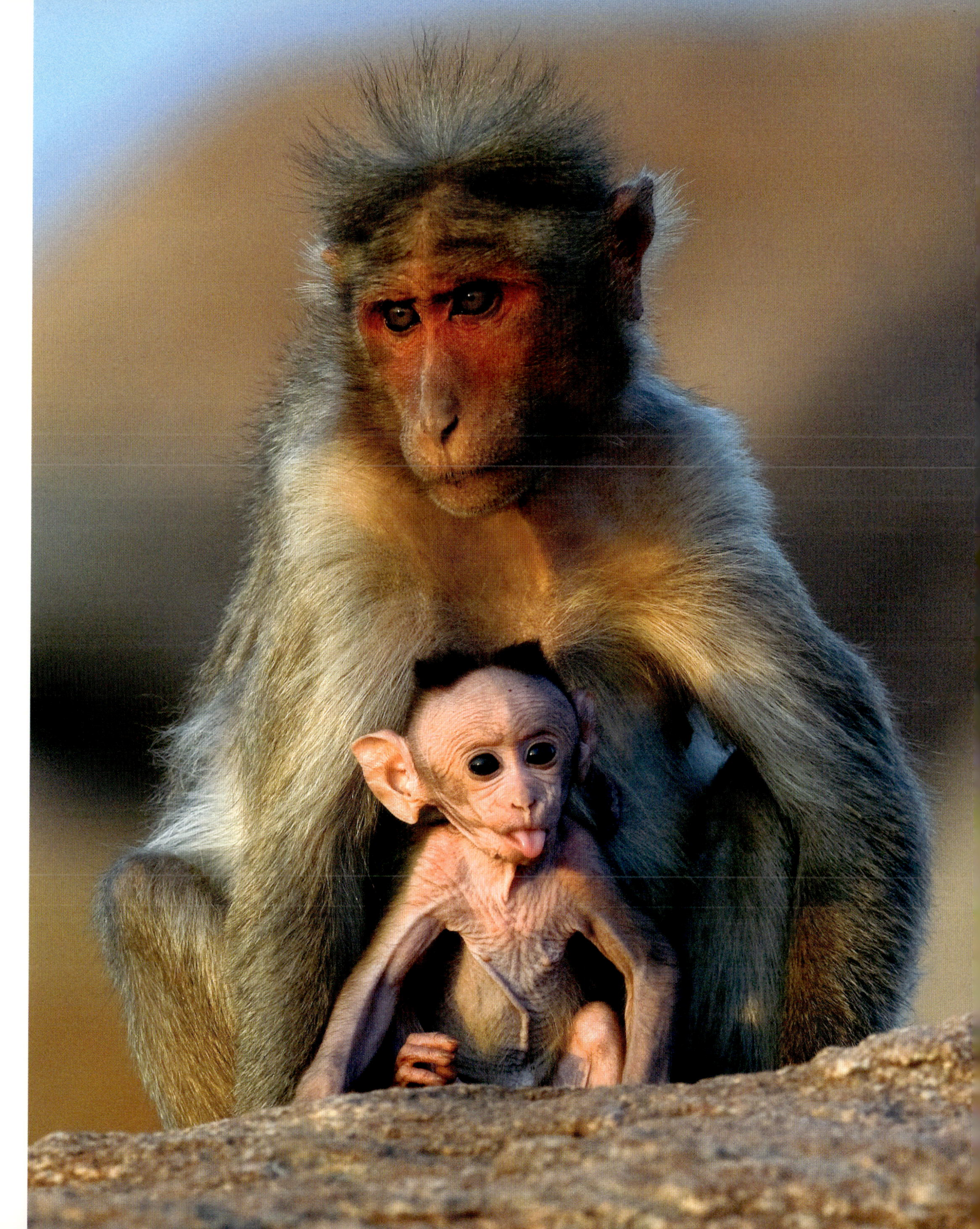

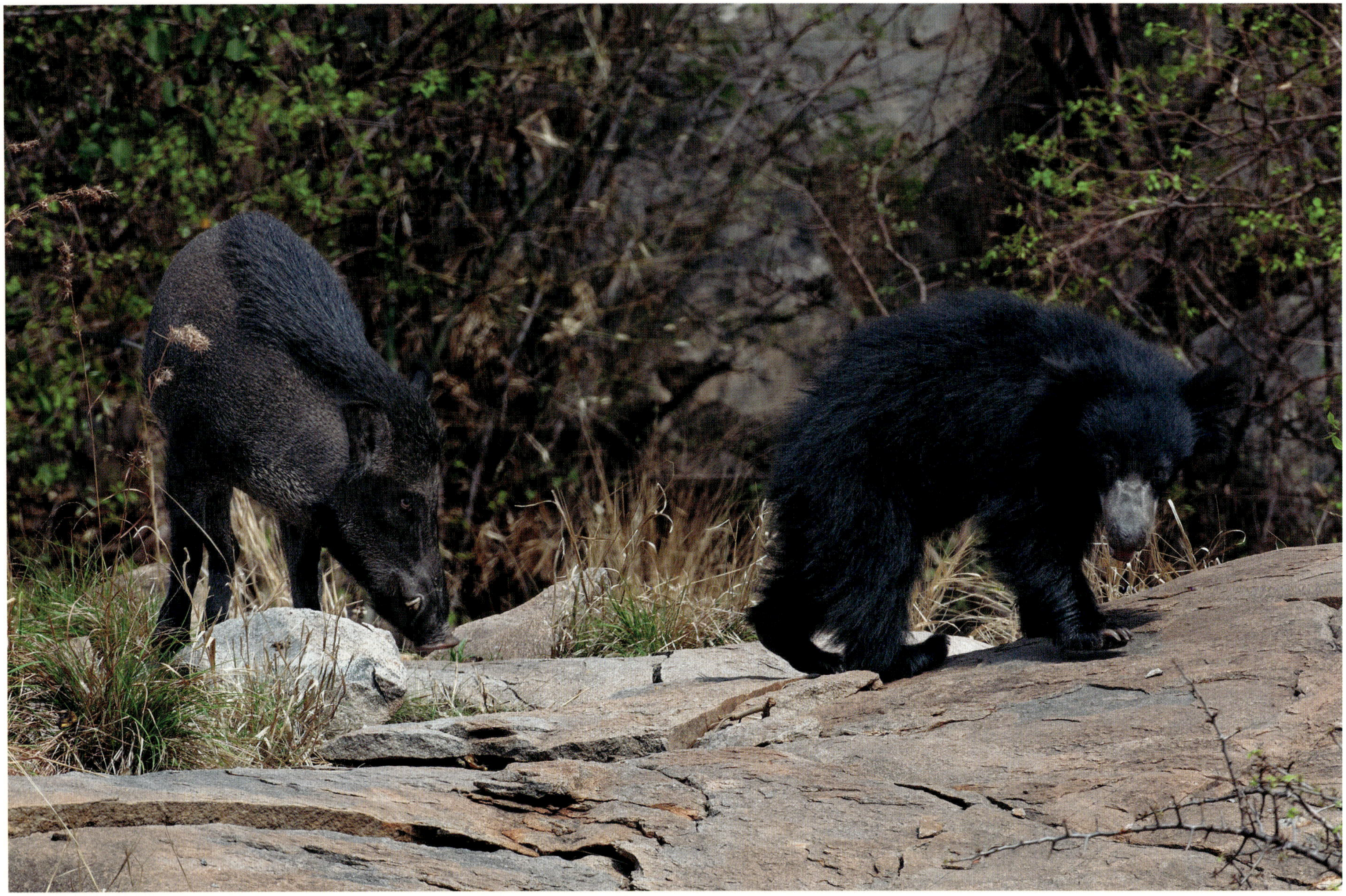

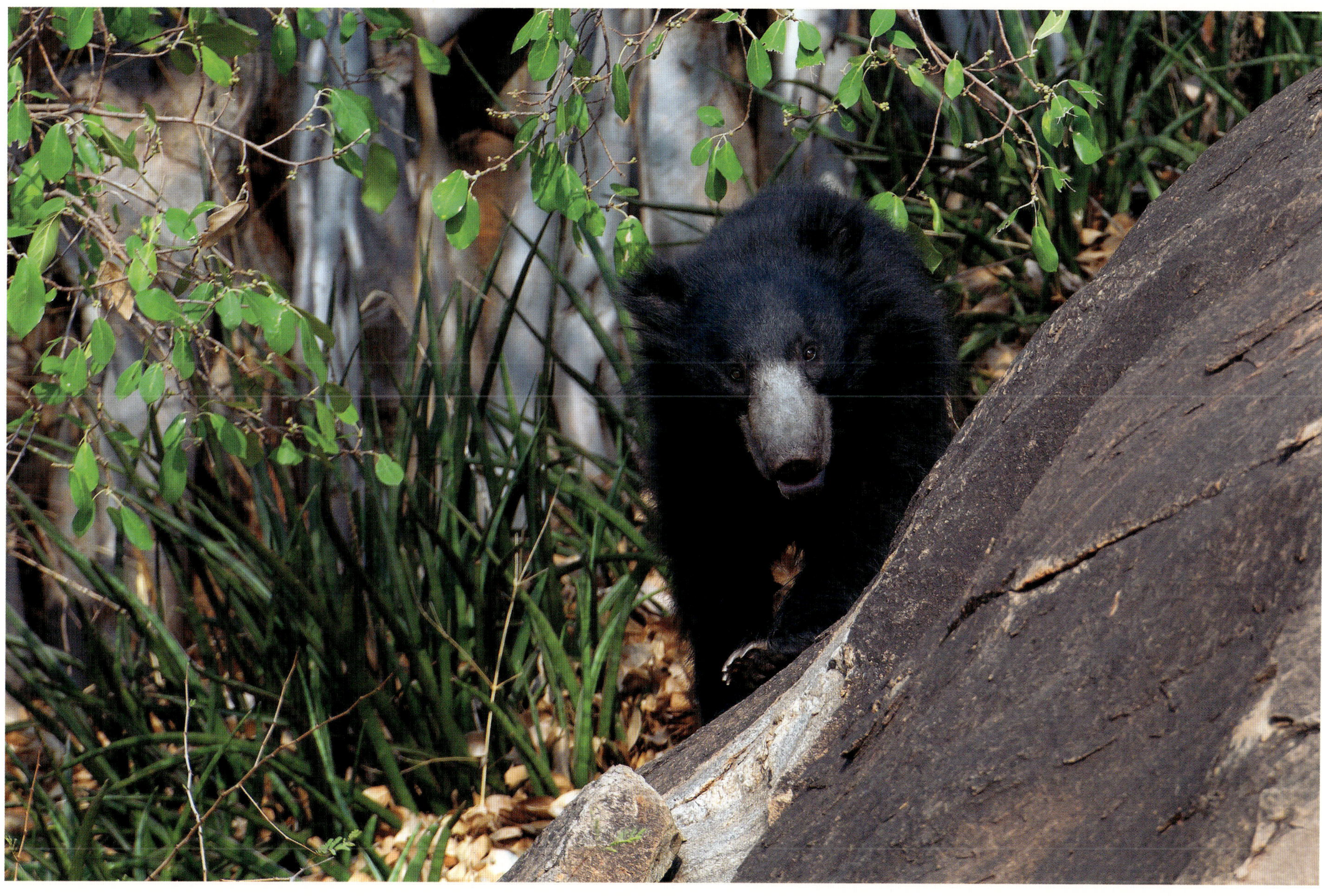

Sloth bear cubs become independent and start to fend for themselves at anywhere between one and a half to two and a half years old (above). At this age, however, they will have not reached their full body size, and sometimes, all that it takes to push them out of the way is a self-confident wild boar (opposite).

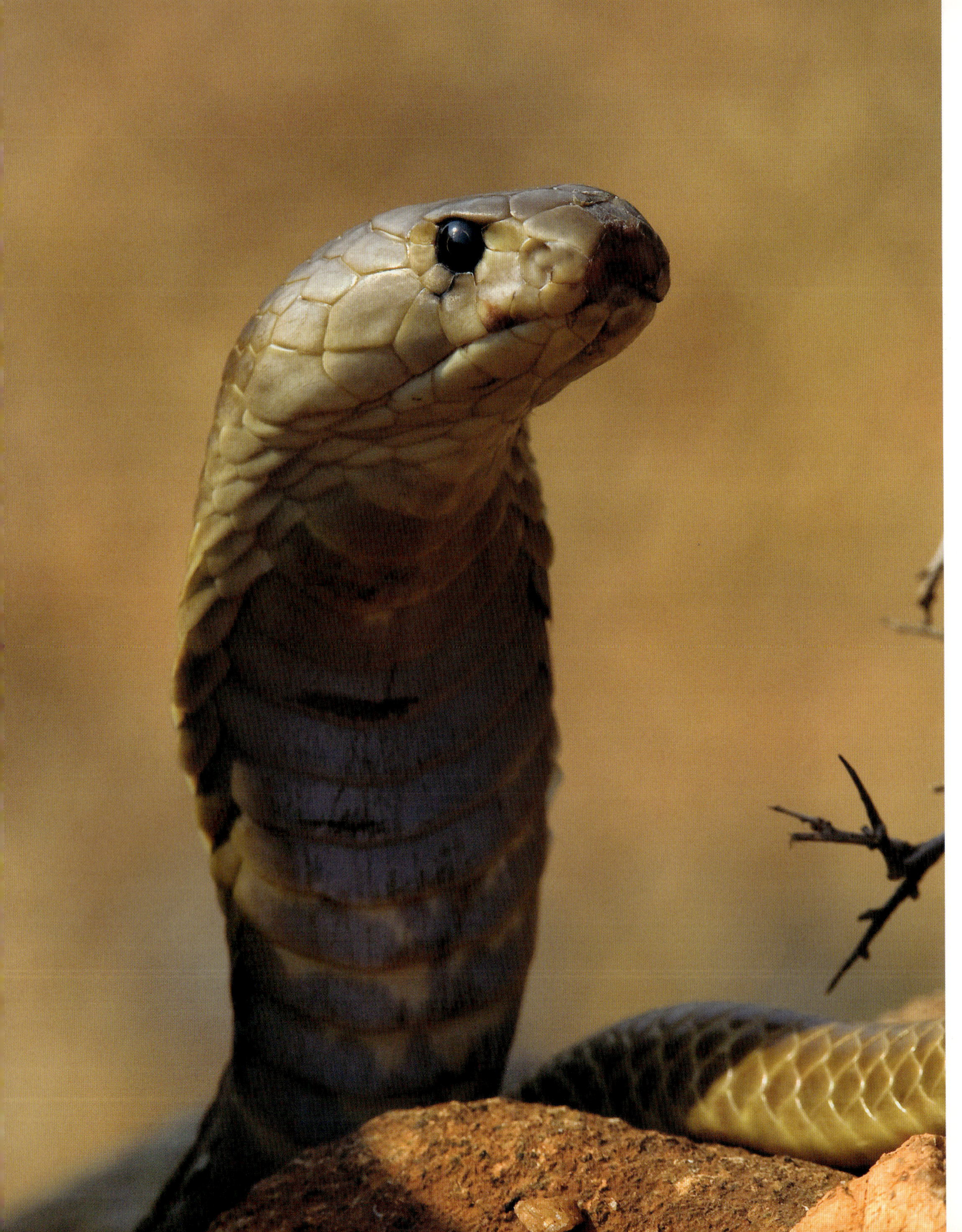

Many animals take refuge in the rocky hills of Karnataka. The highly venomous Indian cobra or spectacled cobra searches for rodents, reptiles and amphibians (left), however, its poison does not deter the swift ruddy mongoose (opposite) who is a skilful snake hunter.

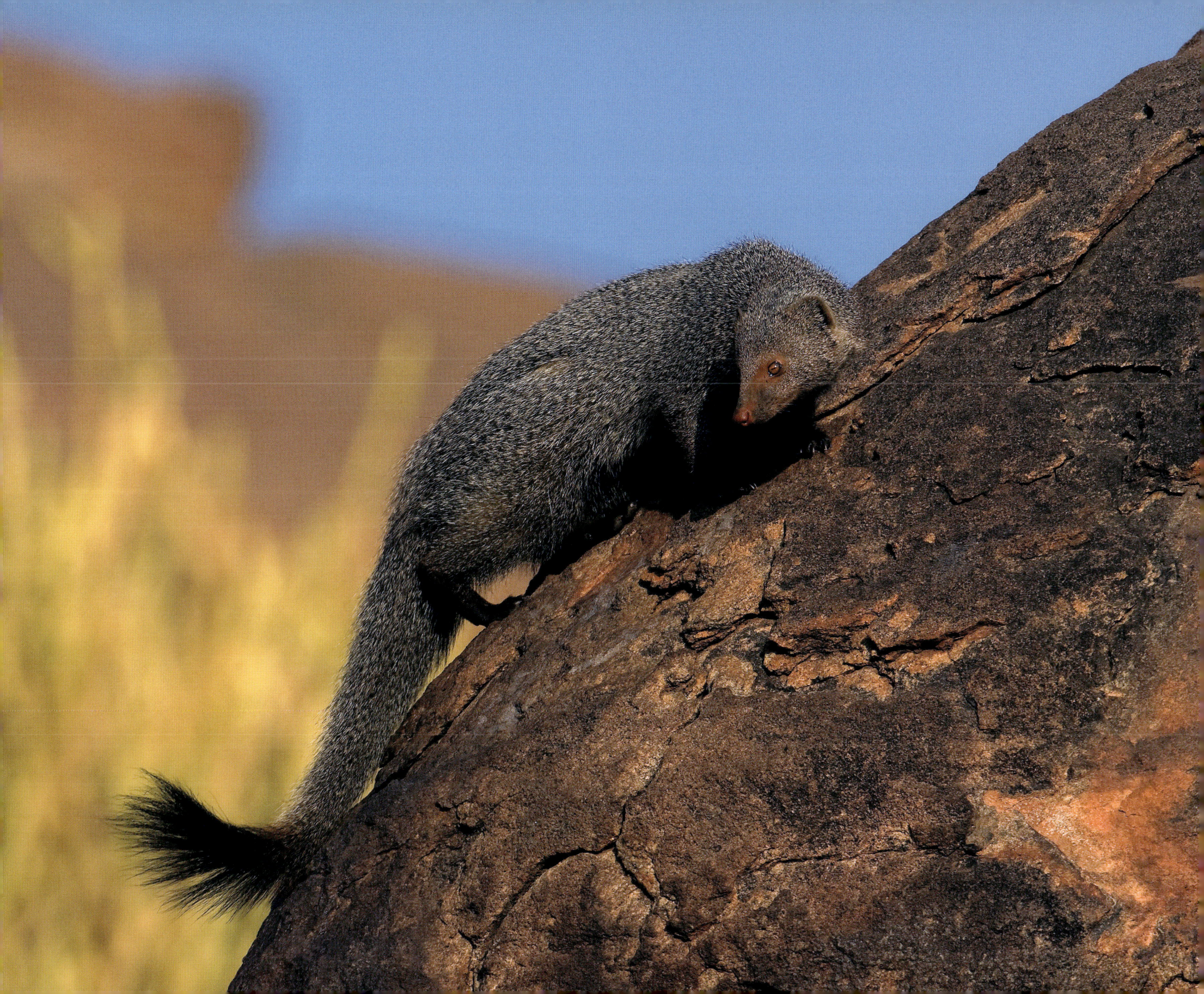

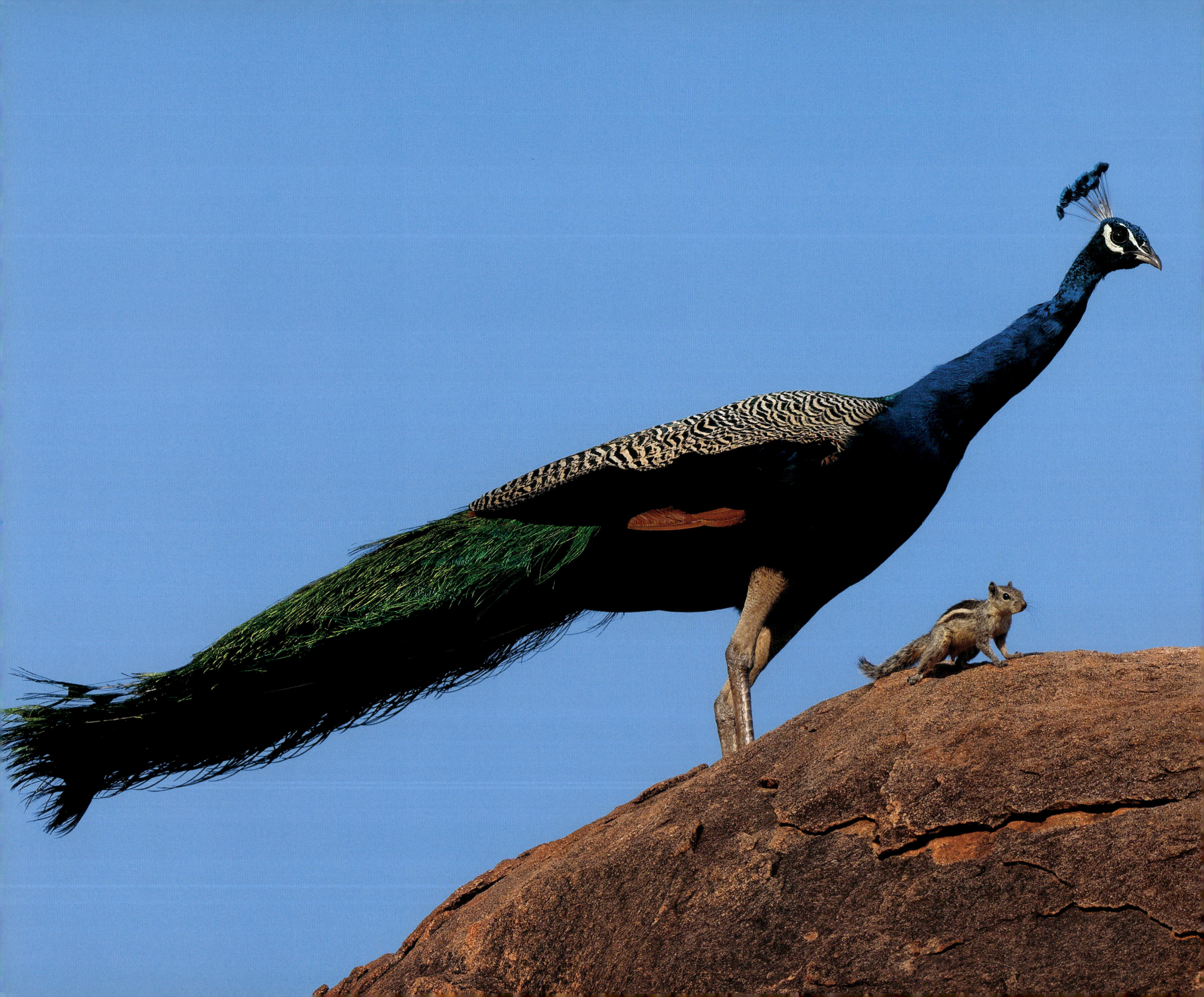

The male of the Indian peafowl can measure up to 230 centimetres in length, due to its lavish and extravagant plummage. The palm squirrel, though dwarfed by the impressive bird, is not at any risk.

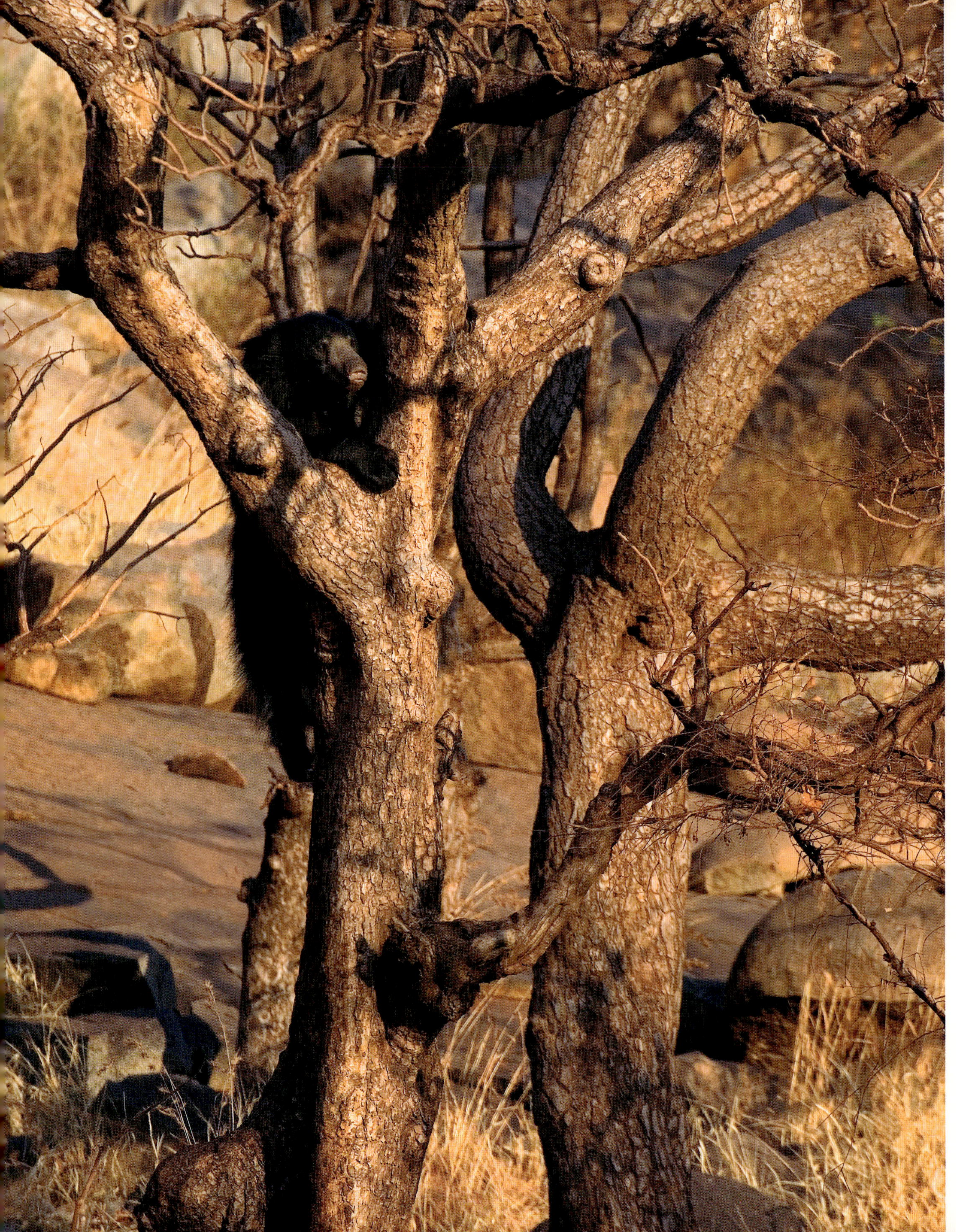

Despite their weight and clumsy appearance, sloth bears have strong claws and are nimble climbers (left). They keep a watchful eye on leopards, who also live in the rocky hills, especially as these big cats could be dangerous for any young bears (opposite).

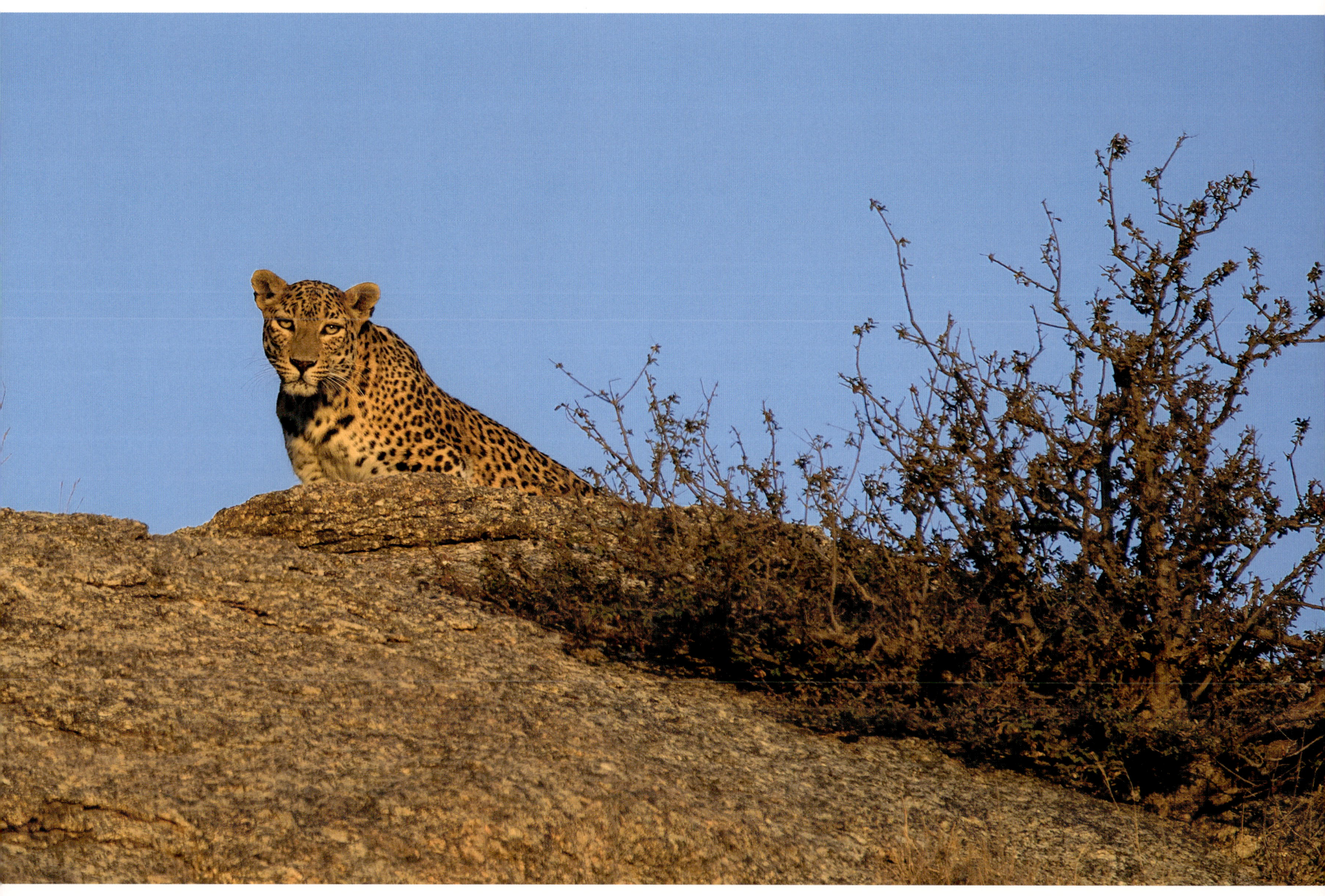

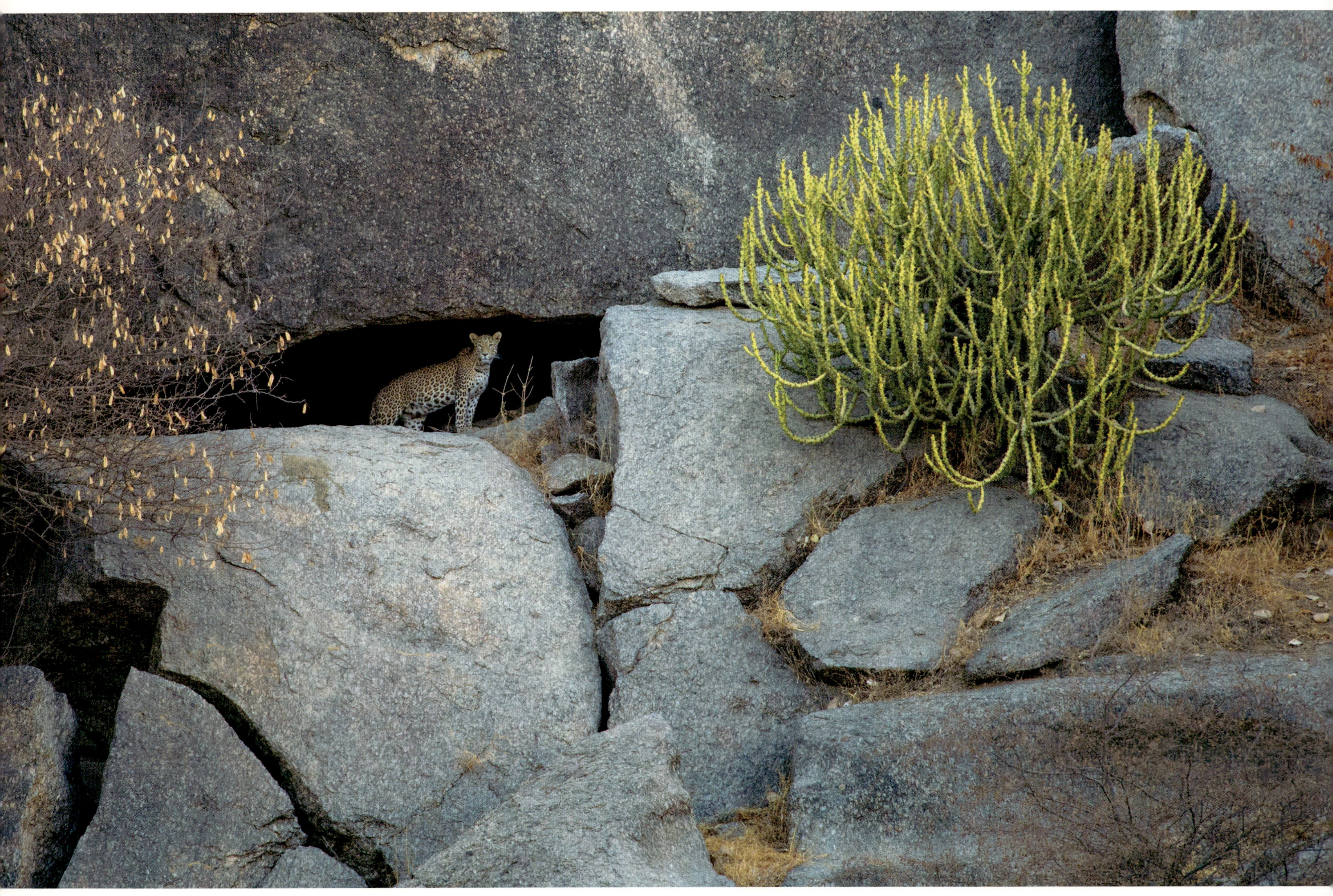

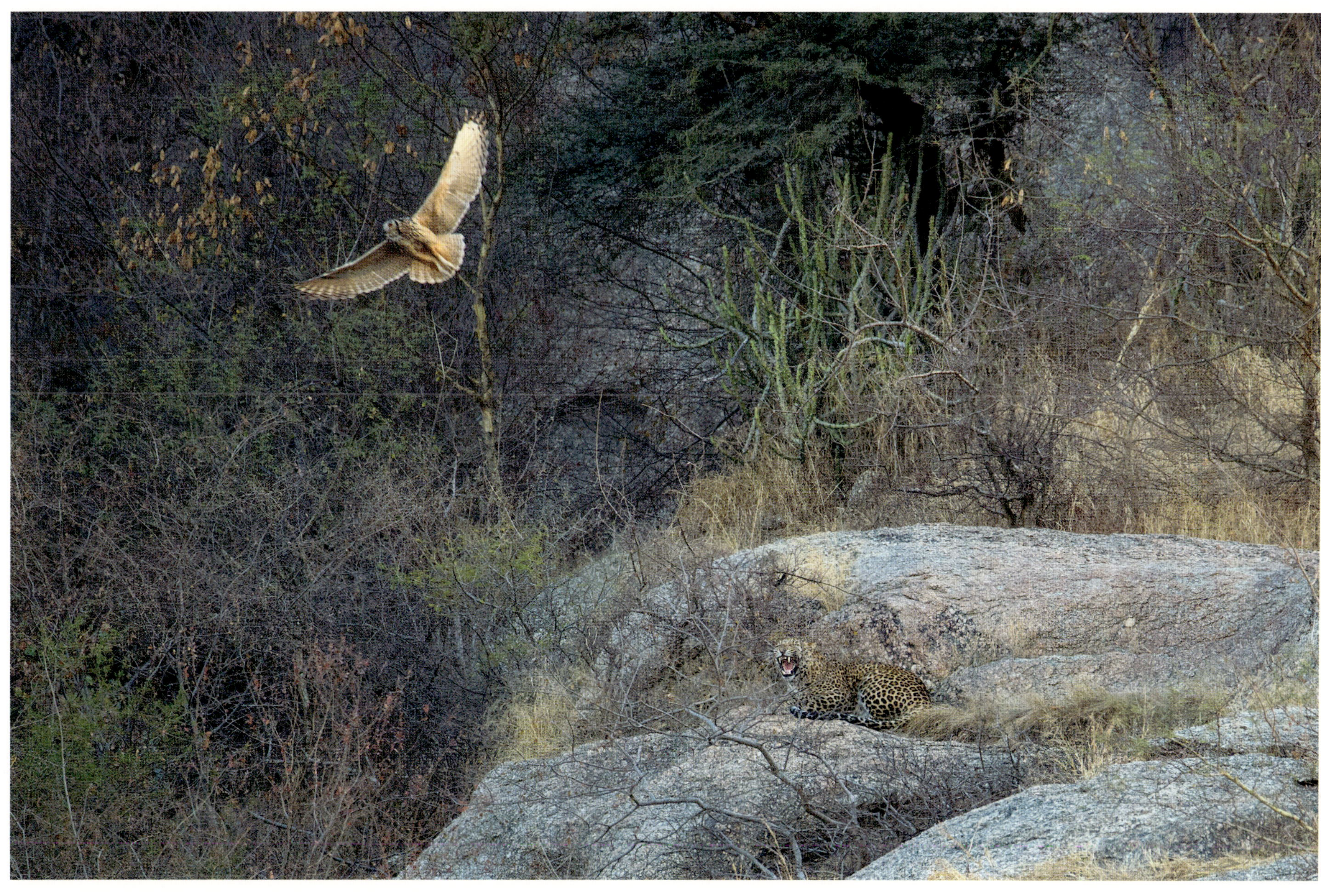

A female leopard watches from the entrance of a cave which she has used as a safe retreat for her family, in a remote region of Rajasthan (opposite). One of her older sons sees off the mock charges of an Indian eagle owl (above). Such behaviour by the eagle owl is very rare, and it is likely that the bird saw the big cat as a threat to its nest.

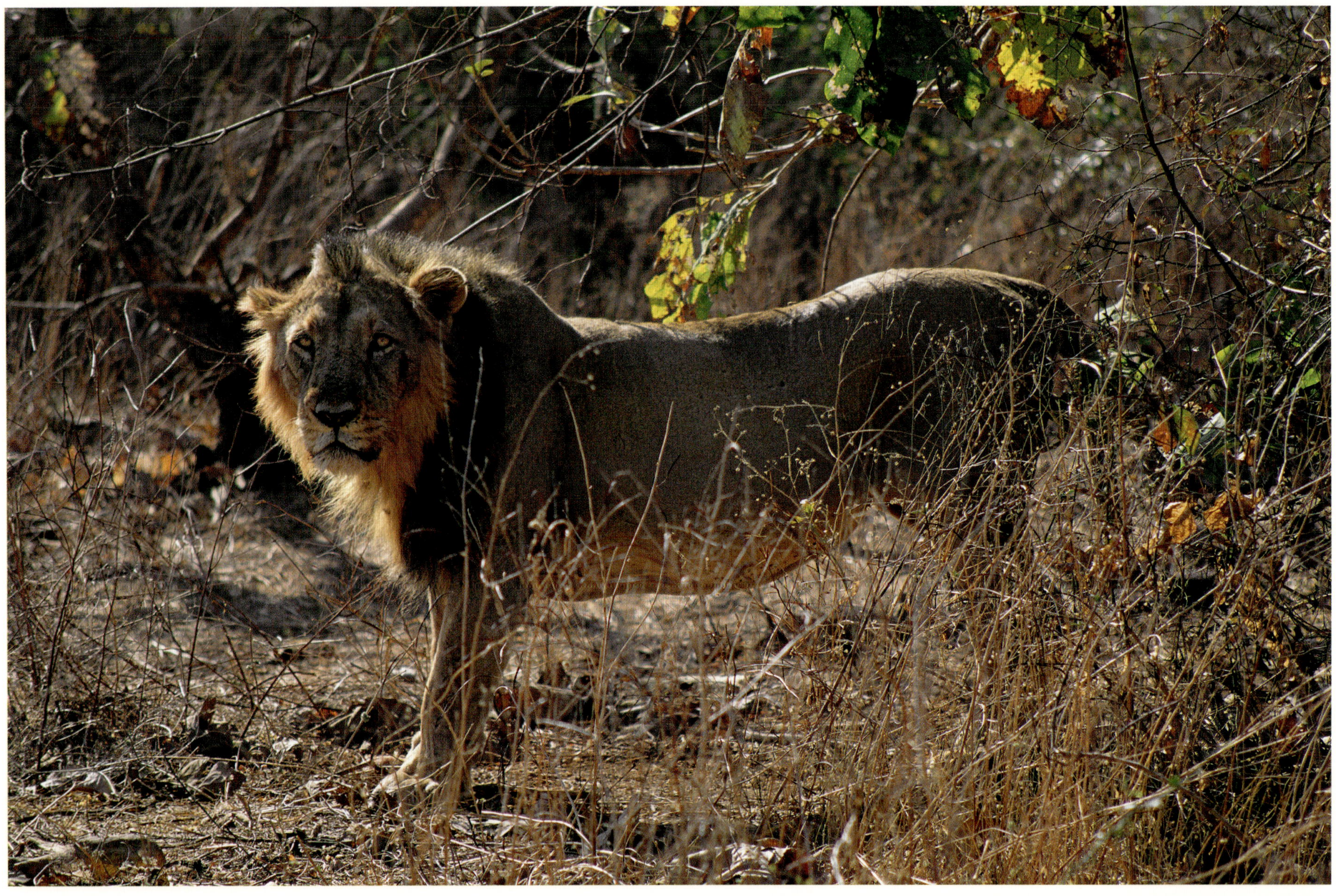

In historic times, the Asiatic lion (opposite) ranged from south-eastern Europe to central India. Today, the last relict population is confined to an area in and around the Gir Forest National Park in the Indian state of Gujarat. They resemble their African counterparts, although the males from Asia (above) have shorter manes.

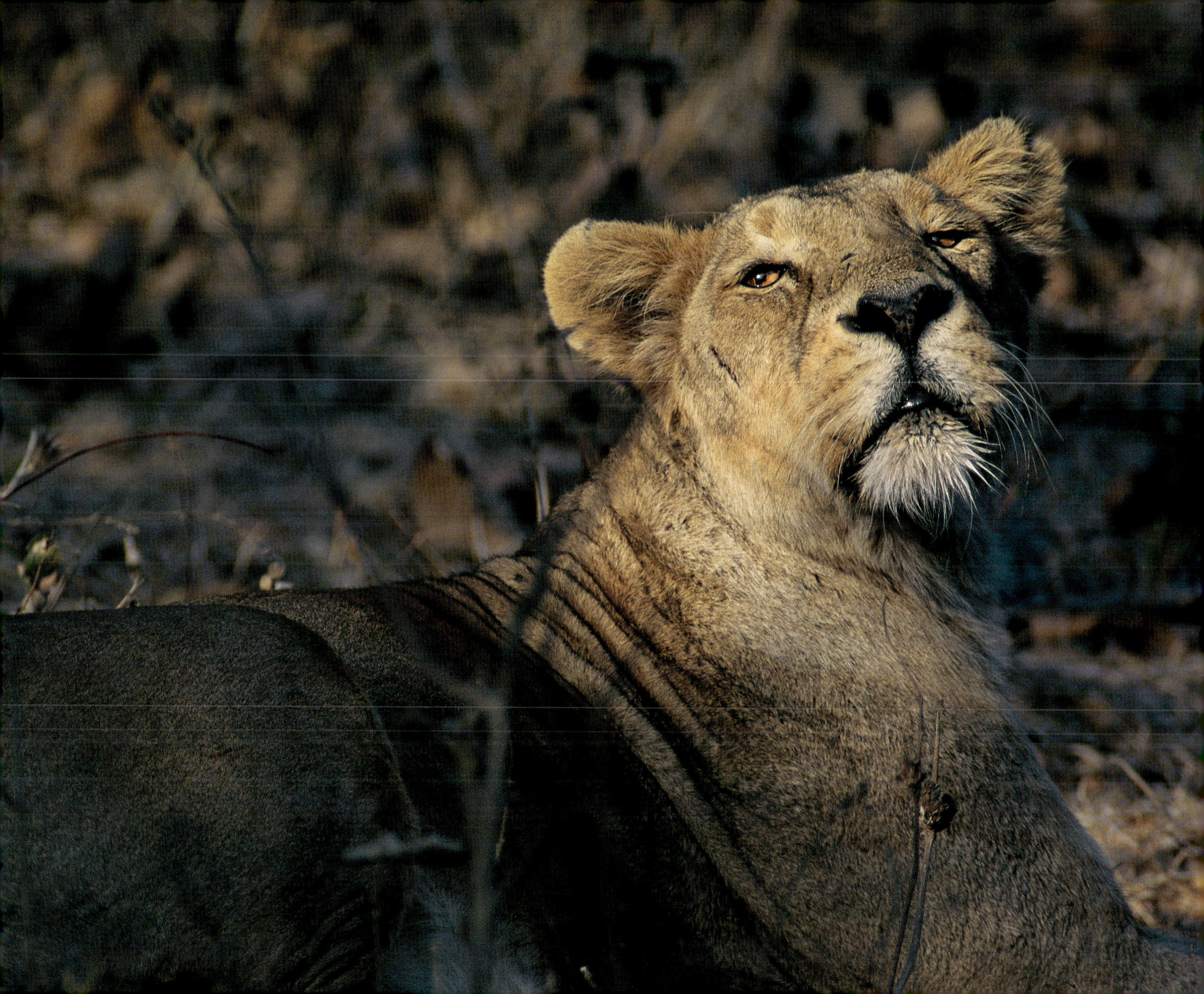

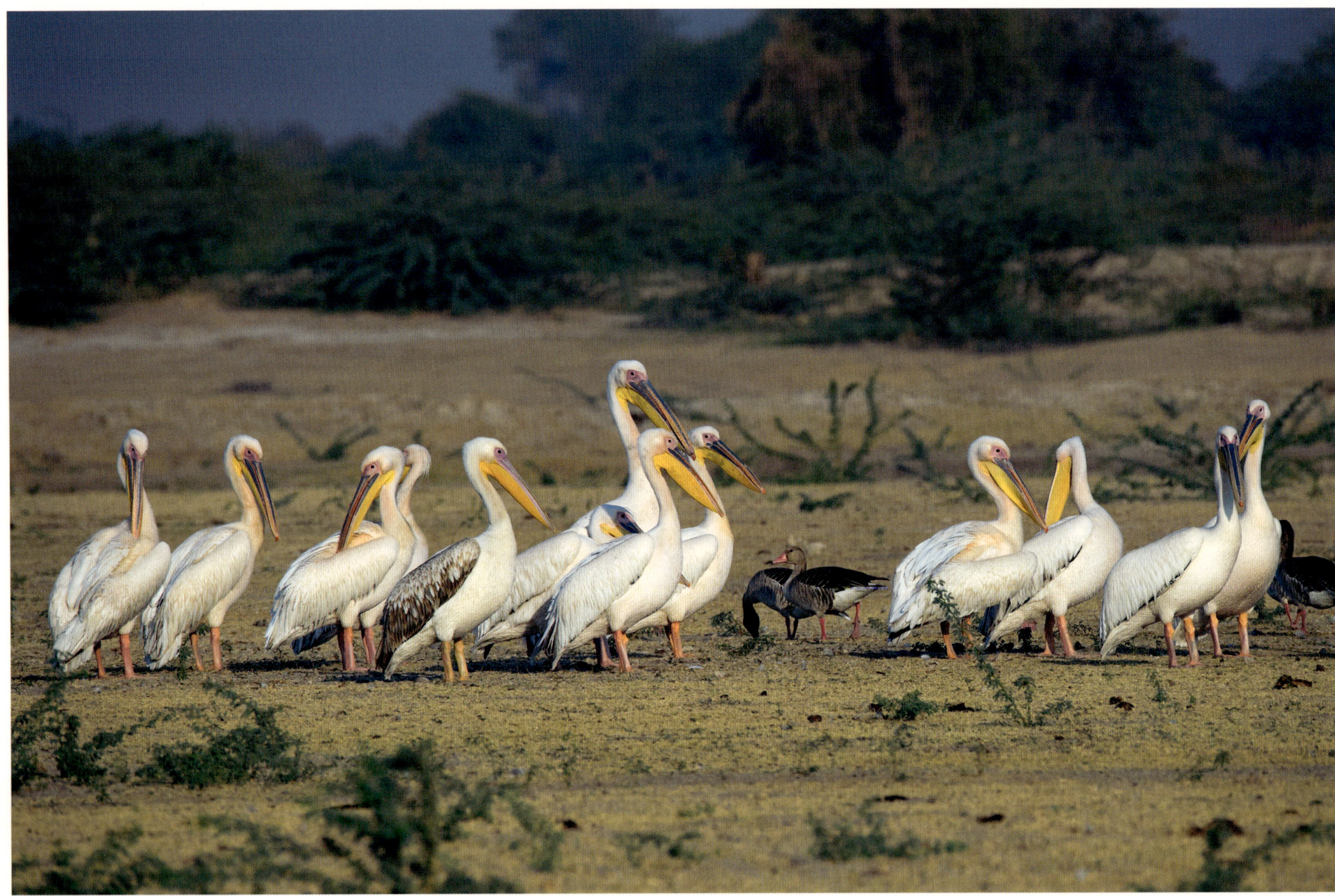

Great white pelicans are pioneers when it comes to discovering new habitats. They rely on fish as their food source, but will appear at small lakes in dry areas in order to explore new feeding grounds (above). Greater flamingos are also attracted to such areas, however, they mainly feed on microorganisms which develop faster in seasonal water bodies (opposite).

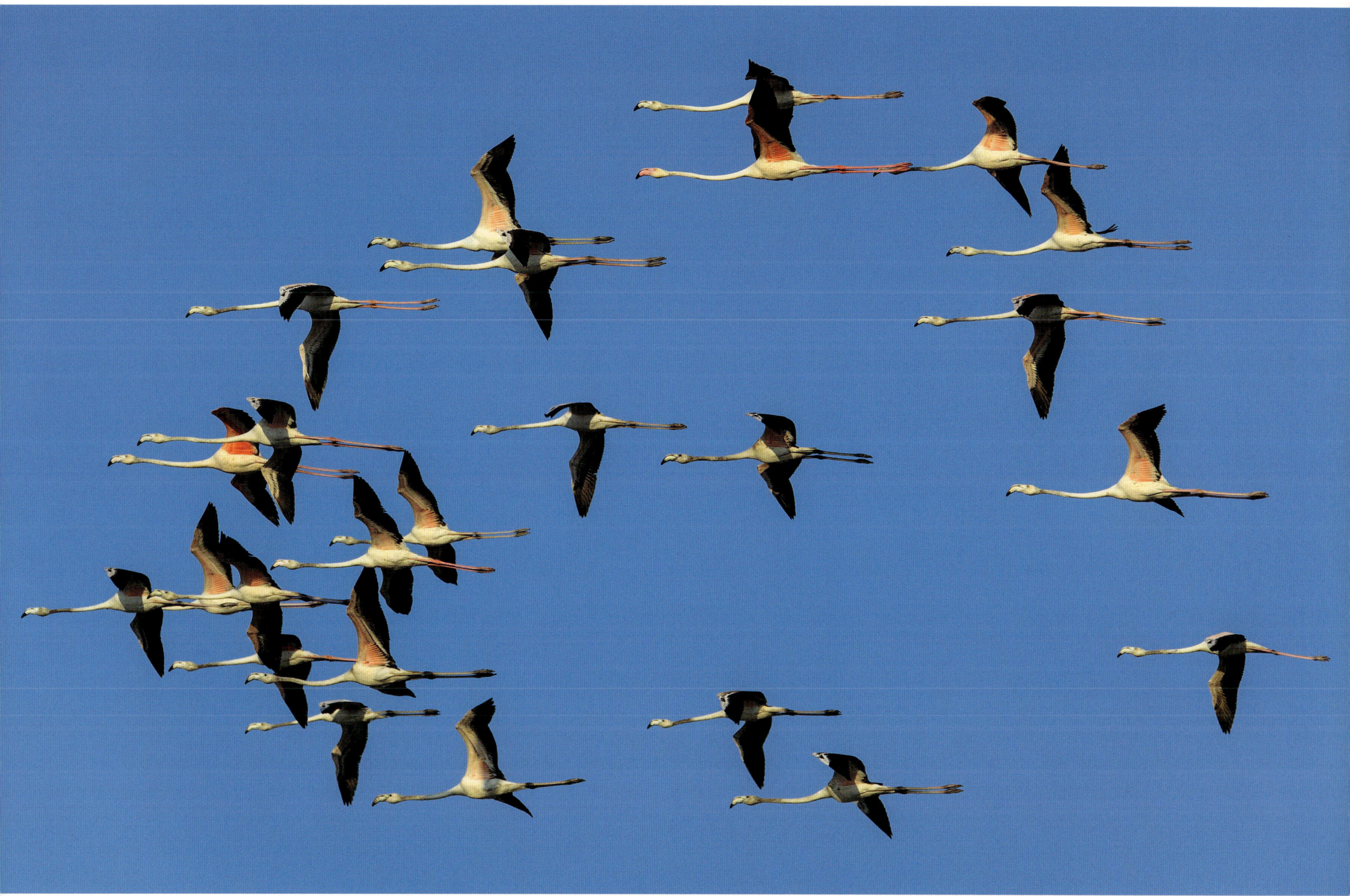

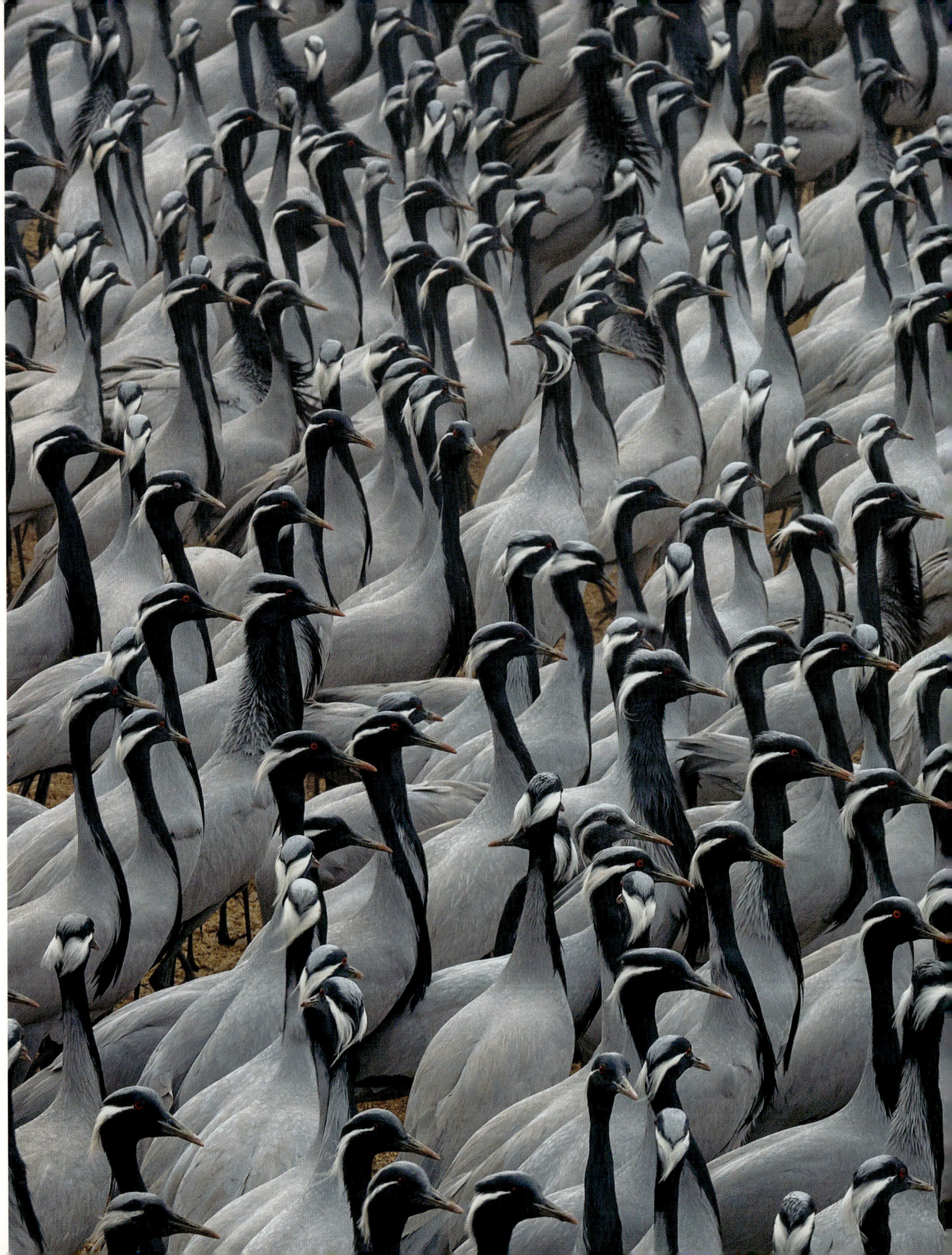

Demoiselle cranes are delicate birds with no means of defence. Their only way to avoid danger is to escape. Gathering in flocks is safer for them as they are more likely to detect danger and a single bird is less likely to be attacked.

Overleaf:
Demoiselle cranes are migratory birds, who escape the cold winters of their central Asian breeding grounds to spend several months each year in the warmer climes of northwestern India.

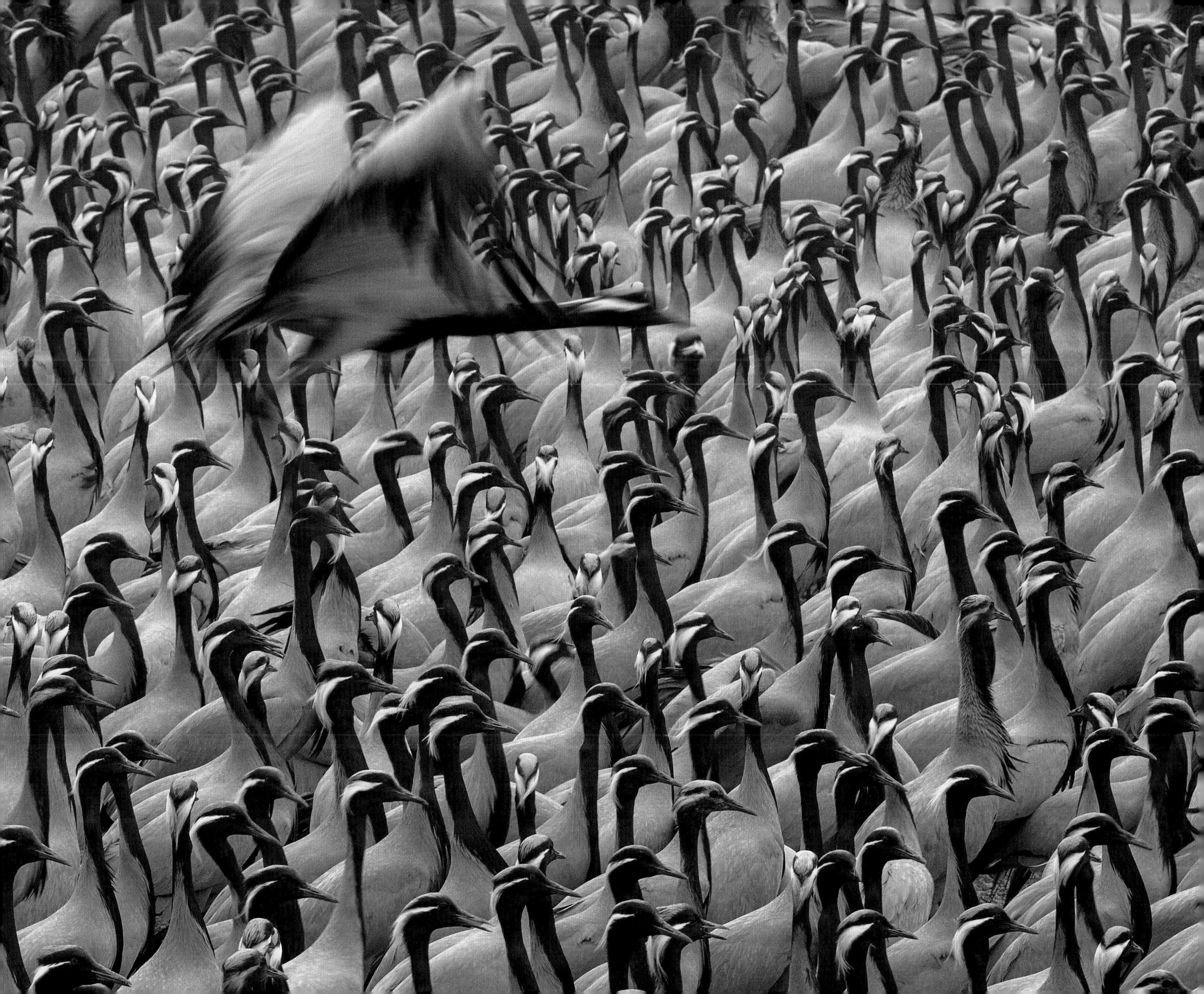

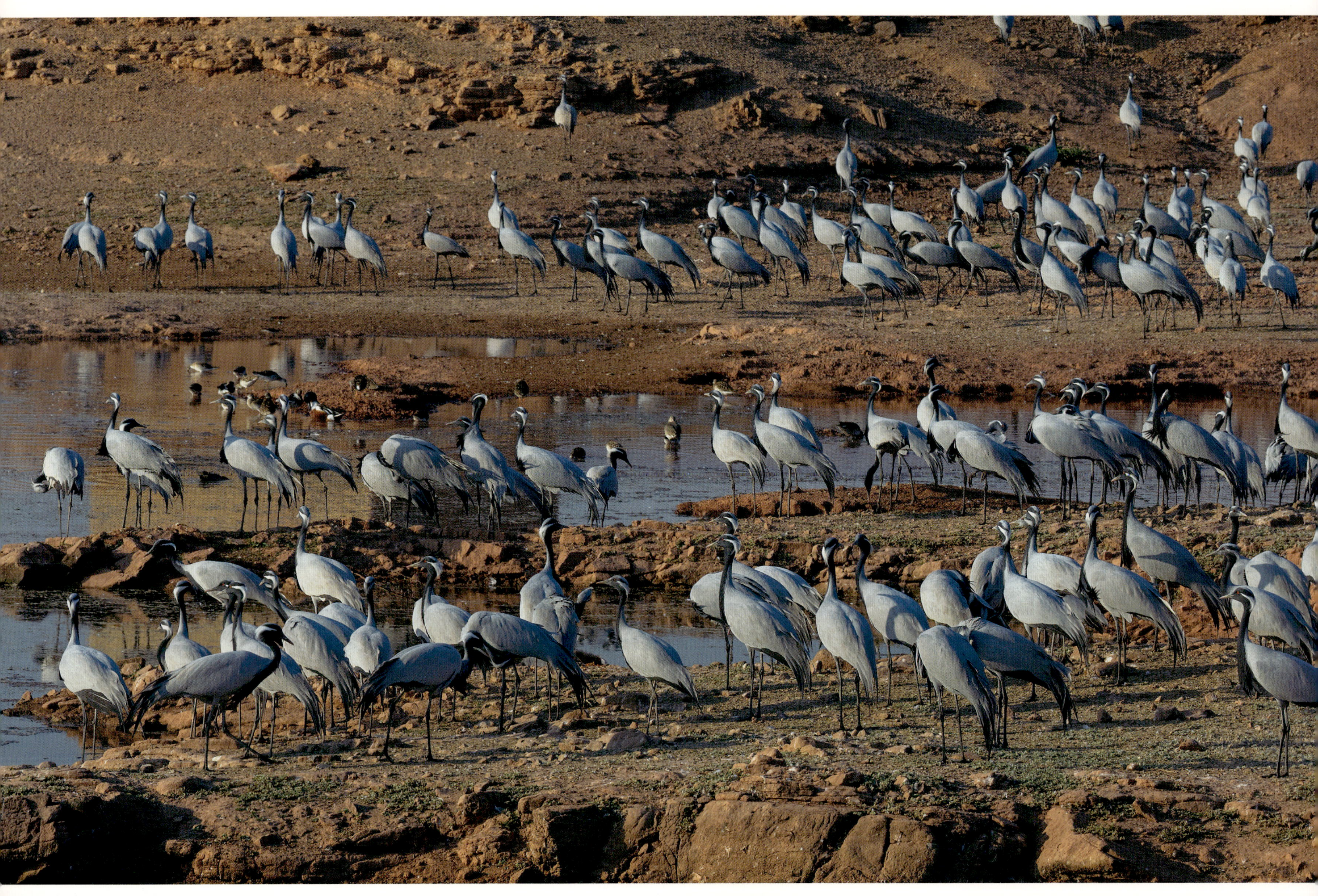

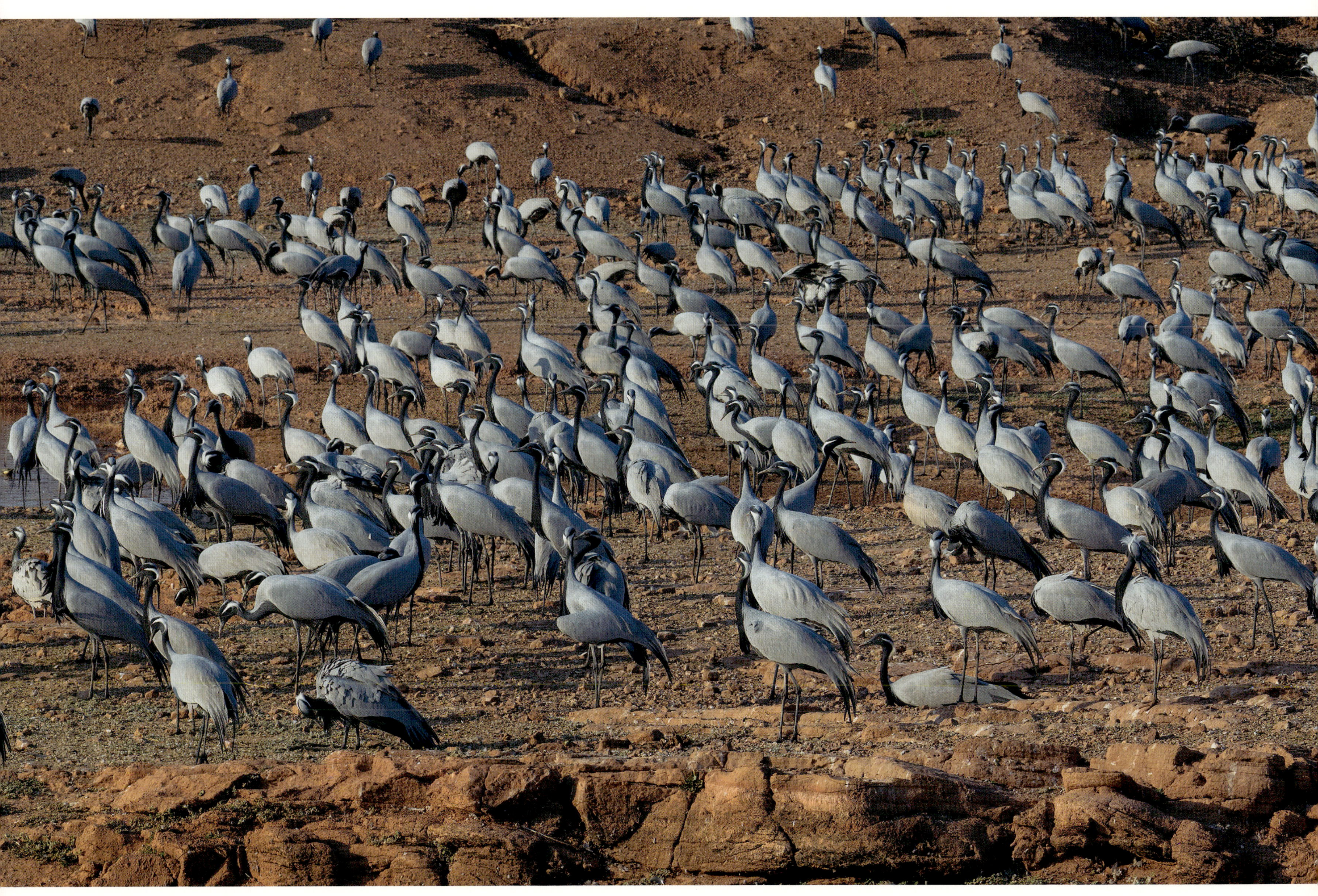

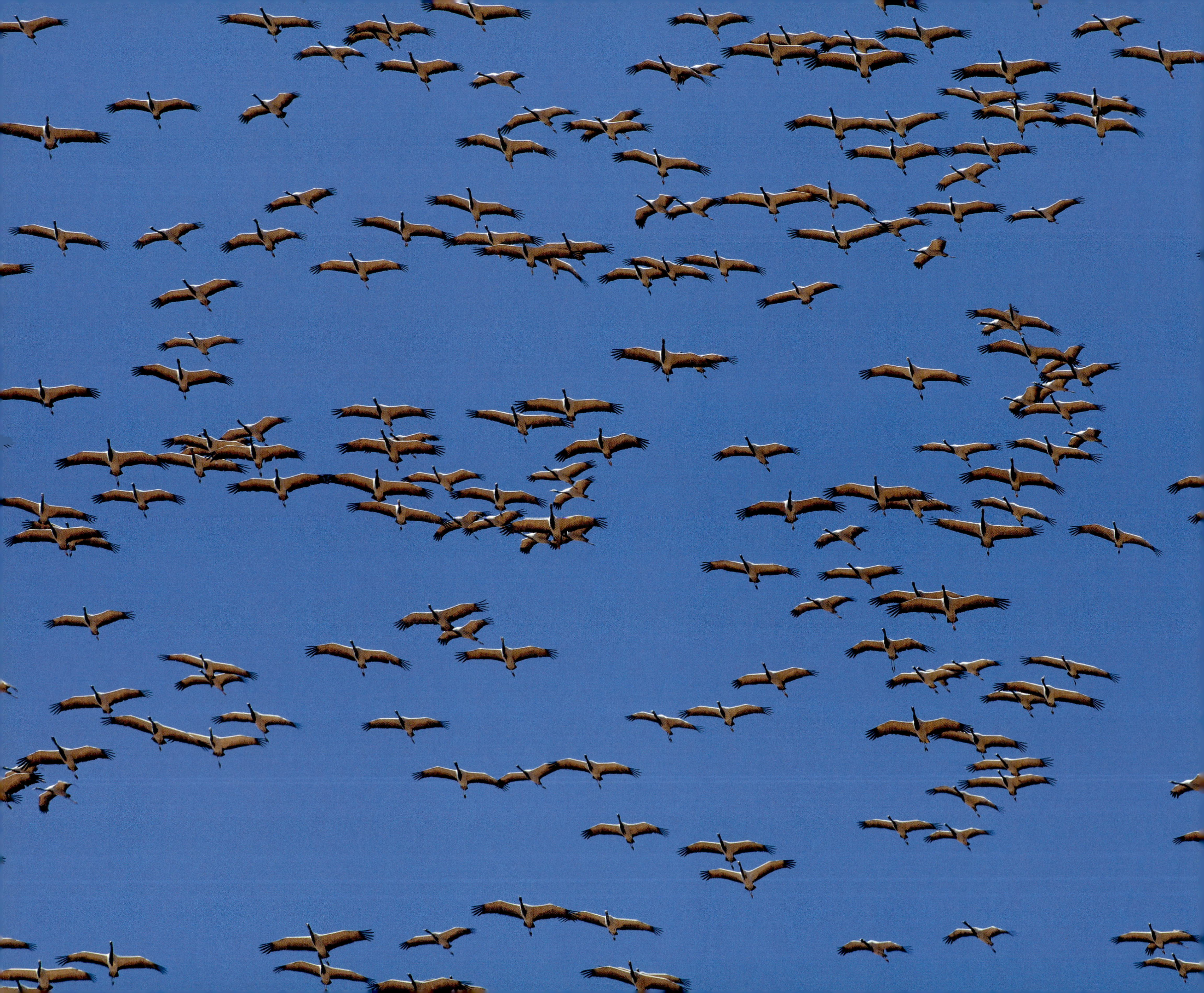

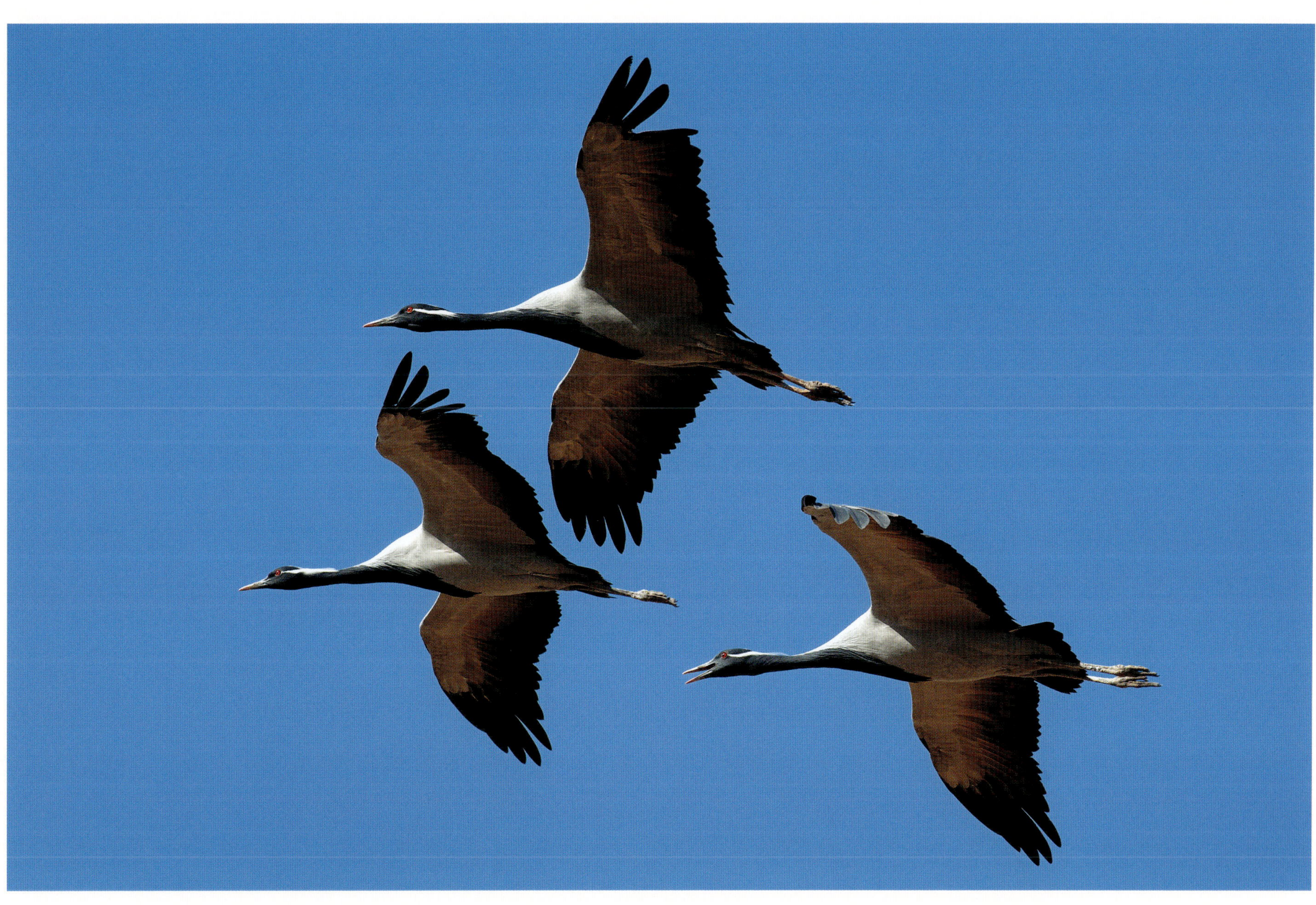

Mid-morning brings rising temperatures, where thermals start to build up. The demoiselle cranes spiral high up in the air, extend their broad wings, creating a huge avian ballet as they all ride the same thermals.

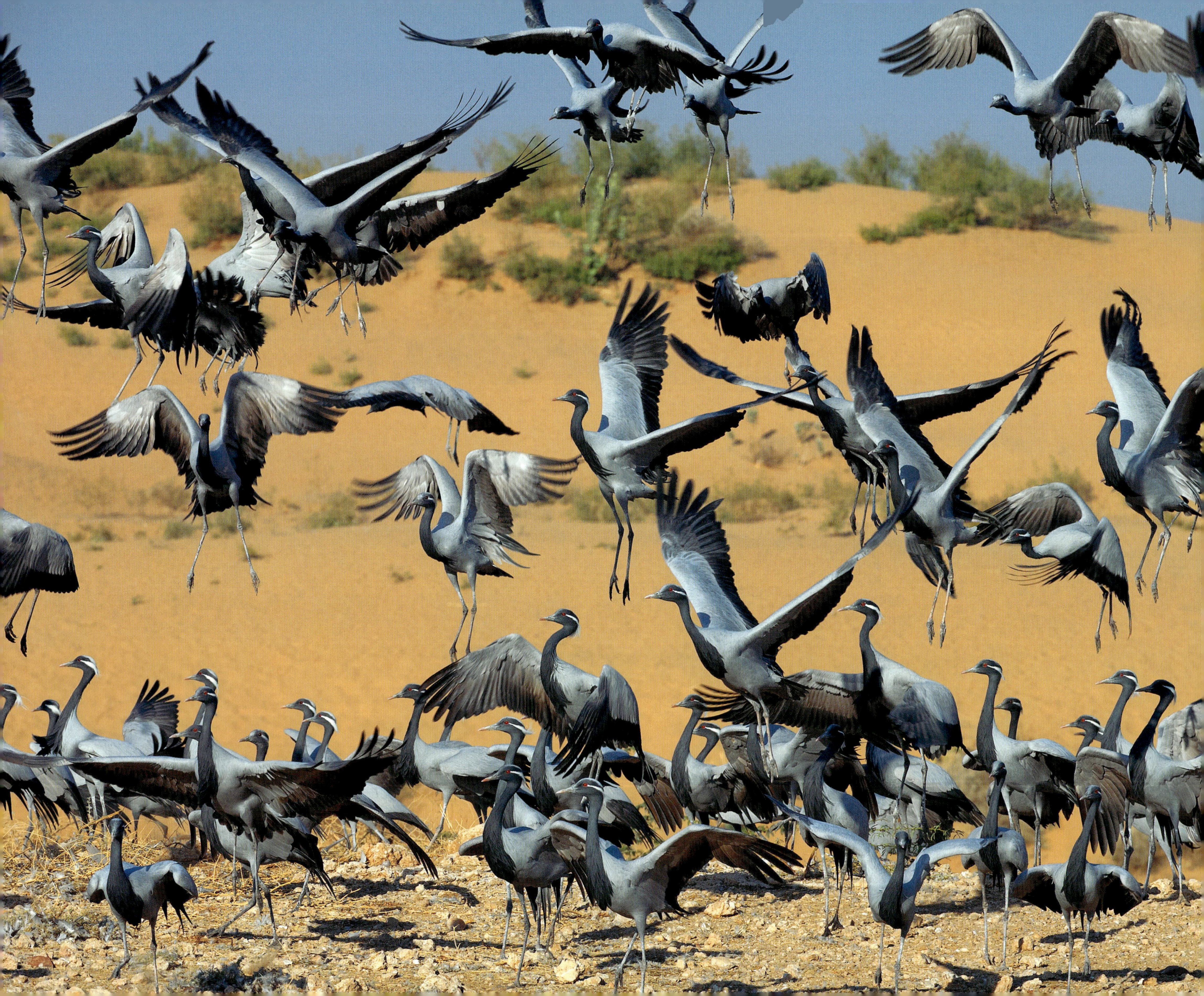

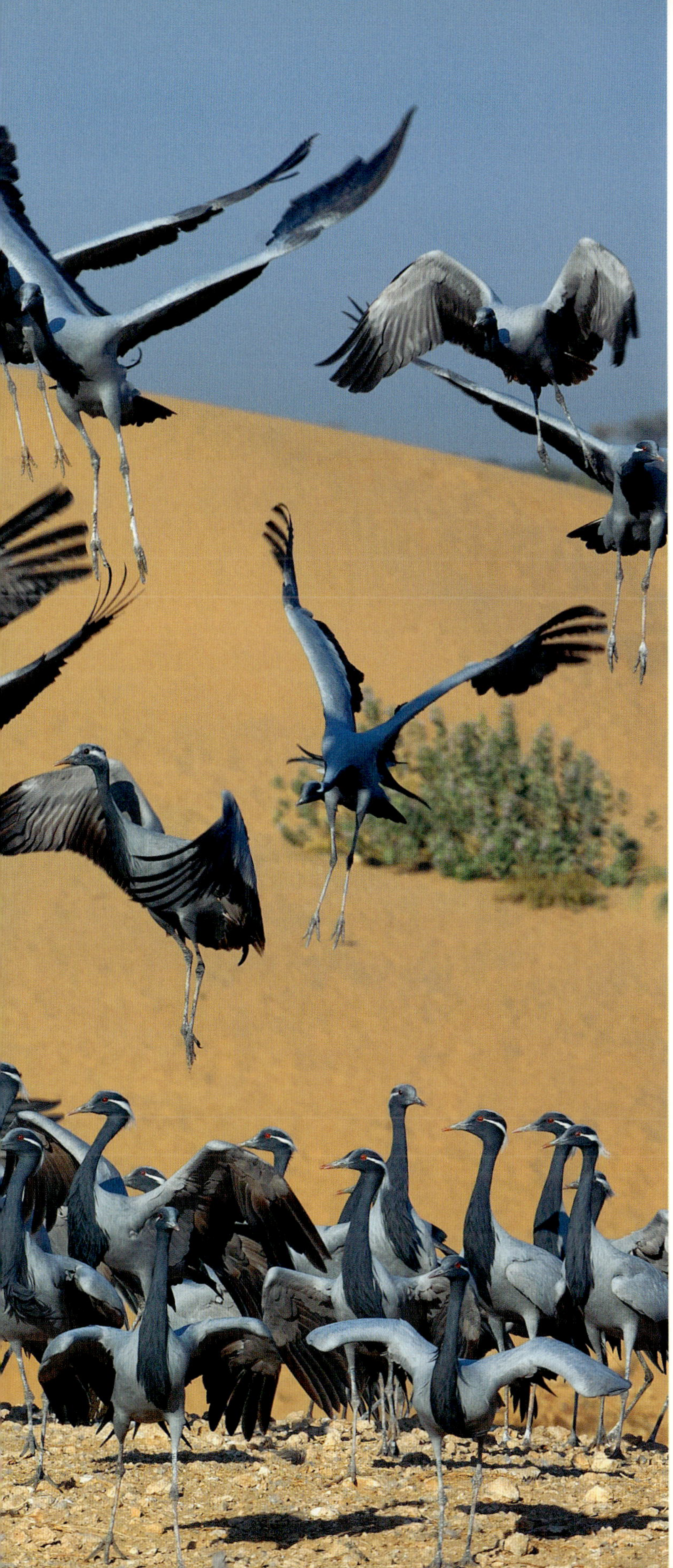

Cranes are mostly associated with wetlands, but many demoiselle cranes spend their winter in the semi-desert of Rajasthan. This environment forms a strong contrast to their breeding grounds in central Asia.

Overleaf:
An enormous diversity of landscapes and habitats can be found in India, including vast stretches of sand dunes in the Thar desert in Rajasthan. Part of the area is protected as the Desert National Park, situated in the far northwest of India, close to the border of Pakistan.

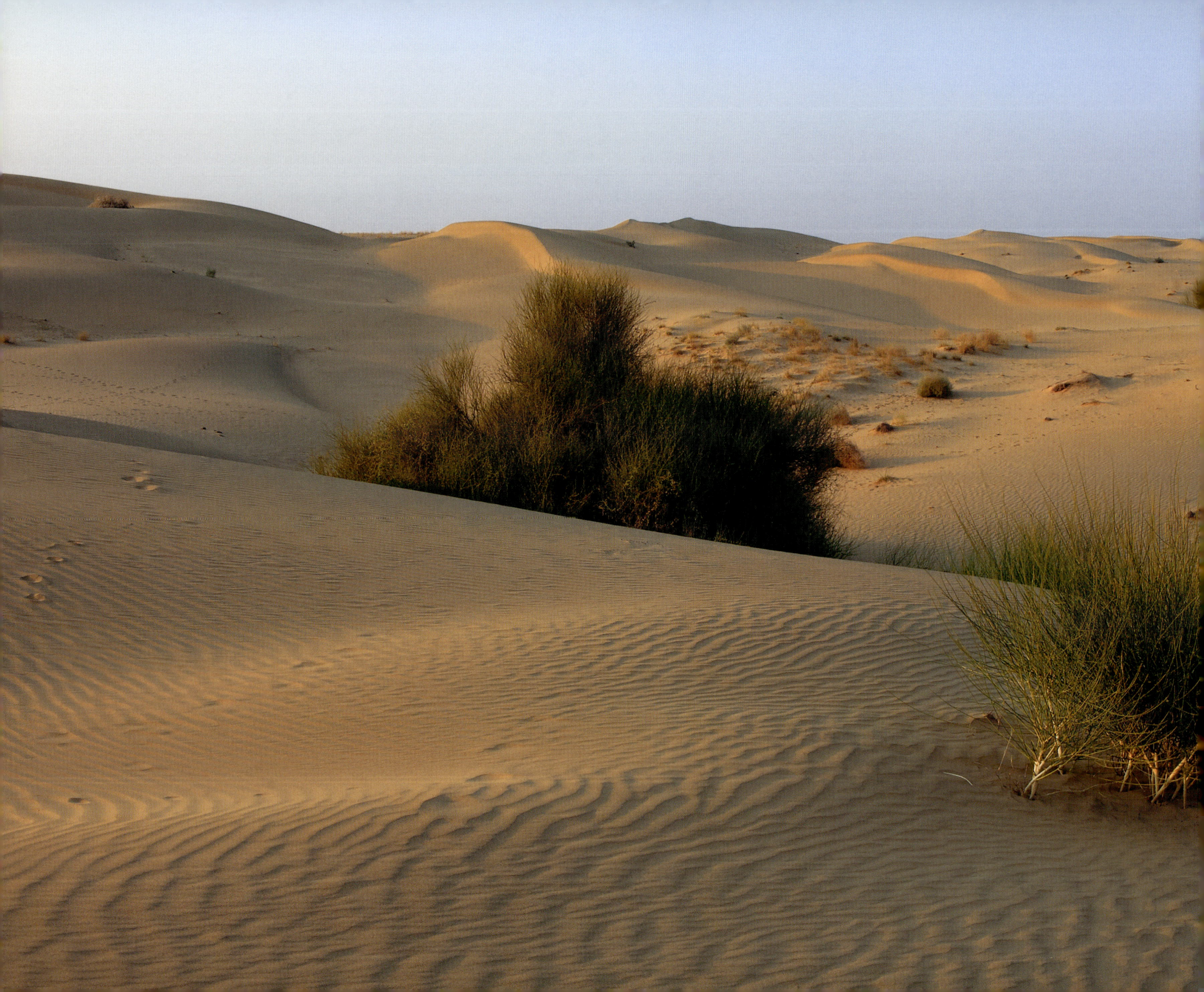

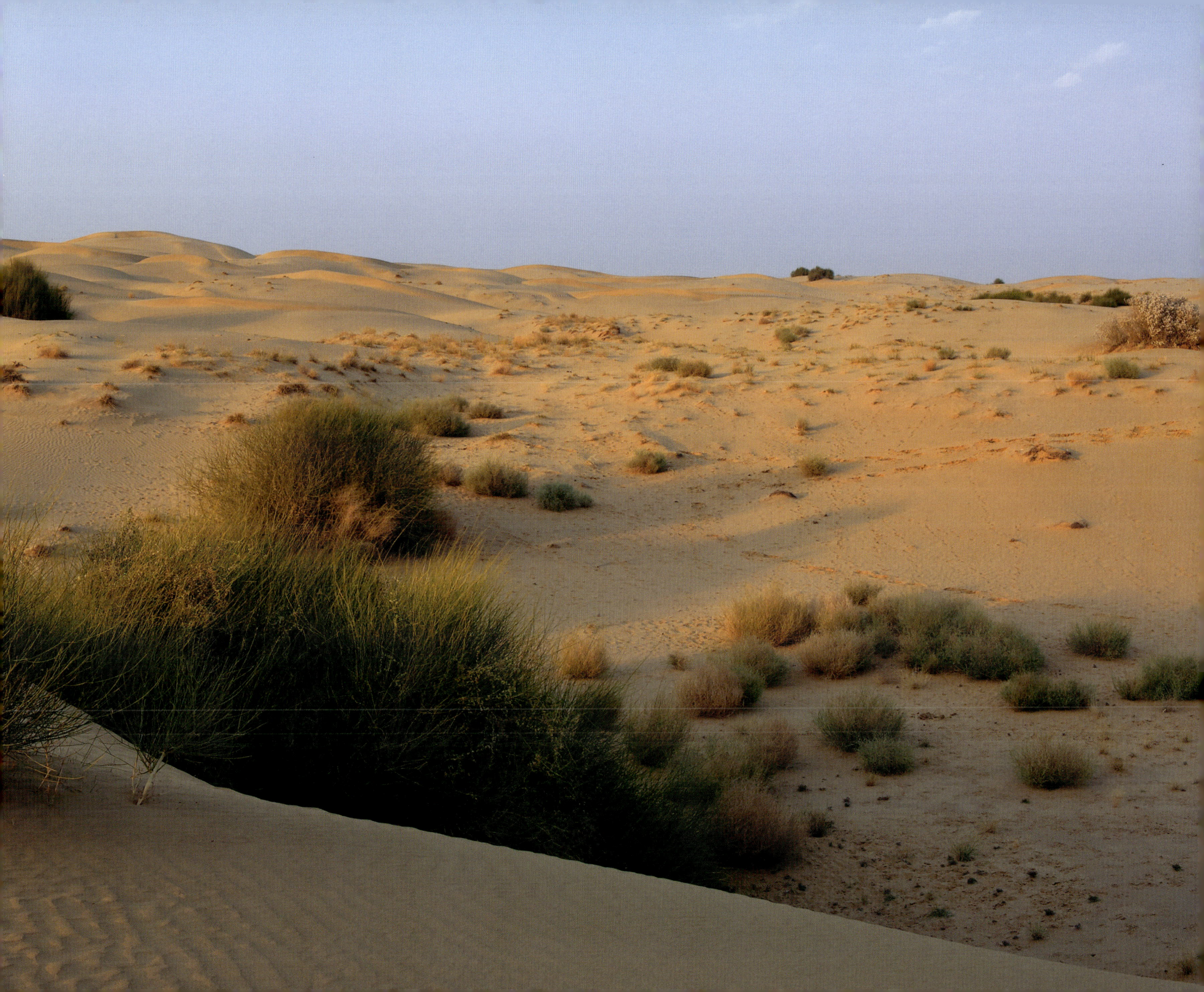

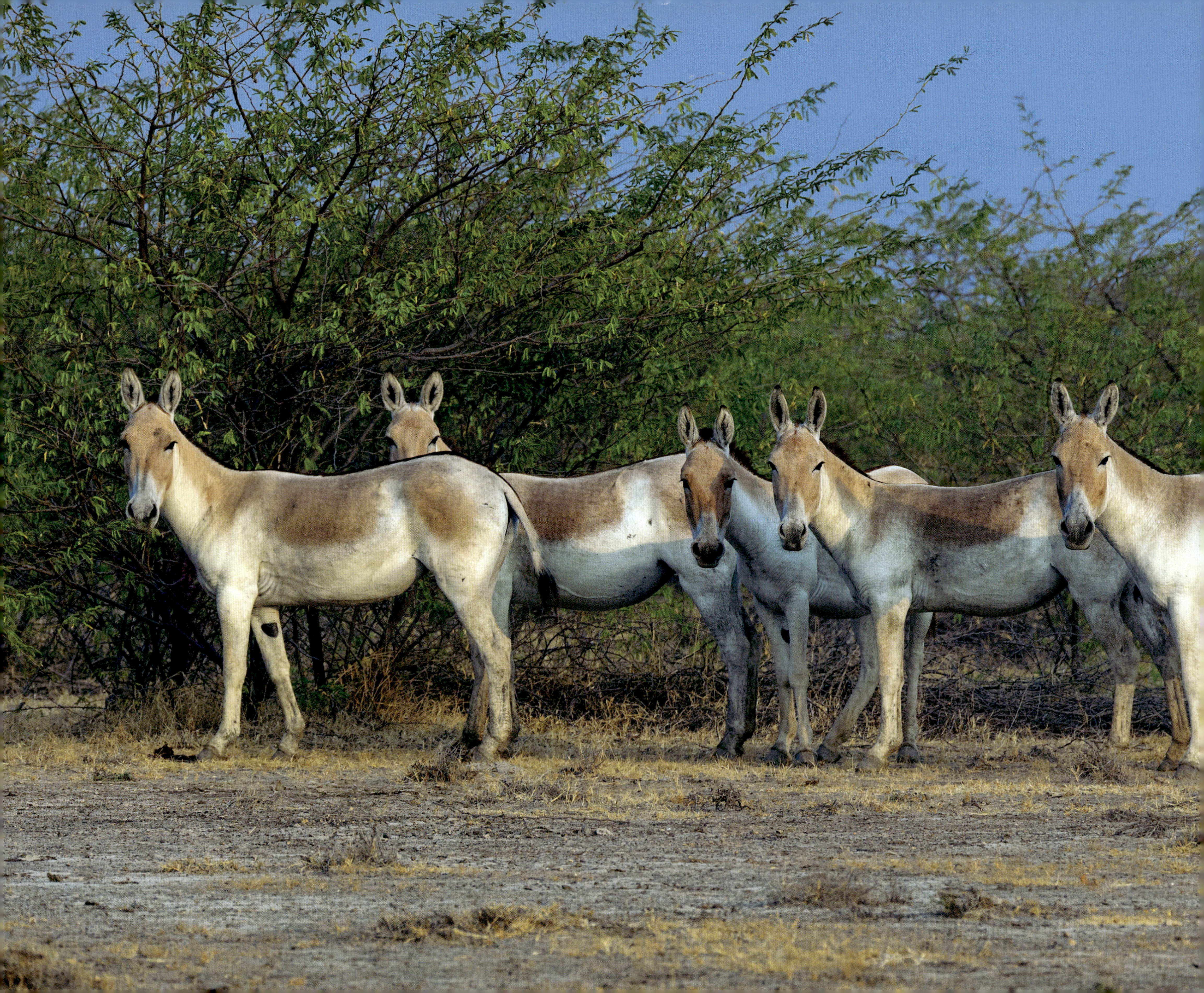

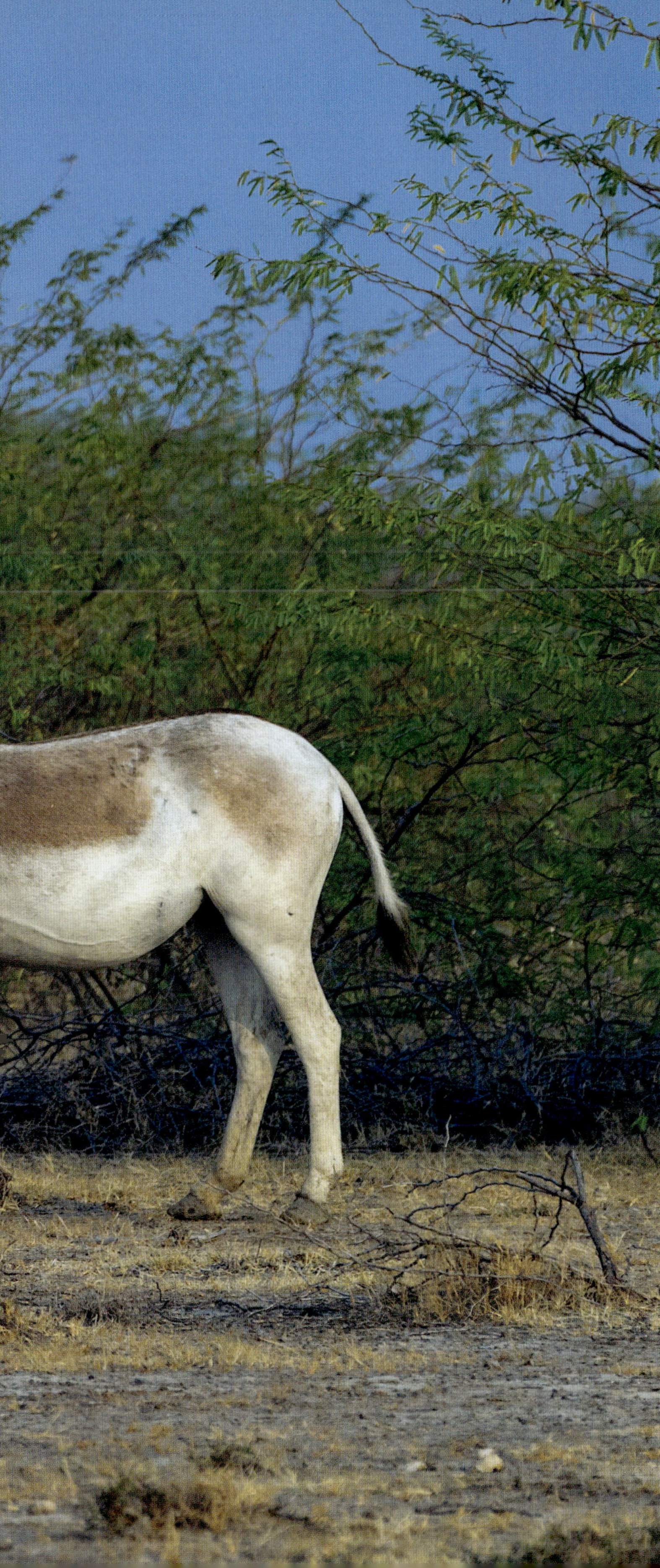

A group of Asiatic wild asses pauses at Little Rann of Kutch in Gujarat. This species of equine was once widespread in the semi-deserts of Asia. Although their numbers and range have dwindled dramatically, the sub-species, also known as khur, is still locally common in parts of western India.

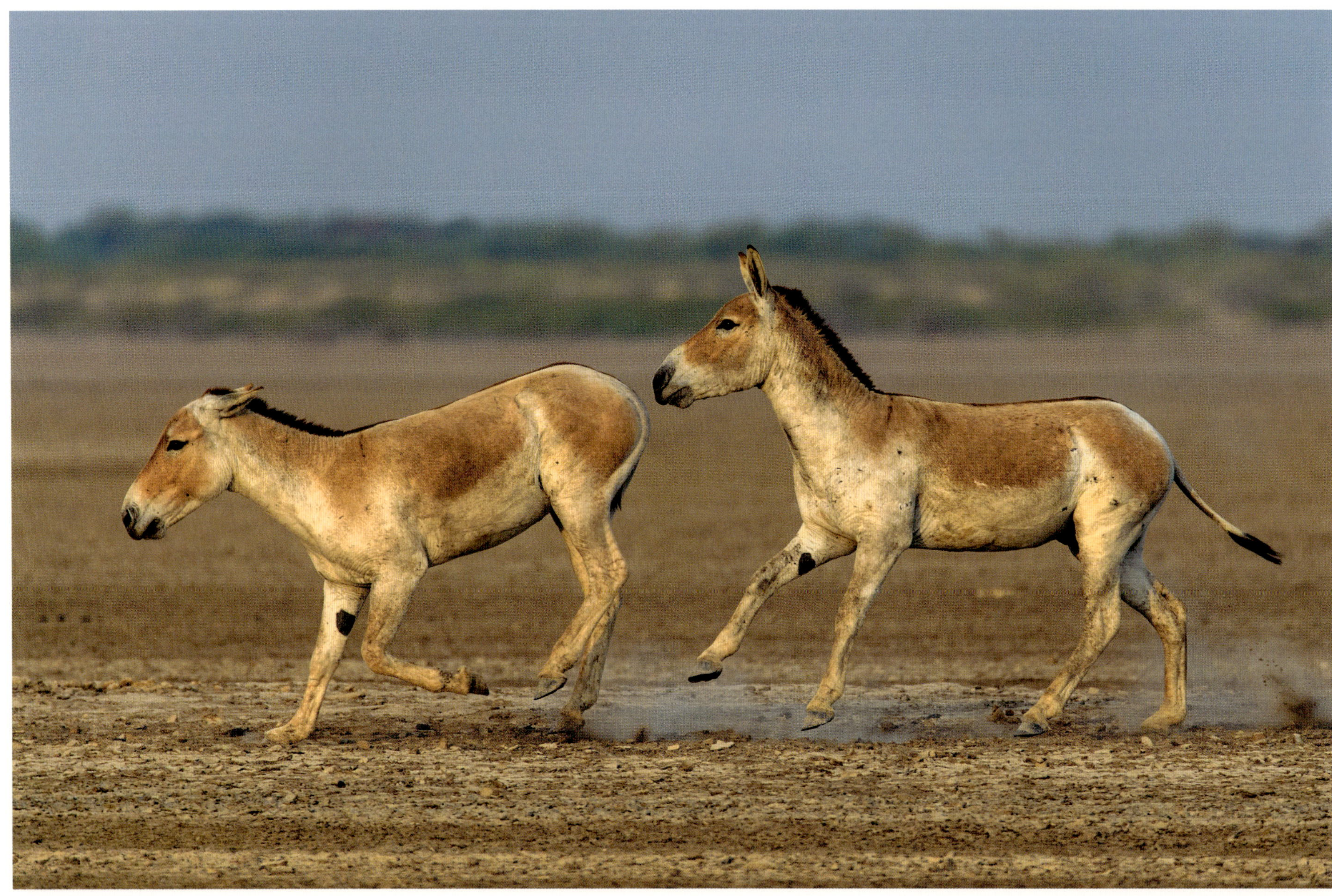

Male Asiatic wild asses, that are unable to defend their own territory, often live in bachelor groups. Tensions among them can lead to chasing and biting (above). If one animal feels exceptionally constrained, it can kick the pursuer with its hind legs, sometimes inflicting serious injury (opposite).

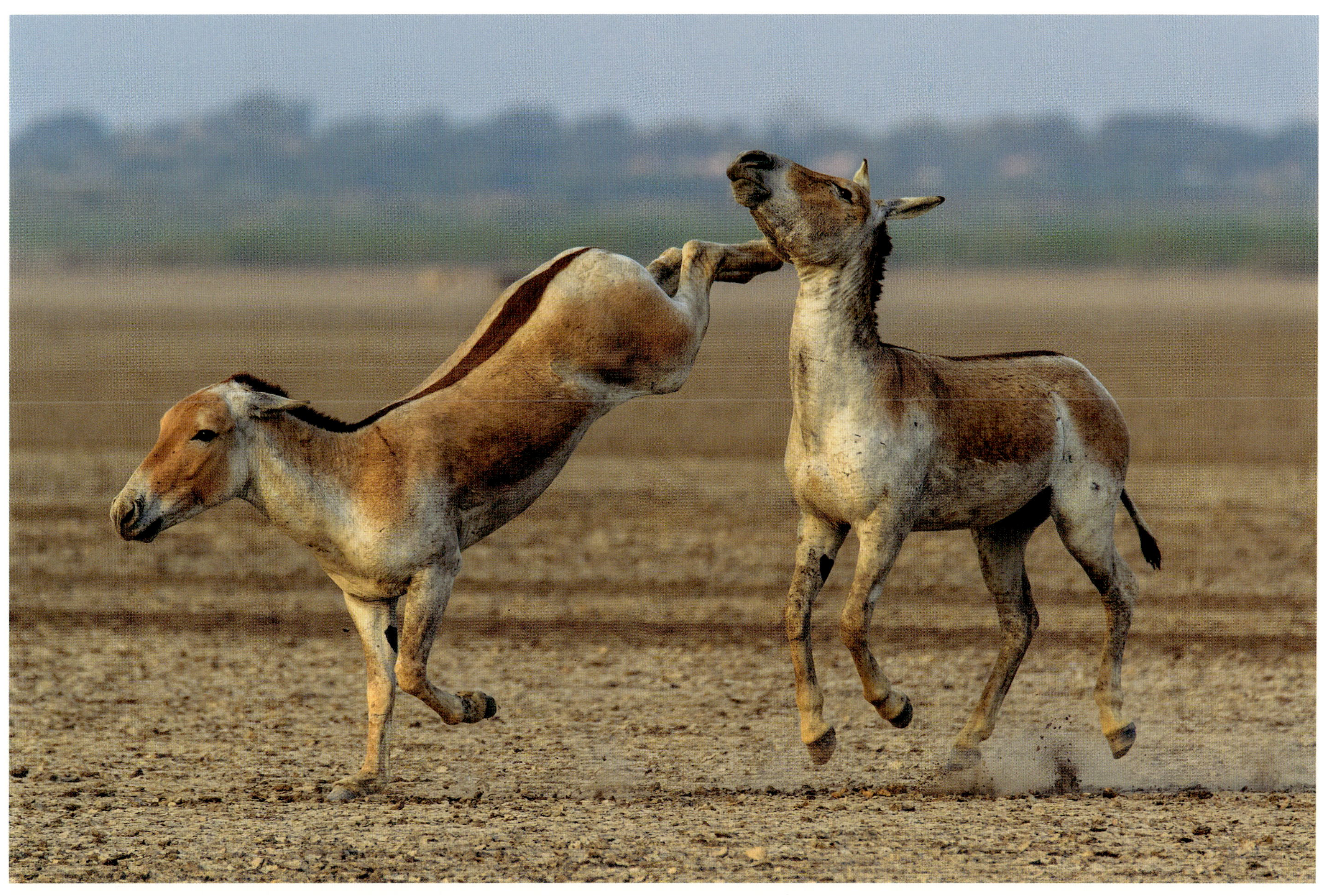

Overleaf:
The Little Rann of Kutch is a barren saltpan, which is very dry for most of the year, receiving erratic rainfall. It is a safe retreat for animals who are able to cope with such conditions, the Asiatic wild ass being one example, however, long distances must be travelled in order to find enough food.

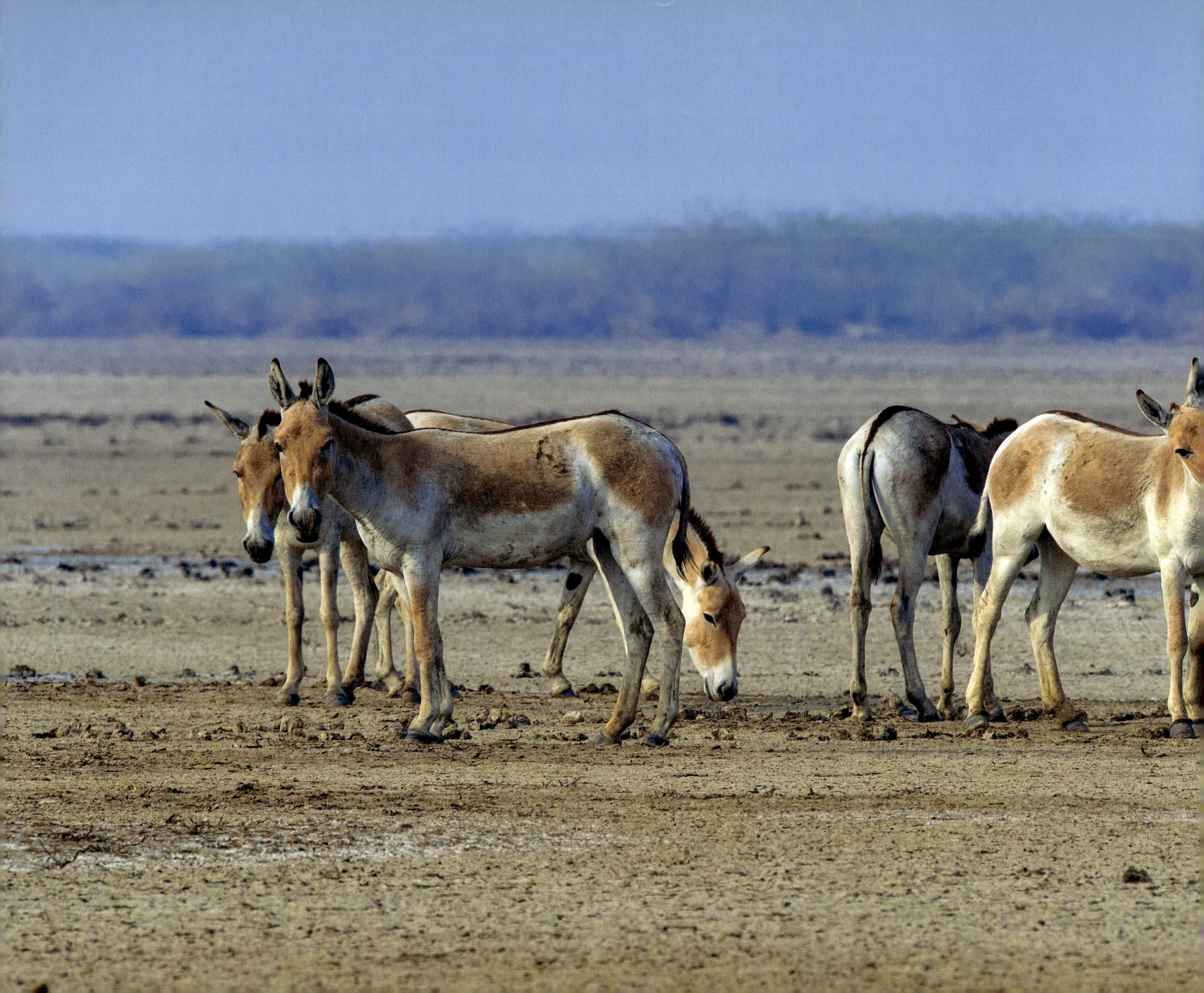

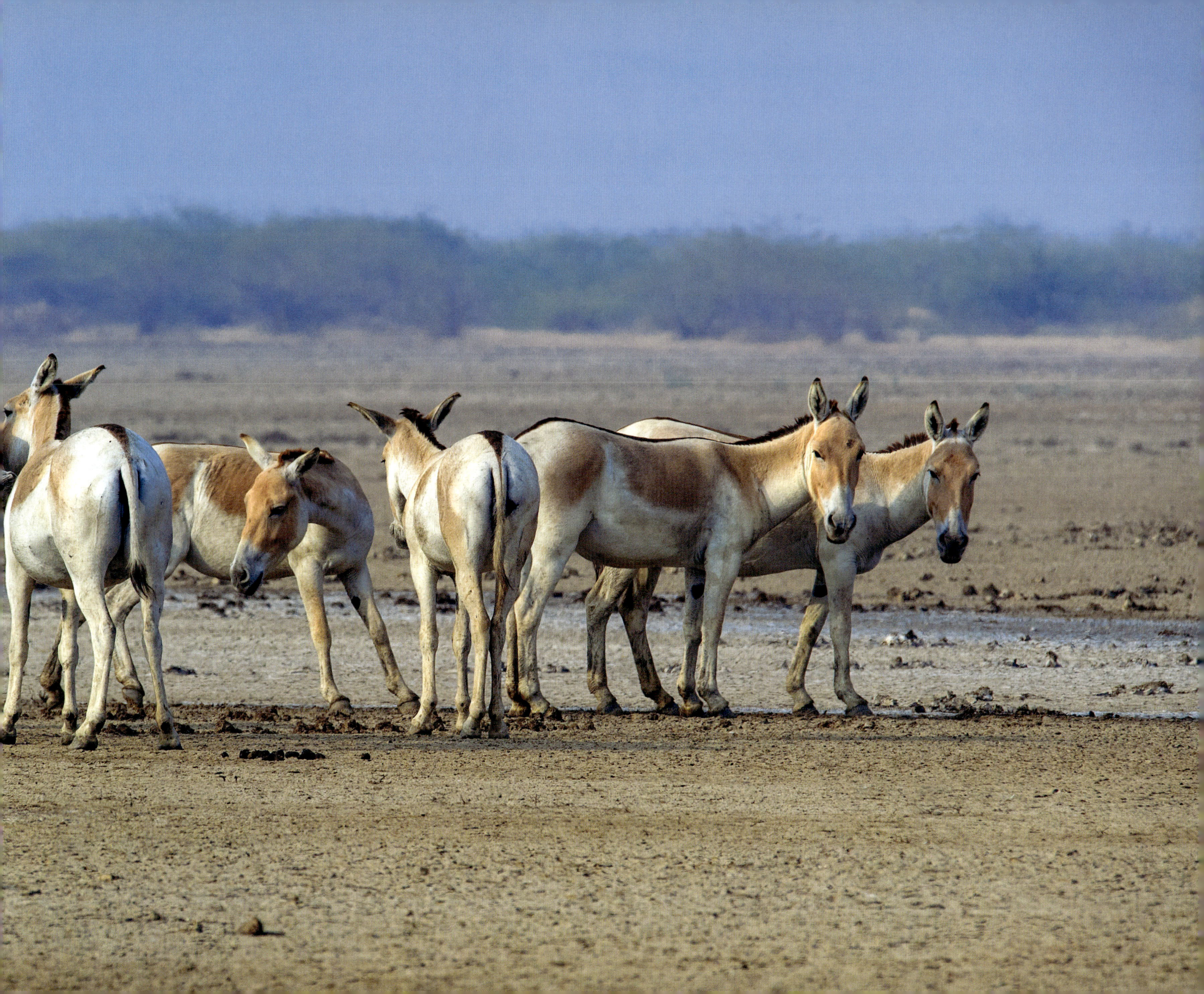

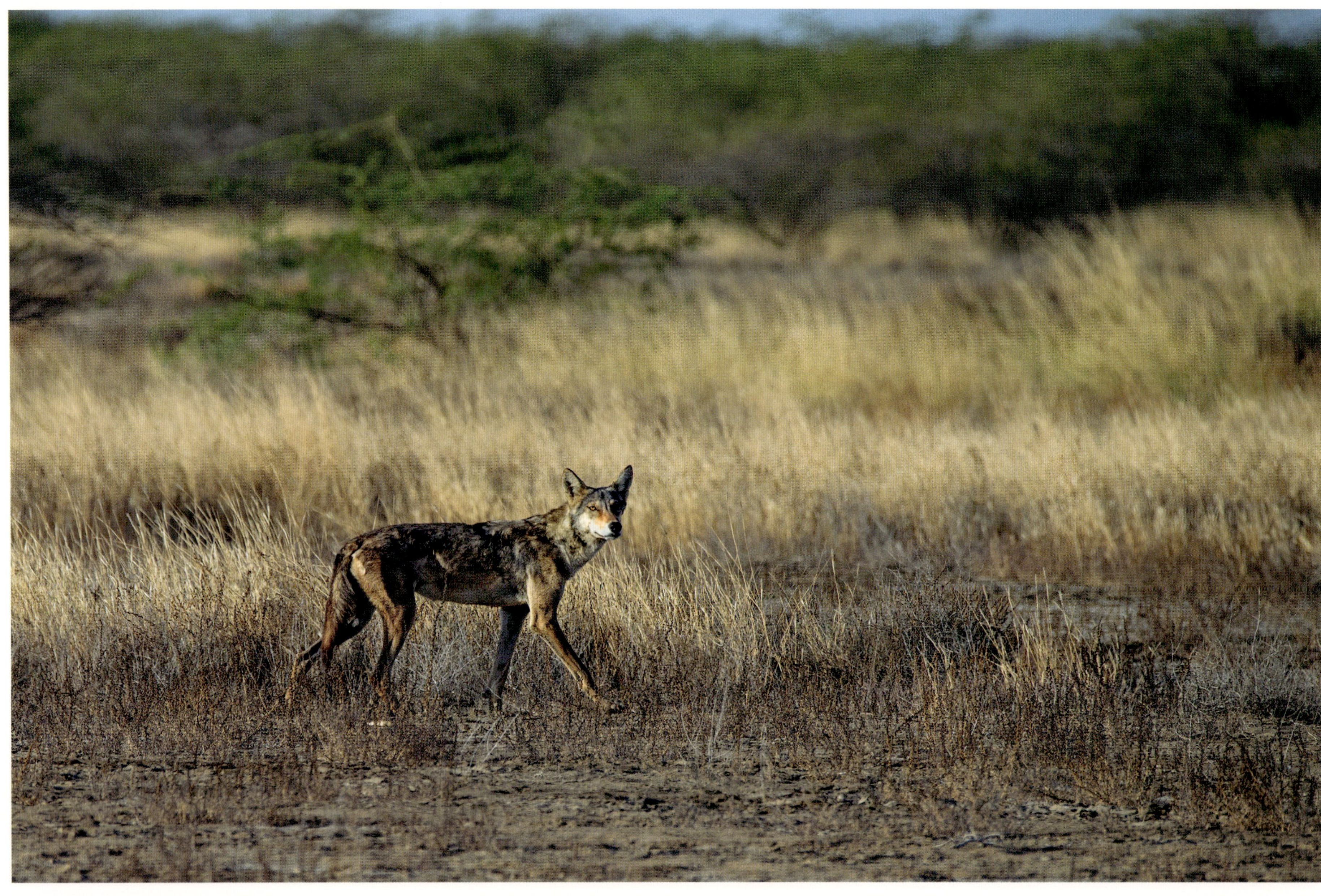

Wolves from the Indian peninsular, though not as large or as heavy as their kin living further north, are very effective predators (above). It would be unusual for them to attack an adult Asiatic wild ass, (opposite) however, they can pose a threat to their foals.

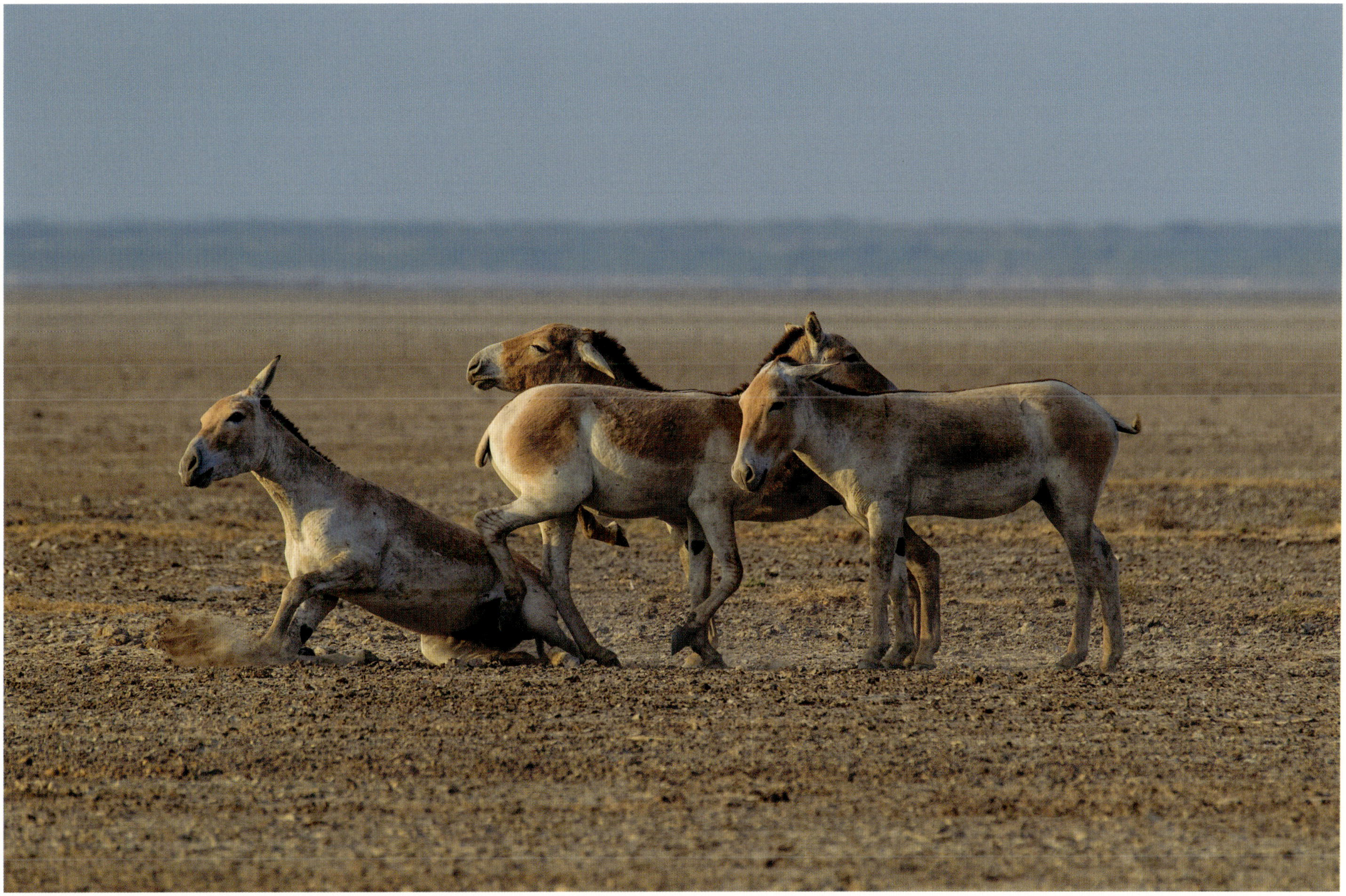

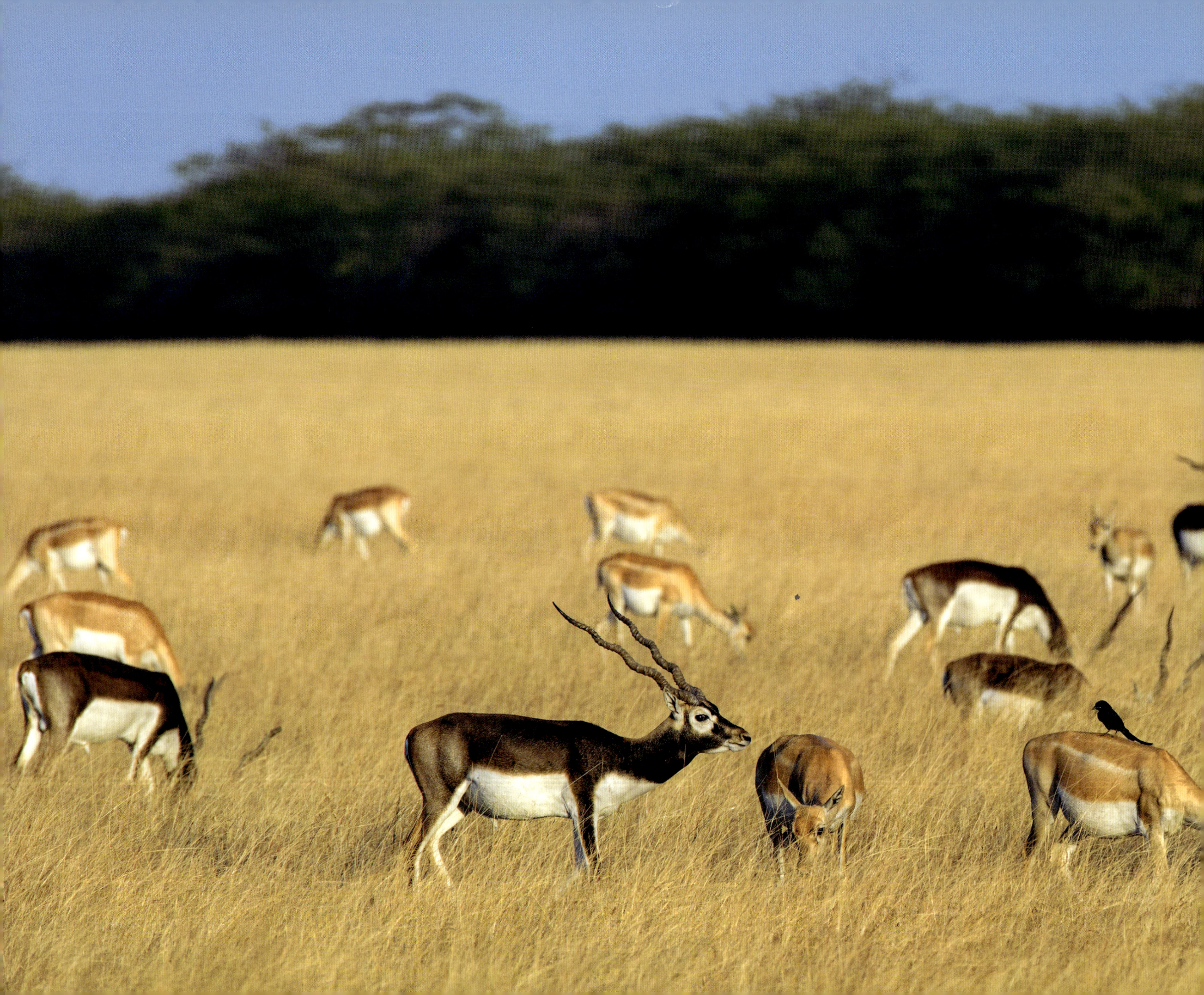

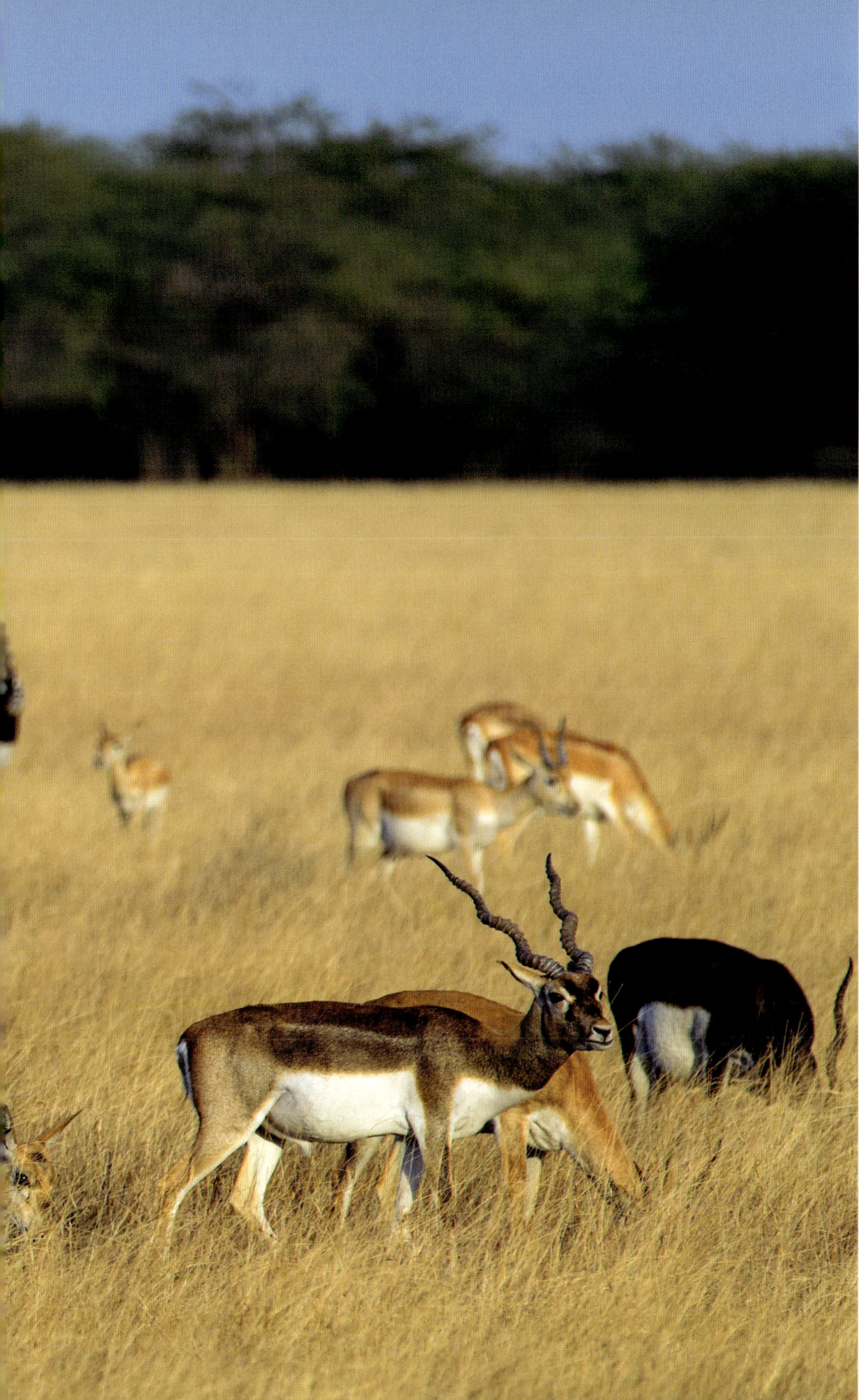

Open grasslands, reminiscent of African savannahs, are found in the Velavadar National Park in Gujarat. This is a window into the past, showing how areas of India would have looked before being cultivated. Large herds of the beautiful blackbuck are characteristic of this habitat.

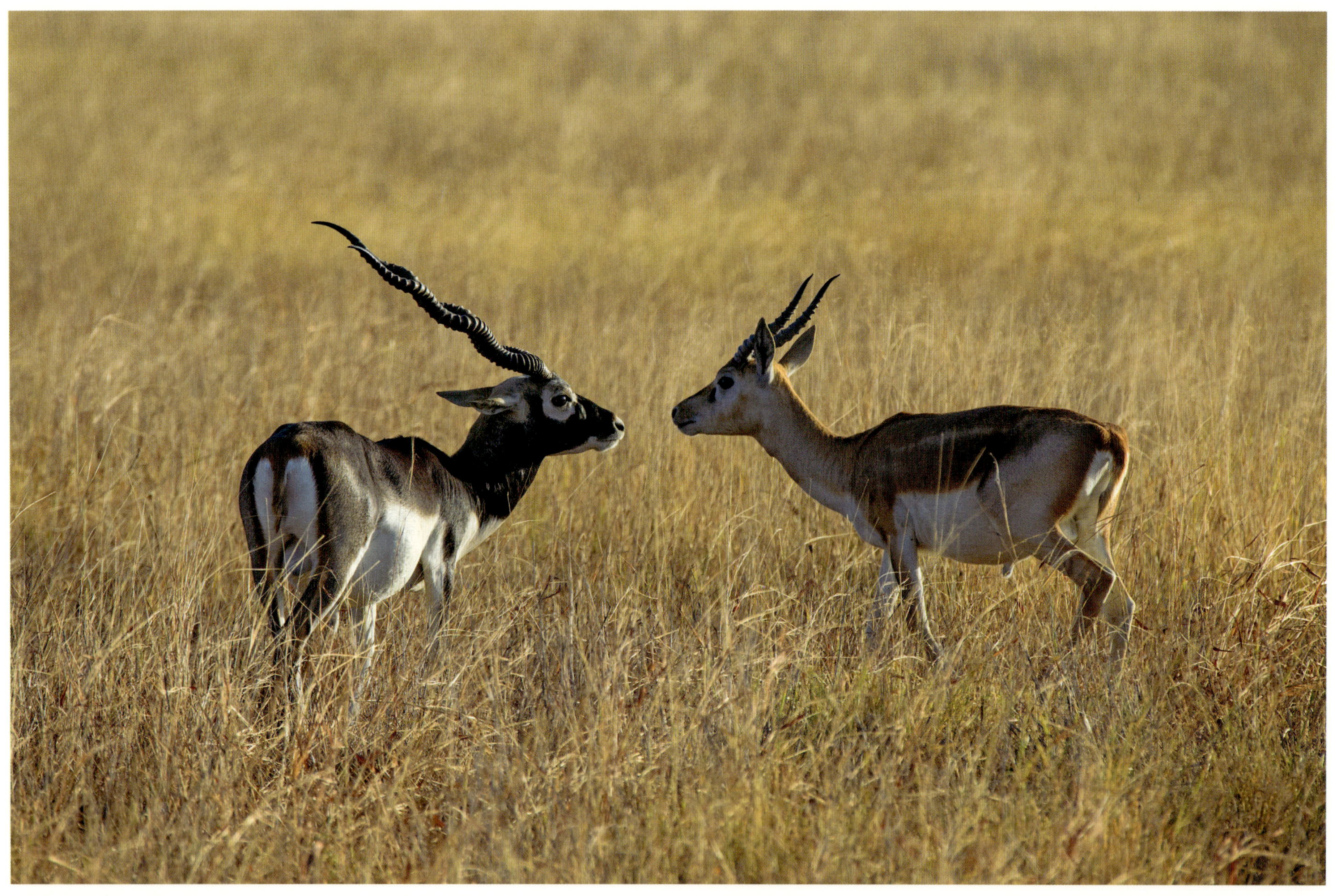

Wolves are the apex predator in the Velavadar National Park. If blackbucks spot one, they will immediately be on full alert (opposite), although social activities (above), may make them an easier target while they are distracted from any potential threat.

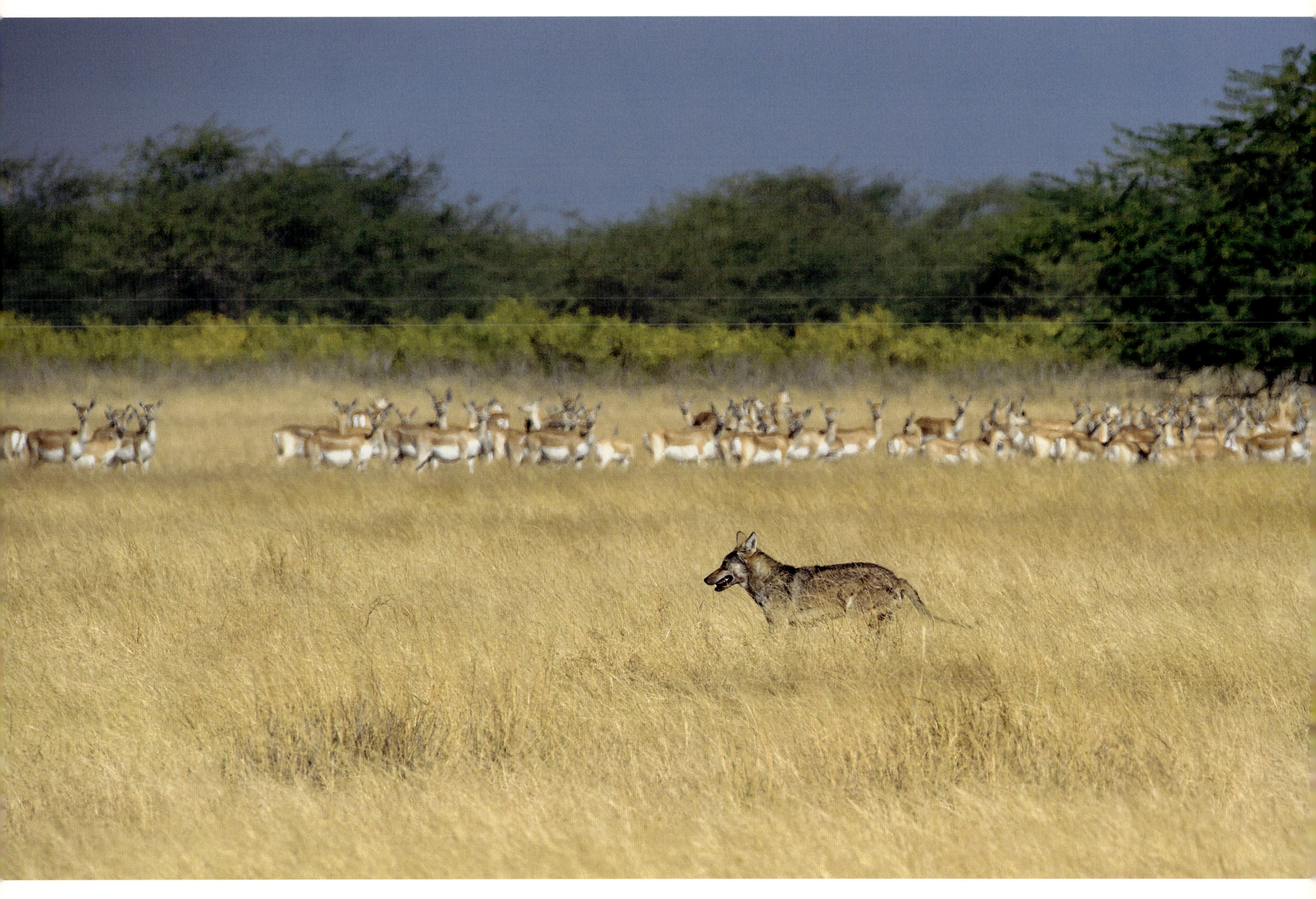

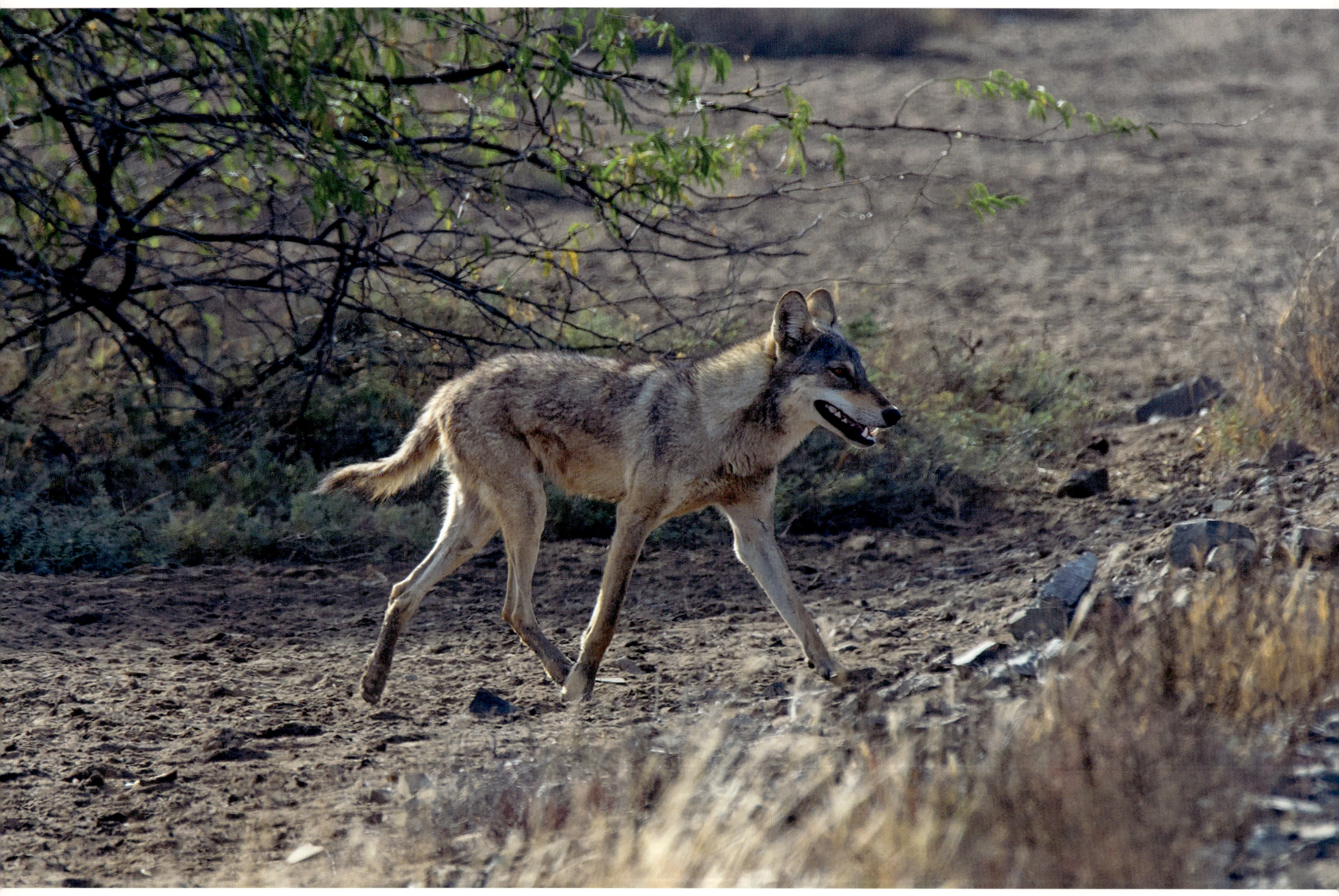

Wolves hunt alone and in packs. The pack is there as a social unit and a family. Family ties among wolves are very strong and a typical pack will consist of the breeding pair, this year's offspring, and older cubs from the previous year.

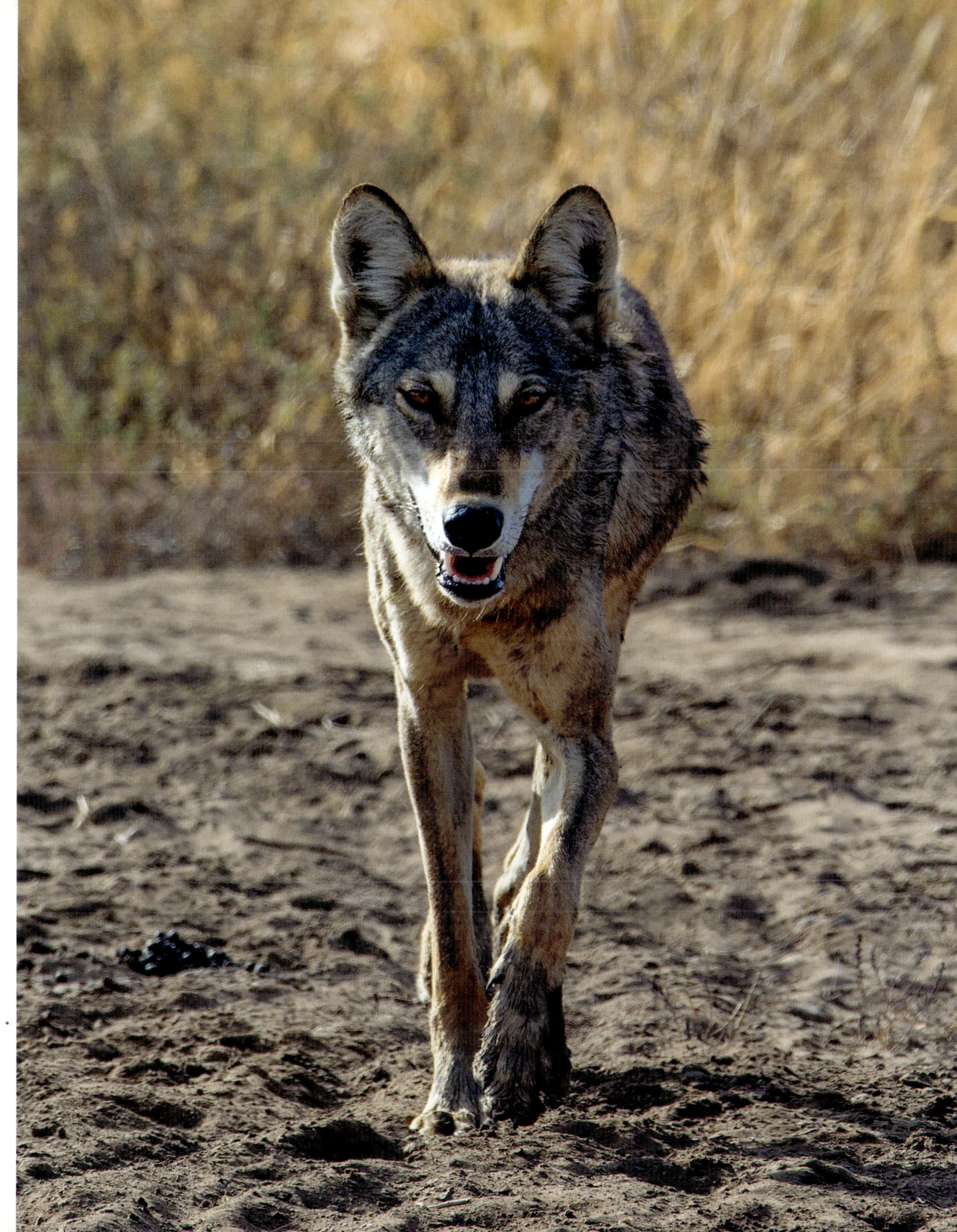

The conflict between wolves and herdsman is as old as livestock farming itself. In many regions of India, wolves attack sheep and goats if they cannot find enough natural prey. Retaliation killings, along with habitat destruction and a lack of natural prey, have all taken their toll on the population, resulting in wolves becoming rare and endangered in India.

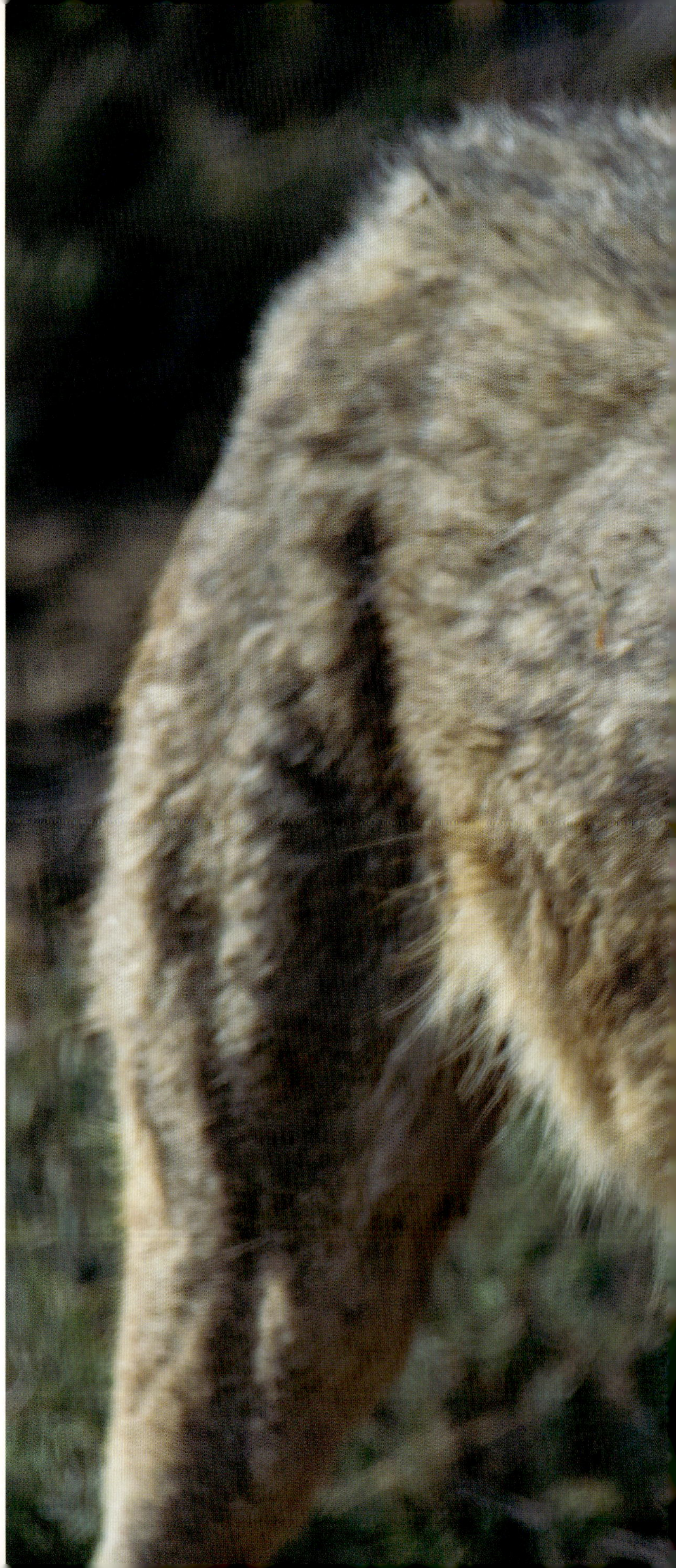

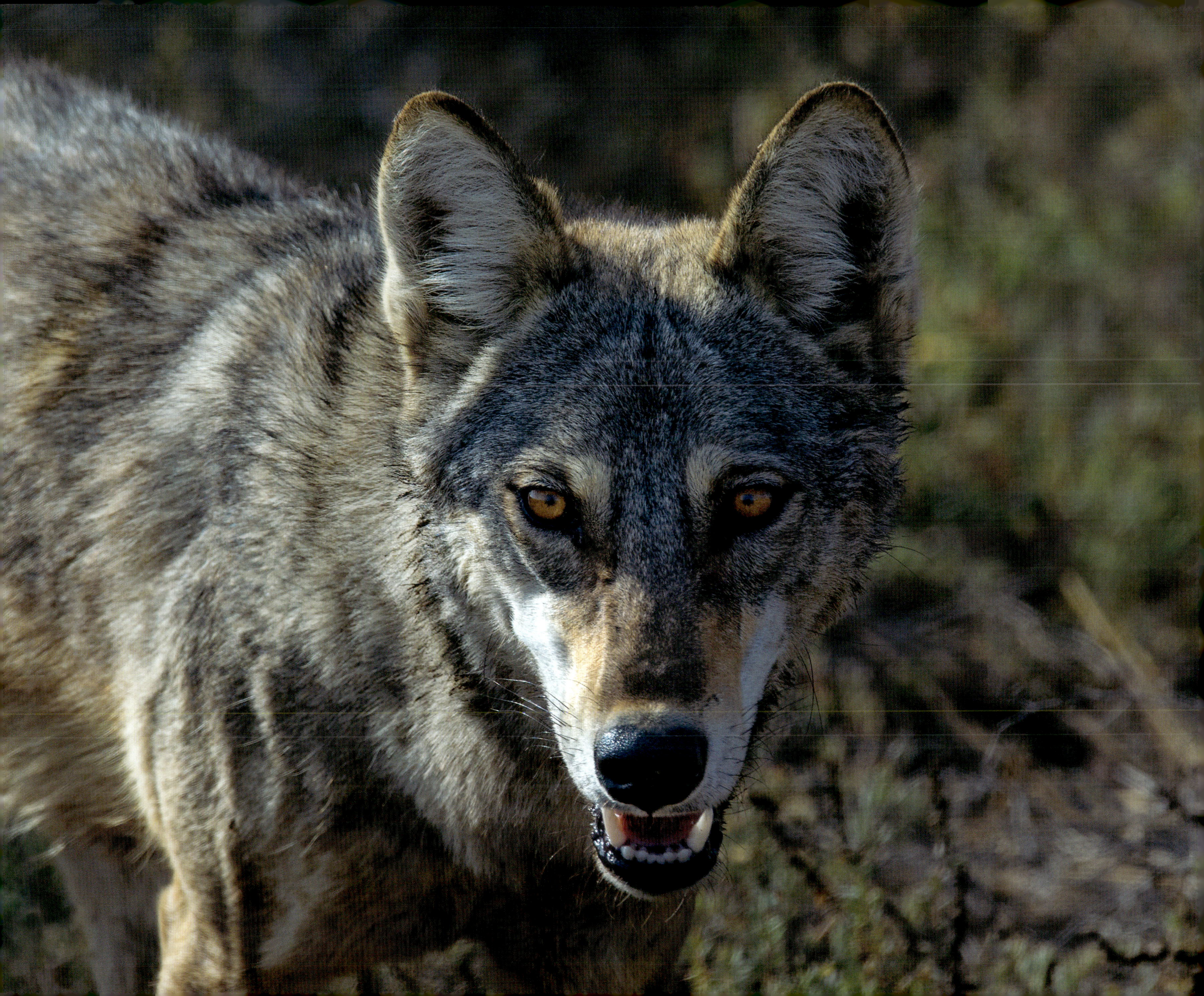

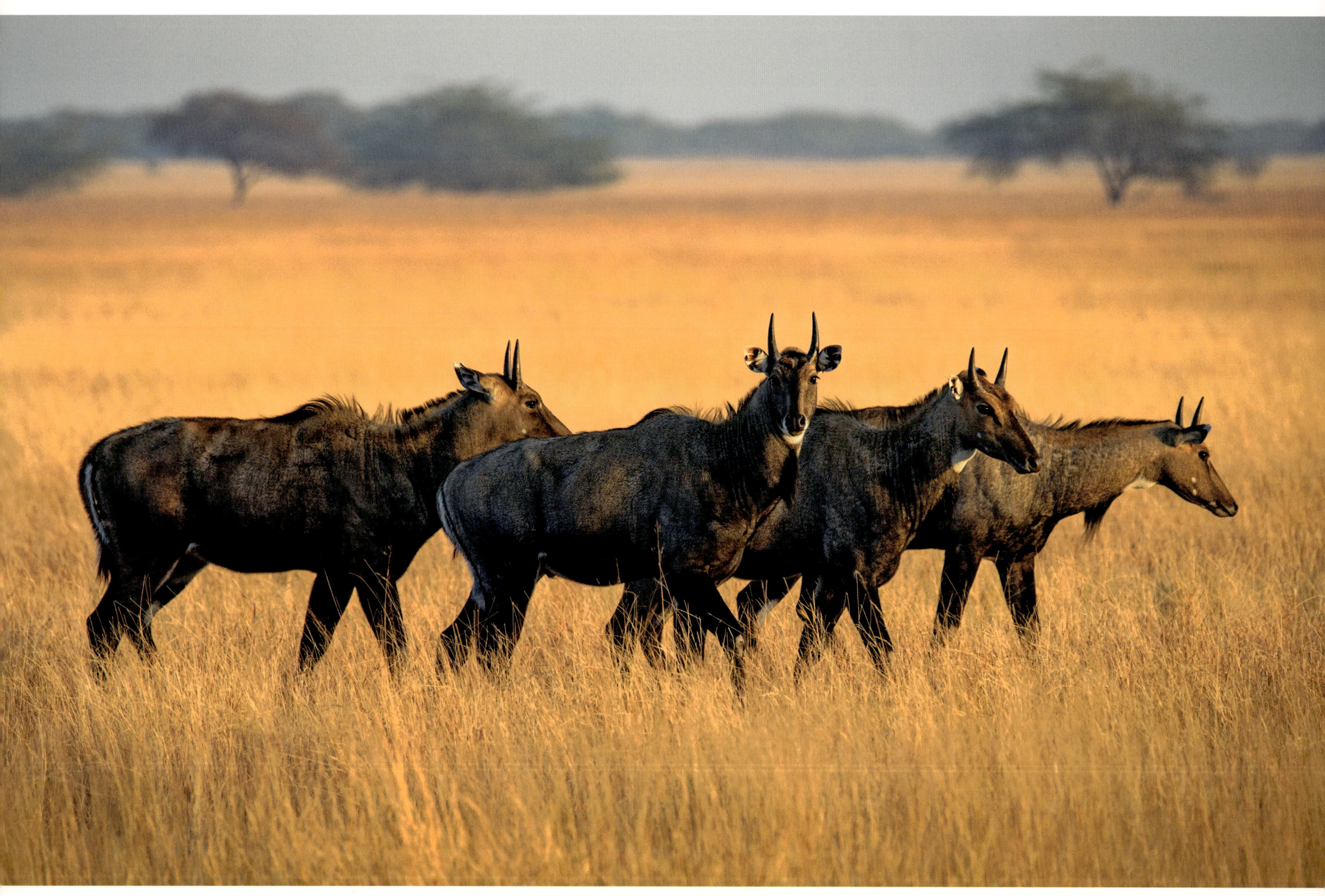

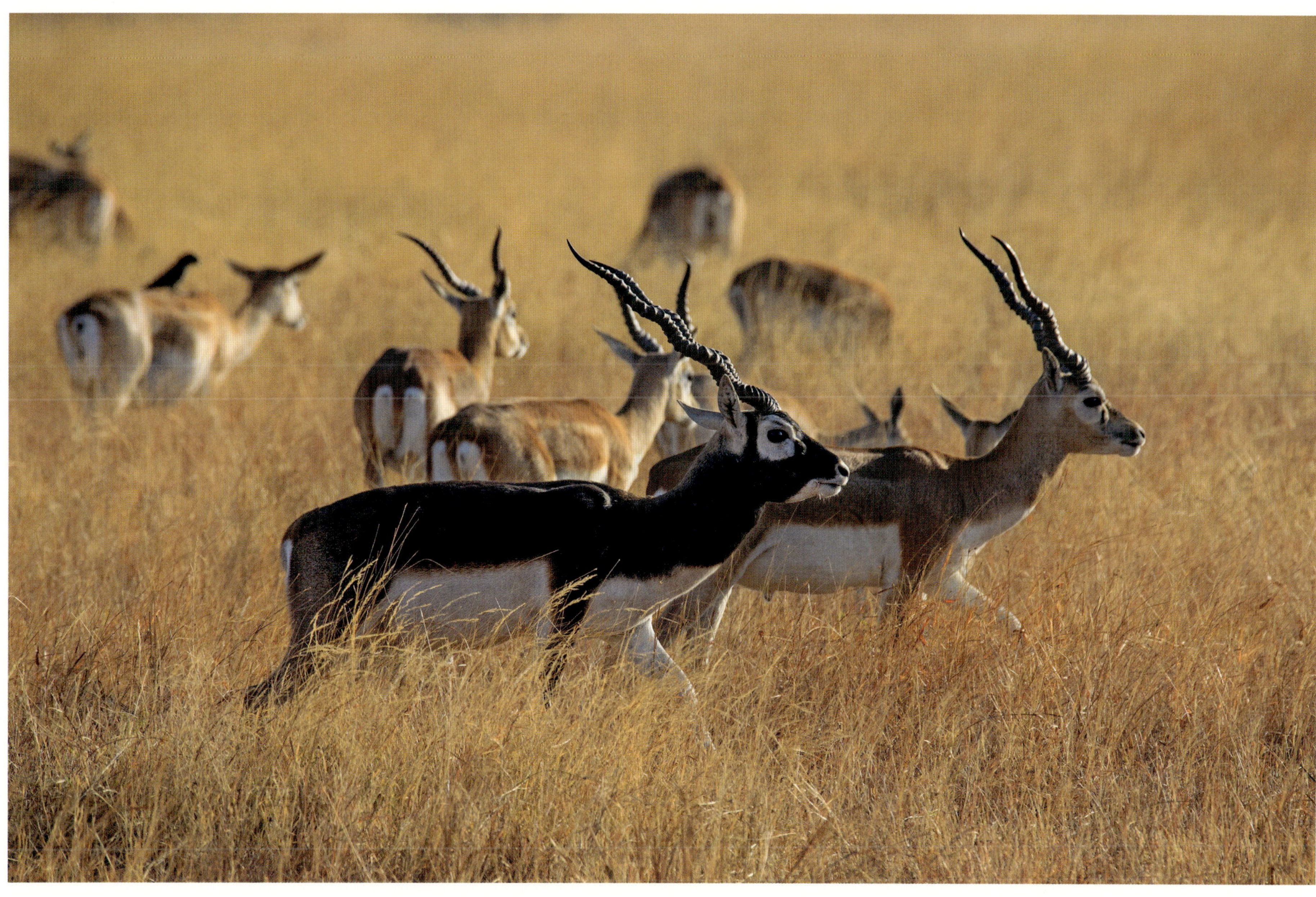

A group of male nilgai cross through the Velavadar National Park (opposite). This large antelope is adaptable and lives in a range of habitats, unlike the blackbuck who prefer open grasslands (above). Their spiralled horns and the prominent coloration are key characteristics of blackbuck, who are endemic to the Indian subcontinent.

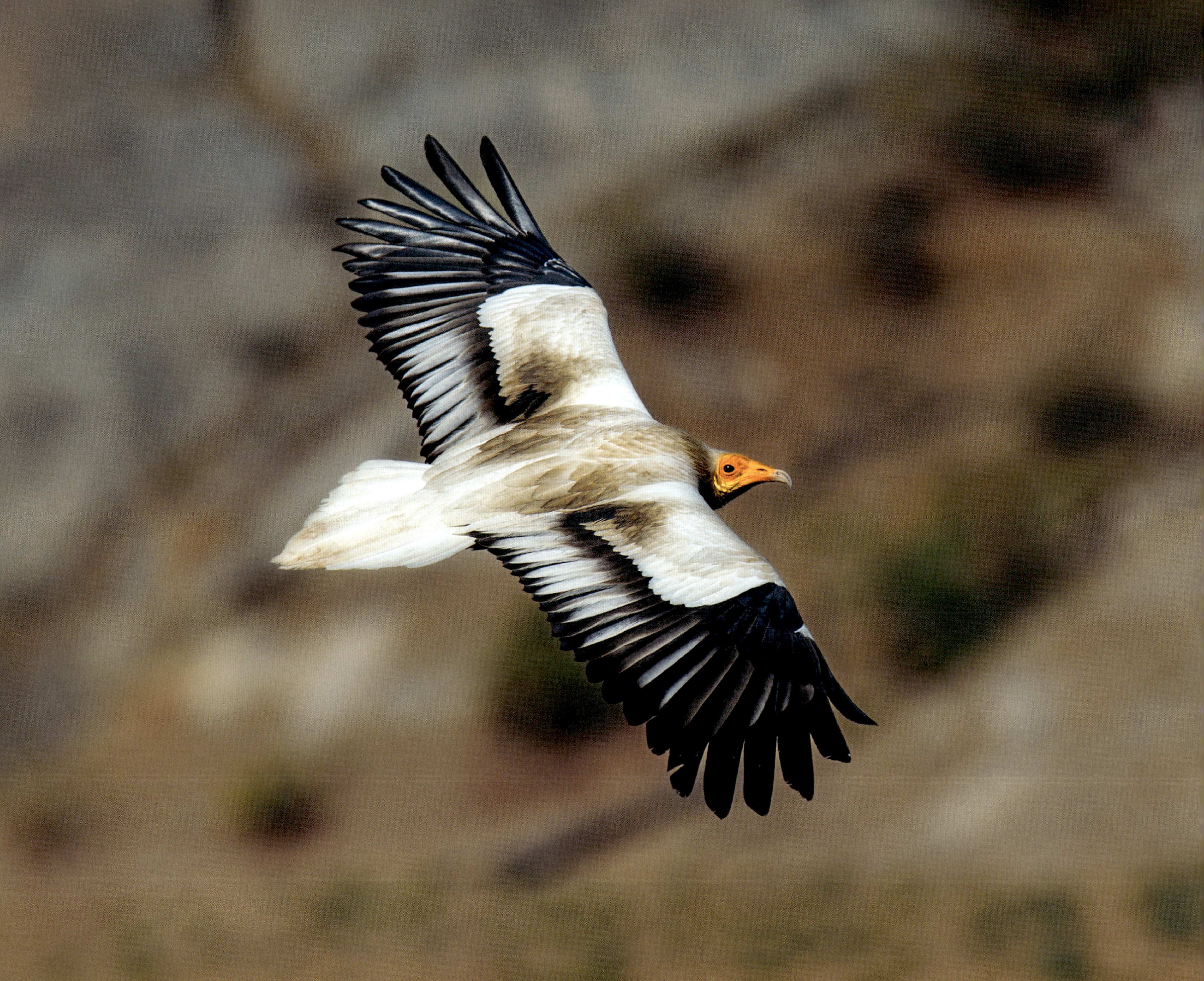

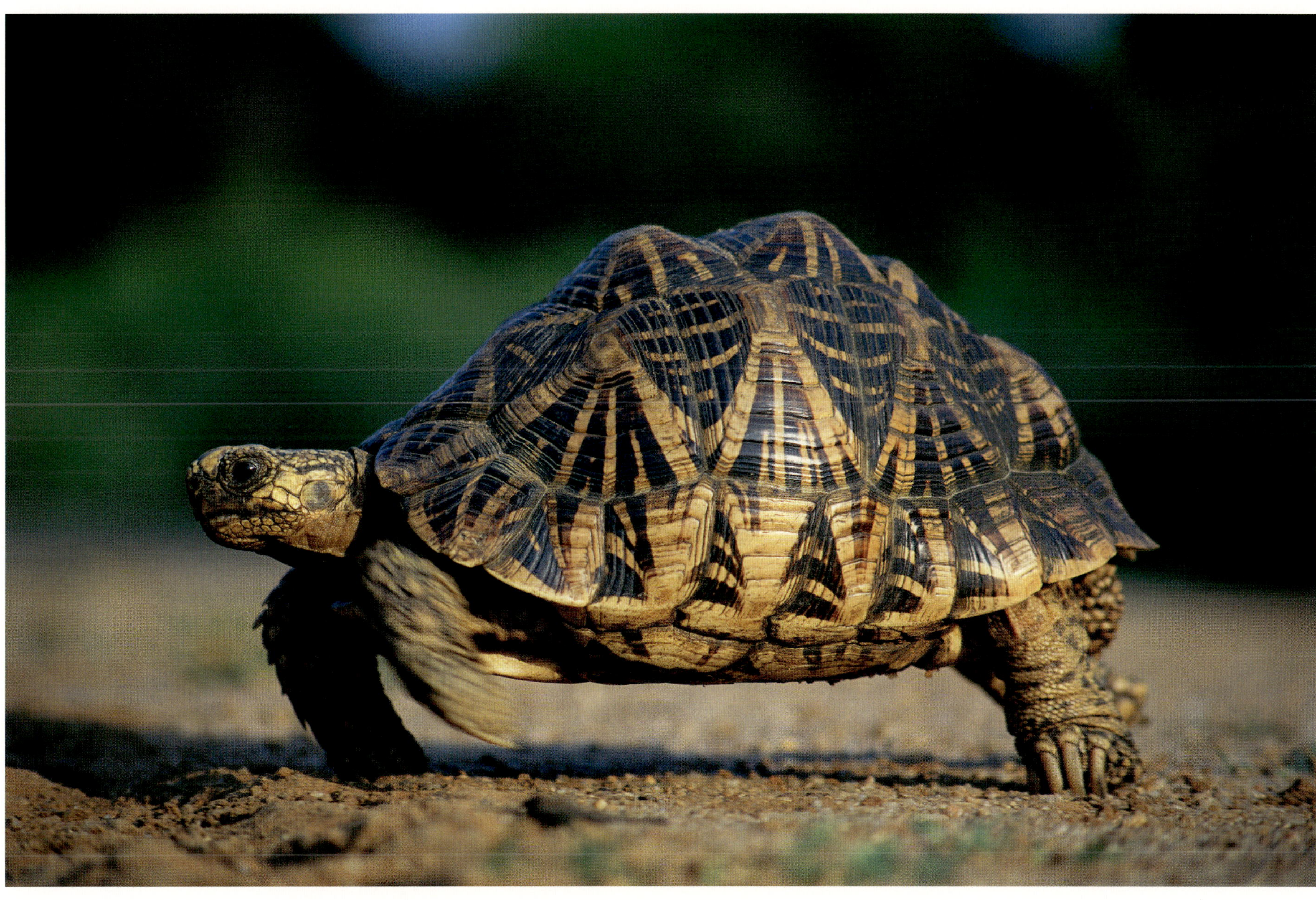

An Egyptian vulture (opposite) soars over the hills of Rajasthan, looking for food. This strikingly coloured bird can cover huge distances with its wings extended, using thermals for lift. Foraging is much more arduous for the Indian star tortoise who, being much less mobile, has to find food in a much smaller area (above).

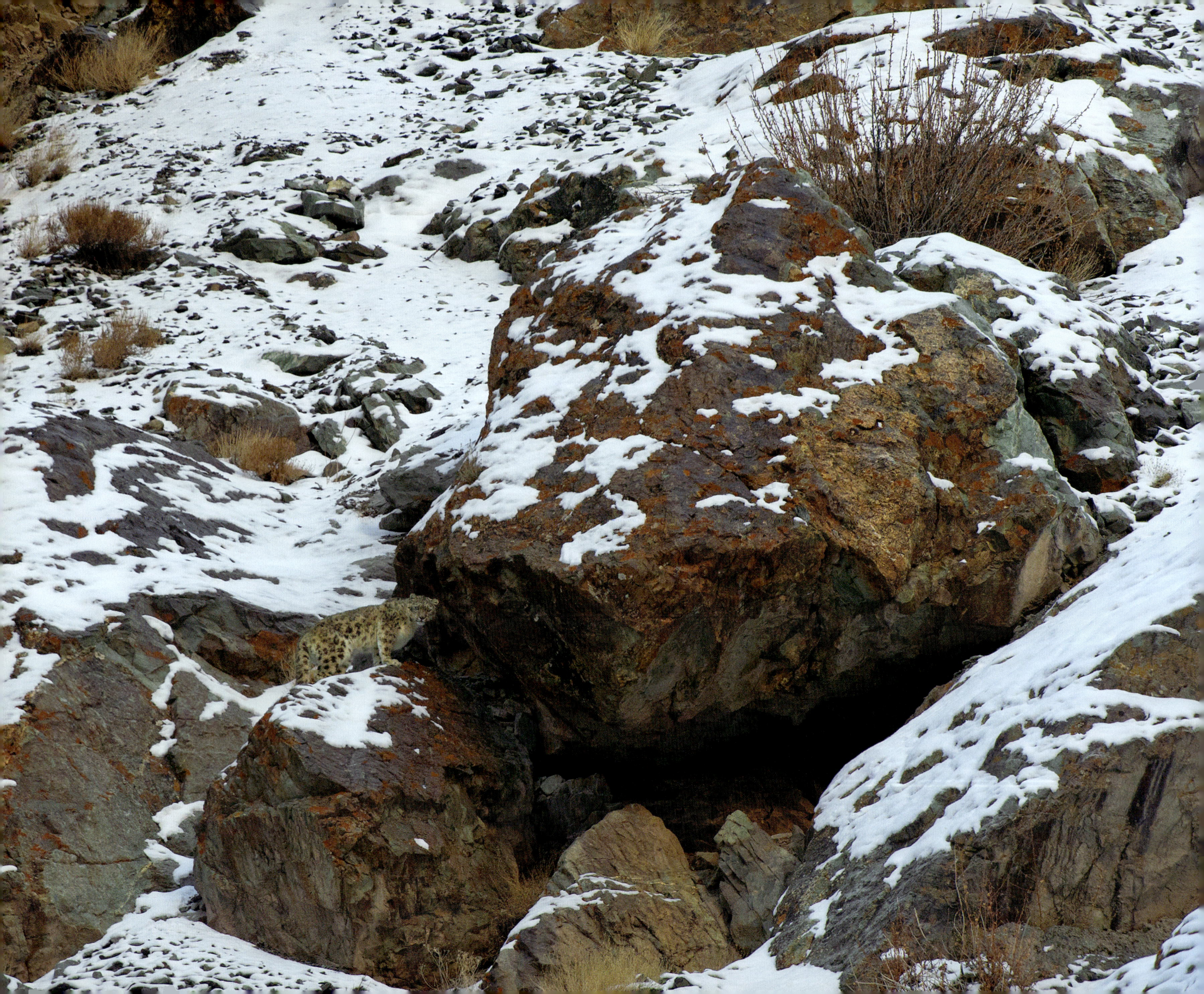

MOUNTAINS

India may be famous for its jungles, but some of the most spectacular and diverse habitats are in northern India, comprising parts of the Himalayan ranges. From the forests at the foothills, to the icebound peaks and mountain lakes, the Himalayas provide a rich and varied habitat for the flora and fauna that inhabit the area.

This is the realm of the magnificent and ghostly snow leopard, and getting a glimpse of this big cat is the holy grail of all wildlife watching in India. Ladakh, in the far north in the Indian state of Jammu and Kashmir, is the best region in which to attempt to see the snow leopard. It takes a small expedition to get there, and with no infrastructure, one has to camp in the snow. While this may be a challenge for many humans, the Himalayan blue sheep, a favourite prey of the snow leopard, can cope well with these climatic conditions and search for the scarce vegetation across rocky terrain.

Buddhism is the prevailing religion in this part of India, and Buddhists impose a great deal of importance upon the mountains of the Himalayas, with many peaks regarded as being sacred. Poaching is contradictory to religious beliefs. The region is not easily accessible to people, and the land cannot be used efficiently for cultivation or cattle breeding. Together with the harsh climatic conditions, these reasons have proven to be the best protection for this remote wilderness.

A snow leopard scans his territory in the Hemis National Park in Ladakh. This remote area in the Himalayas still supports a healthy population of snow leopards.

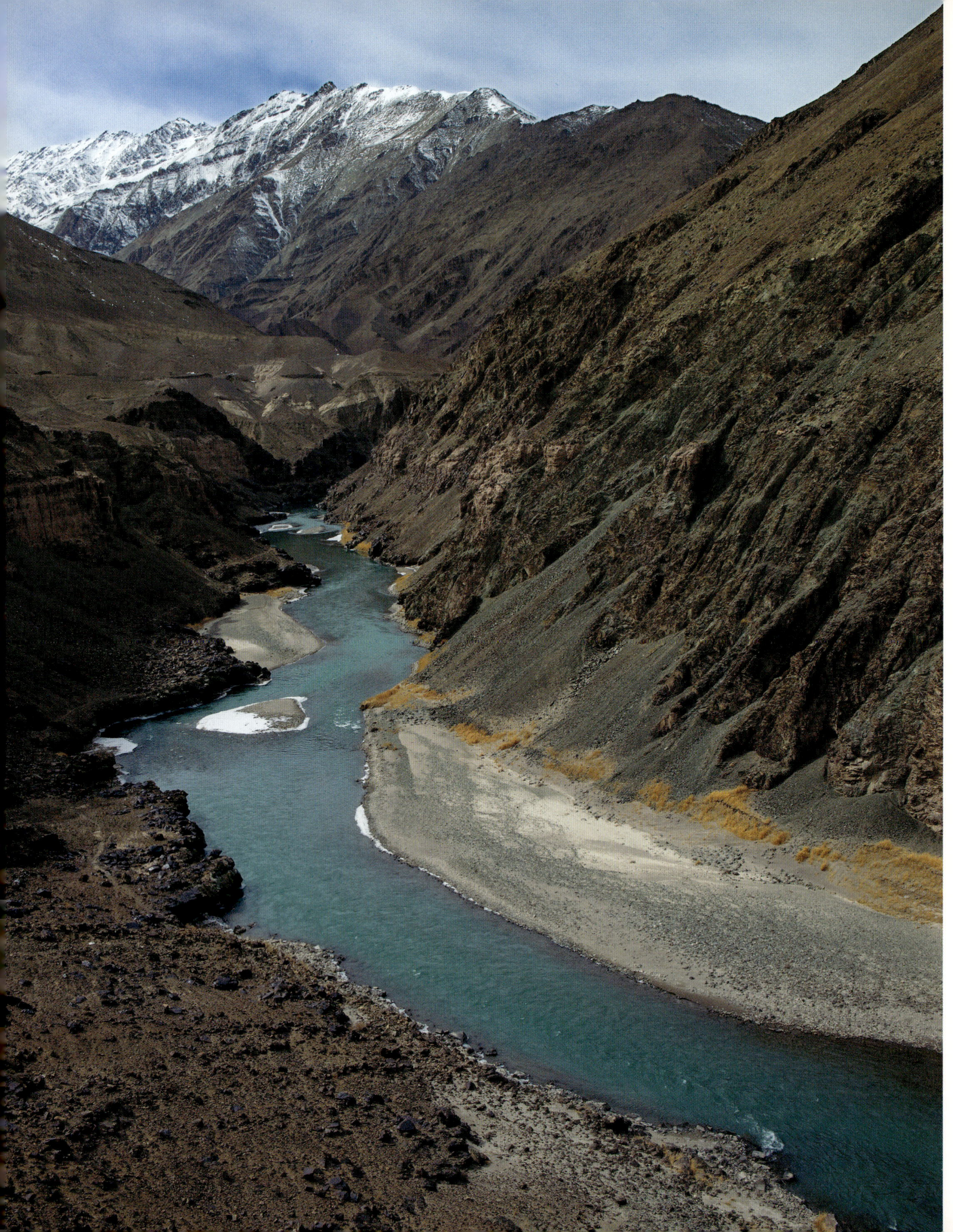

The Zanskar River is a tributary of the Indus, bordering part of the Hemis National Park (left). Strong winds often keep the lower elevations free from snow, yet food is still scarce for the population of Himalayan blue sheep that inhabit the area (opposite).

Overleaf:
The mighty mountain range of the Himalayas has many of the Earth's highest peaks. Some mountains in the Hemis National Park reach heights of 6,400 meters. The area is so remote and inhospitable that very few people live there, making it a safe retreat for wildlife.

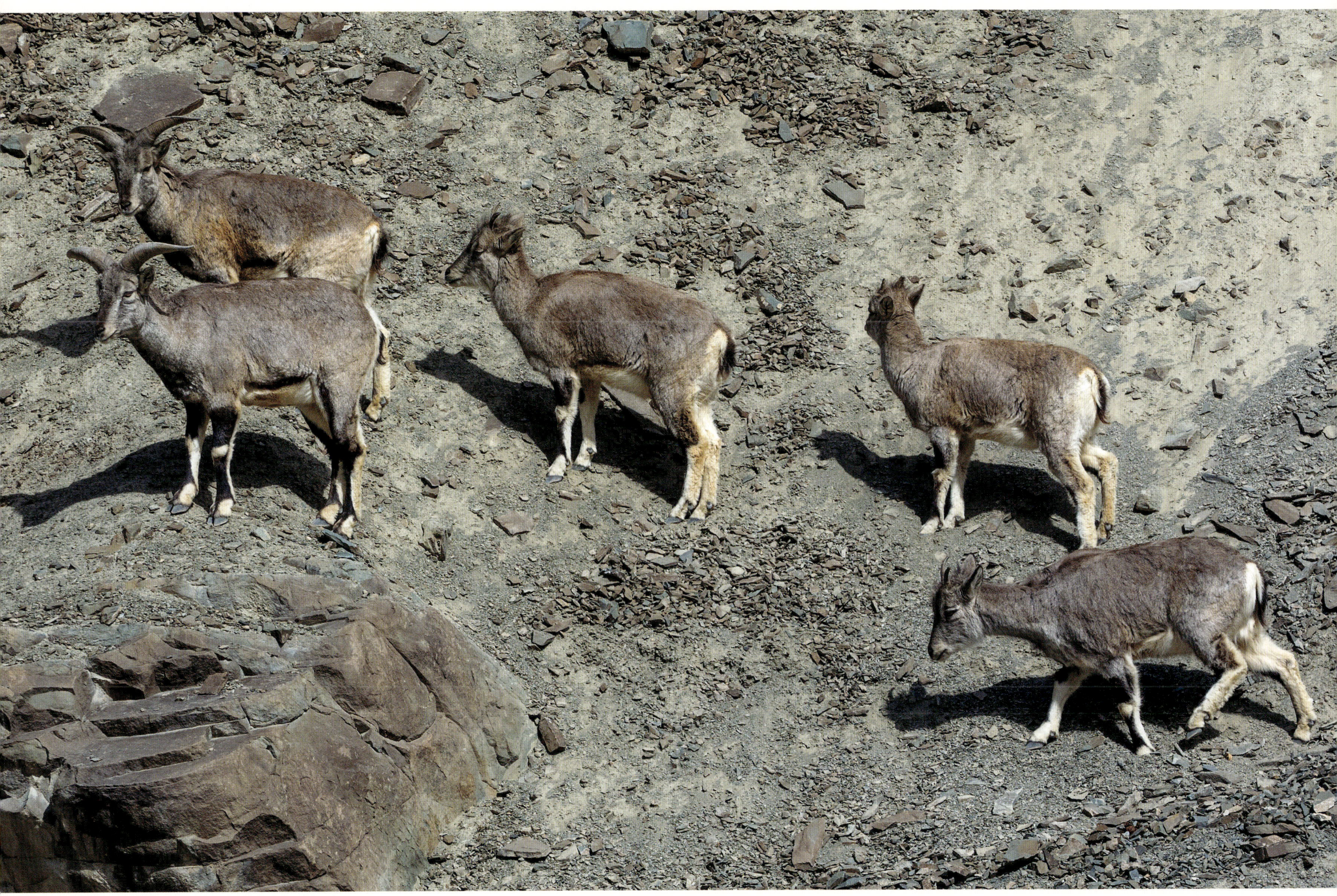

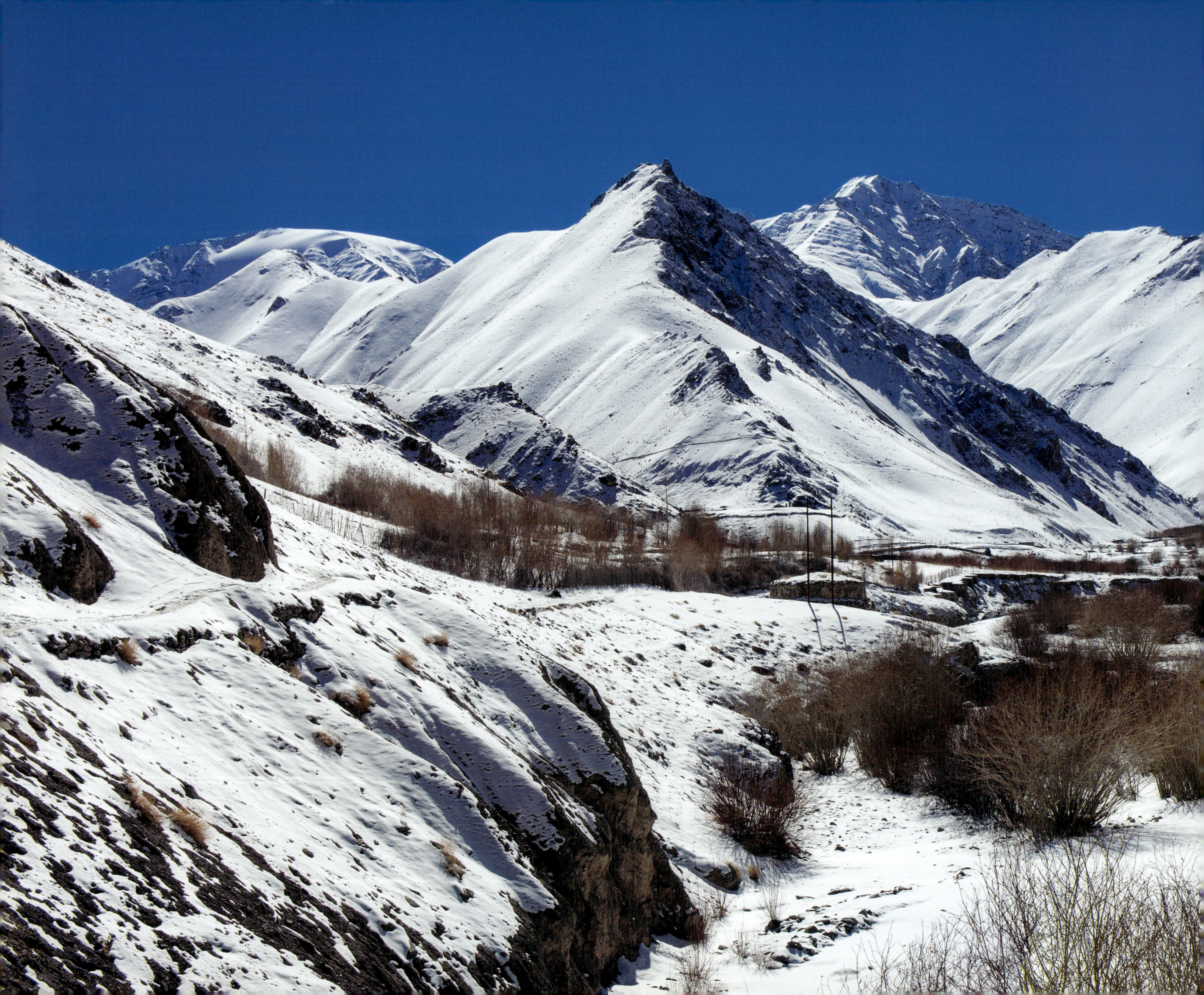

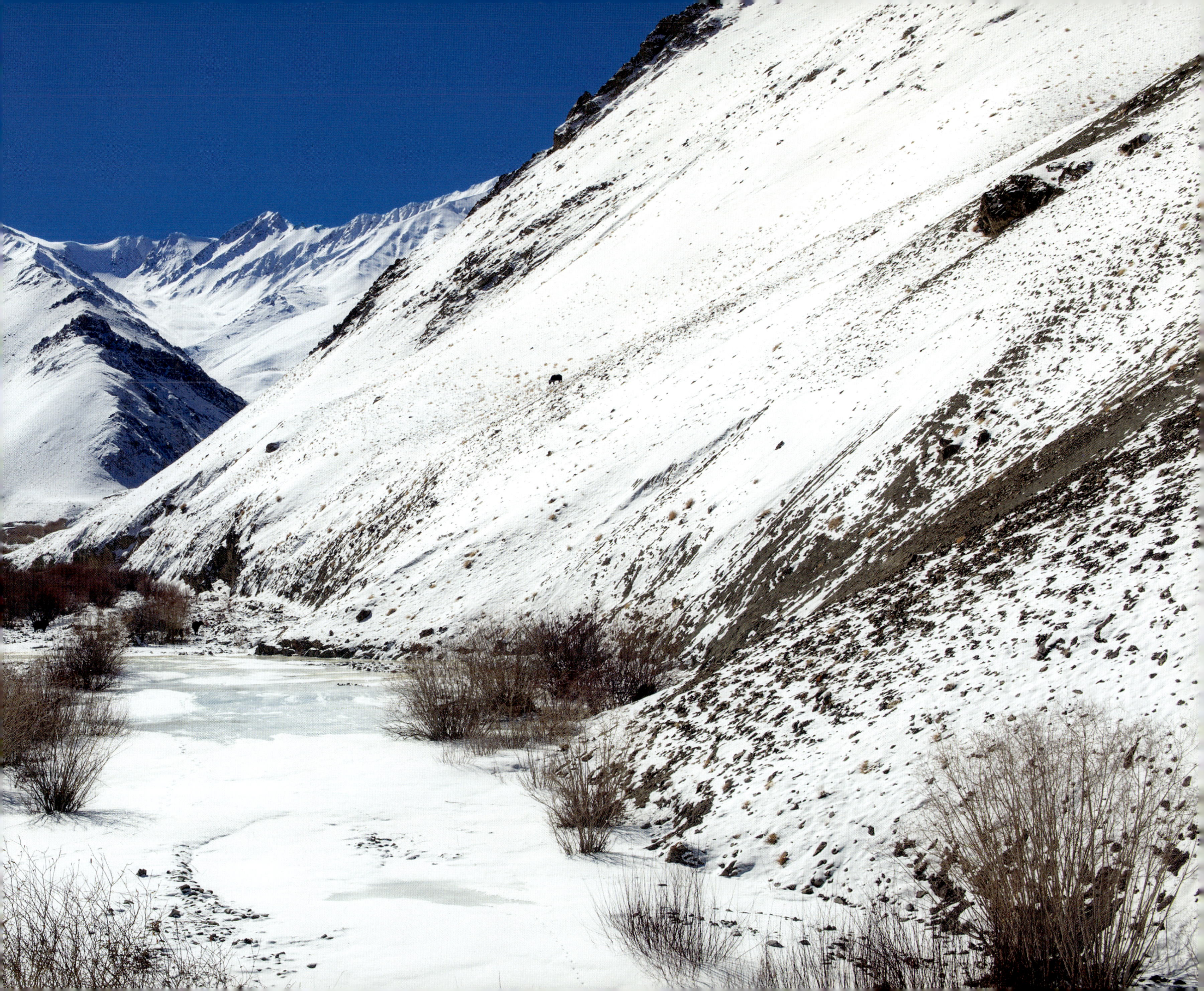

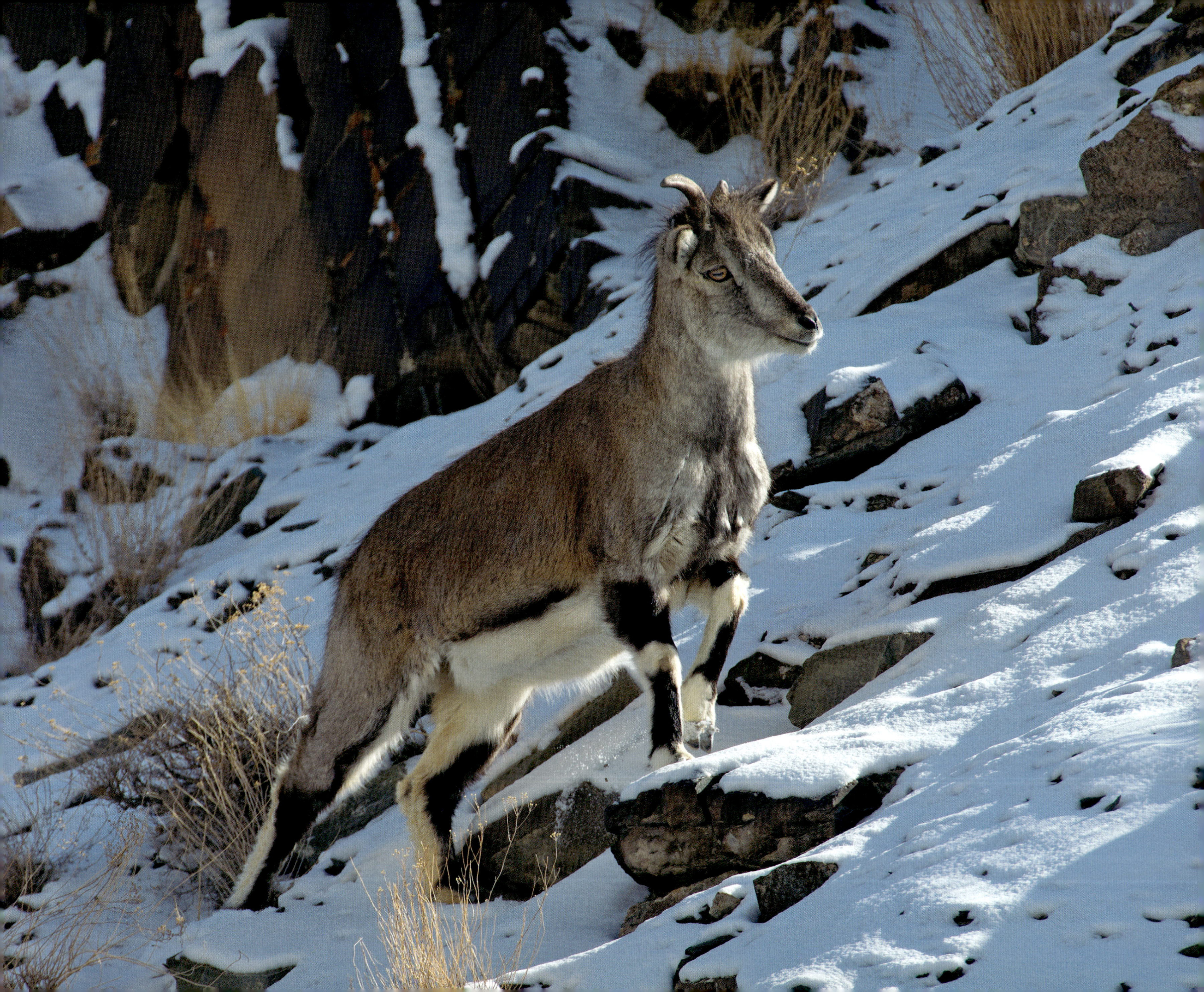

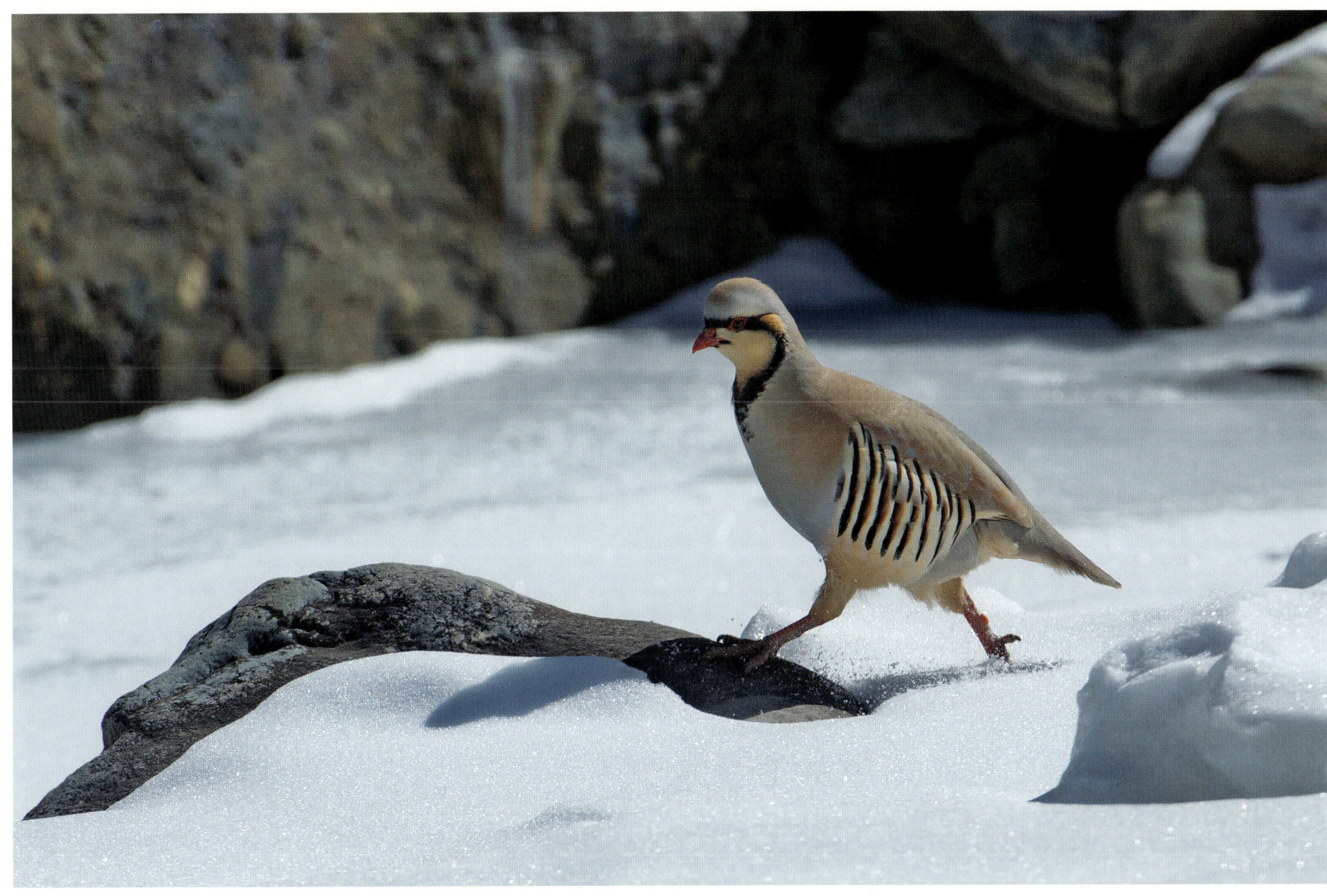

Few animals can cope with the harsh conditions found in the high Himalayas. The Himalayan blue sheep (opposite) is specially adapted to the cold mountain ranges, with its short dense coat and excellent camouflage. The chukar partridge (above) is able to adapt to different habitats, and will also inhabit warmer and lower regions.

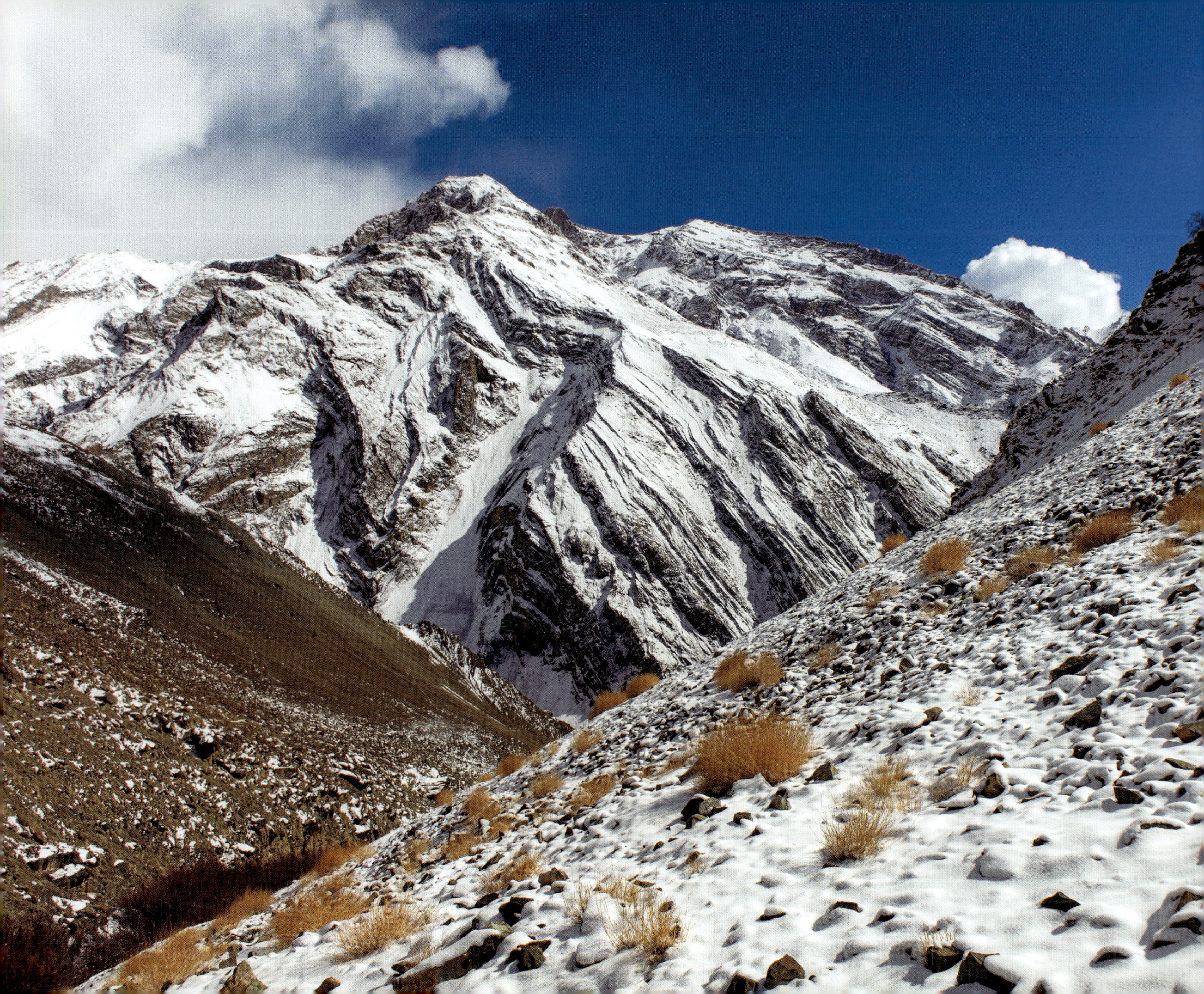

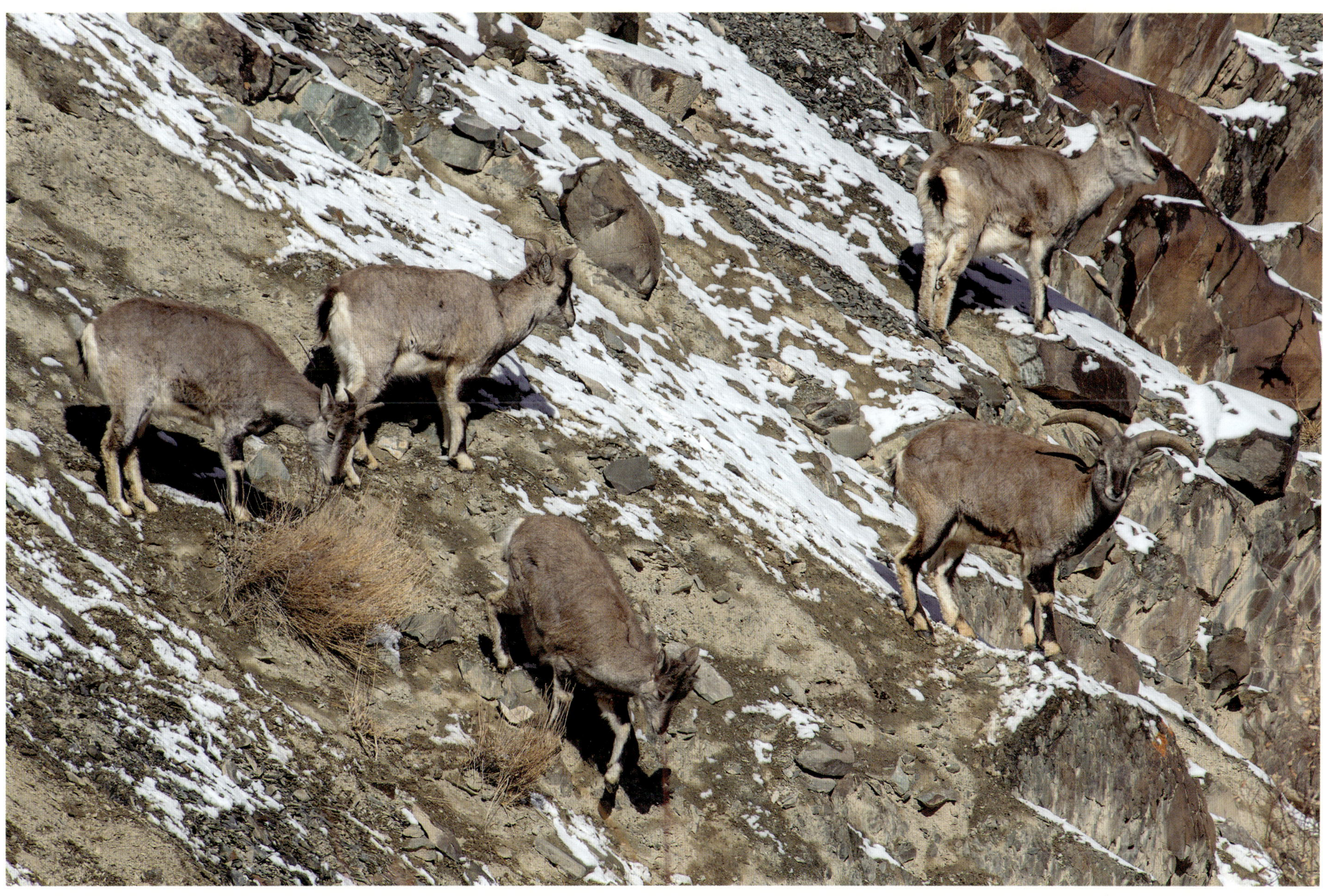

Himalayan blue sheep gather in herds and live in mountainous regions above the tree line. During winter, the snow cover forces them to descend lower elevations in order to find food. The snow leopards, for whom the Himalayan blue sheep are an important prey, also follow them to lower altitudes.

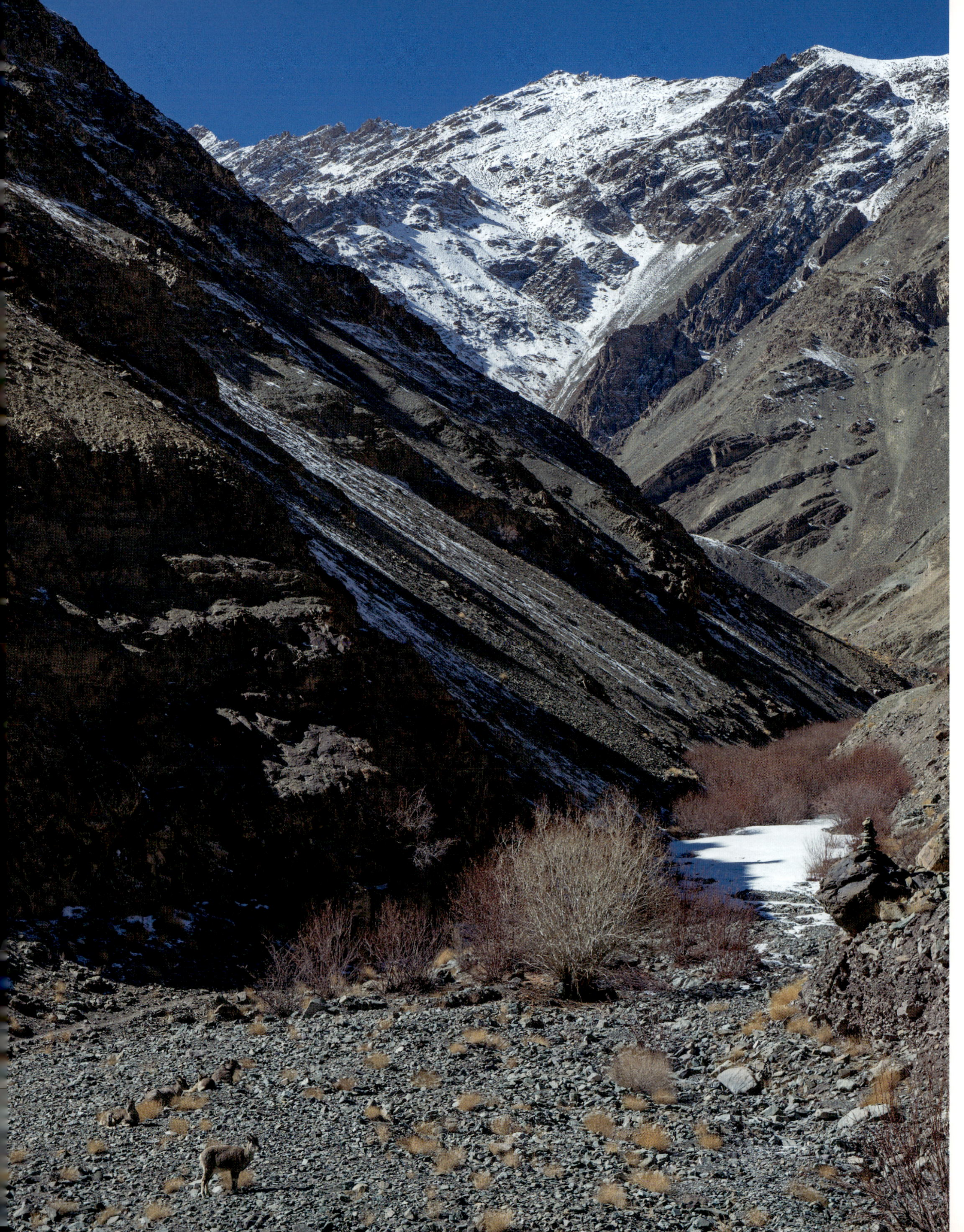

The endangered snow leopard (opposite) is an apex predator, living high up in the mountains. They are solitary animals who prefer to hunt various ungulates, yet the high altitudes offer little food for herbivores such as the Himalayan blue sheep (left), and so densities of prey, and in turn of predators, are low.

Overleaf:
High up in the Hemis National Park, a small stupa symbolises the Buddhist philosophy. Buddhism worships all forms of life, and poaching would be contradictory to religious beliefs.

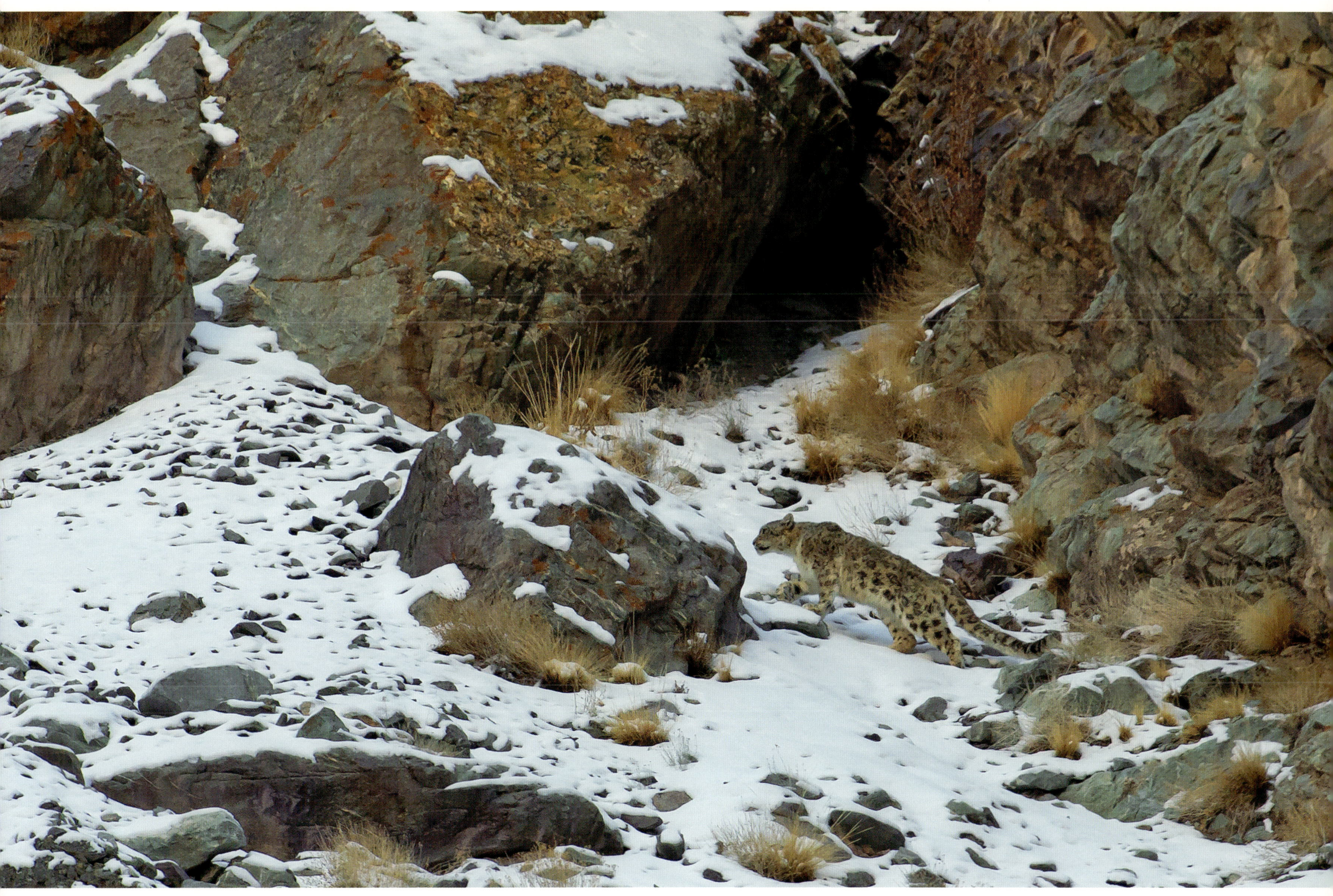

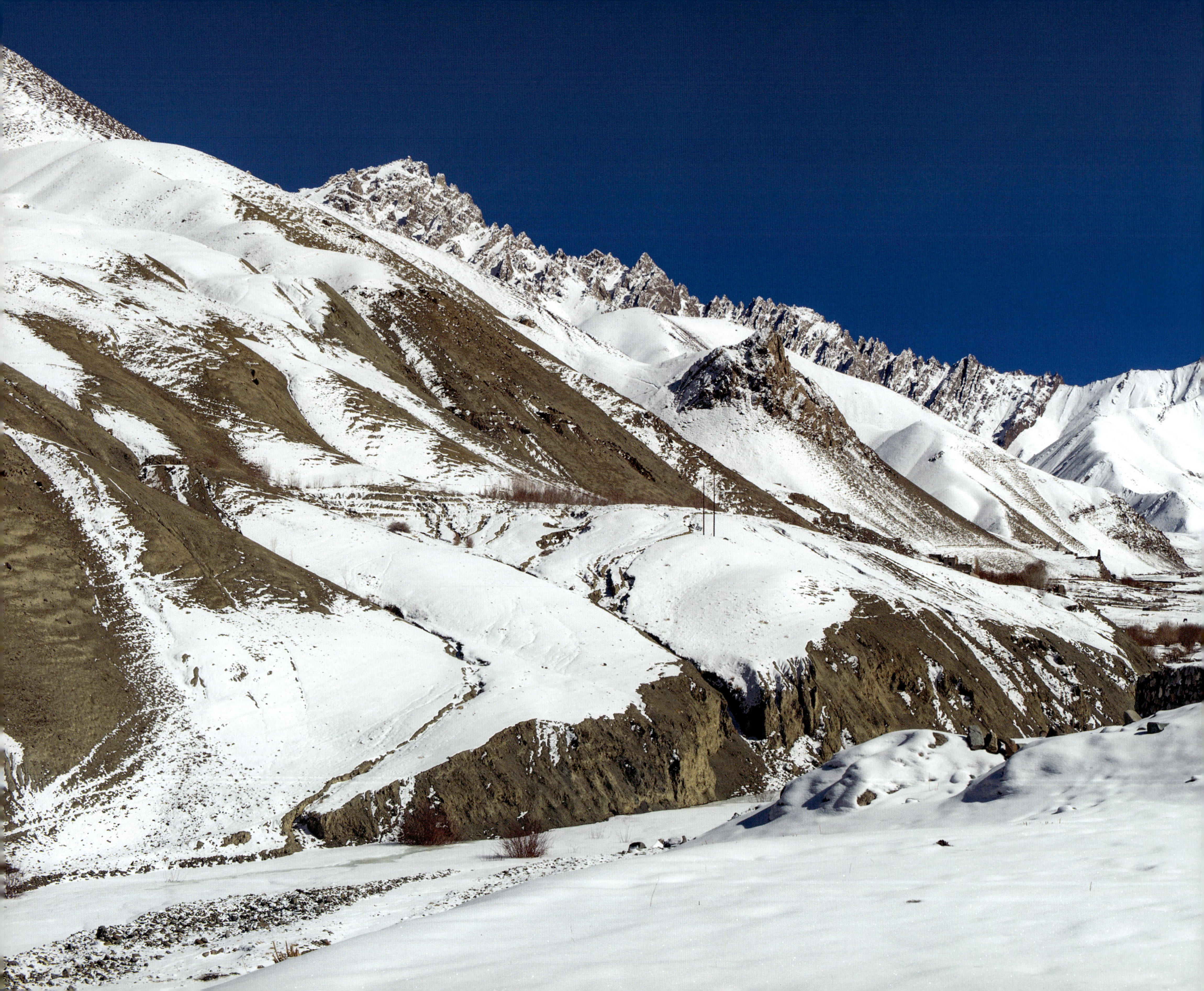

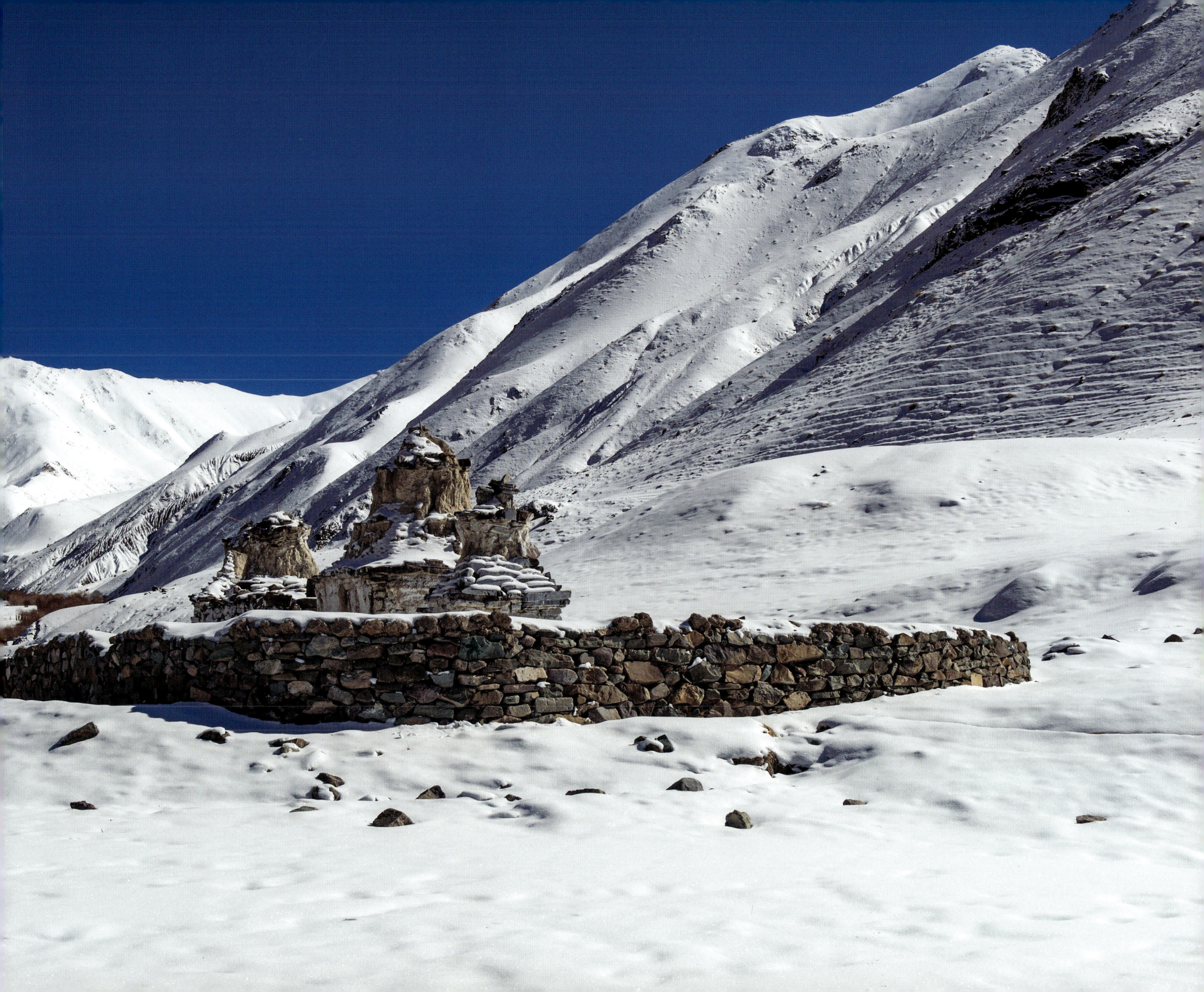

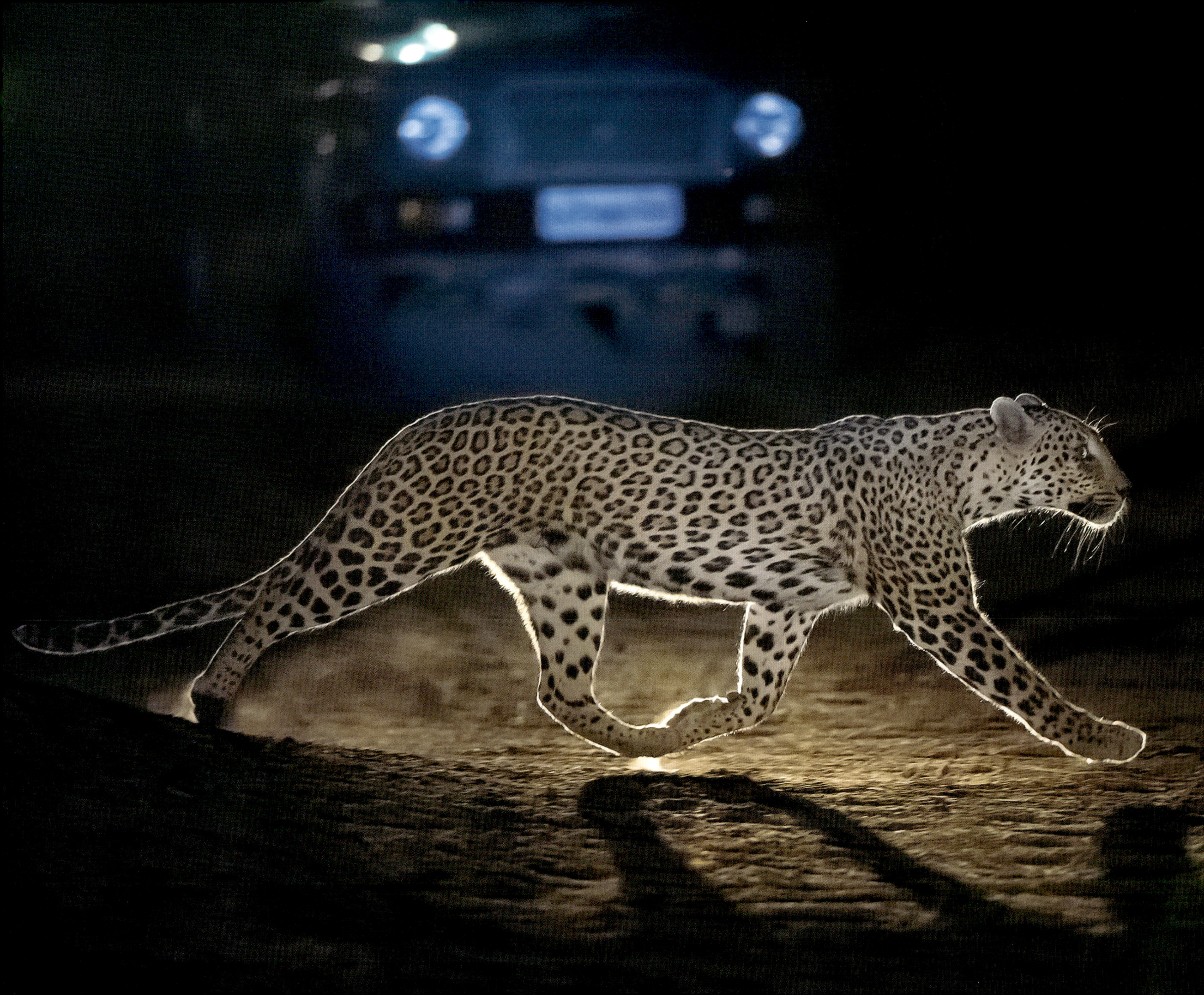

CROSSROADS

Nature and culture, man and wildlife; each are closely intertwined in India. This is why so much wildlife has survived to this day in a country with a higher density of human population than either in Great Britain or in Germany.

The respect for all forms of life is deeply rooted in faith, practised in Hinduism, Buddhism and Jainism. These religions have a profound influence on people's everyday life and on how they treat their fellow creatures. Many people are vegetarian, and most would not kill an animal for either fun or for sport. Tolerance towards wildlife is generally high, and many farmers accept that they will lose a little share of their crops to gazelles or deer. The concept of reincarnation and improving karma by doing good deeds and avoiding evil is still widespread, and especially so in the countryside. One famous example is the feeding of thousands of demoiselle cranes in Rajasthan, which is done so for religious reasons.

The Bishnoi, however, are an extreme case, even for Indian standards. Their religion is founded solely on the principle of conserving nature, where man and animal exist in perfect harmony, and where every living organism has an equal right to the land.

A leopard crosses a village road in Rajasthan. During the day these leopards seek shelter in rocky outcrops, but at night, they can venture into cultivated land and villages, finding easy prey such as goats, poultry, and even dogs.

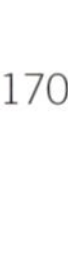

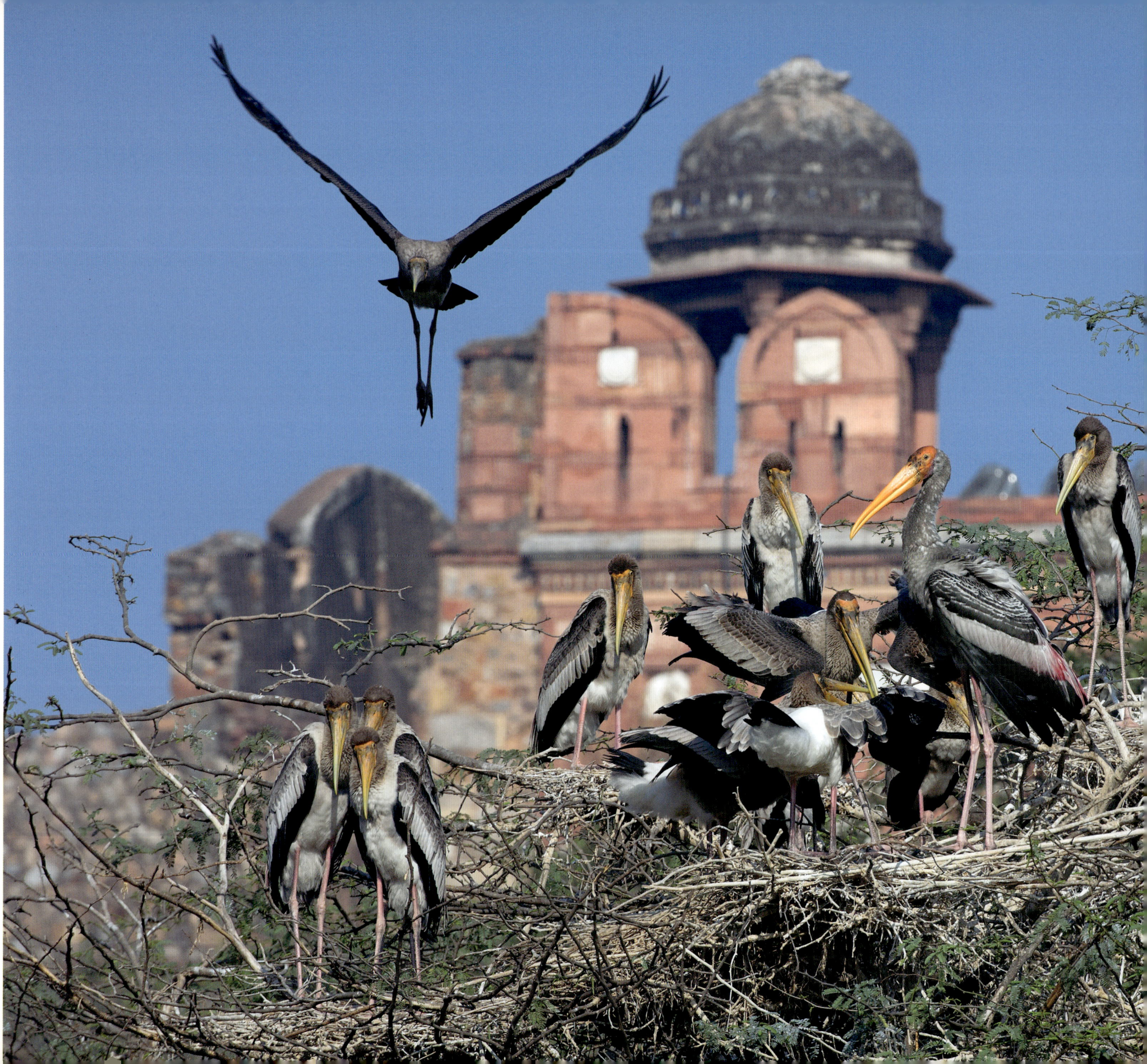

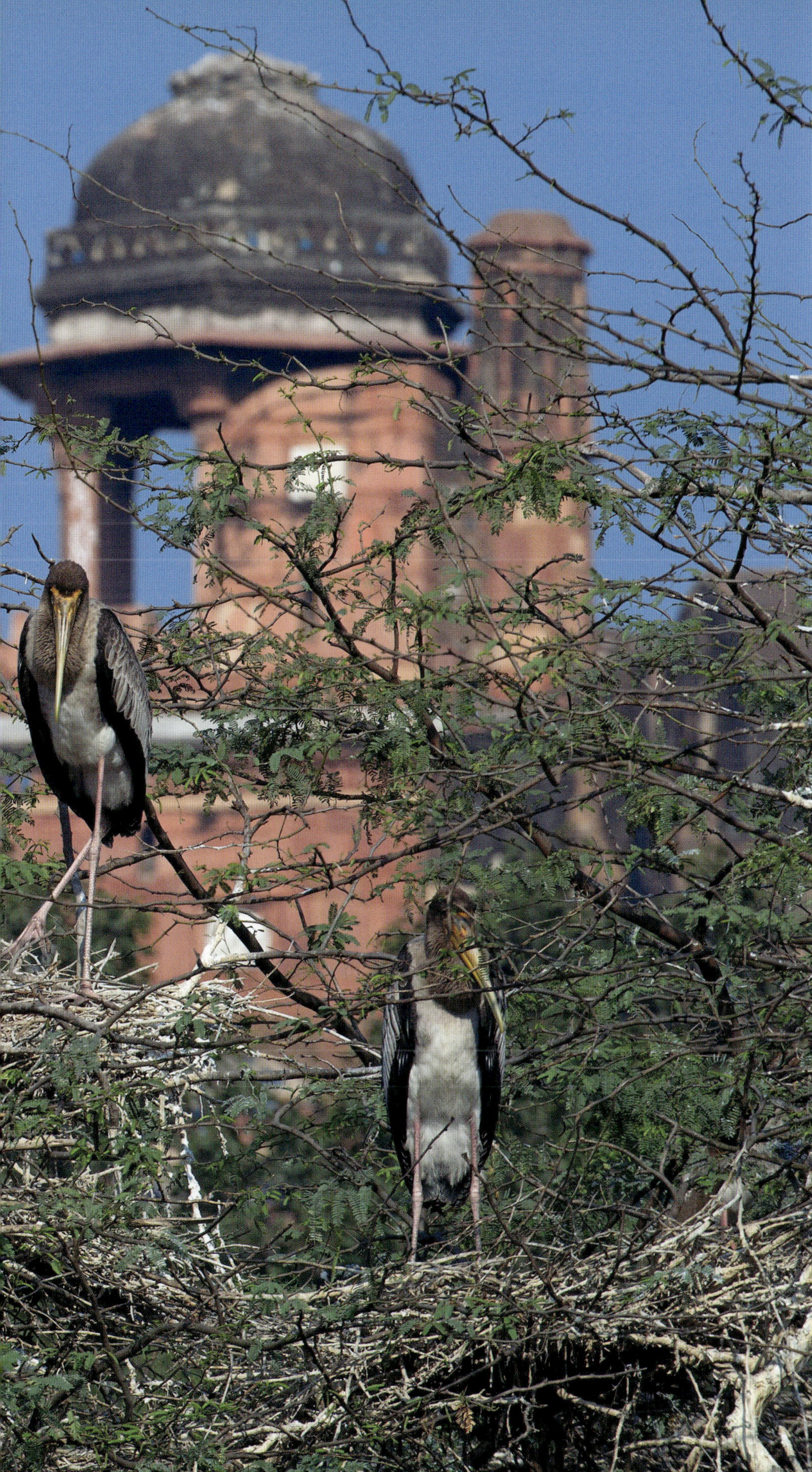

A colony of painted storks is seen thriving in India's capital, New Delhi, showing that wildlife still has a place in modern India.

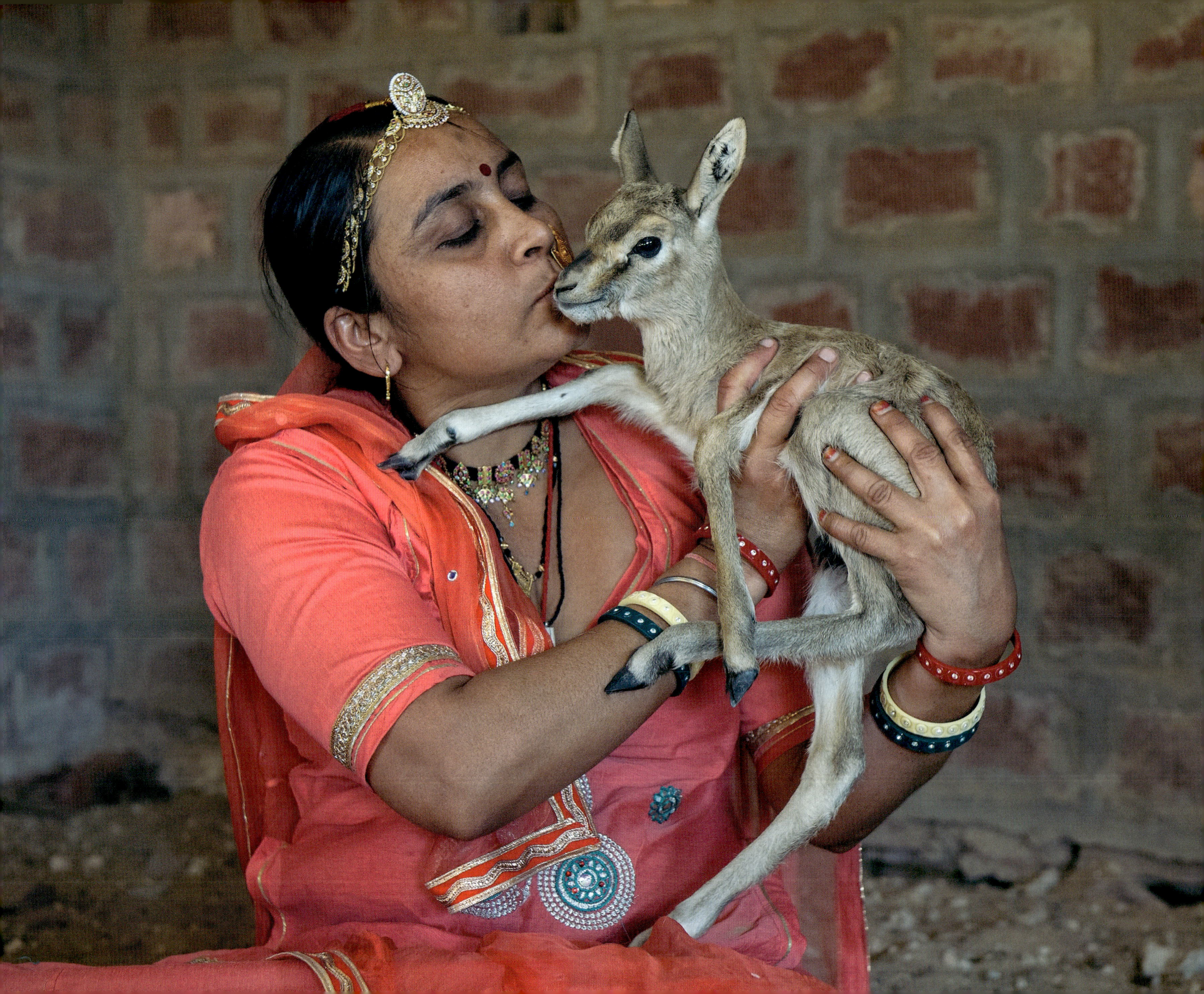

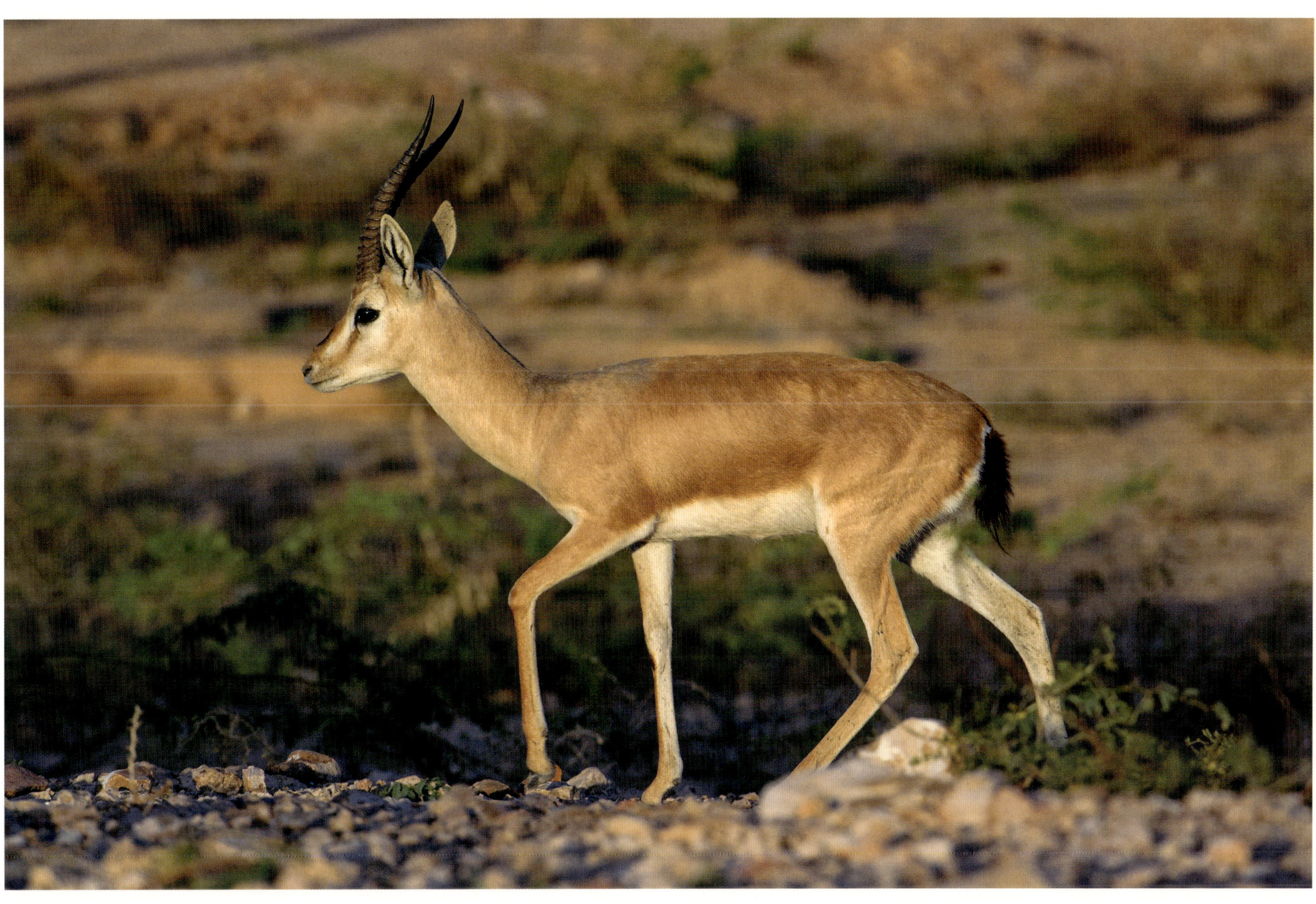

The Bishnoi are a religious community living in northwestern India. They do not treat wildlife as a resource, but as fellow creatures. The Indian gazelle or chinkara is an animal with whom the Bishnoi have very special relations.

Bishnoi women will traditionally take in an orphaned or injured gazelle fawn, breast-feeding them alongside their own children, before releasing the animals back into the wild. The Bishnoi, whose religious beliefs have a direct impact on conservation, refuse to kill animals or cut trees.

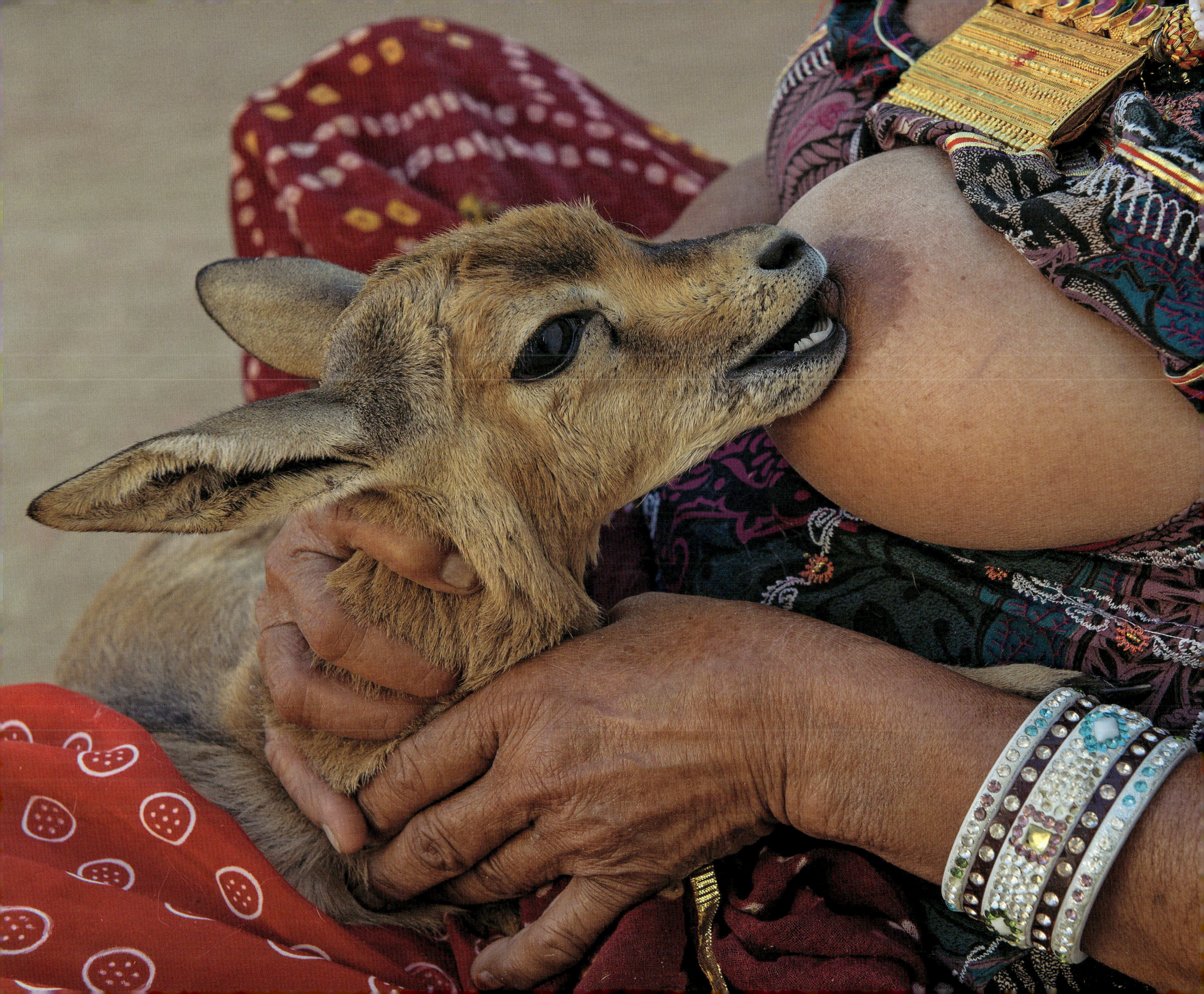

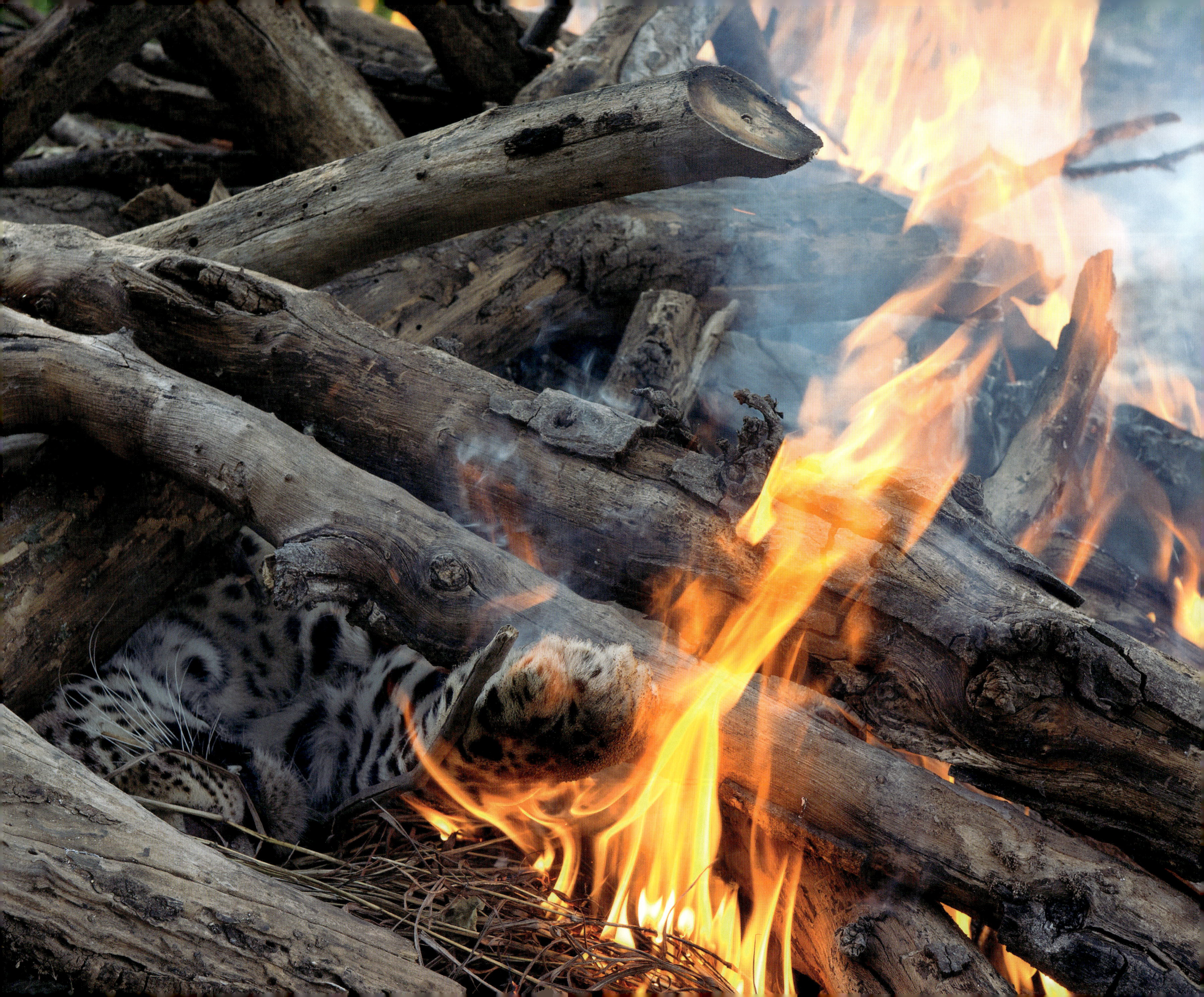

Cremation is not exclusive to humans in India. The body of this dead leopard is committed to the flames outside the Ranthambhore National Park. This not only prevents the potentially valuable fur and body parts from ending up in the wildlife trade, but is also a way of paying homage to the animal, especially as the belief in reincarnation is still widespread throughout India.

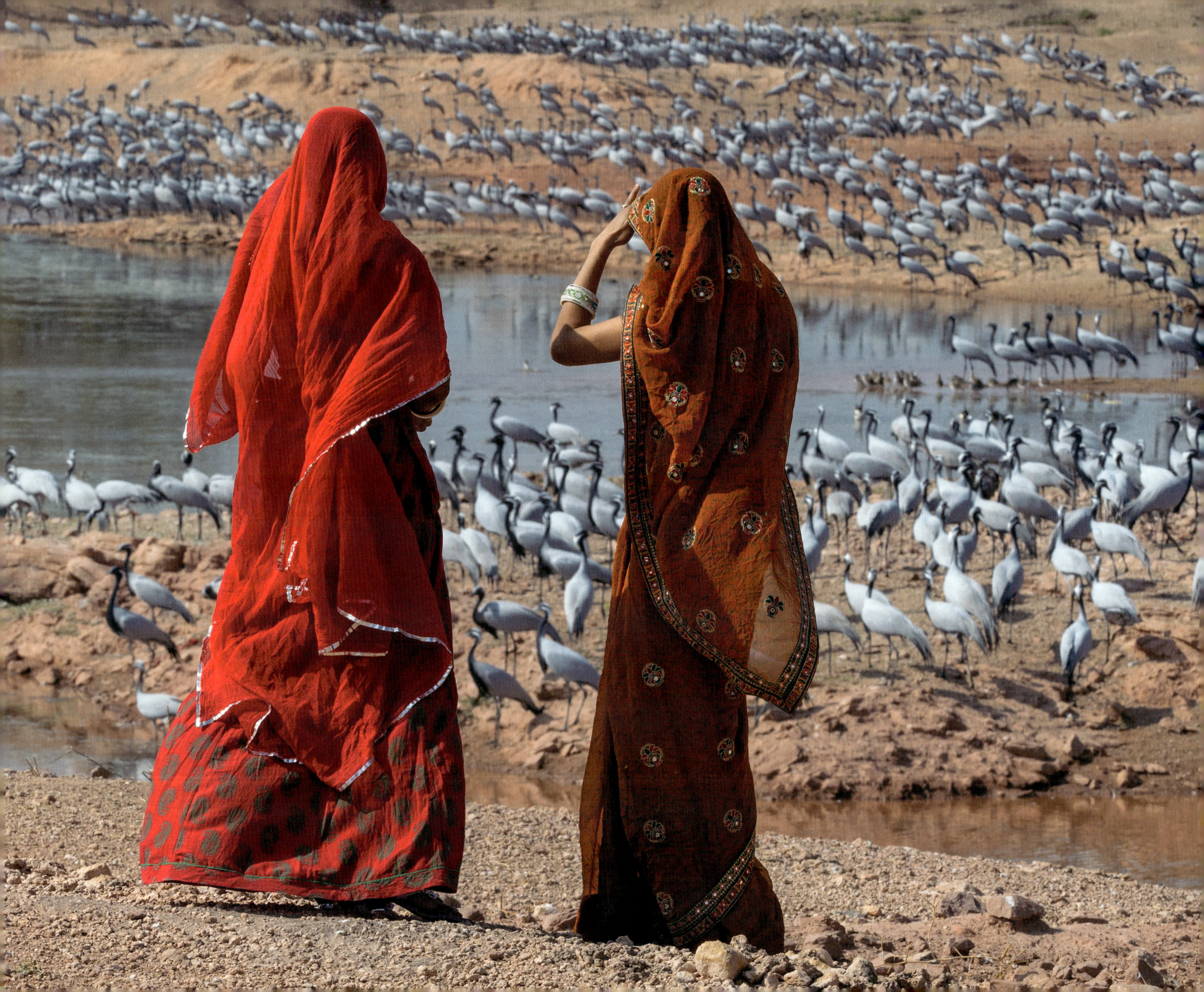

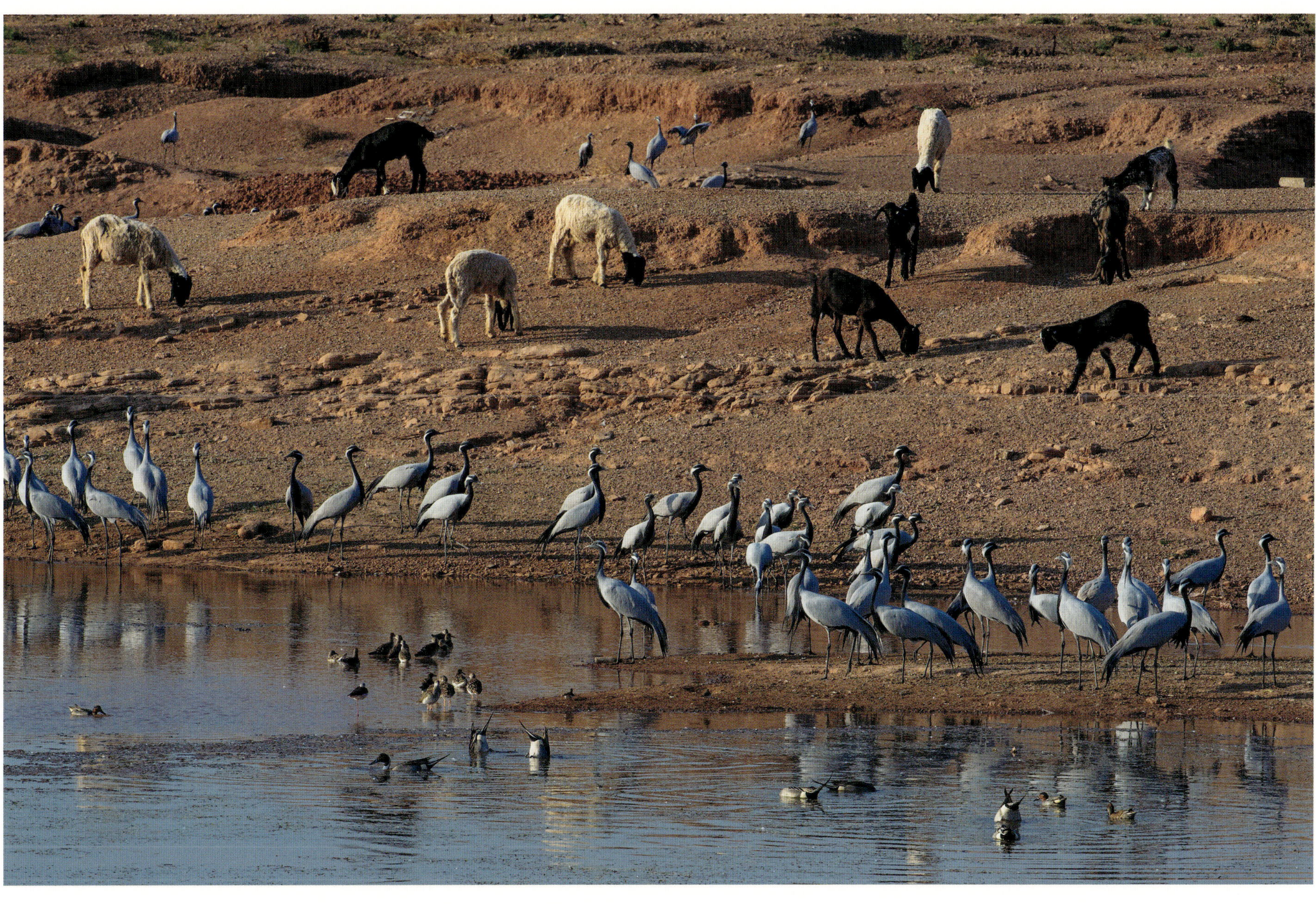

Two ladies from Rajasthan marvel at the gathering of demoiselle cranes outside their village. The birds share the local reservoir with domestic goats and waterfowl.

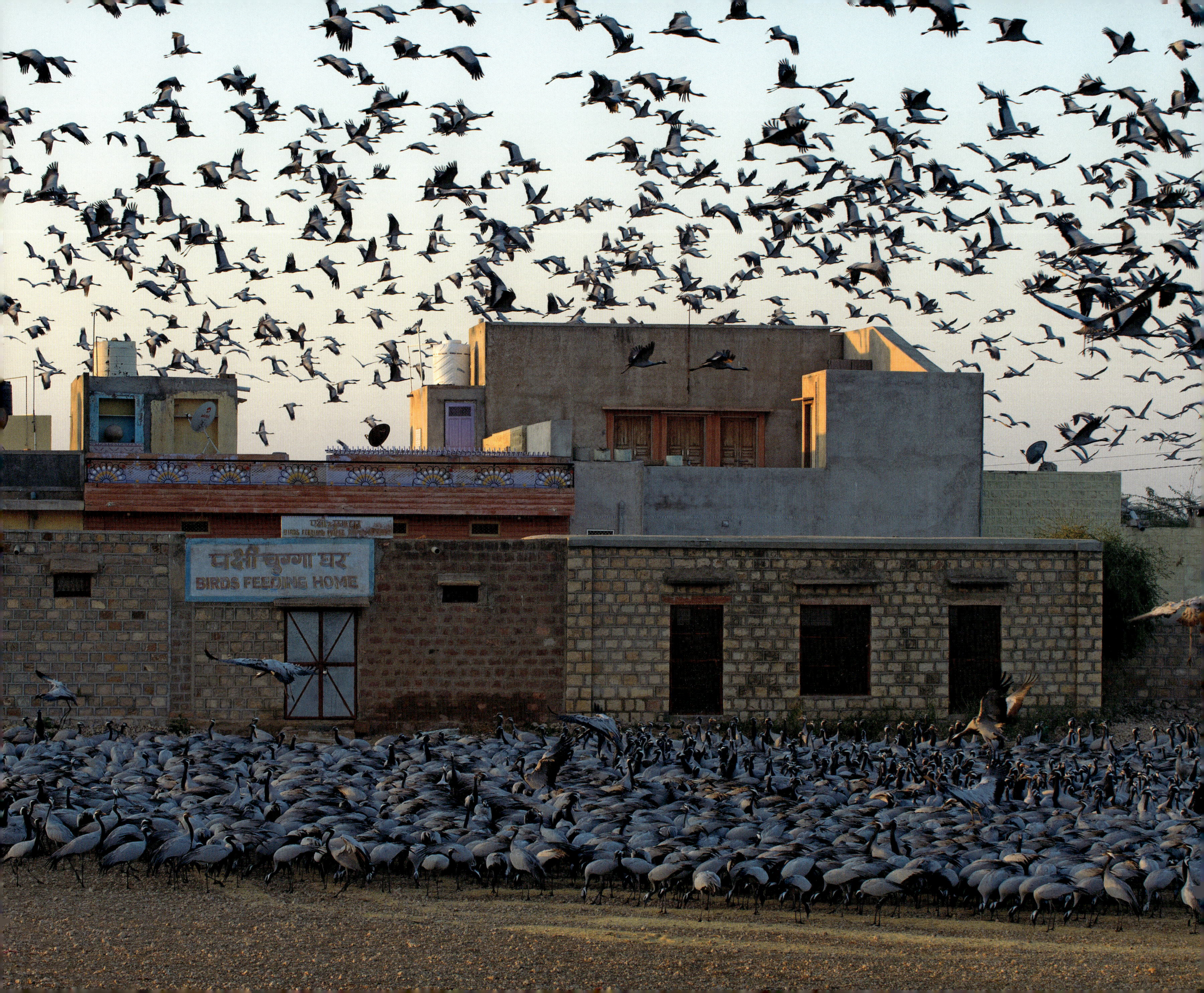
पक्षी चुग्गा घर
BIRDS FEEDING HOME

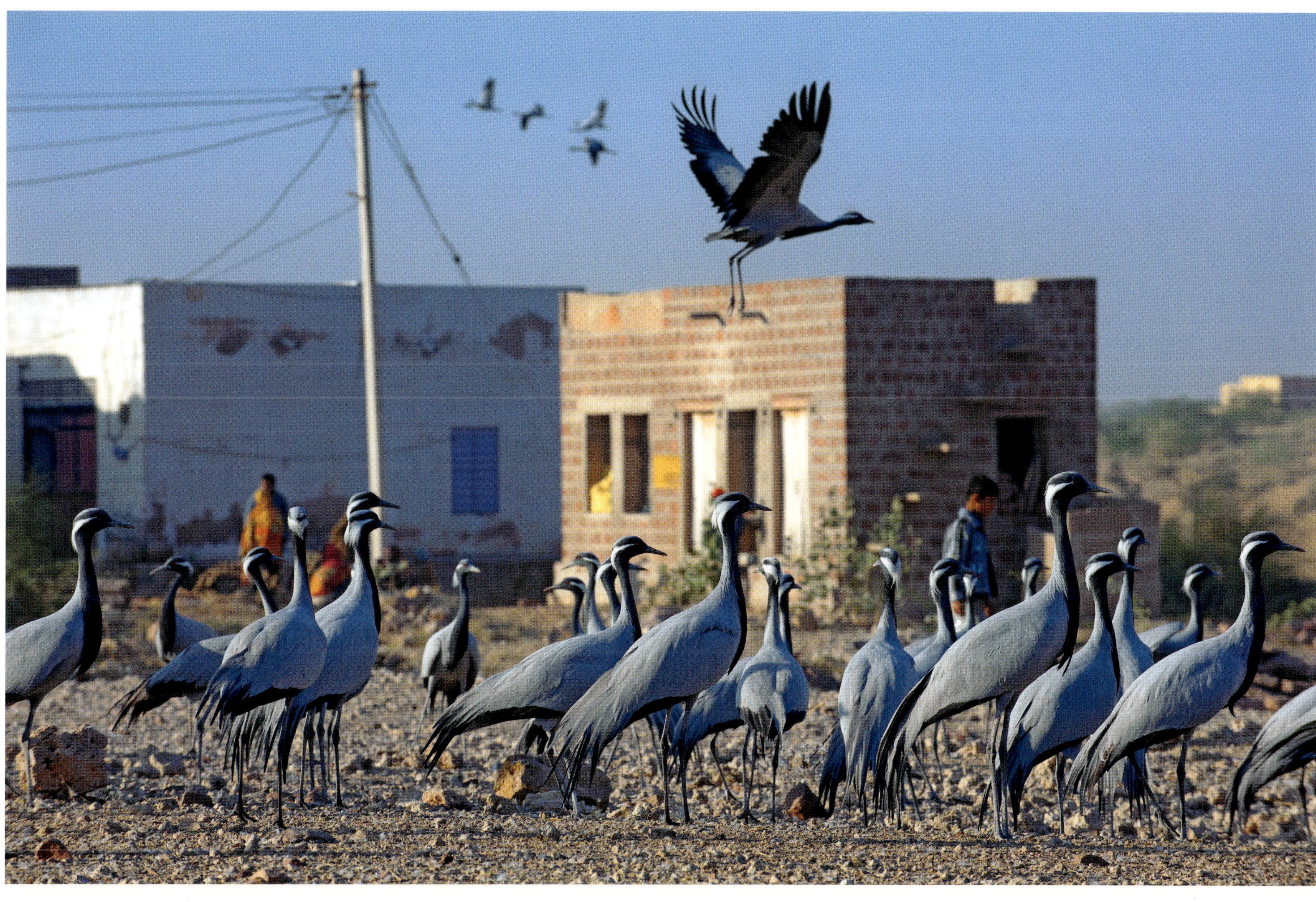

Every winter, thousands of demoiselle cranes flock to the village of Khichan in Rajasthan. The local Jain community feed them vast amounts of grain, as the birds are venerated and the act of feeding them is supposed to bring good karma.

182

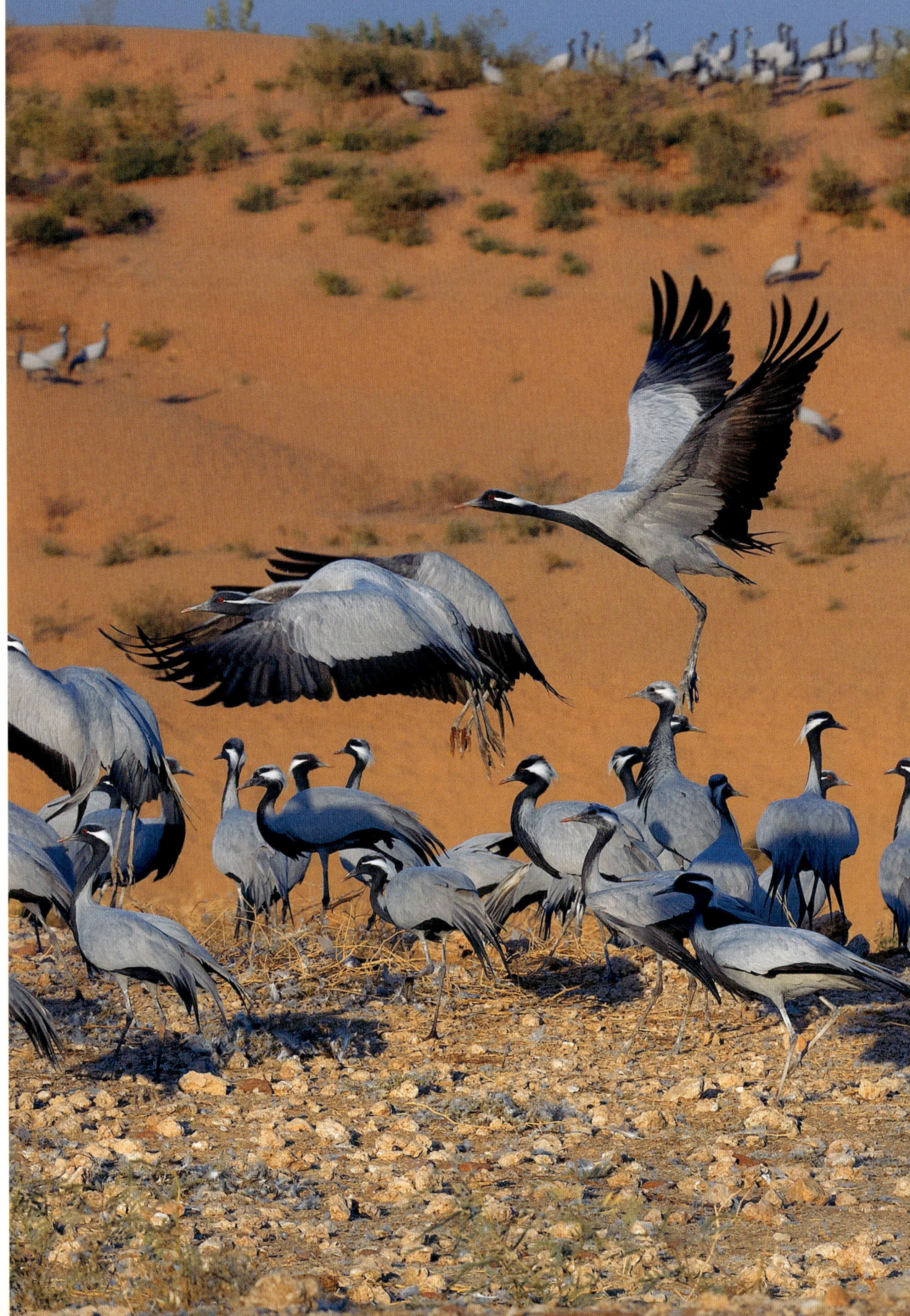

A villager rouses demoiselle cranes that are resting near his house. For the cranes, the benefits of being fed far outweigh such occasional disturbances.

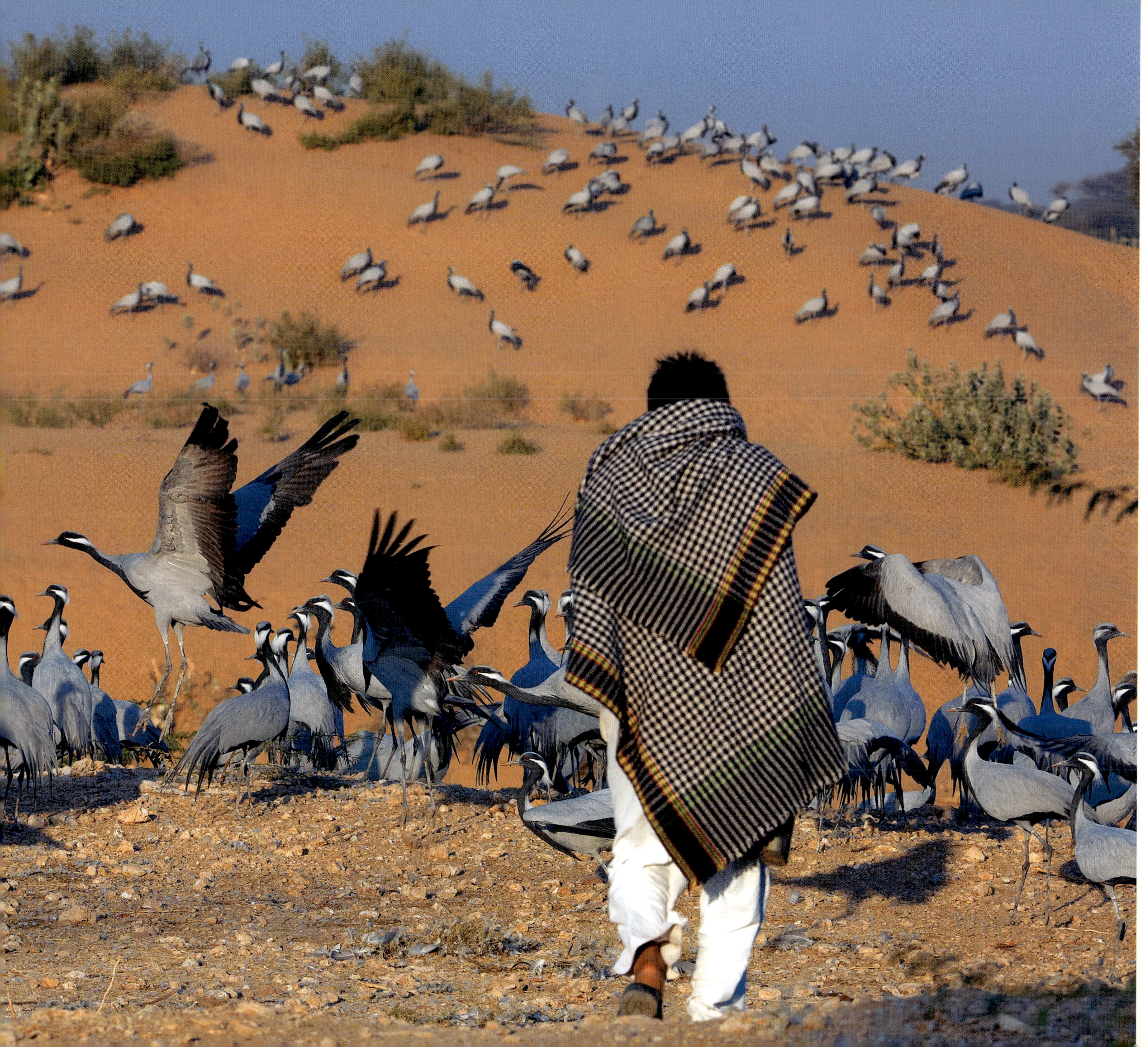

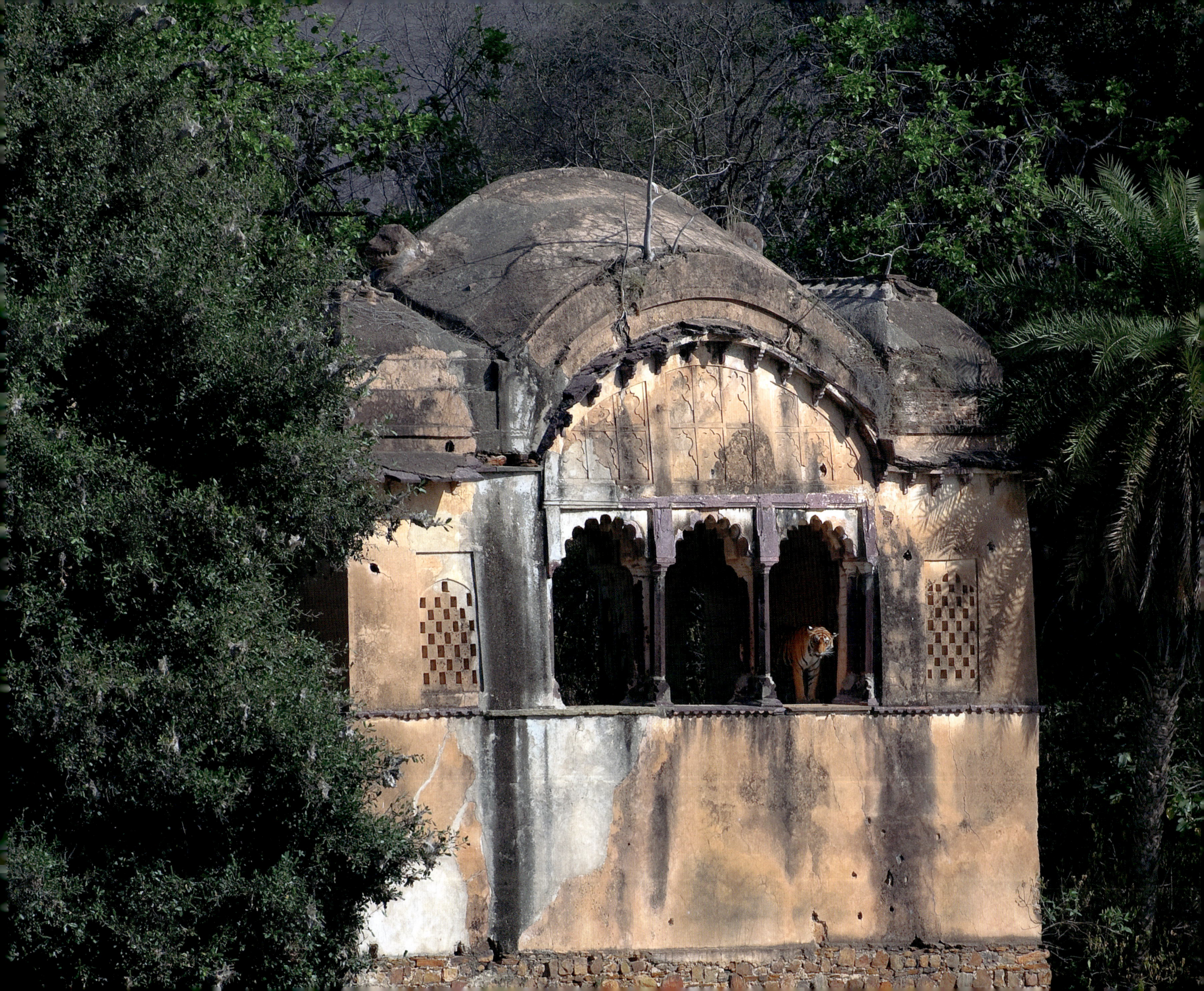

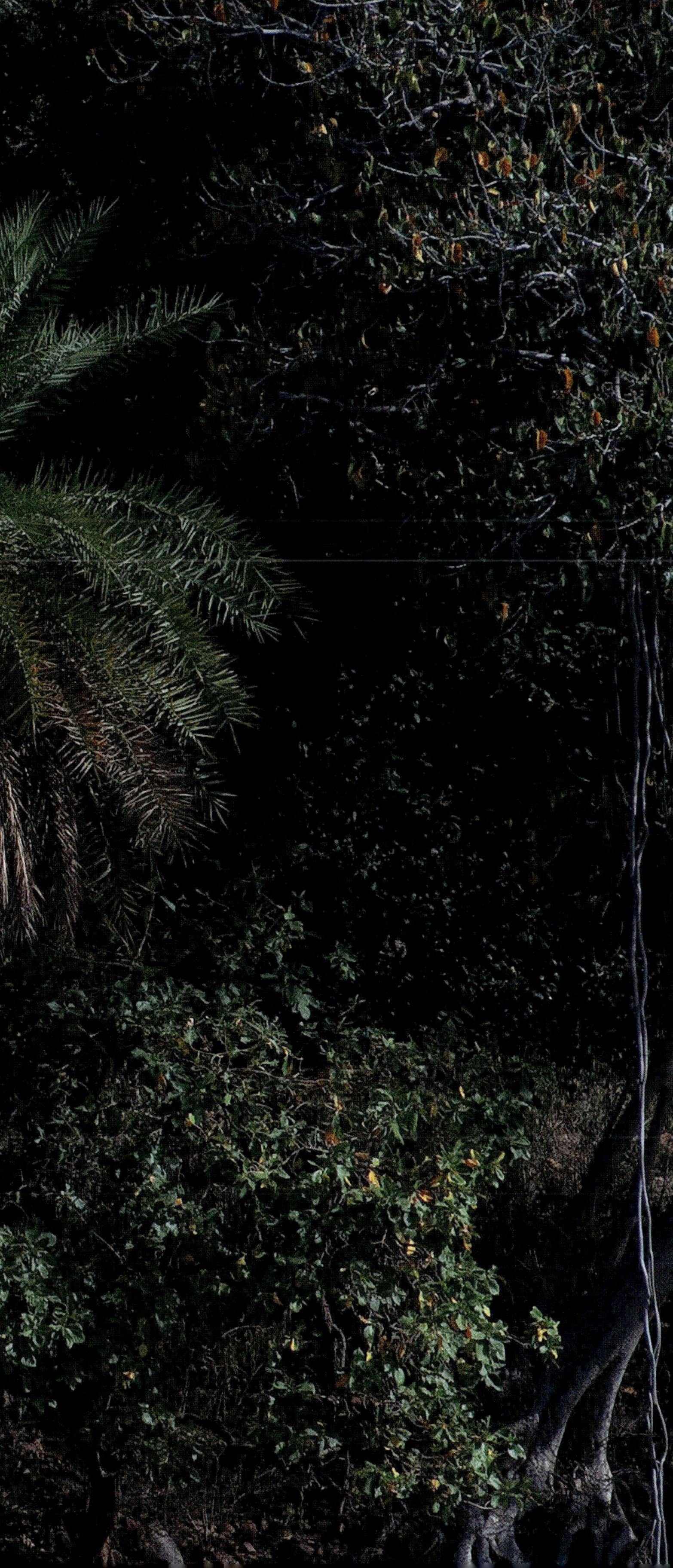

Crossovers between nature and culture are a typical sight in India. The Ranthambhore National Park in Rajasthan sites some impressive ruins that are slowly being overrun by the surrounding vegetation. Here, a tigress has chosen the shady hall of an ancient ruin for her midday rest.

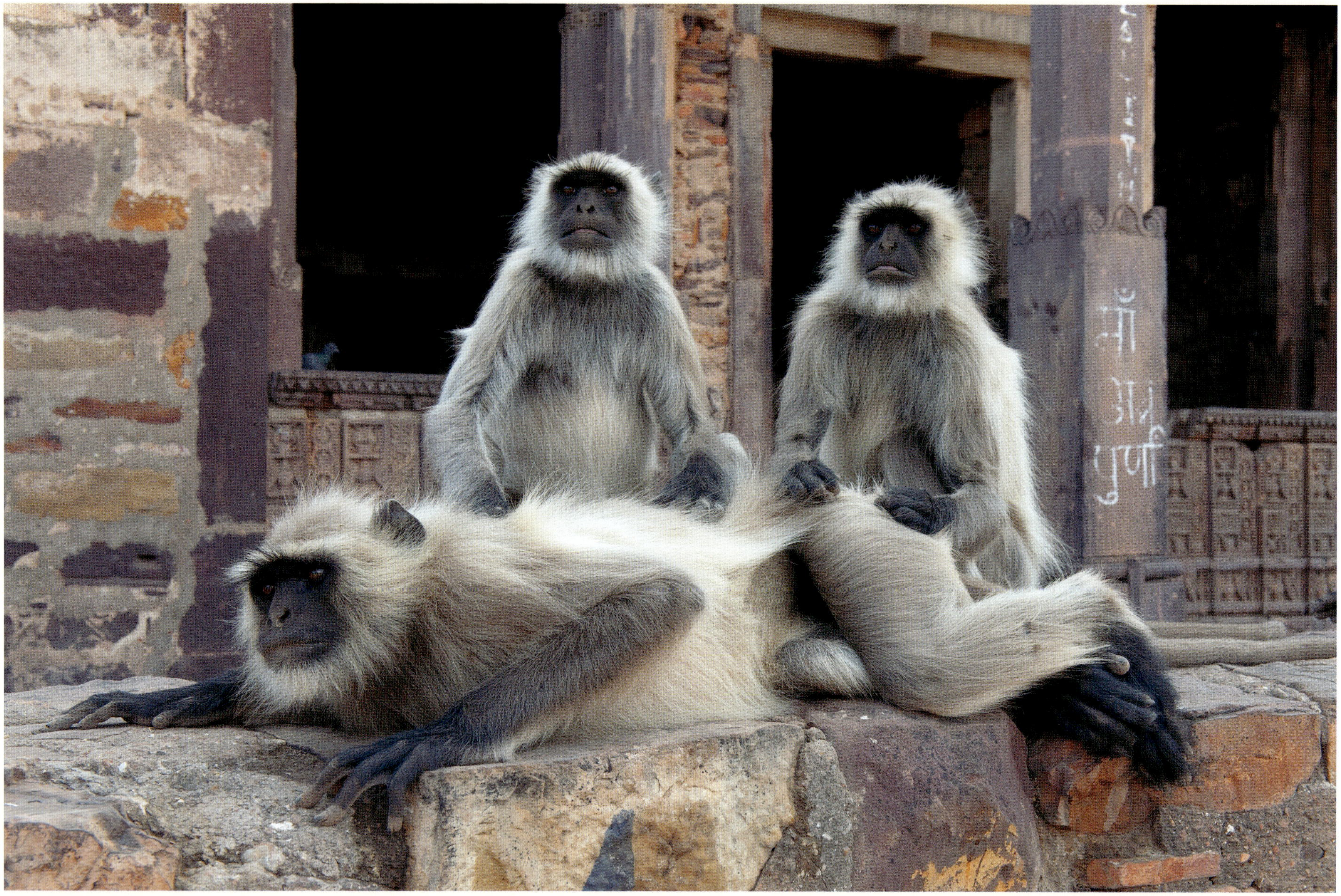

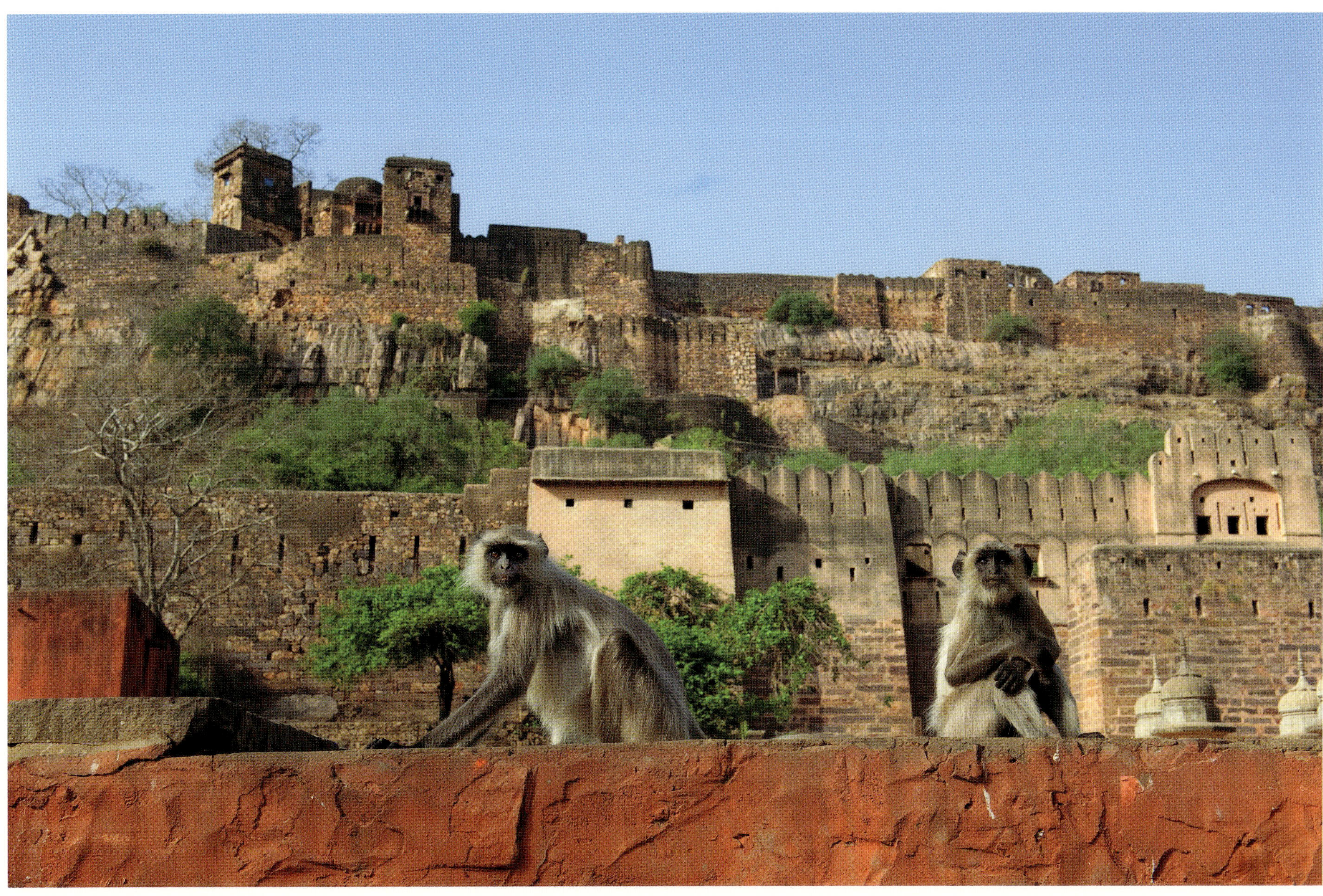

Monkeys such as these Bengal Hanuman langurs have colonised ruins such as the historic Ranthambhore fortress (above). The ruins offer safe lookouts and hiding places, allowing for social activities such as grooming (left).

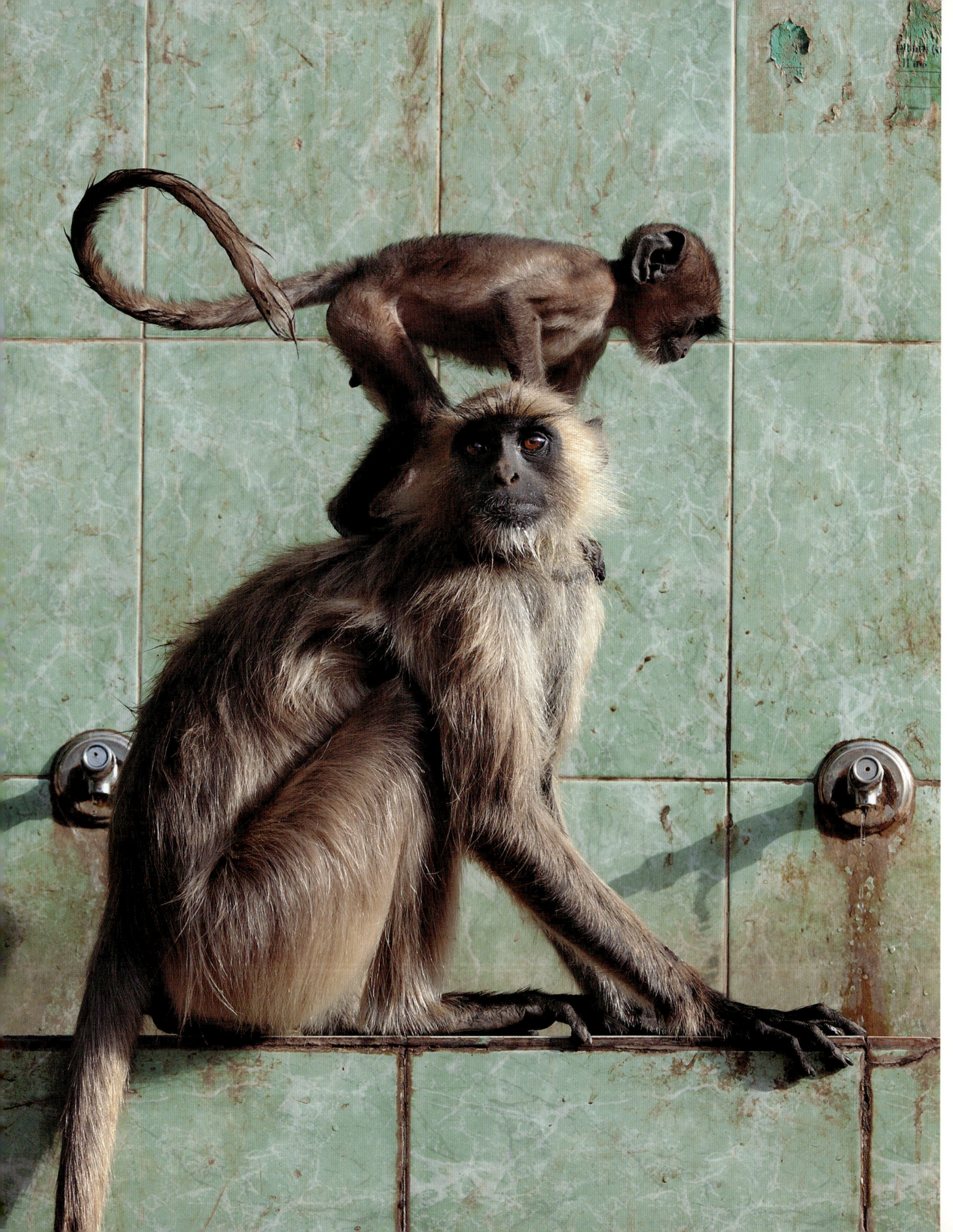

Monkeys, sych as this bonnet macaque (right) are smart creatures that are often found in the vicinity of man. They are highly adaptable and can learn to exploit resources otherwise inaccessible to other wildlife. Here, (left) a young Bengal Hanuman langur is taught to drink water from a tap by his mother.

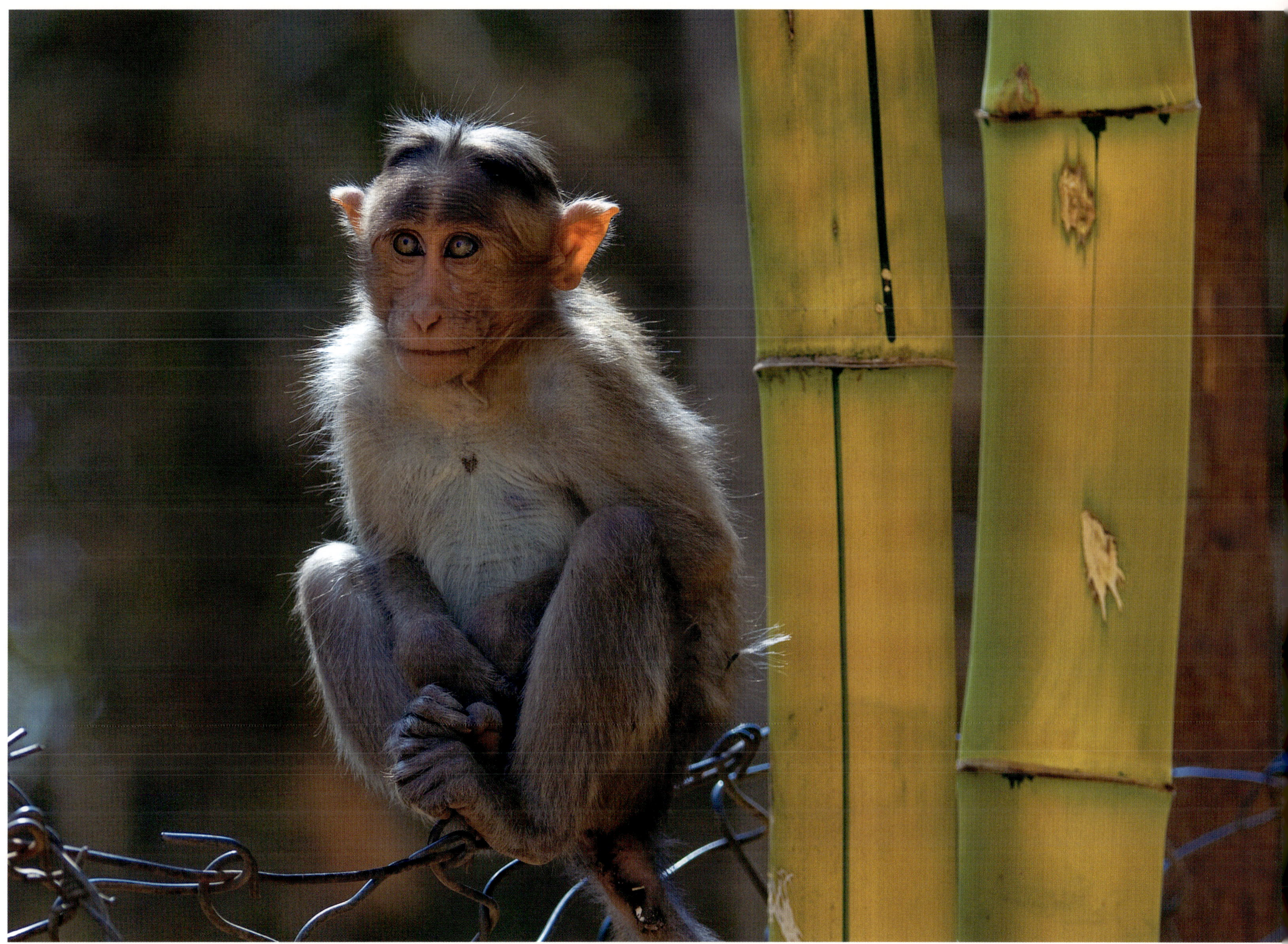

Bengal Hanuman langurs are considered to be sacred animals. Hindus revere them as the symbol of the monkey deity Hanuman. Priests and devotees feed the monkeys, which is why they are commonly found around temples.

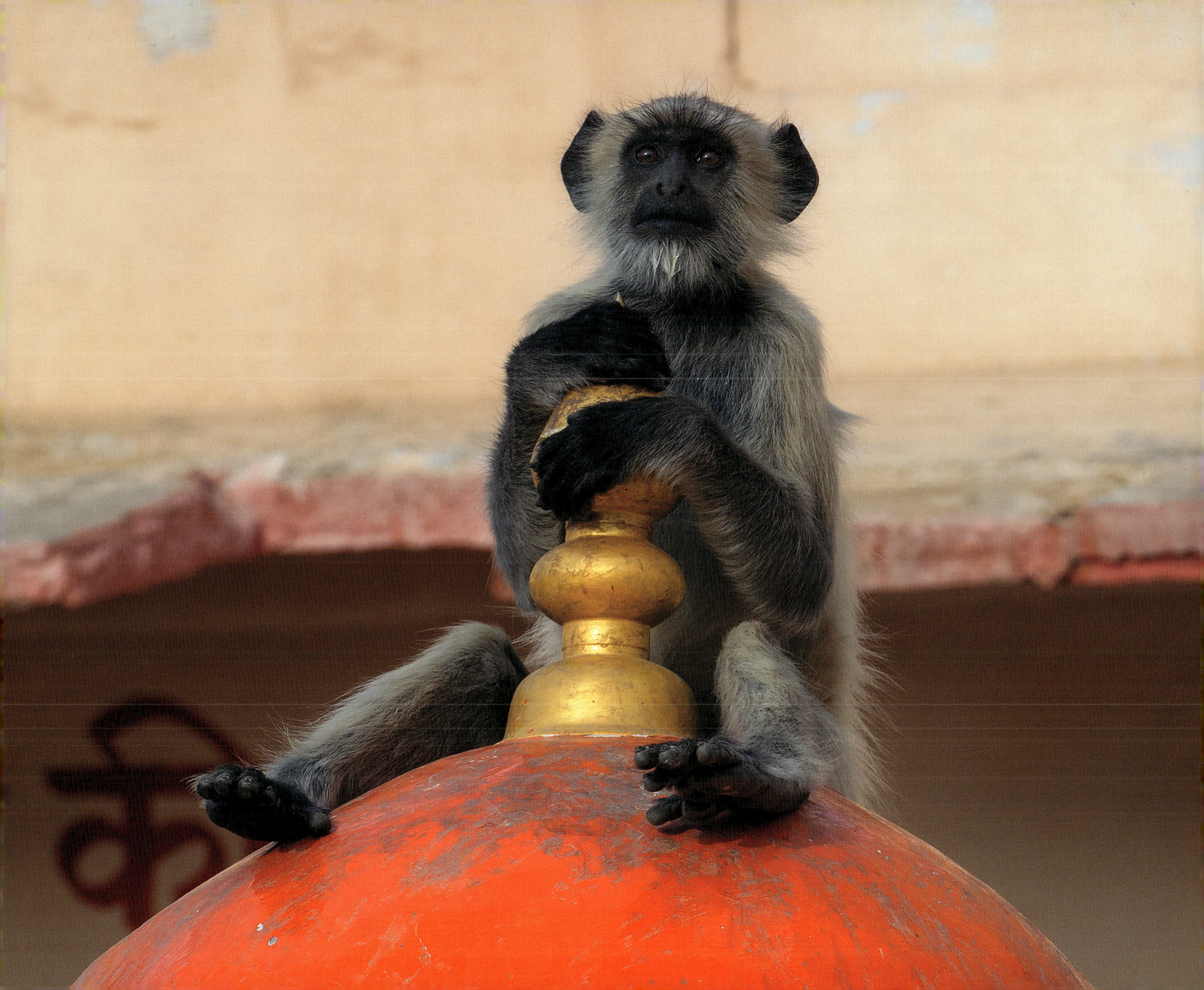

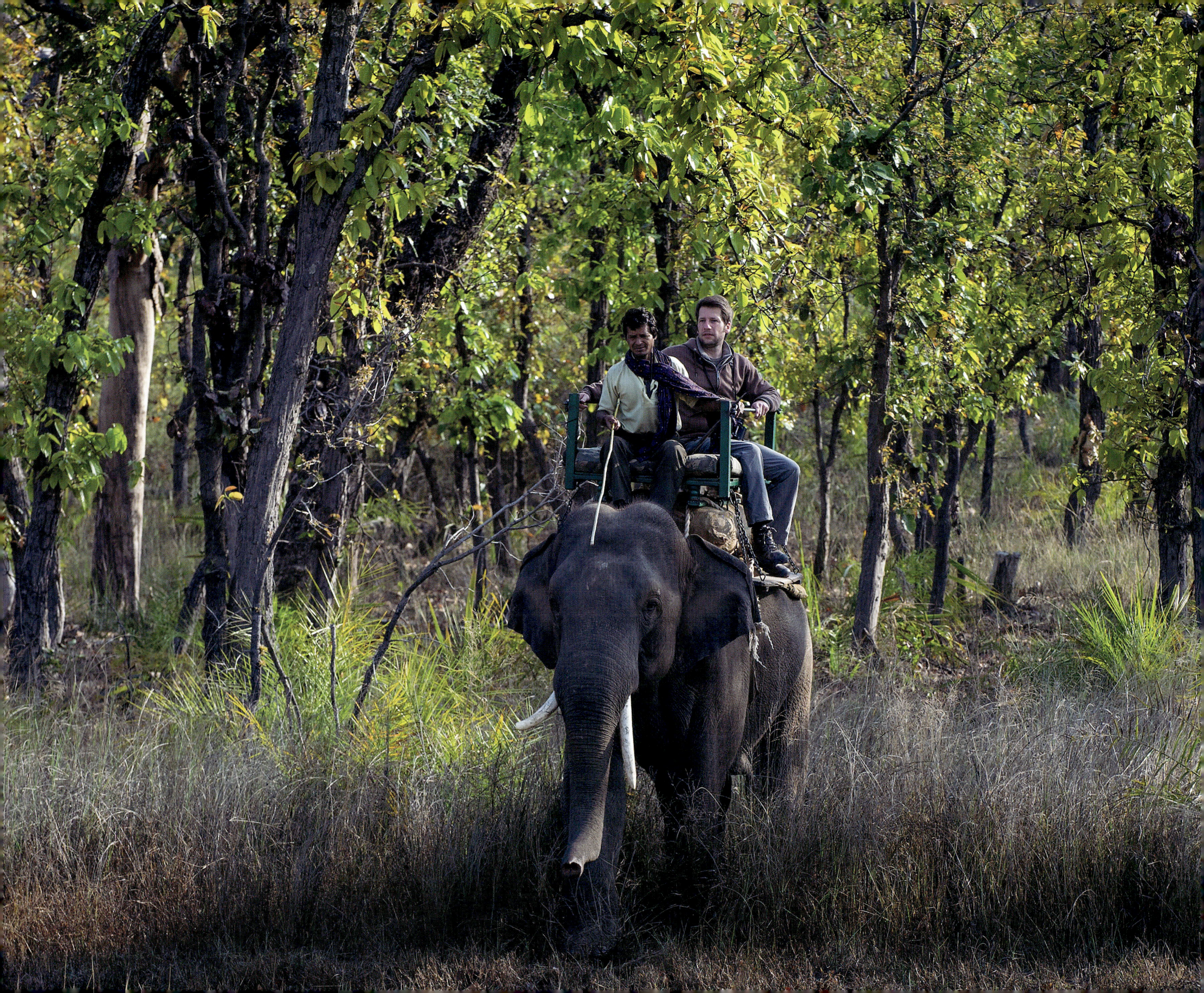

BEHIND THE SCENES

There are many photographs of wildlife to be seen when turning the pages of *Wild India*. What is not apparent, is the time that is involved in order to take them, and what went wrong along the way. Very often, the animals were not to be seen. There were many reasons for the photographer to fail: sometimes they were just too far away, other times the vegetation was too thick to give a clear shot, and sometimes the light was just not good enough.

In order to get good photographs, it is always important to know about the behaviour of each of the animal species, as well as the surrounding ecology. This enables the photographer to decide where and when the best chances are to see them. Axel Gomille is an avid walker, however, walking is not allowed in many of India's protected areas, due to the potential danger posed to humans by animals such as some of the big cats or large herbivores that are around. Four-wheel drive safaris are common as a result, with the limitation being that the cars have to stick to roads. Tame elephants, however, can go anywhere, and it is a remarkable experience to encounter tigers or Indian rhinoceros from the back of one.

Axel Gomille is a long term user of professional Nikon equipment with light-sensitive lenses – reliable gear that works in extremes of tropical heat and bone-chilling cold. Taking these photographs was a challenge, but to get to see these incredible animals in the wild, is in itself an immense reward.

Trained elephants were a valuable way for Axel Gomille to explore the jungle of the Bandhavgarh National Park in Madhya Pradesh. These huge pachyderms are driven by a mahout through all types of terrain – albeit at quite a slow pace.

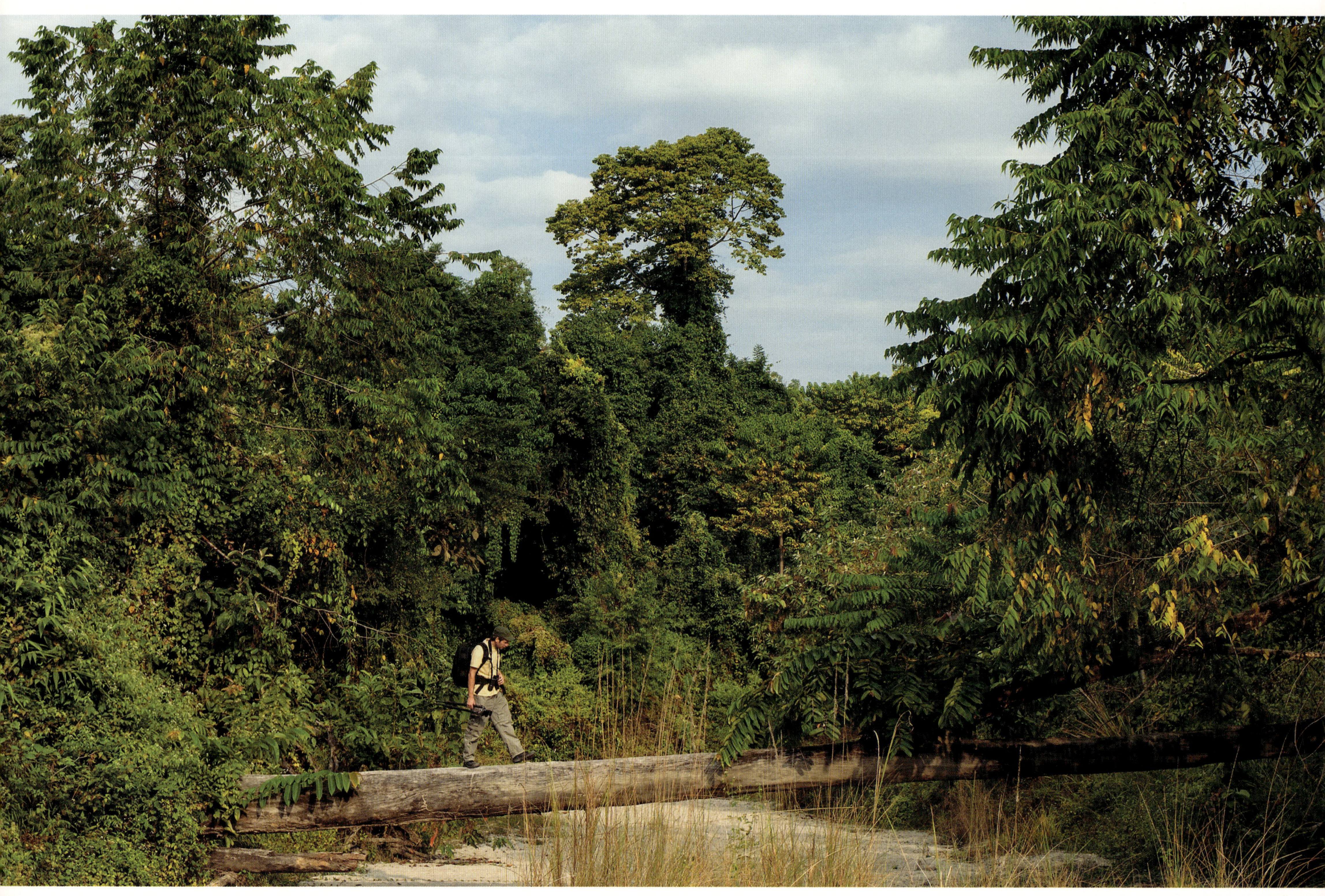

A mahout and an armed ranger take Axel Gomille to photograph an Indian rhinoceros from the back of an elephant in the Kaziranga National Park in Assam (right). With potentially dangerous wildlife around, most protected areas do not allow walking safaris, however, some walks are possible in regions such as Manas (opposite). Hiking in the jungle offers the opportunity to discover small creatures, which cannot not be seen from the back of an elephant or from a vehicle.

Overleaf left:
An Indian python is basking outside its hole, looking on at Axel Gomille. Great care must be taken, as the snake will react sensitively, and just one wrong movement could send the reptile back into its hole.

Overleaf right:
A male Bengal Hanuman langur stands his ground against the photographer. These monkeys are self-confident, especially around temples where they are treated as sacred animals and where they are used to seeing pilgrims and devotees.

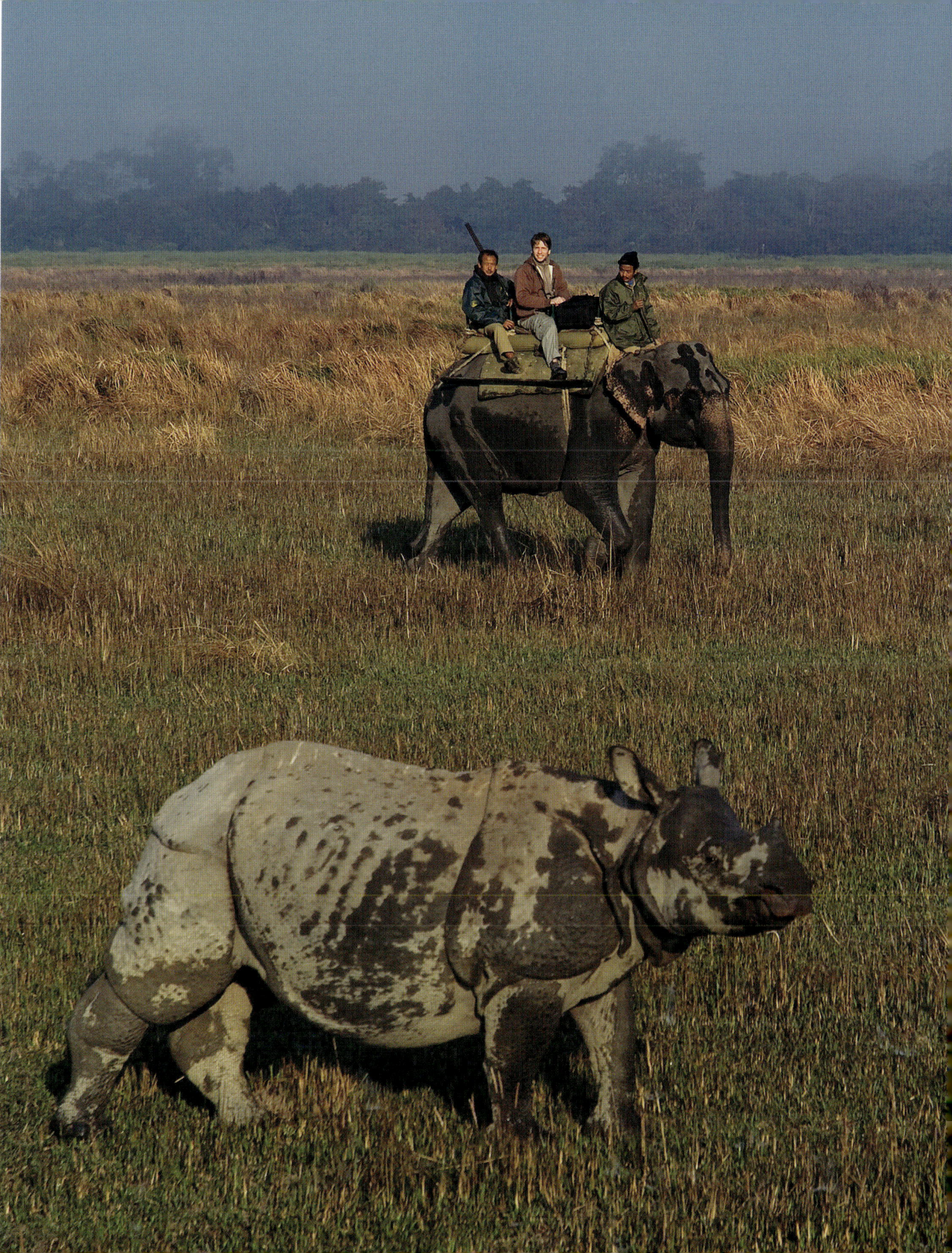

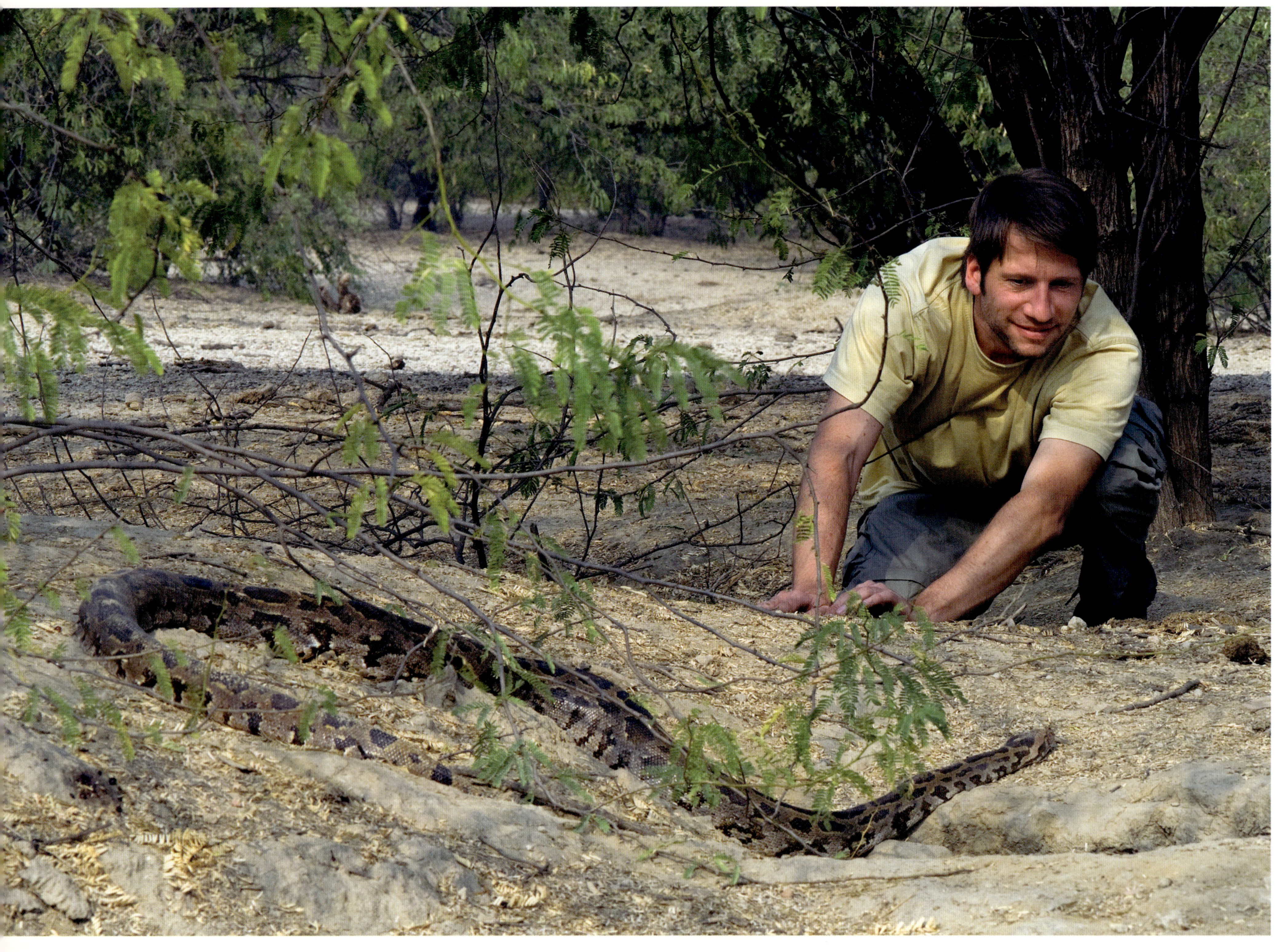

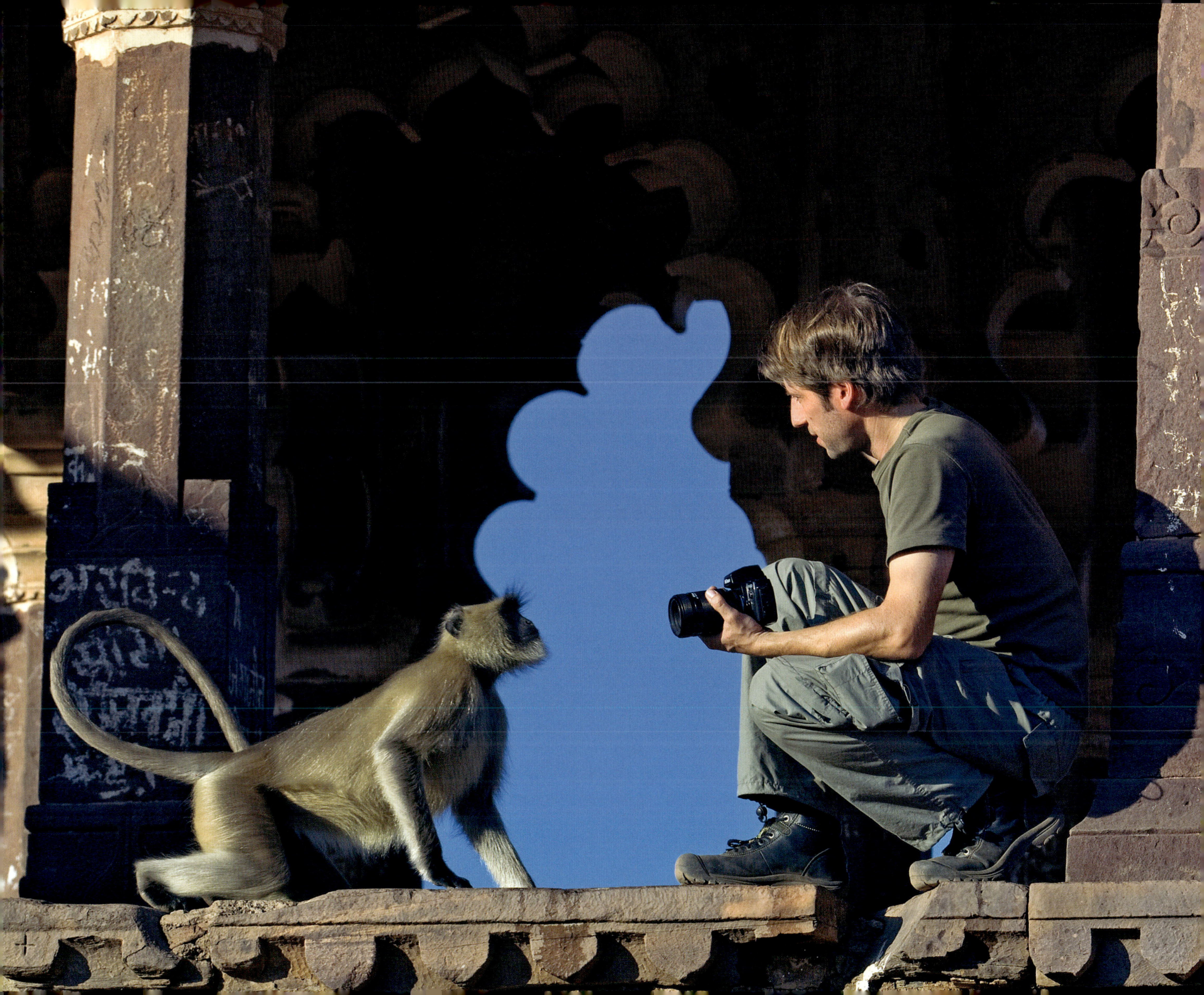

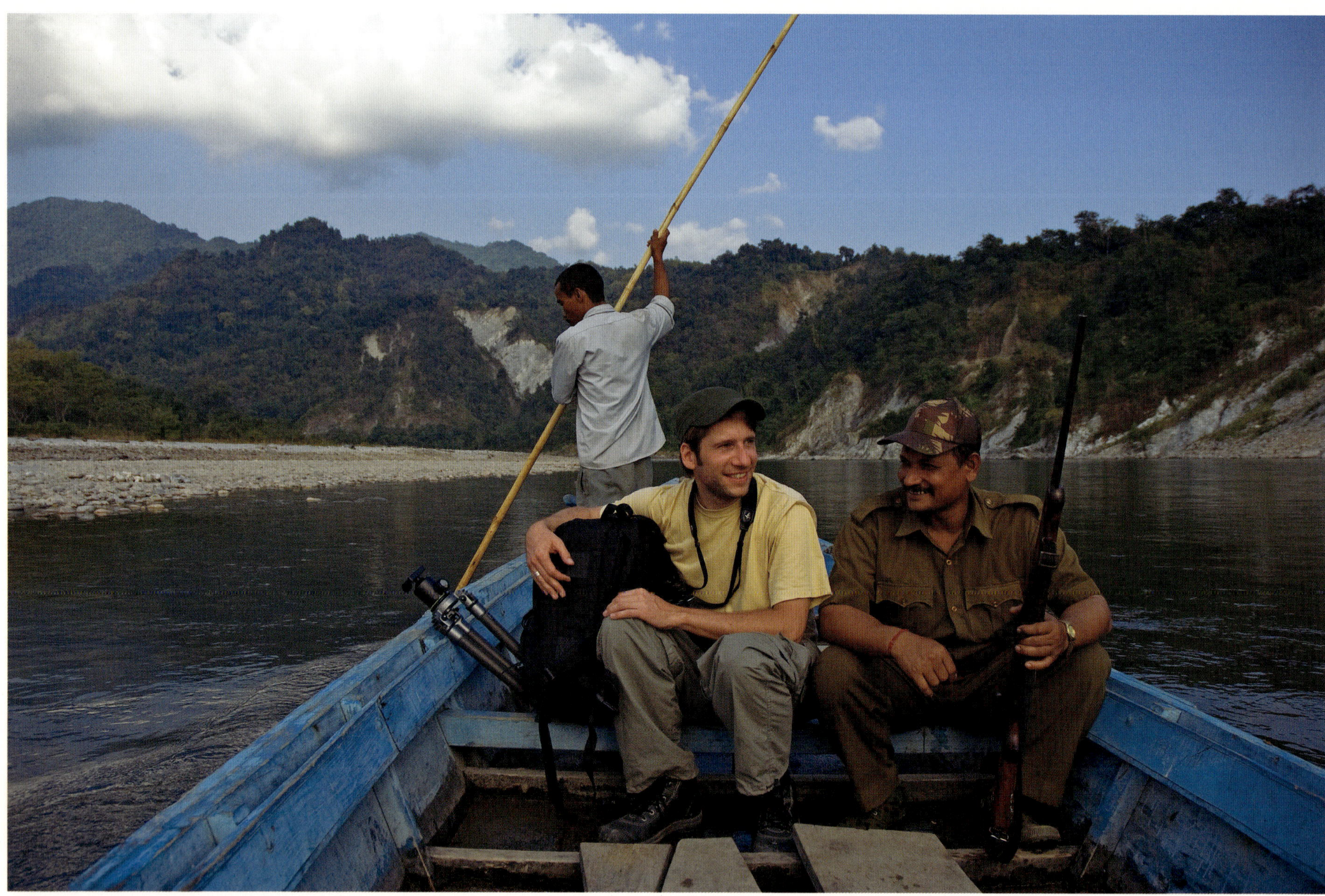

Above:
A boat can be an excellent vantage point from which to view wildlife, especially as it can float along while barely making a sound. In some areas in Assam, where there are large herbivores and big cats, such as in Manas, an armed guard is mandatory for safety reasons.

Opposite:
Searching for the elusive snow leopard in the Himalayas must be done in winter. Snow cover forces herbivores to descend to lower elevations, with snow leopards following their prey. This can mean camping in temperatures dropping to -20°C, requiring the photographer to be in very good physical condition.

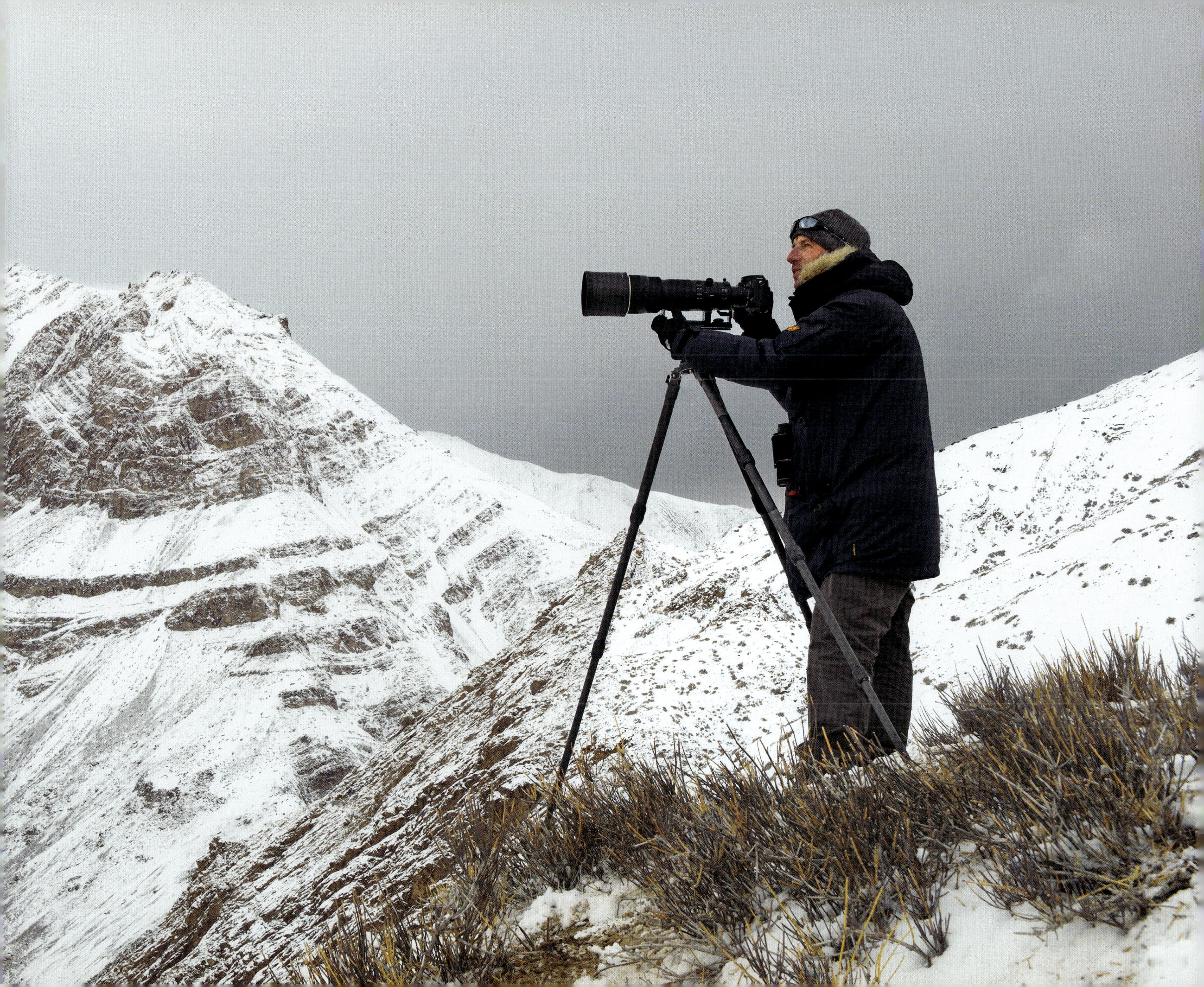

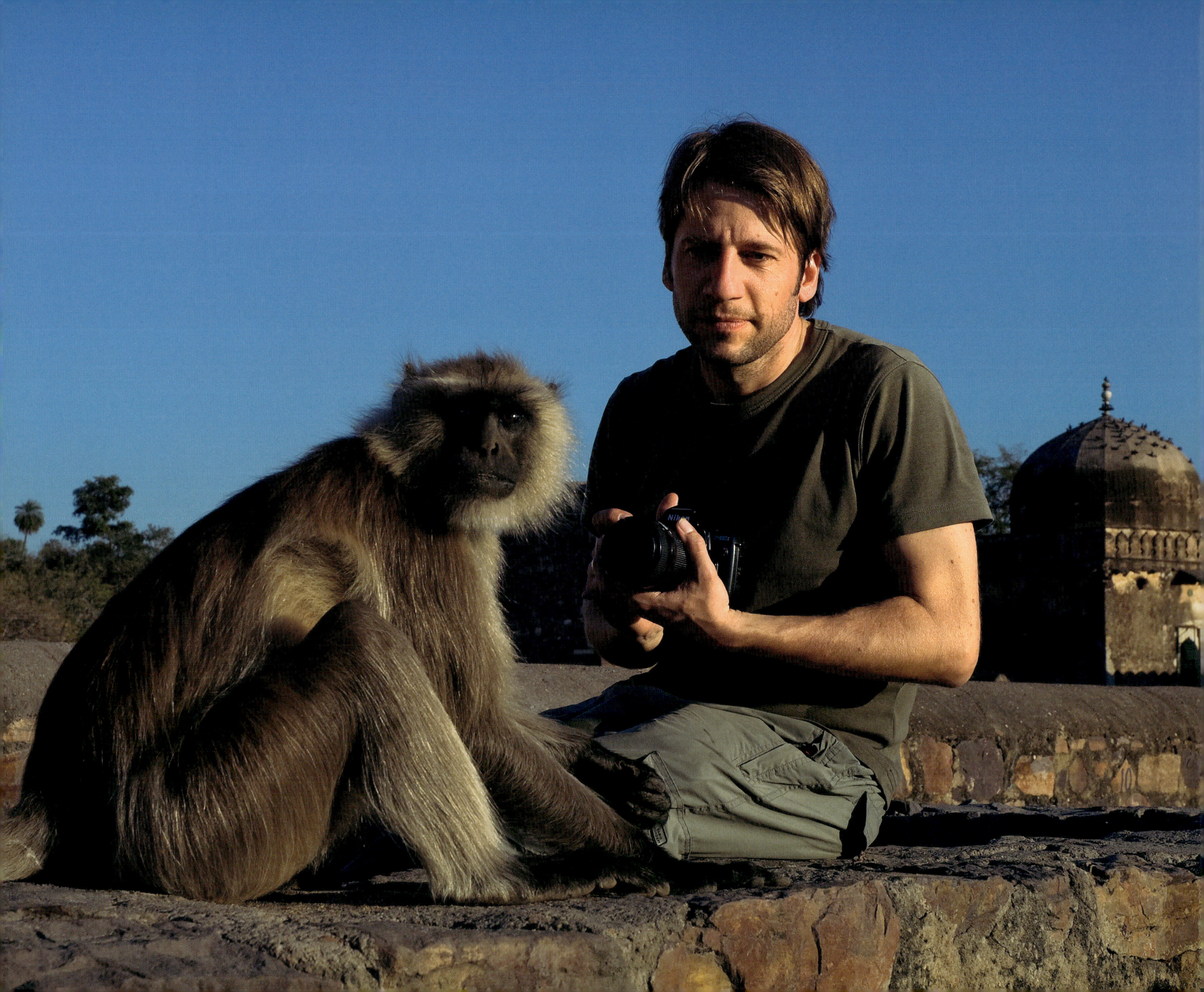

ABOUT THE PHOTOGRAPHER

Axel Gomille is a biologist from Germany with a passion for Indian wildlife. He studied zoology in Frankfurt and in Lakeland, Florida, and works for the German public television broadcaster *ZDF* as a journalist and filmmaker, specialising in topics on wildlife and conservation.

He sets out on the trail of wild animals whenever possible, and has been travelling to India on a regular basis for the past 25 years. Working as a biologist in the tiger reserves of Kanha and Bandhavgarh was a defining experience for him, giving him the opportunity to learn more about the ecology and behaviour of Indian wildlife.

As a photographer and author, Gomille's work has taken him to some of the most beautiful reserves around the world. A key question on his mind is how people and wildlife will continue to coexist in the 21st century.

Axel Gomille's photographs and TV documentaries have received multiple awards. He shot the first photo story on wild sloth bears, which was published in magazines worldwide, including *BBC Wildlife*, *GEO International* and *Asian Geographic*, while his documentary *The Tiger Experiment* portrayed conservation efforts for tigers in India. *Wild India* is his sixth book.

www.axelgomille.com

Axel Gomille has always been intrigued by India's rich wildlife and the close links between nature and culture that are so typical for this country. He has photographed a vast range of animals, from the most common, such as the Bengal Hanuman langur, to very rare species such as the snow leopard.

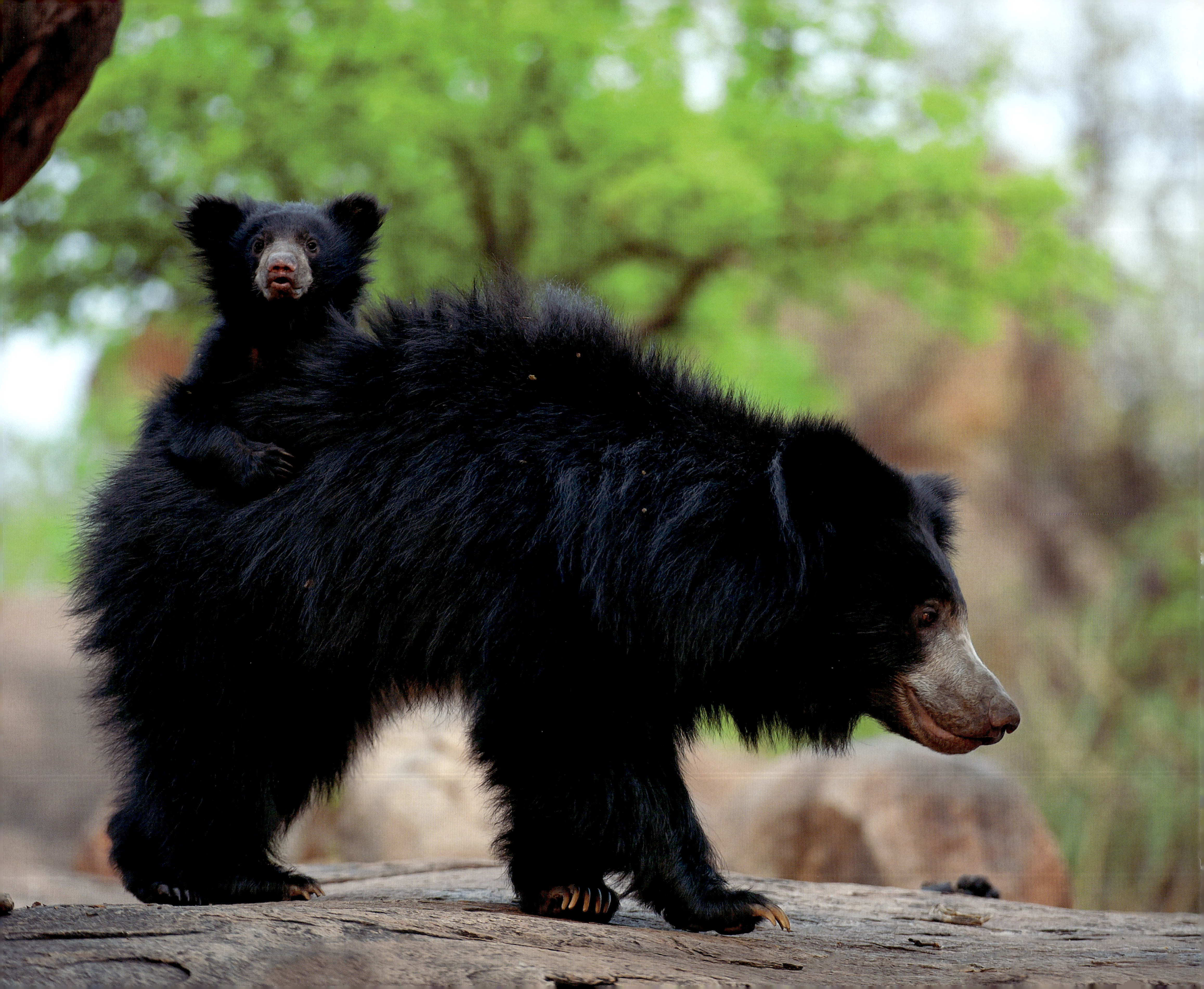

ACKNOWLEDGMENTS

Getting the right opportunity to photograph wildlife is crucial when working on such as book as Wild India. Many experienced people helped me over the years to get access to animals such as tigers, sloth bears and Asian elephants. Among them were local villagers, wildlife biologists, trackers, drivers, mahouts and photographers. K.S. Abdul Samad, Sandesh Kadur and Nalla Muthu were especially helpful. Without their help I would never have been able to see many of the animals that are portrayed in this book and I am very grateful to all of them.

I met Kailash Sankhala during my first visit to India in 1993. He was the first director of *Project Tiger* and did so much for the conservation of this endangered animal. I later worked for his son Pradeep Sankhala, in the tiger reserves of Kanha and Bandhavgarh. Meanwhile, his grandson Amit Sankhala runs the 'tiger resorts', namely the Kanha Jungle Lodge and Bandhavgarh Jungle Lodge, situated in the tiger reserves of the same name. He has proven to be a knowledgeable and reliable partner whenever I am in search of wildlife in India.

I am very thankful for the support of my publisher, Alexandra Papadakis, who has always encouraged me with this project, while keeping an open mind when it came to the content and material, and I am grateful to Aldo Sampieri, the designer of the book, for crafting such a beautiful layout, and to Thieme MapDesign for creating the map at the beginning of the book.

Whenever time was getting short, my wife Yvonne offered understanding and moral support. I am very grateful to everybody who has contributed to making *Wild India* a success.

Watching and photographing the sloth bear, the inspiration for the fictional character *Baloo* from Rudyard Kipling's *The Jungle Book*, was an early dream of Axel Gomille's. After years of attempts and numerous setbacks, Axel finally succeeded in shooting the first photo documentary on the wild sloth bears.